Al-Haq

Al-Haq

*A Global History of the First Palestinian
Human Rights Organization*

Lynn Welchman

UNIVERSITY OF CALIFORNIA PRESS

University of California Press
Oakland, California

Suggested citation: Welchman, L. *Al-Haq: A Global History of the First
Palestinian Human Rights Organization*. Oakland: University of California
Press, 2021. DOI: https://doi.org/10.1525/luminos.102

Library of Congress Cataloging-in-Publication Data

Names: Welchman, Lynn, author.
Title: Al-Haq: a global history of the first Palestinian human rights
    organization / Lynn Welchman.
Description: Oakland, California: University of California Press, [2021] |
    Series: New directions in Palestinian studies; 2 | Includes bibliographical
    references and index.
Identifiers: LCCN 2020043226 | ISBN 9780520379756 (paperback) |
    ISBN 9780520976900 (ebook)
Subjects: LCSH: Law in the Service of Man (Organization: Rām Allāh)—History. |
    Human rights—Palestine—History. | Human rights—West Bank—History. |
    Human rights—Gaza Strip—History.
Classification: LCC KMK2095.W35 2021 | DDC 342.5694/2085—dc23
    LC record available at https://lccn.loc.gov/2020043226

25   24   23   22   21
10   9   8   7   6   5   4   3   2   1

To Al-Haq

CONTENTS

In a 1995 interview, the iconic Palestinian poet Mahmoud Darwish said: "Palestinian poetry has, for little less than a decade, become conscious of the necessity of humanizing its themes and passing from Palestine as a topic or an object, to Palestinian as subject." This ontological shift in poetry also holds true, I believe, for shifts in the political imagination, in institution building, and in knowledge production. The establishment in 1979 of the first Palestinian human rights organization, Law in the Service of Man (later known as al-Haq), is a prime example. The change in focus from Palestine to Palestinian is evident in the name itself. "Man" (writ large, but male nonormative, nonetheless) became the subject on three levels: the individual, the collective (Palestinians as a political community), and the human (universal citizen with inalienable rights).

Al-Haq's founders dared to reimagine politics by initially taking a "nonpolitical" stance in defense of the "rule of law." This, in itself, is not highly unusual, until one is reminded that they did so in the context of a dominant nationalist political culture that saw itself as leading the struggle against a settler colonial project which steals Palestinian land and builds Israeli Jewish colonies while incarcerating Palestinians and brutally repressing them. As the first Palestinian organization of its kind and one of the earliest in the Middle East and the world, al-Haq had an outsized influence locally, regionally, and internationally in terms of its innovative forms of self-governance and methods of data collection, seasoned by working under the very difficult long-term conditions of foreign military rule. In its reports and published self-reflections, al-Haq produced insightful forms of knowledge about the external pressures on and internal contradictions of the Palestinian condition. The rise and inevitable crises experienced by al-Haq, especially after the 1993 Oslo Accords, have profound lessons to teach all of us about the forms of political mobilization that are opened and foreclosed by human rights frameworks, and about how the Palestinians' experience enriches our understanding of larger global trends in struggles for justice, equality, and freedom.

Scholars have recognized the importance of al-Haq, but Lynn Welchman's intimate "insider/outsider" positionality and unparalleled access to sources and people make this book the definitive and most compelling study. Her elegant and tightly structured writing have yielded a page-turning book that humanizes, so to speak, this human rights work. Moreover, her professional expertise on law and society issues provides the analytical scaffolding that links this bottom-up view to larger international issues and debates.

By looking at the world through the eyes of Palestinian legal activists, Welchman's book contributes to the mission of the *New Directions in Palestinian Studies* (NDPS) book series. Among other things, the series seeks rigorous works of scholarship that center the Palestinian experience, introduce new narratives and actors, and utilize locally generated vernacular sources. NDPS values justice-centered academic works that, at the same time, do not shy away from critical analysis of internal problems. One of the important dimensions of Welchman's book is her judicious and honest account of the conflicts –political, personal, institutional, and ideological—which rocked al-Haq, especially after the tragedy of the Oslo Accords and the failures of the Palestinian Authority came into full view. In hindsight, these conflicts were inevitable considering the historical moment of al-Haq's formation, which straddled third-worldist anticolonial worldviews concerned with social and economic development and a universalist liberal conceptual vocabulary concerned with international law and human rights. Welchman's book, therefore, offers a prehistory of human rights work that globalizes the Palestinian experience.

In focusing on Palestinians and the discourse of human rights more than on Palestine and the discourse of national liberation, al-Haq was, in many ways, ahead of its time. It inspired the formation of dozens of similar organizations, became an incubator of legal activists, and anticipated the rise of the Boycott, Divestment, and Sanctions movement. Palestinians are the canary in the mine for many of this world's most pressing challenges, and Welchman's in-depth and textured study of al-Haq is rich with insights about the possibilities and limits of making universal human rights a central arena of struggle, and a welcome intervention in long-running debates about the relationship between law, social movements, and political power.

Beshara Doumani,
Series Editor

ACKNOWLEDGMENTS

I am indebted to a large number of people who helped with the initial stages, lengthy progress, and eventual completion of this book. It was a joy to be back in touch with so many friends and colleagues from al-Haq, many of whom are quoted in this book and to all of whom I owe thanks for giving me their time and insights, whether on or off the record, demonstrating just that commitment to the idea of the organization that characterized al-Haq in the period examined here. In particular, I thank Raqiya Abu Ghosh, Afaf Abu Nakhlah, Sami 'Ayad, George Giacaman, Zahi Jaradat, Mustafa Mar'i, Hanan Rabbani, Mouin Rabbani, Naser Rayyes, Mervat Rishmawi, Mona Rishmawi, Ghazi Shashtari, Randa Siniora, and Issam Younis. Special thanks to Nina Atallah, who tirelessly followed up my many inquiries at the start of the research; Nidal Taha for providing copies of the correspondence between al-Haq's founders and the ICJ in Geneva in the late 1970s; Raja Shehadeh for providing hard copies of his 1980 testimony (as "M") at the UN; and Khaled Batrawi, Iyad Haddad, and Abdel Karim Kan'an, for going so many extra miles to help the research along. Fateh Azzam and Said Zeedani shared insights into some difficult days at the organization. Charles Shammas was responsible for recruiting me to LSM in 1983 (thanks, Charles!), and intense parts of my al-Haq time were shared with Mona Rishmawi, Joost Hiltermann, and Jacqueline Shahinian ("once an al-Haqqer, always an al-Haqqer!"). Enormous thanks of course also to Shawan Jabarin, general director of al-Haq, who invited me to write the book in the first place and then with remarkable good humor accommodated its delayed appearance; and Shawan and the al-Haq board for allowing me to draw on and quote documents from al-Haq's archives and other internal material. Emma Playfair read every chapter as it emerged, and other al-Haq friends also read chapters and provided insightful and encouraging feedback: Charles Shammas,

Raja Shehadeh, Jonathan Kuttab, and Joanna Oyediran. Nina Dodge and Jim Fine helped with memories from the earliest days of the organization.

Maggie Beirne, Margo Picken, Marc Shade-Poulson, Joyce Song, and Wilder Tayler read chapters and gave feedback and food for comparative thought. At the International Commission of Jurists, I was assisted enormously by Illaria Vena, Gerald Staberock, and Wilder Tayler, then secretary-general, who located and gave permission for me to quote documents from the ICJ archives. I am also grateful to Anne Fitzgerald of Amnesty International and Claudio Cordone, then Amnesty's acting secretary-general, for assisting with locating documents at Amnesty, and to the organization for permission to quote said material. Iain Guest directed me to his insightful report. Other helpful readings were suggested, and encouragement provided, by friends and colleagues from the School of Law at SOAS, University of London: Samia Bano, Catriona Drew, Ron Dudai, Kate Grady, Paul O'Connell, Lutz Oette, Nimer Sultany, Iain Scobbie, and Sarah Hibbin, along with Stephen Hopgood, Adam Hanieh, and Dina Matar. Lucy King cheered me up. Abdullahi An-Na`im, Randa Alami, Laila Asser, Sara Hossain, Ziba Mir-Hosseini, and friends at EMHRF (especially Bahey el-Din Hassan and Hanny Megally) offered encouragement all the way. Charles Shammas and Susan Rockwell accommodated me in the MATTIN space next door to al-Haq for extended research visits; and Susan and Shari Lapp, as well as Charles, hosted my husband Akram and me and, with Salwa Duaibis, Raja Shehadeh and Penny Johnson, shared long evenings of good food and laughter as well as reflection. Diala Shammas and Yara Hawari updated friendships with their parents forged in the 1980s at the al-Haq fortieth anniversary events in 2019, where it was also a joy to see Riziq Shuqair demonstrate the depth of his knowledge of the Palestinian human rights movement and the challenges facing it. I take this moment also to pay tribute to the work of Issam Younis of Al Mezan and Raji Sourani of the Palestinian Center for Human Rights, and to the memory of Maha Abu Dayyeh, for many years the director of the Women's Center for Legal Aid and Counselling. Likewise, I pay tribute to the memories of al-Haq staffers Paulein Hanna and Khamis Shalabi.

Sarah Bowes good-humoredly undertook the cutting of the manuscript in an effort that went far beyond the normal limits of friendship, neatly closing the circle of her original introduction of me to Charles Shammas (and thus to LSM) in 1983. My thanks to Sarah and to Alistair Davison, James Dickins, and John Steinhardt, friends since we studied Arabic together at Cambridge and shared extracurricular times and spaces in Damascus and downtown Cairo, and who helped the finishing of this book with some Zermatt air in 2019. I am grateful to Penny Johnson for telling Beshara Doumani, lead editor of the New Directions in Palestinian Studies series, about the book project, and to Beshara for his enthusiastic response and sustained engagement; to Anthony Chase, Mouin Rabbani, and an anonymous reviewer for their constructive comments on the text; to Niels Hooper and Robin

Manley at the University of California Press; and to Nicholas Padfield QC, whose advice reassured me in the final stages.

Two closing points here. Firstly, the usual caveat applies: I am indebted to each and every one of the friends and colleagues who helped me when I was researching and writing this book, but any errors in fact, interpretation, or representation are of course mine. Also, while I have tried to present differing perspectives on some of the contentious issues and periods in al-Haq's history, there may well be some who feel under-represented in the narrative that I tried to construct here, and I regret it should that be the case. This book is, in the end, an attempt at *a* history, not *the* history, of al-Haq.

And finally, my thanks go to Akram al-Khatib, beloved husband, who read chapters and accompanied me on research visits to his homeland Palestine, and whose depths of integrity, compassion, and insight continue to inspire. He has lived with this project since 2009 with the best of humor, and it literally could not have been completed without him.

Introduction

This is a study of the origins of al-Haq, the first Palestinian human rights organization, and of the wider significance of the methodologies and approaches it instigated as it developed under Israeli occupation and into the early years of the Palestinian Authority. I was invited to write about al-Haq by Shawan Jabarin, who joined as a field-worker in 1987 and became general director of the organization in 2006. I worked intermittently with al-Haq from 1983 to 1993 in different capacities and, in common with many former staffers, have an enduring affection and respect for the organization and the people who worked there. For the record, I am hugely proud to have been a tiny part of it. The insider/outsider dynamics of this research affected the writing process somewhat, but I was not engaged in "participant observation" at al-Haq: I was working there, and those were different times. Thus, I step into this study in the first person very sparingly.

The book examines how al-Haq initiated, in areas of law and practice, lines of thinking and methodologies that were ahead of their time, and to which can be traced the origins of many foci of human rights work in Palestine and elsewhere today. It looks at the founders, the organization, its staffers ("al-Haqqers"), its work over its formative first decade, and its legacy. It considers the stresses placed on the young organization by developments under Israeli occupation including the first intifada, the Oslo process, and the arrival of the Palestinian Authority, and how such factors combined to force structural change in al-Haq in the 1990s and beyond. It is a study of some importance to the growing scholarship on the practice (and praxis) of local (as compared to international) human rights organizations and, incidentally, their impact on international groups. It is also a study of the origins of the Palestinian human rights movement and the increasing permeation of the law and rights discourse into the Palestinian public and political sphere. It is an account of Palestinian voices on their choice to work with international law and human rights under occupation, despite the odds, and before human rights first became fashionable and then fell out of favor. This book examines the immediate times and places of al-Haq—that is, I do not present the longer history of Palestine or its people's struggles to stay on their land—and the West Bank (including East Jerusalem) is the main geographical focus, as it was al-Haq's.

In this study, I set the memories of those involved next to public and previously unpublished documents from the time, exploring how the organization formed, applied, and explained its founding principles, methodologies, and strategies. Al-Haq has been written about by its founders, by former staffers, and more recently by external researchers. It has also written about itself frequently; indeed, as a young organization, it engaged in a reflective practice that sought to explain itself to its friends and allies, to the local and the international communities with which it sought to engage. I have drawn on these sources as well as on documents from al-Haq's fading paper archives, the records of other organizations (the International Commission of Jurists [ICJ] and Amnesty International), and, from the personal archives of Nidal Taha (head of al-Haq's Board of Trustees), correspondence spanning the years 1977–80 to and from the ICJ in Geneva and a group of correspondents in the West Bank who became founders of Law in the Service of Man (LSM), as al-Haq was first known. I have also drawn on and been guided by my meetings, discussions, and interviews with a wide range of individuals—colleagues and friends—who worked at and with LSM/al-Haq in its formative period.[1]

The most prolific source of written record and reflection alike is cofounder Raja Shehadeh, several of whose publications are key to this study. His authoritative legal research and analytical works include the seminal *West Bank and the Rule of Law* (1980, with cofounder Jonathan Kuttab), which was al-Haq's first publication. It was critical to the fledgling organization's profile and development and indicative of its approach.[2] At the time he was assembling the material for this work, however, Shehadeh was also keeping a journal, extracts from which (from 1979–80) were published as *The Third Way* in 1982. They provide a vivid contemporary glimpse into life in the West Bank at the time when Shehadeh and friends were setting up LSM/al-Haq. Shehadeh has published three other sets of journal extracts since,[3] as well as a memoir (*Strangers in the House*, 2002), on which I draw for its reflections on establishing al-Haq. The book *Palestinian Walks*, which won the Orwell Prize in 2008, voices other memories and musings about the organization and its work that are the more poignant for being prompted by Shehadeh's walks in what the subtitle calls "a vanishing landscape," in a sense the epitome of what al-Haq was established to prevent. In addition, Shehadeh's recollections are presented in a number of journal articles and interviews. As well as reflecting the phases through which his own thinking has passed, these provide insights on the earlier times informed by perspectives developed and knowledge accrued over the decades.[4]

Al-Haq's first anniversary publication, *Twenty Years Defending Human Rights* (1999) includes an interview with Shehadeh as well as contributions from staffers and former staffers talking about campaigns, events, and projects such as the 1988 International Law conference. In 2005 al-Haq published *Waiting for Justice*, which doubled as a substantive annual report (along the lines of those issued in the first three years of the first intifada) and as an anniversary publication (*Al-Haq: 25 Years Defending Human Rights*). The report includes a retrospective about the organization and its work by Fateh Azzam, who joined in the late 1980s and who recalls with admirable brevity not only substantive work but some important organizational moments: for example, the time when the board resigned and the organization became staff-run, and the crisis of 1997 when the board sacked all but a handful of employees and al-Haq had to more or less start again. Azzam also summarizes the "very hot debates" over the killing of collaborators in the first intifada, and armed attacks against civilian targets inside Israel in the second.[5] In 2009, a distinctive, hard-backed anniversary publication (*Al-Haq: 30 Years Defending Human Rights*) includes testimonials from current and former staffers, the text of the first affidavit, a chronology of al-Haq's early years (based on its Newsletter), photos of events and awards, a list of all publications (except the *Know Your Rights* series), and what tries to be an exhaustive list of everyone who ever worked at the organization. This publication was produced under the directorship of Shawan Jabarin, whose "Detention Memoirs," smuggled out of prison and published in the organization's third annual report, *Protection Denied* (1991), illustrates what an al-Haq field-worker would consider of relevance to the organization at that time.

There are other documents, particularly from the 1980s, which help situate the young organization. A promotional brochure from 1983 endeavored to explain LSM's goals and activities to the public. This was followed by the Newsletter, published bimonthly in English and Arabic from May 1984 until the end of 1987, when the first intifada made it impossible to sustain. For three-and-a-half key years, the Newsletter diligently reported on activities, interventions, and developments in the legal environment. It also took the space to reflect on the organization's identity (hence, "Philosophy of LSM," "The Role of a Human Rights Organization under Occupation," and "Twenty Years of Occupation: A Time to Reflect").[6] Some of these pieces came out of collective discussions as the organization worked through persistent challenges in the 1980s. They are indicative of a fairly consistent pattern of institutional reflection, engaging management and workers across the organization. Those involved were more or less conscious of doing something new, something extraordinary, and explained themselves accordingly. Also from the 1980s, I draw on internal documents concerned with such issues as the establishment of a paid position as director, orientation/reorientation sessions for staffers, the methodology behind the database, and misplaced queries and interventions from external allies in the international human rights movement in whose education al-Haq invested considerable time and energy.

SCHOLARSHIP: AL-HAQ AND HUMAN RIGHTS

Al-Haq staffers also wrote about the organization. Joost Hiltermann published a number of pieces based on work he was doing with LSM/al-Haq in the 1980s, explaining in the *Twenty Years* anniversary publication that he was "forced to engage in extracurricular activities" such as writing these articles (and taking supplies to families whose homes had been demolished) by his frustration with the "infuriating but indispensable legalese of [al-Haq's] analysis."[7] A 1994 study of the organization by Mouin Rabbani is an informative and critical analysis, drawing on al-Haq publications and Rabbani's own experience in the turbulent years of the first intifada.[8] Two further examinations come from academic researchers who were not al-Haq staffers. The first study of the local human rights movement, and al-Haq's place in it, appeared in Lisa Hajjar's important 2001 article, which she opens by insisting that "to understand the history and politics of the human rights movement in [. . .] Israel/Palestine, it is necessary to highlight the politics of law."[9] Hajjar identifies LSM as playing the central role in the mid-1980s in the process of reframing in legal language issues previously considered as political. In her analysis, "this served to politicize law itself."[10] Later, in her compelling study of the Israeli military court system, Hajjar examined how "human rights provided new ways of thinking, talking about, and intervening in the conflict."[11] Her thinking about the work of human rights and law in reframing the political struggle underpins her finding that "framing resistance as demands for human rights [. . .] serves to internationalise local conflict"; this was key to the advocacy of LSM from its earliest years.[12] And the concept of human rights work as resistance was raised by a number of LSM/al-Haq colleagues interviewed for this current study. The debate on the impact of the recasting of "political" matters in legal/human rights language—specifically, whether this contributed to "taming" Palestinian resistance—is considered in chapter 4. But LSM/al-Haq's contribution to building the Palestinian case in law and human rights was enormous.

The second major examination of al-Haq comes in Lori Allen's anthropological study *The Rise and Fall of Human Rights: Cynicism and Politics in Occupied Palestine* (2013). Allen spent considerable time on field research observing different areas of work; her interest is in how, nowadays, human rights officials and professionals act "as if" human rights actually matters and works—that is, "acting as if the human rights industry could stop abuses outside of real political, structural change."[13] Through interviews with the founders and a number of staffers, she constructs a sensitive narrative of the early years of the organization, its practices and priorities. Indeed, it may begin to sound as if, over the decades, these narratives have settled into something of an official version. "It is true," says Tom Buchanan, explaining his interest in examining the origins of Amnesty International, "that organizations tend to develop versions of their past which serve their current needs and purposes."[14] In the narratives of al-Haq's origins there is no "one man's flash of inspiration,"[15] even if the pile of Israeli military orders awaiting scrutiny by

Shehadeh in his father's law office in 1977 is a compelling image. It is interesting how closely the narratives (sometimes grand narratives) are reflected in sources from the time. To be sure, some issues are more nuanced than usually presented: the role of non-Palestinian researchers at al-Haq, for example, needs unpacking. There are other stories that almost everyone knows (or knows bits of) but nobody wants to talk about—and that, I think, is a quality of discretion and compassion that is to be honored in the collective. But the focus on accuracy, evidence, building credibility, and documentation (Allen's "faith in evidence") does indeed reflect the impetus of the founders and the training and methodology of al-Haq workers, at a time when this was ground-breaking.

Allen notes that the dominant critiques of the "human rights industry" that interest her (inter alia, professionalization, NGO-ization and lack of accountability, legalization, subordination to foreign donor funding, and displacement of political activism proper) came after the early years when al-Haq was developing.[16] Nor indeed were the other criticisms of human rights that now preoccupy scholars so widespread during that period. As O'Connell observes, "it is now, in certain circles, in vogue to be 'against', or to dismiss human rights."[17] Human rights was still relatively new as a discourse and as activism in the late 1970s and 1980s, and it was certainly unfamiliar in Palestine. Christine Bell traces a trajectory "from social movement outside academia, to praxis involving academics, to accepted status as a new (multi-disciplinary) field, to new established field to be critiqued." En route she feels that something is lost, perhaps, through "the academic crushing of law's possibilities for good as doomed to inevitable co-option in the quicksand of legalisation."[18] Philip Alston has paid tribute to the lessons provided by critical scholarship on human rights while observing that "critical scholars too need to take account of the 'unintended consequences' of a lot of the work that they do."[19] A key scholar in the debate, Makau Mutua, notes that he has been "othered" by "the human rights project" but that as a TWAIL thinker (Third World Approaches to International Law), he does not "seek to throw the baby out with the bath water" and neither does he find himself "vexed by the inherent contradiction" in the way he views human rights: "My project is to deconstruct, reconstruct, and build a world without hegemonies where conditions of underdevelopment—especially in the South, but also in the North—can be eradicated."[20]

For his part Fateh Azzam, who moved from al-Haq to human rights roles as funder, academic, UN representative, and consultant, has responded to critiques with a certain amount of exasperation.[21] Anthony Tirado Chase, as editor of the *Routledge Handbook on Human Rights and the Middle East and North Africa* (2017), argues that human rights are not in and of themselves a goal or an ideological world view:

> To the contrary, human rights are more about processes than ends—processes that can restrain state dominance, empower peoples and social groups, and advance individual and group agency. What is accomplished with that empowerment and agency

is not determined by human rights; it is determined by those who claim, use, and transform human rights.[22]

FRAMING THE WORK

Process is certainly a better description of the initial interest of al-Haq's founders in setting up the organization. All were (are) fundamentally practitioners looking for practical ways forward. The rule of law (not human rights) is the focus in their correspondence with the International Commission of Jurists in Geneva over the period 1977–79 examined in chapter 2. Like international law and human rights, the concept of the rule of law is the subject of critique, notably by law and colonialism scholars: "If the legal order is based on some originating violence, as it often is, the legitimacy of legal rules tends to be undermined."[23] Nevertheless, Chimni notes that "even critics of the positivist, formal and a-cultural conception of the rule of law concede its value. [. . .] A sanguine take on the rule of law is thus not in contradiction with the claim that law can legitimise a system of domination and exploitation." This last would appear to describe the approach of al-Haq's founders.

Many in the initial founding group were legal professionals operating in a West Bank environment where Israel as the occupying power had a clear monopoly on the idea of the "rule of law" and forcefully presented itself as the epitome of a rule-of-law state. "Indeed," as Hajjar observes, "it was Israel's enthusiasm for law and the ornate legalism of official discourse that catalysed and propelled the development of a local human rights movement, which served as the harbinger of legalistic resistance."[24] A flavor of what this meant at the international level can be read in the 1977 report of the London-based *Sunday Times* on Israel's torture of Palestinian detainees.[25] The *Sunday Times* team directed its five-month investigation at Israel, according to the paper's editorial, "because Israel occupies a special place in our world. Israel itself has always made justice, the rule of law and the fair treatment of Arabs central to its claim to nationhood."[26] The report writers underlined that Israel was "part of the West—and thus to be judged by Western standards," and that indeed this was "fundamental to Israel's ethos and to its claims for international support."[27] The editorial noted a "reticence" in "international bodies" and in the press (including the Israeli press) to report on allegations of human rights violations by Israel.[28] Concluding that "torture has become, on the evidence, an accepted Israeli practice," the INSIGHT team predicted that "some will reject our evidence as literally unthinkable [. . .] a paradox so distasteful as to demand better evidence than would be needed against other countries."[29]

Israel's constant pursuit of internal and external legitimation of its image and conduct was critical to the motivation and methodology of LSM/al-Haq's founders. In this ideological environment, the founders focused on the rule of law as articulated principally by the ICJ. This focus included human rights, but most importantly required a structural focus on cause (not only consequence) that resonated with the founders' immediate concerns. As the decades have passed, frameworks other than belligerent occupation and rule of law have been proposed in response to Israel's developing policy and practice in the West Bank (including East Jerusalem) and Gaza Strip, then routinely referred to (inter alia by al-Haq) as the occupied territories.[30] Israeli scholar David Kretzmer has argued that Israel's rule (in view of the settlers and their treatment by the Israeli state) is "much closer to a colonial regime than one of belligerent occupation."[31]

The interdisciplinary frame of settler-colonialism is also applied, with its focus on the "elimination of the native" or the "erasure" of natives' presence by the settler-colonial power.[32] Sparked by a 2007 report from John Dugard, then UN Special Rapporteur on the situation of human rights in the Palestinian territory occupied since 1967, the international legal framework of apartheid was the subject of a major international research project led by a South Africa–funded team and involving researchers from al-Haq.[33] As illustrated in the epilogue, it is now routinely invoked by al-Haq and other human rights NGOs to frame aspects of Israel's conduct and propose mechanisms of redress. It is easy to point to predictions of these frameworks in early al-Haq work. In 1985, Raja Shehadeh concluded, in regard to Israel's defense of its "land acquisition policy," that "thus, colonialism is to be formalized and made permanent in the guise of autonomy."[34] Al-Haq drew attention to the "massive Israeli colonisation effort that is underway in the Occupied Territories," obscured from outside view by the structure of military legislation, in its reflection on twenty years of occupation.[35] Both Shehadeh and Kuttab made public comparisons with South Africa's apartheid system in the early 1980s.[36]

These early invocations of legal frameworks other than occupation through which to assess and resist Israel's conduct resonated with the broader nationalist discourses of the Palestine Liberation Organization (PLO) alongside its alliances with the Non-Aligned Movement, Afro-Asian states, national liberation movements and post-colonial states, anti-apartheid struggle in South Africa and anti-colonial activism elsewhere, and the demands being made of the international system by "Third World" states and the Global South. In *Justice for Some* (2019), Noura Erakat "explores the role and the potential of law in the pursuit of Palestinian freedom" and applies Duncan Kennedy's concept of "legal work" ("the work that the legal actor performs to achieve a desired outcome") to survey achievements by the PLO and by Israel in shaping the law.[37] In a chapter titled "Pragmatic Revolutionaries," she reviews the "fundamental legal achievements" of the PLO during the 1970s, the period during which LSM's founders were completing their education and entering professional life, and which framed the discourses and expectations of the time.[38] In that sense, the founders of LSM (examined in chapter 3) were very much situated in time and place. They articulated ways in which they considered themselves nationalist, and their vision of LSM as part of the national struggle; in this regard, George Bisharat attributes such sentiments to lawyers in general:

> Both striking and working factions regard themselves as active participants, if not vanguards, in the struggle against Israeli power. This conviction is sometimes articulated frankly in nationalist terms, other times, more indirectly, through slogans concerning the defense and promotion of the general principles of the 'rule of law'.[39]

LSM/al-Haq field researchers also explained how they considered their human rights work to be part of the national struggle and a form of resistance. Shammas frames the work as struggle, while Shehadeh's non-LSM publications underpin Tripp's observation of *sumud* as a "recurrent theme in Palestinian resistance narratives."[40] But the founders deliberately distanced themselves from internal (factional) PLO politics in the occupied territories and the wider national movement. This was for professional reasons (the directive discussed in chapter 4 to "leave your politics at the door"), for organizational sustainability and personal security; but also as a result of personal disinterest and, it appears, a certain impatience with what they considered the limits of the prevailing nationalist discourse and tools. Insisting on not being affiliated with any particular tendency was novel at the time, and unsettling for some in Palestinian society. Instead, the founders proposed the rule of law as a framework for examining and resisting Israel's conduct as an occupying power; human rights, as shown in the correspondence examined in chapter 2, was a secondary discourse.

AL-HAQ CONTRIBUTIONS

Also in chapter 2, we see the innovative nature of LSM's organizational setup (as a not-for-profit company), designed to avoid, at least structurally, what Bisharat termed "over-control" on the part of the Israeli occupation authorities (control over funding by the designated Israeli army officer) and the various PLO factions (via partisan takeovers from a packed membership).[41] LSM's founders shared definite ideas about institutional governance that revolved around active participation and learning from staff, with the aim of growing together to build a "cadre of human rights activists," as Shehadeh put it. Chapter 4 examines how, once the organization outgrew its initial tight group of members and the need for change came, the organization's leadership reminded themselves that LSM/al-Haq was still to "serve as an institutional model to the community," inter alia with its all-staff general meeting remaining as "the highest decision-making body on programme-related matters." This model did not survive the turmoils of expansion and tensions of Oslo, although the underlying values are reaffirmed by some still in the field today. For LSM/al-Haq, seeking to set an institutional rule-of-law and participatory structure went alongside a declared commitment to attending to human rights issues in Palestinian society. This was manifested on the one hand in educational work about rights and legalistic resistance to the occupation, and the provision of the first public law library in the occupied territories; and on the other, in an early attention to an "internal" agenda including the rights of workers and women within Palestinian society. The rule-of-law agenda here was extended to underpin individual and societal relations.

Human rights as a main reference for the founders developed alongside the ICJ's thinking on the right to development. In his introduction to the ICJ's 1966 publication *The Rule of Law and Human Rights: Principles and Definitions*, ICJ's then secretary-general Seán MacBride referred to the "new dynamic concept of the rule of law" developed through a series of meetings, congresses, and seminars in different parts of the world, mainly in the Global South. Jan Eckel considers initiatives at the UN in the 1970s by the Non-Aligned Movement and the Afro-Asia bloc of states to "frame their concern for economic development in human rights language" with the assertion of the right to development as a set of "human rights claims to expose the injustice of the post-colonial world order."[42] Here, LSM's founders can be seen to have been firmly in the corner of the Global South (and peers from "Third World" states and struggles), taking up the right to development in terms of collective as well as individual rights and attending to structure and causes of human rights violations (as discussed in chapter 5). In LSM's case, this was a consistent focus on the ways in which Israel was pursuing an annexationist agenda, itself unlawful, and which gave rise to other human rights violations against the civilian population when they manifested resistance to this agenda. The field research methodology developed by and with the fieldwork unit was groundbreaking, as was the way in which the organization sought to organize and retrieve the data it was collecting. LSM/al-Haq's lessons in field research methodologies and database development were drawn on by domestic and international human rights organizations around the world, and the organization was critical to the development of a number of other Palestinian human rights organizations in the occupied territories.

At the same time, as already noted, the concept of human rights was not familiar in the region; distrust of the human rights discourse was fueled by its selective deployment against the Soviet Union in the Cold War, and field researchers recruited in the early years recall initial concerns about serving a liberal Western agenda by joining LSM. LSM was among the first human rights organizations established in the Arab region, and although contact was limited during the early years, as shown in chapter 1, some of these concerns about the liberal discourse were shared with Arab peers. At the same time, the concept of human rights includes the right to self-determination, affirmed in both of the International Human Rights Covenants and discussed further in chapter 1. The founders of LSM refrained from attending to self-determination in any detail or calling for an end to the occupation as such. Others saw even in LSM's very early work the inevitable conclusion that occupation had to end, but the organization did not explicitly make that call at first; the correspondence with the International Commission of Jurists examined in chapter 2 demonstrates an extreme reluctance to be perceived as making any pronouncement that might be considered "political." It was in its 1987 editorial on twenty years of occupation that al-Haq produced a sustained reflection on Israel's "systematic colonisation of the West Bank and Gaza."[43] "What first looked like a temporary military occupation," said al-Haq, "has been transformed into a long-term Israeli effort to colonise the Occupied Territories."

This 1987 piece reflected the thinking behind al-Haq's preparations for the first international law conference to be held in the occupied territories, which it convened in Jerusalem in January 1988 against the background, as it transpired, of the opening weeks of the first intifada. The impetus for this conference was a learning process—there were simply too many questions arising under international humanitarian law (IHL) from what was already then (at twenty years) being called a long-term or prolonged occupation. Al-Haq's plan was to invite experts in the field to help the organization think through some more obscure but absolutely vital implications of the laws of war for occupied territories under prolonged hostile military rule. For a still relatively young Palestinian NGO to engage in this way with a range of international scholars and practitioners was unusual, and there was a lasting impact from the collection of papers later published and contributing to the wider legal debate on the development of IHL.[44] The work of al-Haq's Enforcement Project arguably had an equally impactful effect in developing the thinking and debates on the implications for third-party states of their obligation "to ensure respect" for the Fourth Geneva Convention by the occupying power (evidenced in certain policy statements by European states) in the early nineties.

The innovative nature of this fledgling Palestinian organization and the creativity that sparked from the engagement of those involved meant that as well as setting standards for monitoring, investigating, documenting, and analyzing information on human rights violations in the West Bank, LSM/al-Haq was engaged in work that was to become a staple of human rights advocacy (Palestinian and international) in future decades. This included, for example, a call in 1984 for the question of Israel's Road Plan No. 50 to be referred to the International Court of Justice for an advisory opinion, and initial efforts, early in the first intifada, to document "grave breaches" of the Fourth Geneva Convention with a view to stimulating prosecutions under third states' domestic legislation.[45] Across the region, and indeed internationally, al-Haq is credited as an incubator for human rights activists, with many who worked there in its early years going on to hold senior and leadership human rights positions in Palestine, regionally and internationally.

LSM/al-Haq learned its trade in the moment of struggle that the West Bank and Gaza lived in the 1980s. Possibilities and challenges looked different. This study explores what that meant for those involved and for the organization. Interviewed for al-Haq's thirty-year anniversary, Raja Shehadeh reflected on the photos that had been assembled for the publication:

For my generation of founding members these pictures bring memories of happy, hopeful and tense times when it was still not clear whether the organization would survive and succeed in fulfilling those aims for which it was established. It has. For those who live in these much crueller times without a memory of the past early years of the organization these pictures provide a window into a past when resilience and hard work defeated defeat and pessimism.

This study begins with those earlier times, before moving to al-Haq's present and "crueller" times, which includes the political and populist pillorying of the human rights and international law discourse on which the idea of LSM/al-Haq was based—indeed, before what currently appears to be a defeat for the realization of those principles through the systems apparently available to protect them. Erakat reminds us that "law's ability to oppress is evidence not of its failure but rather of the fact that it can be strategically deployed."[46] It was upon their understanding of this that LSM's founders acted, and in full knowledge of this that al-Haq continues its resistance today.

1

Context

In the late 1970s, a group of Palestinian professionals from the West Bank (including East Jerusalem) initiated a lengthy correspondence with the International Commission of Jurists (ICJ) in Geneva. It resulted in the establishment of Law in the Service of Man (LSM, later to become al-Haq), as the West Bank affiliate of the ICJ, in 1979. In the next chapter, I examine the challenges identified by the group through this correspondence, and how they rose to them; this chapter is a short reminder of the times insofar as they are raised by the narrative. I focus on the immediate context of the West Bank at this time, not to erase the longer and still violent histories that preceded the 1967 Israeli occupation.

THE OCCUPIED TERRITORIES, ISRAEL, AND THE PLO

The group's initial approach to the ICJ was sent in April 1977. The West Bank (including East Jerusalem) and Gaza Strip—those parts of Palestine remaining outside the Israeli State since its establishment in 1948—had been under Israeli military occupation for just shy of ten years. Jordan, which had ruled the West Bank since 1948, retained its claim till the first intifada, and still maintains authority over its Ministry of Awqaf and Islamic affairs and *shari'a* courts in occupied East Jerusalem, where Israel refuses to countenance Palestinian Authority jurisdiction and over which Israel has asserted sovereignty. US President Trump's 2017 decision to recognize Israel's position on the city as its capital challenged decades of international consensus against recognizing Israel's claims to territory acquired by force.[1] Egypt for its part had governed the Gaza Strip as "administrator" until the 1967 war. The leadership of the Palestine Liberation Organization (originally founded by Arab states in 1964) was taken over by Fatah (headed by Yasser Arafat) after the 1967 war. In 1970, the PLO was ousted from its bases in Jordan after "Black September" and armed engagements between the PLO and the Jordanian army. The PLO was now headquartered in Beirut. It was to be ousted in turn from

13

Lebanon after the Israeli invasion of 1982, removing its last armed bases in a country bordering on Israel, and was thenceforth headquartered in Tunis until the signing of the Israel-PLO Gaza-Jericho Agreement in 1994. In the occupied territories, membership of any faction in the PLO and any contact with the organization were illegal, as were such manifestations of nationalism as raising the Palestinian flag. In LSM's first publication, *The West Bank and the Rule of Law*, Shehadeh records the following example:

> In April 1980, several students from Bethlehem University were arrested and accused of wearing T-shirts which carried the emblem of the Bethlehem University Student Council. The emblem contained streaks of green, black and red on a white T-shirt. The authorities claimed that this added up to the four colours of the Palestinian flag. The University was warned that wearing these T-shirts was illegal, and the students were tried and convicted by a military court under Military Order No. 101.[2]

Gabi Baramki, who was acting president of Birzeit University after the 1974 deportation of the standing president Hanna Nasir, recalls in his memoir the frequency with which the Palestinian flag was raised by students and the hostile responses of the Israeli military.[3] Charles Tripp has pointed out that this kind of repression (whereby "it is forbidden to raise, exhibit or attach any flags or political emblems except after obtaining a licence")[4] made it "perversely easy to commit multiple small acts of resistance" which could involve large numbers of people.[5]

The charge of *tanzhim*, short-hand for membership in an illegal organization (i.e., a PLO faction), was leveled at activists involved in the nationalist political struggle. By no means were they all involved in or accused of involvement in the armed struggle that remained part of the resistance strategy of the various PLO factions (although not of the Communists).[6] Lisa Taraki stresses the formative background of many future leaders of the women's, union, and student movements in the voluntary work committees of the 1970s.[7] Writing in the first intifada, Joost Hiltermann traces the emergence of a "nationalist movement of classic design" in the West Bank and Gaza to the 1970s, after the PLO made a decision in 1974 to focus its energies on the occupied territories:

> The local movement consisted of two branches: the underground military-political branch, whose members adhere directly to one of the factions of the PLO and carry out resistance operations on the orders of their commanders, who are usually outside the area; and the semilegal social-political branch, consisting of institutions and popular organizations set up by local activists who have attempted to mobilize the Palestinian masses by offering them services that were otherwise not available, while articulating nationalist concerns and aspirations as part of their day-to-day work.[8]

Hiltermann refers to an "intensive recruitment drive [that] took place among students, workers, professionals and others." The PLO's decision to focus on the occupied territories came after the Arab League's recognition of the PLO as the "sole legitimate representative of the Palestinian people" followed by Yasser Arafat's historic address at the UN General Assembly, both in 1974 and, as recounted by Noura Erakat, significant outcomes of the PLO's legal work at the UN.[9] Arafat was presented (by then Algerian foreign minister Bouteflika) as chairman of the Executive Committee of the PLO and commander-in-chief of the Palestine Revolution; this was the speech he ended with his dramatic appeal: "Today I have come bearing an olive branch and a freedom-fighter's gun. Do not let the olive branch fall from my hand."[10] Erakat describes the intense efforts that led to this occasion, "the first time a non-state actor had taken the international podium," and describes the General Assembly at that time as comprising an "automatic majority of non-aligned states in a global context of ongoing, armed liberation struggles."[11] In the West Bank, those tied to the "old guard" of the Jordanian regime lost ground to the nationalists; in the 1976 municipal elections, "pro-PLO candidates were re-elected or swept into office in all the major towns except Bethlehem,"[12] and with the formation of the second National Guidance Committee (in 1978) there emerged "the first non-clandestine political framework" in the occupied territories.[13] Hamas did not exist, although its parent movement, the Muslim Brotherhood, was likewise engaged in broadening its constituency and institution-building during this period.[14] The West Bank (including East Jerusalem) and Gaza were known as the occupied territories (sometimes the Israeli-occupied territories); today's nomenclature of the occupied Palestinian territory (oPt) did not appear until the first intifada, with Jordan's renunciation of its claim to the West Bank and the PLO's recognition of and entry into negotiation with the state of Israel.

The Israeli government declined to recognize its status as an occupying power under international law, and preferred the term "administered territories"; it had illegally annexed East Jerusalem and applied the biblical names Judea and Samaria to the West Bank. In the West, Israel had been largely successful in "presenting its occupation of the Palestinian territories as the most benevolent in history." This realization, in the face of the situation he found when he returned home from his law studies in London, was one of the factors to provoke Raja Shehadeh into "agitating"—getting a group together to write to the ICJ.[15] The idea of a "benign occupation" and the assumption that what Israeli officials presented as truth was just that or a fair approximation dogged the attempts of Palestinians and their allies to present the facts as otherwise. This was perhaps the main challenge on the international front that LSM set out to meet.

Writing about the West Bank in the mid-1980s, George Bisharat reflects on the politically unresolved status of the territories and the issues of authority to which this state of "indeterminacy" gave rise:

> Indeterminancy has also given rise to the phenomenon of "over-control," the subjugation of the West Bank to multiple external authorities exerting contradictory pressures on the local community. Israel exercises direct control through the

agency of the military government. Jordan exercises indirect influence through its control of the flow of people and goods between the East and West banks, and through its network of client-notables. The PLO commands some quasi-governmental resources and enjoys the political loyalties of the majority of the Palestinian community. The result is a combination of suffocating control in matters that involve the interests of the three external authorities and a breakdown in the system of social accountability and near anarchy in realms implicating only or primarily local community interests.[16]

Reflections of this situation appear in the initial correspondence from the would-be founders of LSM. The deleterious situation of the court system in the West Bank, with all matters of interest to the Israeli occupation authorities being transferred to the military courts or army-headed Objection Committees, exemplifies Israel's effective power and lack of legitimate force.

WEST BANK LEGAL PROFESSION

Bisharat's study focuses on the legal profession and the challenges and dilemmas it faced during these times, not least its internal division between striking and working lawyers. The strike by West Bank lawyers had begun with the 1967 occupation, when the legal profession in the West Bank as a whole went on strike in protest against Israel's annexation of East Jerusalem, its transfer of the West Bank's Court of Appeal to Ramallah from Jerusalem, and its noncompliance with the Fourth Geneva Convention. As Shehadeh explains:

> The general feeling among the lawyers was that to appear before the newly organized courts would give legitimacy to the annexation of Jerusalem, because the Jordanian law specifically designates Jerusalem as the seat of the Court of Appeal. It would also, they thought, imply that the other changes carried out by the military authority were being condoned and legitimized, if they continued to work as usual.[17]

The Jordanian Bar Association—the professional organization for West Bank lawyers—supported the strike and undertook to pay stipends for the loss of professional income. Striking lawyers could practice—as appropriate—before the *shari'a* courts (where the judiciary had refused to give any recognition to the Israeli authorities) and the different courts of the Christian communities, but not in the military courts, which were gaining in jurisdiction, nor in the regular court system now under the control of the Israeli occupation authorities. Practicing West Bank lawyers were expelled from the Jordanian Bar Association (JBA) or else not allowed to join when they qualified. In the early 1980s, Bisharat estimates that some 60 percent of the profession were striking in the West Bank; there was no strike by lawyers in the Gaza Strip, where the separate system administered previously under Egypt's control had been unaffected by the changes to the judicial system in the West Bank.[18] Bisharat considers in detail the factors that, over the years since 1967, brought some lawyers back into work and kept others committed to the strike or encouraged them to join it upon qualifying. In regard to the system of justice administered by the occupation authorities, he observes:

> In the minds of local practitioners, these laws are a reflection of the very power of the military legal system, which is not to dispense justice, but to further the policy goals of suppressing Palestinian nationalism and facilitating Israeli settlement of the West Bank. In this view, the underlying objective of the military courts is less to affix guilt to specific individuals for violations of security regulations than to exact a steady toll from the community in general for acts of resistance, in the hope that pressure will develop within the community itself for the disciplining of its members.[19]

From the early 1980s there were attempts on the part of practicing lawyers in the West Bank to come to some kind of accommodation with the Bar Association in Amman, and/or to set up a branch of the JBA in the West Bank. These developments were followed closely by LSM in its formative years, given the deleterious effect on the coherence and standards of the profession of the absence of a professional association. The JBA threatened to have tried for treason those involved in negotiating with the Israeli military government for permission to establish a West Bank branch.[20] Shehadeh's journal records a striking lawyer telling him, "All of you lawyers who work here are collaborators. Every move you make is used to consolidate the Israeli occupation."[21] I return to these tensions in chapter 3.

The Palestinian population included rural and urban dwellers and the residents of refugee camps established after the 1948 *Nakba*, with other refugees added from the internal displacements of the 1967 war; there were also scattered Bedouin encampments. Travel within the West Bank, between the West Bank and Gaza, and between the West Bank and Israel was comparatively unimpeded in light of today's barricades of the Wall and permanent checkpoints to control movement of Palestinians between Areas A, B, and C. Although the whole of the occupied territories was a closed military area, flying checkpoints and closures after particular incidents were qualitatively different from the overall closures and partitions that characterize the areas today. The movement of Palestinians was controlled through the ID card system; in 1980, Shehadeh explained the wider significance of this form of control as follows:

> The agony of the exile and the dispersion of thousands and thousands of Palestinians can be stated in terms of their inability to obtain from the Israelis an identity card, evidence of their acceptance and status as residents in the country they were forced to leave. On the other hand, the humiliation of the million Palestinian holders of these coveted cards and the discrimination to which they are subjected is symbolised by this card which may at any time be confiscated, terminating their right to stay in the area.[22]

Palestinian vehicles were identified through the distinctive area-specific license plates the military authorities assigned. There were checkpoints—some regular and others flying—but none of today's Israeli-controlled terminals marking the end of "Area A" urban centers under Palestinian Authority jurisdiction; all this was to come after Oslo. Provided you were not wanted by the Israeli authorities and had not been placed under particular movement restrictions, you could get a blue-plated (West Bank) *servis* (shared seven-passenger taxi) from Ramallah all the way into East Jerusalem and back, something that is no longer possible even for those Palestinians who have the requisite Israeli permits allowing them to enter occupied East Jerusalem. West Bank Palestinians holding East Jerusalem ID cards had relatively easier passage with their yellow-plated vehicles.

Snapshots of life in the West Bank can be glimpsed in Raja Shehadeh's published extracts from his journal written over 1979–80.[23] Israeli settlers could be seen driving through the main towns of the West Bank, on their way to settlements, sometimes buying supplies, sometimes smashing up cars and committing other acts of violence against Palestinian civilians and their property. The road network that links up the settlement colonies with Israel's municipal areas and fractures the West Bank into atomized enclaves was not yet built, though in its original form it was to be the subject of one of LSM's early reports. Settler violence was an early focus of the organization's monitoring activities. The settlements were growing, with the active support of Israeli Prime Minister Begin. The settlers were armed, as were the Israeli soldiers who patrolled in jeeps or on foot through the Palestinian towns and villages, living in barracks and guarding the prisons and the headquarters of the military governor in each district. Palestinian students and schoolchildren were involved in protests and clashes with Israeli settlers and soldiers. The Palestinian population was not armed, with the exception of those members of the "military-political branch" of the PLO factions referred to by Hiltermann. A different exception comprised those Palestinians collaborating with the Israeli occupation authorities, notably members of the Village Leagues established by Israel to foster an alternative leadership and described by Shehadeh in one of his nonacademic pieces as "a criminal collaborationist grouping."[24]

CAMP DAVID

The Village Leagues were established after the conclusion of the 1978 Camp David Accords between Israel and Egypt, the negotiations for which had been hosted and the agreement brokered by US president Jimmy Carter. These accords were a critical part of the context in which the idea for LSM/al-Haq arose, and they are obliquely referred to in the correspondence with the ICJ examined in the following chapter. Carter had thrown himself into intense Middle East peace efforts since taking office in January 1977. In Israel, Likud came to power for the first time, and in November 1977 Egypt's President Sadat made the first ever official visit by an Arab leader to Israel, speaking before the Israeli Knesset; Erakat notes that the surprise visit derailed ongoing diplomatic exchanges between the United States and the PLO at the time.[25] The following month, Begin presented his plan for nonterritorial "administrative autonomy"—that is, "autonomy was to apply not to the land but only to the people who lived on it."[26] The first of the two Camp David Accords provided for the implementation of "autonomy" or "self-rule" arrangements for the Palestinians of the territories, with the exception of occupied East Jerusalem.[27] The PLO had not been a party to Camp David, nor had the Palestinian population been consulted, and Egypt's declared goal of achieving Israel's agreement to Palestinian self-determination was not realized.[28] Jordan refused to cooperate; Israel and Egypt signed a peace treaty the following year (1979), and Egypt was suspended from the Arab League, which moved its headquarters from Cairo to Tunis. By the time Shehadeh was writing his journal (1979–80), Likud was pushing the "administrative autonomy" concept that Hiltermann attributes originally to Moshe Dayan, looking for cooperative Palestinians to administer Palestinian affairs while Israel kept control of the territories, in accordance with the Israeli government's interpretation of the Camp David agreement.[29] In 1981 the Israeli occupation authorities established a civilian administration alongside its military government in the territories; LSM responded with an analysis of the substance and implications of Military Order 947 for the West Bank that set up the civilian administration.[30] Raja Shehadeh was later to tell an interviewer from the *International Review of the Red Cross* that this was "the most important legal change" and "this was how apartheid was introduced to the Occupied Palestinian Territory."[31]

The processes and conclusion of the Camp David arrangements were rejected by "national congresses" in the West Bank and Gaza, under the slogan "No to self-government, yes to the PLO."[32] They were protested and resisted by school and university students and the burgeoning number of politically affiliated voluntary committees and professional institutions that had been forming since the mid-'70s.[33] Amnesty International's annual report for 1977 highlights an increase in the number of convictions of Palestinians for alleged security-related offenses, and frequent demonstrations against the occupation.[34] The PLO, as already noted, had been investing in the mobilization of the population of the occupied territories, building on existing organizational structures of the PLO (such as trade unions), voluntary work committees established locally to provide social services for the occupied population, and encouraging the creation of new professional associations and popular groupings. This was "to serve as an infrastructure for a future Palestinian state" and in the meantime to constitute an "institutional infrastructure of resistance" to the occupation, including the authorities' plans for Israeli-controlled administrative autonomy.[35] Hiltermann theorizes this as a strategy of "out-administering the enemy."[36] This was not, however, a time of consensus among the factions of the Palestinian national movement in the occupied territories, but rather one of "acrimonious competition" over influence and control, notably among Fatah, the Democratic Front for the Liberation of Palestine (DFLP), the Popular Front for the Liberation of Palestine (PFLP) and the Communists.[37] Although membership in these political groups was illegal, Hiltermann explains the implications for local committees and associations as follows:

> In each of these organizations and movements, individuals tend to identify with a particular political current in the national movement headed by the PLO, or else the

organization has set itself apart from similar organizations, becoming for example the workers' branch of a particular current in the national movement.[38]

Everyday references to a particular person (or group) "being" PF/DF/Fatah thus intended and intend to convey that the person spoken about supports or sympathizes with that faction over others, rather than alleging the individual to be a "member." There was also the matter of money. Shehadeh opens his preface to *The Third Way* with reference to the 1978 decision of the Arab States' meeting in Baghdad to establish a Steadfastness Fund "to help us combat the collapse of our social and economic fabric, caused by the Israeli colonization of our land."[39] The fund was controlled by a joint PLO-Jordan committee, an arrangement which "became the focus of sharp criticism from nationalist leaders in the West Bank, who had little faith in the intentions of the king of Jordan"; according to Hiltermann, "the issue of Joint Committee funding was to become the main cause of contention in the national movement in the late 1970s and early 1980s."[40] This exacerbated tensions between the inside and the outside—the nationalist movement outside the occupied territories, and the local leadership within. Writing about the late 1970s, Hiltermann describes this as a "war of the institutions."[41] This forms part of the background to a key concern articulated in the letters from LSM's founders to the ICJ by those who built the institution: the insistence on a nonpartisan positioning for LSM. In 1978, the Joint Committee took over from the Jordanian government the payment of the stipends of striking West Bank lawyers.[42]

HUMAN RIGHTS ORGANIZATIONS

There was a gap among the popular and professional associations developing at this time. In his contribution to al-Haq's *Twenty Years Defending Human Rights* publication, Hiltermann notes that around the same time that the initiative to set up LSM began to take shape, other professional and intellectual institutions had begun to "come into their own," including Palestinian universities, the Arab Thought Forum, and the Arab Studies Society.[43] As already noted, there was no functioning professional association for West Bank lawyers that might have provided a forum for legal challenges. There was no local Palestinian human rights group. From the early seventies, Quaker Peace and Service ran legal advice services for Palestinians from an office in East Jerusalem.[44] In Israel there was the Association for Civil Rights in Israel (ACRI), which did not deal as a rule with matters in the occupied territories and, according to Hajjar, neither challenged the occupation per se nor took a position on the applicability of the Fourth Geneva Convention to Israel's rule in those territories.[45] There was also the Israeli National Section of the ICJ, which was not involved in challenging Israeli measures and policies in the West Bank and Gaza. One source of information was the Israeli League for Human and Civil Rights, chaired by Israel Shahak, publishing information (often culled from the Hebrew Israeli press) on human rights abuses inside Israel and in the occupied territories; in 1973 this group had been disaffiliated as a member by the New York–based International League for Human Rights.[46] Hajjar traces the "departure point for a local human rights movement" to politically motivated Palestinian and Israeli lawyers working in the military court system and increasingly making reference to international law and issues of legality of the nature of Israel's conduct of the occupation.[47]

Of less direct influence were developments in the human rights movement internationally.[48] Relatively recent academic reevaluations of the historiography/ies of human rights have cogently critiqued presentations of human rights and/or the "human rights movement" that were concentrated on Europe and/or the United States. Samuel Moyn and others identify breakthroughs in the seventies, with Eckel identifying Eastern Europe and South America as regions where "human rights came to the fore as a protest language."[49] Moyn has proposed that "the best general explanation for the origins of this social movement and common discourse around rights remains the collapse of other, prior utopias, both state-based and internationalist"[50]—more generally, he argues, a move from politics broadly stated to a morality that sought to stand apart from (and indeed above) the politics of the past and of the day. This last proposition is oddly resonant with the positions articulated by the founders of LSM in 1979. This is not to detract from the cogency of Moyn's critics, for example Joseph Slaughter, who prefaces his intervention with a quotation from Upendra Baxi: "An adequate historiography will, of course, [. . .] locate the originating languages of human rights far beyond the European spacetime."[51] Nor indeed would al-Haq locate "international" or "human rights" as coterminous with concepts, movement, or histories in the West or Global North, but would be more likely to agree with Vasuki Nesiah that "the human rights tradition is internally diverse and even internally conflicted, and a singular history does a disservice to the counter-hegemonic projects that have framed their claims through human rights language."[52] Still, in its origins, LSM/al-Haq (or at least the three founders) tended to look west (rather than south), and to the conventionally recognized and established international human rights organizations, for initial support and alliances, because of their personal familiarity with these groups and their contexts, but also for pragmatic assessments of the potential impact such groups offered in their interventions with the Israeli occupation authorities: To whom would Israel listen? Whose voice would Israel hear? As noted, they paid close attention to the struggle against apartheid in South Africa, noting the structural underpinnings of apartheid rule.[53] As for Arab organizations, Joe Stork and Susan E. Waltz consider the turbulences elsewhere in the region that unsettled existing ideologies and allegiances and made space for a human rights discourse to emerge. This is explored briefly below, but as a number of interviewees for this study made clear, their real, sustained engagement with

Arab human rights groups and actors elsewhere in the Global South came after the Vienna meeting of 1993 considered in chapter 6 (and, of course, after Oslo).[54]

In 1977, David Weissbrodt published one of the first articles on the international human rights movement, looking at a number of human rights NGOs with national sections in different countries, including the oldest of them, the Paris-based and primarily Francophone International Federation of Human Rights (FIDH) founded in 1922.[55] FIDH was to become an international partner for some of the first Arab human rights groups, those setting up in the Maghreb around the same time as LSM. Amnesty International, founded in 1961, is described by Weissbrodt as "one of the largest and newest of the nongovernmental organizations concerned with human rights."[56] Amnesty's International Secretariat assigned a full-time research assistant to work on the Middle East region in 1970 and undertook an extended research visit to Israel and the occupied territories in 1978; a twentieth-anniversary account of Amnesty's achievements does not cover its work here.[57] As the model of a membership organization, Amnesty's activism revolved around national sections, which existed overwhelmingly in the West and did not, at that time, work on human rights violations in their own countries.[58] The award of the Nobel Peace Prize 1977 to Amnesty is part of the standard narrative of the 1970s as the breakthrough decade in the international human rights movement, although in Palestine, the following year's award to Menachem Begin and Anwar Sadat (for the Camp David Accords) made more of an impression, and not a positive one.[59] Greater impact from an external actor on a human rights–related story was generated in Palestine by the publication the same year of the *Sunday Times'* report on allegations of torture of Palestinian detainees by Israeli forces.[60]

In the United States, the Lawyers Committee for Human Rights—since 2003 Human Rights First—was established in 1978 and was one of LSM's earliest institutional interlocutors in the States.[61] Another of today's players, Human Rights Watch, did not exist as such. Its first structure, Helsinki Watch, was established in 1978, to follow up on the commitments to human rights and fundamental freedoms made by state signatories to the Helsinki Accords of 1975.[62] Other watch committees were established during the course of the 1980s, with Middle East Watch the last in 1989.[63] In Europe, the International Commission of Jurists (ICJ) was established in 1952, solidly on one side in the context of the Cold War, but its Geneva-based secretariat later moved determinedly and innovatively into a more international position considering a broader range of human rights issues, including social and economic rights. The ICJ had national sections, again mostly in Western Europe, and was best known among lawyers for its focus on rule-of-law issues and its governing commission of prominent judges and lawyers.[64] The ICJ produced its first report focusing on Israel/Palestine in 1970, in the wake of a funding scandal that is discussed in chapter 2 in the context of its repercussions in the West Bank. The ideological counterpart to the ICJ (at least historically) was the International Association of Democratic Lawyers, which Weissbrodt described in

1977 as finding "the large part of their members and support in socialist countries and in allied groups in nonsocialist nations."[65] One of the first substantial human rights reports on Israeli violations in the occupied territories was published in 1978 by the National Lawyers Guild, a US organization affiliated with the IADL.[66]

INTERNATIONAL LAW

International human rights organizations in the 1970s did not address issues of international humanitarian law (IHL) as a matter of course, if at all.[67] IHL was then mostly the concern of the International Committee of the Red Cross (ICRC) and military lawyers in different parts of the world. Israeli law journals were among the few academic venues for publications on this body of law at the time, and Israel and the occupied territories constituted the main case study for contemporary application of IHL.[68] It was in the *Israel Law Review* that Yehuda Blum published his arguments in support of the Israeli government's decision early in the occupation that it was not legally bound to apply the Fourth Geneva Convention Relative to the Protection of Civilian Persons in Time of War (1949), a position central to Israel's annexationist agenda and part of its "lawfare" work discussed further in the epilogue.[69] Beyond this context, however, it is hard to convey the overwhelming lack of interest, then, among both international legal scholars and human rights groups in the principles of the law governing military occupation and, indeed, armed conflict. There has been an explosion of scholarship and other material on IHL since the 2003 US-led invasion of Iraq and, to a certain extent, in the 1990s context of the wars in former Yugoslavia. This has included analysis of state practice-led developments in IHL to accommodate changes to existing governance and legal systems in occupied territory necessitated by the "transformative goals of certain occupations" (as the occupation of Iraq is presented). These contrast with the "conservationist principle in the laws of war," certain underlying rules of which, according to Adam Roberts, "set a framework of minimal alteration of the existing order in the occupied territory."[70] In the late 1970s, the lack of academic interest in IHL was matched by a lack of intellectual resources to support those (such as the founders of al-Haq) struggling to understand and work with it. By contrast, Noura Erakat maps considerable efforts invested by the PLO in securing admission with other liberation movements to the ICRC-convened Diplomatic Conference charged with reviewing what became the 1977 Additional Protocols to the Geneva Conventions. However, she also reports key figures from the time as recalling that the PLO was not technically engaged with the law, but rather, "its strategy was to enter every available space in order to enhance its international standing."[71] This approach was also to mark the PLO's engagement with the negotiations of the Oslo Accords in the early 1990s, to the documented despair of Raja Shehadeh.

As for international human rights law (IHRL), the two International Human Rights Covenants had come into force in 1976, developing into international treaty law the principles established in the 1948 Universal Declaration of Human Rights (UDHR). Human rights–related activity at the United Nations proliferated in consequence, including the establishment of the UN Centre for Human Rights and the drafting of additional human rights treaties.[72] However, the extension of this body of law to occupied territories and war zones was not yet under investigation. In 2006, Roberts was still describing the "applicability of the international law of human rights to military occupations" as "a relatively new and controversial issue."[73]

On the other hand, the Covenants share a common Article 1 that begins, "all peoples have the right to self-determination," a principle that the colonial powers had kept out of the UDHR when it was proposed by Egypt and supported by Lebanon. Anthony Tirado Chase observes that the context of the 1960s, particularly the greater involvement of states from the developing world and the Non-Aligned Movement in UNGA debates, allowed arguments led by Middle Eastern states in committee to ensure inclusion of the right to self-determination. Tolley notes further that "new Afro-Asian members reformed Human Rights Commission procedures to hear black African and Palestinian demands for self-determination."[74] The right of self-determination, says Chase, has been "particularly instrumental for grounding the South African and Palestinian struggles in international law," and the fact that it is there in the first article of the Covenants is "due, in good part, to the Palestinian case."[75] Samuel Moyn considers self-determination to have been the "chief and threshold right" in the anticolonial struggle.[76] In the case of Palestine, the "threshold right" of self-determination had not been achieved, and there was no national state from which to seek the promotion and protection of the human rights of its citizens. The argument that an occupying power would be bound by treaty obligations under international human rights law had not at this point been made, let alone won, and Israel had yet to sign on to the two International Covenants.

It is unsurprising that the founders of LSM mostly steered clear of the principle of self-determination, focusing rather on violations of the rule of law to meticulously build a picture of the occupation very different from that projected by Israel as the occupying power. Mouin Rabbani, a researcher with the organization during the first intifada, observed that this risked an "emphasis on micro-violations to the detriment of the bigger picture."[77] Nevertheless, as Hajjar has pointed out, the Israeli authorities clearly regarded "most Palestinian attempts to mobilise round a collective national identity" as a security risk and could be expected to react accordingly.[78] In the initial correspondence with the ICJ in Geneva, examined in the next chapter, and against the background of Camp David, the would-be founders of the new organization explicitly distanced themselves from expressing any view on what political arrangements should prevail in the occupied territories, provided the rule of law was respected, and declared themselves free of partisan political affiliation. That the rule of law for them would include implementation of Palestinians' right to self-determination was not made explicit.

HUMAN RIGHTS IN THE REGION

In such positioning, those who became the founders of Palestine's first human rights organization were different from counterparts in the Arab region moving towards human rights initiatives. The founders of LSM did not consciously work on enabling political pluralism or on the promotion of democracy, although they insisted on their vision of the "rule of law" entailing internal processes of inclusion and equality in Palestinian society. The circumstances of occupation (and IHL) framed priorities here differently. It was not until Oslo and the arrival of the Palestinian Authority that al-Haq was advised, by Chilean human rights leader José Zalaquett, that it might need to make a "certain declaration of principles about the connection between human rights and democracy" were it to treat such matters as fair elections as human rights issues.[79] Nor were the three founders political activists, as many of their counterparts were.[80] The first human rights organization in the Arab region not set up by a political party was the Tunisian League of Human Rights (LTDH), formally authorized by the Tunisian authorities in May 1977.[81] Others followed: in Morocco, the Moroccan Association for Human Rights (AMDH) in 1979 and the Moroccan Organisation for Human Rights in 1988; different Algerian Leagues in the mid-1980s; the regional Arab Organization for Human Rights in 1983;[82] and the Egyptian Organisation for Human Rights in 1985. The circumstances of their emergence depended on the domestic context, but there were common regional factors. Several of these related to Israel/Palestine: Israel's defeat of the Arab forces in 1967 and the "subsequent ideological decline of Arab nationalism," according to Chase, and the 1982 Israeli invasion of Lebanon and siege of Beirut, when Arab governments failed to assist and also repressed demonstrations by their own nationals against the Israeli action.[83] According to Stork, it was this latter that "prompted human rights to take organizational form" in Egypt.[84] The solidarity of the Arab human rights movement with the cause of Palestinian rights has been a consistent feature of regional activism since its origins.

The Arab human rights groups also had challenges in common. Their positioning towards their governments, of course, differed from that of LSM towards the Israeli military authorities, but similar balances had to be weighed to survive in hostile political circumstances. The founders of the politically independent Arab human rights groups were as keen as those of LSM to be nonpartisan and to be seen as such in their human rights work. Unlike the LSM founders, they often worked directly to create a consensus of space for human rights work among the different parties, sometimes by having representatives of the parties in their governing structures. Also unlike LSM, the groups in Tunisia and Morocco had to deal explicitly with the relationship between Islam and international human rights, and the role that Islamists might play in their organizations.

In common with LSM, on the other hand, they found the context for human rights work uncomfortable: "the concept of human rights, it must be noted, was far from fashionable at the time," says Waltz in relation to Tunisia. Leftists who constituted the majority of the intelligentsia "commonly dismissed human rights as a bourgeois notion and dangerously American."[85] In Egypt, a founder of the EOHR, Hani Shukrallah, recalled that "the existence of the [human rights] movement was put in question not just by the government but by the intellectual and political elites, including the political parties, legal and illegal."[86] Talking of the reaction to the establishment of the AOHR, Crystal notes that besides the regimes and the Islamists, "the Arab nationalist left was also historically suspicious of the group's aims, seeing human rights as an issue of Western origin designed to deflect concern from economic and social issues."[87]

Part of the ideological association of "human rights" with the West was the use of human rights language by the United States (and Western Europe) against the Soviet Union during the Cold War. In the States, Congress had in 1974 adopted the Foreign Assistance Act, section 502B of which required reports from the State Department on the human rights record of all those states receiving US aid; this was soon expanded to include all states. LSM's first formal intervention in a third-party state was a response to one of these reports.[88] Furthermore, President Jimmy Carter's January 1977 speech on taking office is framed as one of the key human rights moments of the era.[89] Carter proclaimed "commitment to human rights as the centre of his foreign policy," but implementation of the policy was predictably problematic.[90] Dumbrell notes that in contrast to the way liberals received it, "for conservatives, the policy offered a lever against communism and its abuses" or, as one US administration staffer put it, "to really beat up morally on the Soviets."[91] A distrust of the discourse of human rights among Palestinians—particularly but not exclusively those educated on Soviet scholarships, and the many Communist-aligned activists involved in civil society groups—was to be part of the context of LSM's early years. "The idea about human rights," says Khaled Batrawi, coordinator of al-Haq's fieldwork unit in the late 1980s and a graduate of Kiev, "was that it was a new form of colonialism, or imperialism, a western discourse."[92]

At the same time as declaring his commitment to human rights, President Carter was cosigning the 1978 Camp David Accords that signally failed to secure Palestinian rights and were the object of so much protest in the occupied territories. Jimmy Carter went on, after the end of his presidency, to set up the annual Carter-Menil Human Rights Prize, which in 1989 was awarded jointly to al-Haq and to the then new Israeli human rights organization B'Tselem.[93] Carter remained engaged with the area into which he had put so much energy, and with so few of the results that he apparently anticipated: the title of his 2006 book, *Palestine: Peace not Apartheid*, was designed to provoke a primarily US audience into acknowledging the reality of "the abominable oppression and persecution in the occupied territories."[94] This is part of the current "crueller times" that Shehadeh referred to in his 2009 reflection for al-Haq's *30 Years* publication, including sustained siege on Gaza, the systematic effort to permanently dispossess Palestinians in East Jerusalem, and US president Trump's 2017 decision to recognize Jerusalem as the capital of Israel and move the US embassy there.

2

—————

Beginnings

In the spring of 1977, four Palestinian legal professionals—three lawyers and a judge—wrote from the West Bank to the International Commission of Jurists (ICJ) in Geneva, initiating a correspondence that would culminate in the establishment of LSM as an ICJ affiliate.[1] The ICJ, with its key mandate vested in the judiciary and the legal profession, was an obvious and attractive international partner to this group of legal professionals, and they were seeking to establish a branch of the ICJ in the West Bank, as they explained:

> Sir,
> We the undersigned are a group of lawyers and judges working in the occupied West Bank of Jordan. One of us is a member of 'Justice', the British Branch of the International Commission of Jurists.
>
> The situation now in the West Bank is such that there is no Law Council, Bar, or any other association of lawyers, in operation. There is also no centre for legal research.
>
> All of us the undersigned believe in and uphold the principles of the rule of law. We believe that it is at this time more than at any other time that it is important that these principles be promulgated, developed, and applied, especially since we are on the brink of a new re-organization of our society here.
>
> We also believe in and uphold all the principles of human rights and liberties as set forth in the Universal Declaration of Human Rights.
>
> Therefore and in order to uphold and strengthen these principles which we believe in and in order to help in promulgating these and also in order to assist in every way the existence and maintenance of high principles of justice, we are desirous of establishing a society here to be a branch of your commission and whose objects conform with the objects which your commission was established to help promulgate.
>
> We would however like from the outset to describe to you all the difficulties that we would be facing. The first is that, unfortunately, these objects which both

you and we uphold are not as yet part of the tradition of this land nor are they commonly understood or believed in. We believe that in order to make them common knowledge and in order to win more adherents it is imperative that we should have the means both intellectual and financial to write, publish, translate articles, pamphlets and books and to do whatever else we deem necessary to achieve that goal. Although we would be able to draw to some extent on the means available to us here, yet, due to the unnatural and most difficult conditions we have to operate under, we shall be in need of assistance if we are to operate effectively. We would, furthermore, like to make it absolutely clear from the outset that we have no political affiliations nor would we support or advocate any specific political creed or future. We would advocate and pursue the ideas which the commission was founded to uphold such as the supremacy of the rule of law and which we believe should prevail as the foundation stone upon which any such structure should be constructed. However, and in order that this may be ensured, the ground must be prepared and this we hope with your help to do by establishing here a branch of your commission which would do what it would deem necessary in the way of publishing, lecturing, sponsoring research etc. The Branch would also be active in preparing reports on the administration of justice in the area and would be willing to cooperate with other Branches of the Commission abroad by exchanging literature on jurisprudence and working on joint projects in comparative law.

We would like to know at your earliest convenience your readiness to assist in the establishment here of a branch of your commission and of your readiness to help us financially if not directly then perhaps through the contact of your central office in Geneva.[2]

This is the letter of a group anticipating social and political change and seeking to promote and uphold the rule of law (and "also," in a subsequent paragraph, human rights). They want to do this—and be seen to do it—almost without reference to the highly political context. The impetus is very much focused on rule-of-law issues in Palestinian society, on the need for promotion and dissemination of these principles, despite "the unnatural and most difficult conditions we have to operate under." This oblique reference is the only mention of the Israeli occupation. The insistence on their lack of political party affiliation or a view on the political future (the disposition of the Palestinian territories) may have been included to reassure their ICJ interlocutors (and any Israeli interceptors of the correspondence) of their distance from nationalist (PLO) politics that the Israeli authorities considered a security threat. In fact, the secretary-general of the ICJ at the time, Niall MacDermot, was considerably more politically outspoken on such matters than his West Bank correspondents were able to be.

On receipt of the letter, MacDermot responded with interest. "Our timing was impeccable," Shehadah was later to write: "The respectable human rights organization was looking for partners to work with on the issue of the Israeli occupation."[3] The ICJ already had a section in Israel, headed by Justice Haim Cohn, who was also at the time an ICJ commissioner.[4] It was under the names of Cohn as chairman and the group's honorary secretary that early in 1970 the Israeli National Section of the ICJ had released a statement to "register its protest against the publication in the Review of the International Commission of Jurists, of a Report entitled: 'The Middle East: War or Peace,' because of its being tendentious and misleading."[5] The 1969 ICJ report, its first on the Middle East, was published under the leadership of the previous secretary-general, Seán MacBride.[6] MacBride was an imposing figure who among other things had fought against the British for Irish independence, been a politically committed lawyer and then a minister of foreign affairs in Ireland, and helped Amnesty International get started; he went on to be awarded both the Nobel Peace Prize in 1974 and the Lenin Prize for Peace among Nations in 1977, and to be closely involved in different United Nations initiatives.[7] The Israeli section's statement of protest against the ICJ's 1969 report was a two-page single-spaced defense of Israeli government positions, current and historical. Inter alia, it read:

> As far as allegations of "disrespect for the civilian population" are directed against the Israeli authorities, the Report fails to mention that in Israel, unlike some other countries, every person, without distinction of race or religion, domicile or nationality, political or other affiliation, has free access to independent courts of justice which exercise jurisdiction over all Israeli public officers and which enforce the Rule of Law without fear or favour. [...]
>
> Much capital is made in the Report of the non-compliance (by Israel of course) with various resolutions of the General Assembly, the Security Council and other organs of the United Nations, and several such resolutions are adduced as proof of "flagrant violations" (by Israel) of the United Nations Charter (p. 13), of military action (by Israel) endangering the "maintenance of peace" (ibid.), and even of "the violation (by Israel) of human rights in the Arab territories occupied by Israel" (p. 12). [...] To present readers of the Review with the one-sided picture of censures passed against Israel is to imply that there was, indeed, nothing to censure in the Middle East War but what the Security Council was allowed, without being vetoed, to censure; and to demand respect for such resolutions on the part of Israel is to ask a nation upholding the Rule of Law to submit to political machinations calculated to undermine the Rule of Law and supersede it by procedural and political tactics. Compliance by an innocent party with United Nations resolutions of this kind would amount to a suicidal self-castigation which is morally, legally and politically unjustifiable.
>
> The Israeli National Section of the International Commission of Jurists, which is second to none in its dedication to the Rule of Law, comprises among its members many jurists and lawyers who are, and have for many years been actively engaged in the administration of military justice including, since 1967, the administration of justice in the occupied territories. They deeply resent the wholesale allegations of violations of human rights, even if emanating from United Nations origins and if echoed in publications such as the Review, as slanderous war propaganda. As they will not let themselves be deviated from their duty to enforce the laws justly and impartially, so will this Section be and always remain vigilant for the observance of

the Rule of Law and the protection of human rights. But the purposes and concerns of the Rule of Law appear badly served if its promoters allow themselves to be made the mouthpiece of partiality and prejudice.[8]

This image of Israel as a state firmly based on the rule of law was shared broadly in Israeli society; the Israeli National Section of the ICJ was to become a significant platform for articulating Israeli government positions in this regard.[9] The broad acceptance of this image in the West constituted both major motivation and vital context in and against which the founders of LSM/al-Haq consciously sited their efforts. The Israeli section's disdain for the UN, a little over two years after the 1967 war, seems in part a response to MacBride's own insistence (in the ICJ report) on the necessary role of the international body in resolving the conflict. Also clear in this letter are allusions to the Cold War context in which the Soviet Union championed its Arab allies and the Palestinian cause.

Like his predecessor at the head of the ICJ, Niall MacDermot had come into human rights after a career in law and then in politics, although in this case in the British parliament. A political contemporary recalled MacDermot as "the most surefooted, on-top-of-the-job, confidence-inspiring ministerial performer of all the talented 1964 Labour government."[10] His highly promising political career was stymied after British intelligence (MI5) briefed against him as a security risk to the then Labour prime minister, Harold Wilson, and in frustration he left politics and quite soon took over from MacBride at the ICJ.[11] Tolley reports from a journalist who watched him in action at the UN Commission on Human Rights that "no one talked down to MacDermot, and no one ignored him. Diplomats deferred to him, and dreaded his rebuke."[12] In 1977, *The Review* of the ICJ ran a piece titled "Israeli Settlements in Occupied Territories,"[13] which MacDermot later summarized as follows:

> In our Review of December 1977 we in the Secretariat of the International Commission of Jurists sought to show what we believe to be the fallacies in the Israeli arguments. [. . .] No country supports Israel in opposing the repeated UN resolutions declaring that the settlements have no legal validity. All the permanent members of the Security Council are agreed upon their illegality. To me the Israeli settlements are the touchstone of Israeli intentions.[14]

The ICJ's rule-of-law approach enabled (indeed required) a structural approach to violations that went directly to the concerns of the LSM founders. MacDermot had already robustly told his audience at the UN's Palais des Nations in Geneva that "the Israeli government say they cannot negotiate with terrorists. For my part I am unmoved by this description of those who fight for their liberation."[15] In the same venue the following year he turned his attention to those matters of politics from which his West Bank interlocutors had distanced themselves in their initial communication. He told his audience how a recent study "shows clearly how unacceptable to the Palestinians are the so-called autonomy proposals of the Camp David

Agreement" and closed with the observation that "the PLO should be included" in detailed negotiations that might lead to "an acceptable transition period if, and it is a big if, the people of Israel could bring themselves to accept the legitimate rights of the Palestinians, and accept the idea of self-determination for the Palestinian people and their eventual right to erect their own sovereign state."[16] Very differently placed from the LSM group, MacDermot lost no opportunity to link human rights and international law to a just and durable peace process realizing the goal of self-determination. Carter's Camp David impressed MacDermot no more than it had the Palestinians.

At the same time, MacDermot had to bear in mind that not all of his commissioners—those ultimately responsible for governance at the ICJ—saw things the same way. Hiltermann recalls that into the late 1980s "in the United States a Palestinian was an adjective modifying the noun terrorist."[17] At the 1979 meeting, MacDermot began by noting that "on such a controversial subject as this, it is difficult for me to say anything other than platitudes which would meet with the approval of all my Commission members"; his views and comments were to be taken as his own.[18] Tolley notes that "after MacDermot pressed a reluctant Executive Committee to recognise Palestinian rights, the ICJ became one of the few non-communist NGOs to criticise Israel."[19]

The ICJ had things in its past that would lend themselves to rumor and distrust in Palestine: its own website describes its Cold War origins (in 1952) as "born at the ideological frontline of a divided post-war Berlin." Things changed in the 1960s; with the recruitment to its ranks of more jurists from Asia, Africa, and South America, the ICJ worked for "the endorsement of economic development and social justice objectives" of which, as Richard Pierre Claude points out, "ICJ anti-communist founders heartily disapproved."[20] Tolley notes that "ICJ advocacy of development as a human right sought to bridge a major North-South divide."[21] Despite these principled changes in direction under MacBride's leadership, in 1967 the ICJ was embroiled in a scandal when the press broke what Claude refers to as "the tale of the United States Central Intelligence Agency (CIA) in secretly bankrolling the formation of the ICJ as an instrument of the Cold War" through the "conduit" of the American Fund for Free Jurists.[22] Tolley notes that MacBride "denounced the CIA and asserted that he had no information about covert funding through conduit foundations."[23] The ICJ survived the initial fallout through funding from the Ford Foundation and an energetic battle by MacBride to counter any reputational damage; Neier's assessment is that the organization "was never severely discredited" by the revelations.[24] At the end of 1970, MacDermot took over as secretary-general from MacBride. "Oh paradox!" wrote a reviewer in 1981, welcoming the ICJ's copublication of LSM's *The West Bank and the Rule of Law*: under MacBride and MacDermot, the ICJ had been transformed into a "veritable international power [. . .] whose reports are feared like the plague by dictatorships of the right, totalitarian regimes of the left, in brief by oppressors."[25]

Back in 1977, MacDermot wrote back to his Palestinian correspondents, rais- ing what he must have known would be for them a most political matter, as well as one of principle: the ICJ's Executive Committee, he anticipated, would expect him "to invite the comments of our Israeli Section on your application." He asked his Palestinian interlocutors whether they would agree to MacDermot's forward- ing a copy of their letter to Justice Haim Cohn for his comment or whether they would prefer to approach Cohn themselves.[26] In response, the four replied that after serious consideration they had come to the conclusion that "we have nothing to gain from such contact." They were located in the "occupied territories of Jordan whereas the other Branch is in Israel." And:

> We would therefore appreciate it if you would consider the Branch we intend to establish as entirely separate and independent and that you do not invite the com- ments of the Israeli Branch on this matter. As we are legally-speaking in two different countries you are not under any obligation to consult the Israeli Branch.[27]

There is another reference here to "this occupied area which is approaching a political reorganization." Given that the founders wanted the protection of the ICJ against the likely hostility of the Israeli occupation authorities, along with their sensitivity to being considered to be coming under an Israeli principal in any mat- ter, it was an answer that MacDermot might have anticipated. When he in turn replied, he reported on the meeting of the ICJ's Executive Committee to which he had submitted the West Bank letters and also a comment from Justice Haim Cohn (an ICJ commissioner) whom he reported as writing:

> I welcome the establishment in the West Bank of a Section of the Commission, com- posed of legal practitioners without "political affiliations" whose purpose is not to "advocate or support any specific political creed or future." [. . .] If some formula can be found to recognize this group without (expressly or impliedly) recognizing the West Bank as a state, the Israeli National Section will be glad to cooperate with it in fostering and promoting the Rule of Law.[28]

Clear here is the significance of LSM asserting a nonpolitical stance. The response underlines antipathy to the idea of a "state" in the West Bank (and/or Gaza Strip). Fully in line with official Israeli positions at Camp David,[29] Justice Cohn suggested that the ICJ might furnish him with the names of the West Bank signatories, which MacDermot had removed from the copy: "I would have pleasure in inviting them to an informal meeting in which some patterns of cooperation could perhaps be worked out." MacDermot advised the West Bank group accordingly:

> The Executive Committee fully understand and agree that your organisation should be totally separate from the Israeli National Section. [. . .] However, in view of Mr Justice Haim Cohn's friendly reply, they hope very much that you will agree to meet him, and authorise me to disclose your names and addresses to him for this purpose.

This point was pursued by the ICJ in subsequent correspondence. Given the international context at the time, it is entirely possible that certain Executive

Committee members were keen that a potential Palestinian partner be approved by the established Israeli section, however informally this was to happen, and despite the fact that the author of a history of the ICJ describes the latter at the time as "the inactive Israeli national section nominally headed by Haim Cohn."[30] Shehadeh describes this as getting "clearance."[31] MacDermot himself seems to have viewed it as a matter of practicalities beyond convincing his committee:

> It seems to me almost certain that before the authorities will agree to the creation of your association, they will consult Mr Justice Cohn, since he is one of the Commission members and President of the Israeli Section. It will be difficult for him to lend his support to the application if he has not met you. I think you will find that he fully accepts that your association should be wholly independent of the Israeli national section.[32]

The issue was raised with Charles Shammas when he met with the ICJ in Geneva in the summer of 1978, and he was reminded later that year: "We think the stage has been reached to approach and inform Mr Justice Haim Cohn of the developments, something we understood you agreed on, here in Geneva."[33] The following year, informing Jonathan Kuttab of the Executive Committee's approval of the application, a postscript from MacDermot notes that "The Executive Committee hopes that you will keep Justice Haim Cohn informed of developments and of your activities. They consider that it may prove to be in your own interest to do so."[34] By then, Charles Shammas and Raja Shehadeh had indeed paid an informal visit to Justice Cohn, and engaged an institutional relationship that was to be tested in the next few years. Shehadeh describes the encounter as follows: "With his kind but authoritative manner, he asked us a few questions, which we answered honestly. The verdict he communicated to Geneva was that 'we were okay. But too political.'"[35] Shehadeh assumes that the finding of "political" rested on their view that the building of settlements was in violation of international law. For his part, Shammas recalls that he and Shehadeh were struck by "how completely unaware he [Cohn] was of the practices of the military government."

Back in the West Bank, the group was working on the technicalities of registration. A long letter in early 1978 set out the "three species of corporate entities" that were available: registration as a charitable society, as a cooperative society, and as a limited public company.[36] This first explanation to the ICJ of the choice of a company framework set out the powers of regulation in regard to the first two types of entity over permission to establish, over operations, and over membership of the Executive Committee, as well as, in the case of charitable societies, over "each transfer of funds from abroad." These powers under Jordanian law were now in the West Bank exercised (in the case of the establishment and committee membership of charitable societies) by the delegated Israeli army officer. As the letter pointed out, "for any proposed society whose objects appear to any degree to be problematic from the standpoint of the Military administration, permission to register is simply withheld indefinitely." LSM's continuing interest in this as a rule-of-law issue was to be demonstrated by the publication in 1982 of the collected laws and military orders applying to charitable societies in the West Bank, which like other military orders were not routinely available.[37]

Having set out the legal constraints, the group proposed the option of the limited public company, "not considered as a public trust and therefore [. . .] not subject to the same degree of regulation and control by the relevant minister or, as things stand, the relevant officer of the Israeli army." This option involved technical transactions between the company, the association it would set up, the ICJ in Geneva, the shareholders, and the elected officers of the association. By way of further explanation, the letter observed:

> Incorporating the branch's charter into a contract between the company and a foreign provider of funds for the branch should make it more difficult for local forces to compromise the branch's functional independence and non-political status or to impose modifications in its internal processes or its complexion without precipitating its closure. [. . .] A branch organized as a subsidiary project of a holding company would not be reporting directly to any authority, civil or military.

Although not picked up immediately in Geneva, this paragraph was trying to convey a further concern to do with interference from "local forces." The reply from the ICJ shows discomfort at this proposed setup, which clearly constituted a departure from the normal institutional form of unincorporated membership organizations. "The scheme you propose seems extremely complicated," responded MacDermot, and "I doubt whether our Executive Committee would favour entering into a contract of the kind you suggest."[38] MacDermot offered to "take the matter up with the Israeli authorities in advance" on the assumption that "whatever form of organisation you adopt, the creation of the association is going to require the consent in some form of the Israeli authorities, civil or military."

In the autumn of 1978, with Shammas's visit to the ICJ in Geneva in between, the West Bank group wrote back with a five-page letter addressing the ICJ's concerns and reservations "with respect to our proposal to organize within the framework of a company." This letter revisits some of the points in regard to applicable law and practice but also addresses the "contextual constraints" within which the group saw itself operating and which the proposed institutional framework was intended to accommodate:

> Both our choice of framework and the procedure which we propose to follow in establishing an effective non-politicized affiliate of the International Commission of Jurists reflect, on the one hand, restrictions on freedom of assembly and association that have been in force since the Israeli occupation and, on the other hand, certain problematic characteristics of our society's internal processes which those restrictions have exacerbated.[39]

The authors detailed the restrictions on freedom of assembly and association imposed under the terms of Israeli Military Proclamation 101 that would challenge attempts to hold meetings and activities as an "ad hoc committee," which was one structural suggestion from the ICJ. The following paragraphs are a dense exposition of the challenges the drafters saw themselves facing:

> Economic and political developments to date have provided little impetus or leeway for the generation of modern institutional forms and internal alignments typical of a society organized around production for exchange rather than patronage and subsidy. [...]
>
> Consequently efforts such as ours must be carried out within the context of a still vigorous sectarian order whose subjects have some difficulty accepting at face value a public interest or social development project with whose proclaimed objectives they may wholly identify. This difficulty has been aggravated since 1967 by the prohibition of all organized political activity, the effect of which has been to cause political expression to assume a cryptic idiom, thereby giving sectarian political overtones to even the most loosely organized pro bona initiative.
>
> In light of the above, we strongly believe that the effective promotion of the rule of law within our context requires an organizational vehicle that proclaims as well as assures the non-sectarian nature of the enterprise if it is to attract participants on a non-sectarian basis. An arrangement which lacks either an incorporated institutional foundation or a democratic, constitutional process of internal regulation will not under the prevailing conditions win sufficiently broad participation because it calls for the commitment to a visible group process of individuals whose civil rights are highly circumscribed and precarious, and who have uncertain expectations of each other's conduct and a weak tradition of ad hoc association. Failure to attract participants across sectarian lines would seriously diminish our ability to spread the ideas we uphold within the society at large.

Part of what the authors are referring to here was the tendency in Palestine to ascribe to any group or organization a political character in the sense of associating it (and its actors) with a particular PLO faction or the Communists or, alternatively, with loyalty to the Jordanian regime or to even more dubious allies, foremost among these last the CIA. The fledgling West Bank affiliate did not escape such characterizations, and the effort to establish the organization as "nonpartisan"—as emphasized in its earliest literature—is examined in the following chapters.

The group raised the need to be inclusive of all West Bank lawyers who identified with their objectives, whether they were striking or practicing. The group writing to the ICJ included both, and in this letter informed their interlocutors in Geneva that they had decided not to pursue an earlier idea of including a Gaza branch in their establishment plans: Gazan lawyers had established a functioning professional guild after the Israeli occupation, which constituted "a prospective framework already in existence within which to establish a local Gaza affiliate of the ICJ." Colleagues in Gaza, they reported, preferred to "initiate their own direct contacts with the ICJ to study further the feasibility of a unified West Bank/Gaza framework": and moreover, "some of our colleagues have expressed concern about how the authorities might construe a unified initiative at this juncture."

This long letter is something of a tour de force in its attempt to have the ICJ in Geneva understand the particular challenges of setting up an affiliate in the West Bank in the late 1970s. The creativity of the very idea of LSM was matched by the ingenuity of the response to these challenges in terms of structure (the company framework) and process. The group proposed registration of company shares in the names of four local lawyers, a contractual arrangement with the ICJ, an unpaid executive staff elected from among the unpaid employees (the members) and the employment of paid full-time staff. Variations on this theme appeared in later correspondence once the ICJ's Executive Committee had understood "after some explanation why you choose to operate in the proposed way."[40] In 1979, a letter from Jonathan Kuttab opened with "Good news: We have been officially registered."[41] This letter responded to a number of concerns that had been raised by the ICJ. The complex relations with Gaza had been explained to an intermediary with whom "lengthy meetings" had been held. The form of cooperation "remains to be worked out and depends to a large degree on the preferences of our colleagues in Gaza."[42]

The group were at pains to explain anticipated internal political dynamics requiring, in their view, structural safeguards for the organization:

> The limitation on shareholders is deliberate. It is intended to insure a measure of control over the Company by those who are serious and active. There is a real fear that, if our Company's activities come to arouse a broad interest or achieve any significant impact, we may be flooded with "members" who have neither the dedication nor the willingness to work on behalf of the Company's goals. The procedures followed give a special voice and measure of influence to a core group of founding members, together with those who have proven their interest in the Company by serving as directors. This group of shareholders can exercise pivotal powers, and insulate the Company from partisan take-over attempts. [. . .] We strongly believe that retaining this set-up is wise and necessary in light of the intrusive pressures of internal politics in the West Bank.

This paragraph addresses a key element in the structure that was to characterize LSM: it was not, fundamentally, a "membership organization" in the manner of, notably, the Tunisian league (LTDH). Its idea of "LSM members" referred to all those working with it, not to a formalized membership base. "We wanted to make sure it wouldn't be factionalized" says Kuttab, "so we had to write the by-laws in such a way as to keep people out." The letter points up two related concerns: the desire to maintain the influence of the "core group" and the need to prevent "partisan take-over attempts." Elsewhere in the region, the new human rights groups faced similar concerns, and recruitment mostly proceeded at first through personal contacts. Waltz describes the LTDH as having begun "as an experiment closely governed by a fairly intimate band of professionals who shared a common vision of justice," which had a membership of around a thousand in 1982, tripling by 1985. Despite a measure of control through membership being, at this time, by recommendation, the central leadership became "wary of the loss of control implied by precipitous expansion" and began debate on a charter that would set out the position on a set of human rights, based on the UDHR, to which members would have to commit. Action was also taken against local branches judged to present a partisan political risk, whether from leftist groups or from the government party.[43] In his 1991 study, Kevin Dwyer presents the reflections of two leading LTDH activists on these challenges, and similarly the comments of one of the founders of the AMDH to the effect that the young Moroccan Association also had to find a way to control the membership: "We couldn't let everyone join who wanted to. To remain in control of the work you had to have a pretty tight structure."[44] Groups sought to involve a range of political parties while avoiding their jeopardizing organizational independence and the integrity of the work.

In the meantime, in the West Bank, the limited public and not-for-profit company structure served LSM/al-Haq well for many years, until in 1997 staff shareholders attempted to dismiss the new board. The tangled events leading up to the 1997 crisis are examined in chapter 7. Back in 1979, three more West Bank lawyers had joined the group; eight of the nine signatories were shareholders, with only Shammas omitted as holding neither a law degree nor a West Bank or Jerusalem ID card. The company, LSM, was registered. In October 1979, MacDermot wrote with news that the ICJ Executive Committee had approved affiliation with the ICJ. MacDermot then passed the relevant registration documents to the PLO representation in Geneva. A cover note reads:

> A group of Palestinian lawyers approached the ICJ in 1977 with a proposal to form an organisation in the West Bank to work for the rule of law in that area, and to be affiliated to the ICJ.
>
> The ICJ showed interest and encouraged them to proceed. Eventually the group formed a limited liability company called "The Institute of Law in the Service of Man, Limited." This is known for short as Law in the Service of Man or LSM.
>
> A company was formed because it was the view of these lawyers that in this way they would be able to avoid some of the more paralysing controls imposed on other forms of association by the occupying authorities. [. . .]
>
> Operating Regulations have been prepared, under which there will be an elected Executive Council and three operating divisions concerned respectively with a) research, library and documentation, b) legal reporting, c) legal aid. It is intended to ensure that the Company remains non political.
>
> The founders believe, and the ICJ's enquires support the belief, that the LSM, if it succeeds in getting itself established and in operation, will be widely welcomed and supported by Palestinian lawyers in the West Bank.
>
> November 1979.

The note is on unheaded paper and without attribution. A handwritten note at the top reads "handed to PLO Representative by NMD 19/11/79."[45] MacDermot's experience and diplomatic background likely prompted this initiative to ensure that the PLO, as the major political force in the West Bank (albeit lacking any legal presence there) and specifically Fatah, which held the representative posts in diplomatic missions around the world, need not feel unsettled by developments outside its control. MacDermot certainly seems to have understood the "cryptic idiom" of the group's letter of September 20, 1978, and to have done what he thought appropriate to secure space for "an organizational vehicle that proclaims as well as assures the non-sectarian nature of the enterprise." The note is dry and in the manner of a courtesy; it does not seek approval or permission, nor does it present the ICJ as an intermediary between LSM and the PLO; the LSM correspondents were not informed.[46]

In January 1980, MacDermot paid his first visit to the occupied territories,[47] where with Nidal Taha he signed an agreement between the ICJ and LSM.[48] The ICJ secured seed funding from private sources for its new affiliate.[49] MacDermot also met with others in the occupied territories and in Israel, including an interview with Israeli prime minister Menachem Begin, with unanticipated results. In early spring 1980, a letter from Nidal Taha updates MacDermot on LSM's activities since their meeting,[50] reporting visits paid to introduce LSM to the mayors of Nablus and Hebron. The former, Bassam Shaka'a, was to lose both legs a few months later in a series of bombings carried out against West Bank mayors by underground Israeli Jewish groups after an attack by armed Palestinians on Israeli settlers in Hebron. The mayor of Hebron, Fahad Qawasme, was to be deported after the attack, along with the mayor of nearby Halhul, Muhammad Milhem, and Shaykh Rajab al-Tamimi, judge of the Hebron *shari'a* court. The Israeli authorities' official response included a lengthy curfew imposed on Hebron and conduct by the occupation forces that subsequently gave rise to "shocking revelations" in the Israeli press.[51] The failure of lawyers' attempts to prevent the deportations through recourse to the Israeli High Court—in only the second case of its type—is the subject of Shehadeh's last (and rather despairing) journal entry for 1980.[52]

Nidal Taha's letter also pointed up challenges which the fledgling organization was meeting in the aftermath of MacDermot's visit: questions being raised in the West Bank about who or what was the ICJ and, by extension, its local affiliate LSM. MacDermot had made a speech to the UN Commission on Human Rights which Tolley describes as the moment when "MacDermot began confronting Israel."[53] The speech was selectively reported in the Israeli press, and Taha's letter describes the consequences:

These quotations gave the expression that you are in favour of the Israeli occupational authority; this consumed much of our energy in answering questions from nearly everyone who knows or doesn't know about our group or the commission. But fortunately your report as a whole illustrates this point and we translated it and wanted to publish it in the local magazines. But the Israeli military censor refused to permit the publishing of the Arabic translation of the report which you find enclosed.

> As things stand now there is only one way in which this may be achieved: the publication of your report in some European periodical that is received and/or circulable here, and the local newspapers' subsequent translation and publication of same. Should the censor again refuse permission for its publication we will be in a position to raise an action contesting the censor's ban.

This appears to be the first time that LSM had its material censored; it was not to be the last. The misquoting of MacDermot's statement drew unwelcome local attention to LSM. ICJ protection had been sought against the forces of the Israeli occupation, but in this first challenge it was Palestinian society that was asking the questions.

MacDermot reacted swiftly to Taha's letter. In the June issue of *The Review*, the section on "Human Rights in the World"—contributed by the ICJ Secretariat—included an entry titled "Palestine: Torture in the Occupied Territories."[54] It opened as follows:

> To attempt to write or say anything impartial, objective or balanced about the situation in the occupied territories of Palestine is a thankless task. Either side in the argument will quote and make use of those passages which support its own case so as to give a distorted impression of what has been said.
>
> At the 1980 session of the UN Commission on Human Rights the Secretary-General of the International Commission of Jurists made an oral intervention describing a recent brief visit to the occupied territories and an interview he had had with the Israeli Prime Minister, Mr Begin, who invited him to raise any matters concerning human rights. Those extracts of his speech which seemed favourable to the Israelis were reported in the Israeli English language and Hebrew press with no mention of the criticisms he had made. There is a group of Palestinian lawyers in the West Bank and Gaza Strip affiliated to the ICJ who work to promote the legal protection of persons in the occupied territories. Seeking to redress the balance, they prepared a translation of the full text of the speech with a view to its publication in the Arabic press in Jerusalem. When it was submitted to the Israeli censors, the entire speech was deleted, including even the passages which had already been quoted in the Israeli press.[55]

The piece then turned its attention to "further use of the speech" made by "a distinguished human rights activist in the United States" whose treatment was first quoted and then corrected as being "wholly inaccurate" in one part and containing "other inaccuracies" elsewhere. The specific focus was on allegations of torture and ill treatment of detainees under interrogation. The ICJ secretary-general, said *The Review*,

> did not say he received 'no reports of torture'. He said he had received no reports of *physical* torture in the last eighteen months, but that he believed that unacceptable methods of psychological pressure were being used. Many victims of these forms of psychological torture considered this type of torture more difficult to bear than physical torture.[56]

The Review then proceeded to reproduce in relevant part MacDermot's speech, including his reference to "prolonged periods of sleep deprivation, accompanied by prolonged standing or sitting, bound hand and foot and hooded and in complete isolation" and his invocation of Begin's own account of the effect of sleep deprivation on prisoners.[57] MacDermot had told the Commission, "I urged Mr. Begin and other Israeli authorities to whom I spoke to lay down very clearly what methods of interrogation were permissible and what impermissible, and to have a system of inspection or spot checks to ensure that the rules were adhered to." Some years later, the Israeli authorities—prompted by a domestic scandal over interrogation techniques and General Security Services agents' false testimony about their use—adopted the recommendations of the Landau Commission (1987). These endorsed "moderate physical pressure" and annexed a secret set of guidelines for use by interrogators.[58] Clearly, this was not what MacDermot had had in mind.

There are two things to note here for the purposes of the current study. On the positive side, the ICJ's emphasis on social and economic rights was to influence its colleagues in LSM in terms of the development of LSM's thinking on collective rights and the right to development.[59] On the downside, the story of covert CIA funding (which had been briefly raised again in 1975) surely fed into the questions being asked in 1980 in the West Bank, when for Palestinian nationalists the CIA was on a political par with Shin Bet or Mossad.[60]

MacDermot's early action in response to an appeal from his Palestinian colleagues was indicative of energetic support; he was, of course, also responding in defense of the integrity of the ICJ's own work. Two months after Taha's letter, in May 1980, MacDermot was sitting day after day listening to Shehadeh give evidence to the UN Special Committee to Investigate Israeli Practices Affecting the Human Rights of the Population of the Occupied Territories.[61] This episode, already exciting enough in its own right, was to lead to LSM's first and seminal publication, one that propelled the organization onto the public stage at home and abroad. It had come about during a trip to New York the previous year, when Shehadeh had secured an introduction to an influential UN human rights staffer who worked with the committee. Shehadah had told him that in his view the committee was "doing consequences not causes" and needed to include in its examinations the legal changes being effected by Israel in the Palestinian territories.[62] In April 1980 the committee sent Shehadeh a letter inviting him to appear and to "talk on the matters which are concerned with the property rights of the civilian population in the occupied territories" and "to deliver to us information on the developments of the recent month, involving measures affecting the civilian population and their property."[63]

Shehadeh and Kuttab set to work compiling the presentation, collecting and ordering the myriad military orders and regulations through which the Israeli occupation authorities had been amending the existing Jordanian law, and drawing out their implications. This was the challenge that had first attracted

Shehadeh's attention when he was assigned to sort out the pile of Israeli military orders stacked up behind the door in his father's law office.[64]

Meanwhile, the situation in the West Bank was tense. Shehadeh's journal extracts from the time talk of Israeli settler leader Meir Kahane's "visit" to the Ramallah town hall with members of his Kach movement to announce that "the only solution is for the Arabs to be sent out of here," of everyday clashes between Israeli settlers and soldiers and Palestinian students and schoolchildren, of the attack on settlers in Hebron followed by the deportation of two Palestinian mayors and the imposition of a curfew, and of the confirmation of a massive land expropriation in the Jordan valley.[65] Shehadeh writes:

> Jonathan has been coming here every night for a month. [. . .] The biggest difficulty is keeping it secret, explaining away exhaustion during the day. And at night, as we sit with the lights on, I feel so exposed.
>
> But these documents we are collecting are on the state of law, and it seems too late to speak of law now. They are just words, and it all seems too late. But we can't stop. We must not give in to the fear that silences *samidin*. The world must hear what our legal system has been reduced to—hear about the violation of basic human rights. Whoever cares should know how the Israelis are cloaking their brutality in legal garb.[66]

Together the two of them prepared "*huge* notes," and when it came time for Shehadeh to leave for Geneva, he focused on defiance rather than despair. Looking back at this experience, he recalled:

> I went fully prepared to cover as many of the legal changes and human rights violations as time would allow. I believed that by revealing to the UN Committee the immensity of these violations, they would certainly take action. Israel would no longer be able to proceed as before with its administration of the occupation. Consequently the occupation would crumble.[67]

This wry recounting of his early expectations of international actors is in tune with his belief in the Israeli public's likely reaction to the information in *The West Bank and the Rule of Law*, discussed further below. It also indicates his (and LSM's) understanding of the strategic importance to Israel's conduct of the occupation of its systematic and policy-based violation of IHL rules—these were the causes of the consequences with which the committee had been concerned. At the time, Shehadeh remembers, "I thought I was doing something very heroic and dangerous!" On the plane to Geneva, he reports thinking, "I haven't had any time to think what this will lead to. A report in the *Post*? Twenty years in jail? Banishment?"[68] At the UN, "out of fear of Israeli reprisals, I insisted on being referred to in the document as 'M.'"[69] The meetings were held as closed sessions. In extracts from his journal published as *The Third Way* in 1982, there is no reference whatsoever to this episode at the UN, only to the book *The West Bank and the Rule of Law*, which was already a public document by the time the diary extracts were published.[70]

What happened, according to the records of the committee sessions as well as to Shehadeh's own recollections, was something of a marathon.[71] The meeting began on a Tuesday morning, and the committee called Shehadeh back for a second day, then a third and then a final Friday morning session, with questions to think about in between sessions and requests for follow-up information when he was back. Starting with land seizure and closure, the system of land law in the West Bank, rulings by the Israeli High Court of Justice in land cases, and the obstacles that Israeli military orders placed before Palestinians trying to prove their ownership or usufructory rights to the land, he warned the committee that "there is a programme, a full programme, to settle the whole of the West Bank. I have a copy of this programme."[72] In subsequent sessions, he set out the legal system in the West Bank, the jurisdiction of the Israeli High Court of Justice, and the range of amendments made to Jordanian law. He invoked in support of his argument a ruling by Justice Haim Cohn on the restricted ability of the occupying power to amend local law.[73] He detailed the parlous state of the West Bank judicial system, and the fact that Israeli military orders were not made available to the general public (while "ignorance of the law is no excuse," according to security legislation). The rules on labor law, tax and customs duties, municipalities, and security offenses were all examined. On the Friday morning, Shehadeh delivered a summary of his testimony. The record shows how he tried to get across the enormity of the gap between what Israel was doing in the West Bank and how it was presenting its conduct to the outside world in 1980:

> The intention of the Israeli Military Administration of the West Bank, the intention seems to be as follows: To keep the façade that a legal system is continuing to operate. That this legal system is following Jordanian law. That this legal system is not interfered with by the Israeli Military Administration. That this legal system is run by Arabs who act as judges and who are employed in the various departments and that the lawyers are also Arabs and therefore that the whole system is given freedom to continue to go on as it was going on during the Jordanian time without interference from the Israeli Military. That for security offences, military tribunals have been set up. These military tribunals are dealing legitimately with security offences. That these tribunals follow the Geneva Convention. That when there are any needs for appeal, a decision of the military administration, the local Arabs can be brought to the High Court of Justice in Israel and this is also an addition or something that is unprecedented on the part of an occupying power to make open[ly] available its own courts to the inhabitants of the occupied territories and that in view of all these conditions Israel is doing very well and acting very fairly in its administration of the occupied West Bank. Having painted the picture to the world outside, and as far as my reading goes of literature that is published internationally on the West Bank, this seems very much to be the picture that the writers of these books and papers seem to have.
>
> Whereas this is the picture that is presented, the reality is entirely different. The reality is that one of the first steps taken by Israel was to change the law in order to take the power to appoint judges, to deprive the courts of a whole area of litigation

having to do with administrative law, to reduce the stages, the levels of appeal from four to three, to appoint less judges and employees than are necessary under the conditions and in view of the big number of cases, to control the purchase of land and the laws concerning land and control the land departments and all the departments which are related. To change Jordanian law so that the legal system is deprived of many of the powers which it had originally had under Jordanian law as it stood in 1967. To take many of the offices which previously, and according to Jordanian law, should be held by various individuals who sometimes are controlled or sometimes are related in one way or another to various ministries, to assume all these offices and vest them in the Officer in Charge of the Judiciary, or as the case may be so that the checks and balances which the Jordanian law had provided are no longer available and all the power is united in the hands of one man who under the present circumstance is the Officer in Charge of the Judiciary who comes to hold 14 offices besides all his functions as minister empowered as Minister of Justice. And also to give the military courts the power to look into cases which the military have an interest in so that in cases where a certain employee is not wanted to continue office, he is charged with corruption and he is not tried at the civil court, he is tried at the military court because there is an interest there in making him lose office.

And finally changing Jordanian law to a great extent and in various areas which have no relation to security the most important of which have to deal with the administration of justice, natural resources including land and water, town planning, expropriation, municipalities and administration of the towns and villages, granting of licences of businesses, income tax and fees and value added tax, pensions and rights of civil employees as well as employees of the police force. Also the laws concerning the police force have been amended [. . . .] so that now the police is a branch of the Israeli police and there is co-operation between the two and control by one of the other. The setting up of objection committees which have assumed the powers which previously were in the hands of the civil courts. These are some of the most important areas where there has been change of Jordanian law by military orders. Having taken all these steps the desired outcome has been achieved and the law that is now being exercised over the West Bank is entirely different from Jordanian law as it existed on the eve of the Six Day War. [. . .] If one compares the situation in Jordan now and the level at which the courts operate and the judgements that are made there is great disparity between the Jordanian practice presently and the West Bank practice which is an indication that it is not inherently problematic to the West Bank or the Jordanian system of courts, but it has to do with the effects of the occupation.[74]

The way this summary was delivered gives some indication of the outrage provoked in Shehadeh by his close examination of the military orders and the changes made to the legal system in order to concentrate the Israeli military's control over a huge range of quotidian civilian, infrastructural, economic, and other matters. The international law on military occupation (specifically the Hague Regulations) generally requires a military occupant to maintain local governance and local economic and legal systems unless "absolutely prevented." Israel's narrative—as explained by Shehadeh—was that this was what it was doing, while in fact it was effecting massive transformations with almost entirely prejudicial consequences for the occupied population. Against the 2003 invasion of Iraq and attendant developments in the law of occupation, Roberts observes that "certain occupants—and not only those with a generally transformative purpose—have been able to give cogent reasons" why they were prevented from maintaining existing elements of the legal system. His example is "in the Israeli-occupied territories some significant changes were made to laws, including by abolishing the death penalty."[75]

> Back in Geneva, Niall MacDermot, according to Shehadeh, did not miss a single session. When I finished, he took me aside and let me know that the text of my testimony was destined to stand on the shelf in the UN office in Geneva gathering dust and that nothing would be done about it. He suggested that I write a book based on the material presented, which the ICJ would be willing to co-publish with Al Haq. I was delighted. What better way to start off the organization and let the world know of the Israeli violations.[76]

MacDermot proceeded to review the manuscript line by line with Shehadeh, with the eye of a keen editor as well as a demanding interlocutor on matters of evidence. The result, LSM's first publication, is considered in the following chapter. By the time it was published, most of the original group had left LSM. There were sensitivities over the reporting of MacDermot's meeting with the Israeli prime minister and the allegations of CIA-ICJ links. There had also been a tightening of the fault line between working and striking lawyers. During his testimony in Geneva, Shehadeh had told the committee that a large meeting of working lawyers had recently decided to negotiate with the Jordanian Bar Association in Amman on the issue of the strike.[77] Bisharat records a delegation of "young working lawyers," who had established a Committee of Working Lawyers (CAL) in Jerusalem and subsequently the rest of the West Bank, going to Amman to discuss the establishment of a branch of the Jordanian Bar Association in the West Bank. Not only "rebuffed," the delegation was "violently castigated"; certain working lawyers, it was alleged, had held meetings with US and Egyptian officials:

> The strikers charged CAL with complicity in the 'Camp David Scheme' to circumvent the political authority of the PLO and impose a settlement against the will of the Palestinian people, and with posing itself as an alternate local leadership compliant to Israeli and American interests.[78]

Internal differences in the group led to sometimes acrimonious meetings. Kuttab recalls "the same old political arguments," with someone questioning whether the Shehadeh law office "was really viewed as nationalist," and questioning Kuttab's own standing ("who is he, just back from the US, we don't really know him"). Shammas was even more of an unknown quantity, with his Brooklyn Lebanese origins and his interest in and unusual approach to matters economic. Certainly Kuttab, Shammas, and Shehadeh had very clear ideas of what they did and didn't want the organization to do and to be. "It was a new concept, new to this society," says Kuttab; and new in those days tended to be distrusted. Unlikely as individuals to have been minded to compromise, together they seem to have formed an unsettling alliance in the face of established local figures.

The initial approach to the larger group, says Shehadeh, was made "because we thought we had to have legitimacy." Had it worked, LSM might have developed more along the lines of its counterparts elsewhere in the region, with a broader set of local professionals (at least to some extent representing different political tendencies) involved in its growth. In the event, the striking lawyers withdrew together, and a final meeting voted to dissolve the group. Nidal Taha was one of those to leave. "There were lots of rumours here, lots of us withdrew, it was very difficult." He himself left to practice law in Nablus, returning to al-Haq's board of directors in the difficult days of the internal crisis in 1997, subsequently heading the board. The three who remained, wearied like everybody else from the process, decided to proceed alone. The company shares were reregistered under the names of Shehadeh and Kuttab, who were named as codirectors of the reconstituted LSM, and together with Shammas they went forward as the organization's Steering Committee.

3

——

Founders

This chapter considers the individual concerns and motivations of the three men who cofounded LSM and formed its first Steering Committee—the two codirectors Raja Shehadeh and Jonathan Kuttab, along with Charles Shammas—and how, in responding to the challenges of the time, they articulated and built the values, ethics, and approaches of the new organization. A number of documents are quoted at length, particularly those which are not available online.[1]

RAJA SHEHADEH

Raja Shehadeh described as follows the coming together of what a former researcher refers to as "the Triumvirate," the group of three who succeeded in establishing LSM as a working entity:[2]

> During my stay in London I had learned of an organization called Justice, the British section of the International Commission of Jurists, whose headquarters were in Geneva. This was an organization dedicated to the promotion of the rule of law. I began to dream about the creation of a Palestinian section of the ICJ, to promote the rule of law in the West Bank. It was my good fortune that I then met Charles Shammas, a Lebanese American graduate of Yale University who had come to the West Bank to try out new ideas. He was exceptionally bright with a highly developed ethical sensibility. [. . .] Together we began the difficult process of creating the first professional nonfactional organization in the West Bank dedicated to working on issues of an essentially political nature. We were soon joined by a third partner who proved of immense help to us, Jonathan Kuttab [. . .] He was an American lawyer whose family had emigrated after he finished high school in Jerusalem. He was looking for ways to serve the Palestinian cause through the law and had written to ask me for ideas. I told him about the new organization and he soon left the law office in New York where he had been working and came to help us with our new project.

47

We were an enthusiastic trio. We put all we had into our work, writing letters, meeting people, and devising strategies. With Charles's meticulous mind and Jonathan's flair I was in very good company.[3]

Shehadeh had completed a degree in English literature at the American University of Beirut after two years at Birzeit Junior College. He then qualified in law in London, where he was called to the bar. He began his two years as a *stagier* (trainee lawyer) in the law office of his father and his uncle, who had been among the first West Bank lawyers to leave the strike and return to practice after the occupation. It was the task of preparing a subject index of Israeli military orders that revealed the extent and implications of changes made to Jordanian law by the Israeli military authorities: "all these changes weren't random, there was a method to it," and here, he thought, was a role that he could usefully play. Shehadeh's testimony at the UN and LSM's first publication, *The West Bank and the Rule of Law* (WBRL), were direct results of this examination. The little book sets out the UN position that the West Bank—including East Jerusalem—is occupied territory and explains that Israel has refused to recognize this status and denies that the Fourth Geneva Convention applies, while insisting that it is "willing to be governed" by its humanitarian provisions (not specifying which these might be).[4] Israel insists that "the framework of Jordanian law has been retained and that only those amendments necessitated by humanitarian and security considerations and proper and effective administration were made." Shehadeh then explains:

> It is not a primary purpose of this study to examine the status of the West Bank under international law. Without accepting the official Israeli position as stated above, the intention here is to study the situation now prevailing in the West Bank, using universally accepted standards, to assess whether the principles of the rule of law are being observed. As Israel has declared that Jordanian law continues to be applied in the West Bank, this body of law will be used as the frame of reference.
>
> It must be emphasized from the start, however, that the military occupation itself places the greatest limitation on the rule of law. As long as it continues all essential requirements of a society under the rule of law such as the right to self-determination, representative government and an independent judiciary will continue to be denied. As matters now stand no indigenous central government machinery or legislative body of any sort is in existence. The judiciary is the only national institution that continues to function in the occupied territories. For this reason and for the reason that an essential requirement of a society under the rule of law is the existence of an independent and respected judiciary, and an independent legal profession with a professional body to uphold its standards, this study will focus first on the position of the judiciary and the legal profession.[5]

The systematic debilitation of the West Bank judiciary during the Israeli occupation was a major source of concern and a prime motivator for Shehadeh upon his return from abroad; it also involved the issue of the lawyers' strike. LSM introduced itself as follows on the back cover of the book:

Law in the Service of Man, which became an affiliate of the International Commission of Jurists in 1979, was formed by a group of West Bank Palestinians to develop and uphold the principles of the rule of law in the West Bank, carry out legal research, and provide legal services for the community.

For its part, the International Commission of Jurists (ICJ) described itself on the inside back cover as "a non-governmental organisation devoted to promoting throughout the world the understanding and observance of the Rule of Law and the legal protection of human rights." The omission of *human rights* from the LSM blurb was no doubt deliberate: because the initial focus was very much on law, and/or because the term *human rights* might attract unwanted attention from the occupation authorities, or indeed because the existing legal regime of human rights had less to do with the structures of occupation than did the rule of law. The rule-of-law theme fed into the methodological approach of taking seriously official Israeli claims about the occupation's approach to the law and testing these normative assertions against the facts of the conduct of the occupation: fundamentally, it was about legality, a form of "rightful resistance."[6] Summing up his motivations, Shehadeh explained:

> If we wanted a Palestinian state (and I did, I thought we did), we're going to have to work for it, have the rule of law, different to what I saw around me. So the main thing was: the rule of law, Israeli violations and correcting the record and not letting the Israelis get away with it.

Howard B. Tolley Jr. reports that publication of the book was funded by a Kuwaiti donor (presumably sourced by MacDermot) and translated into five languages by national sections of the ICJ. The UN Human Rights Division bought five hundred copies to distribute to the UN General Assembly; "foreign missions in Geneva made bulk purchases," and "Jordan requested copies for UN Commission members." Israeli representatives, says Tolley, "made outraged denials."[7] Al-Haq's archives contain press clippings of reviews and notices published in international press outlets.[8] This was quite an impact for what Shehadeh spoke of as "our dry little book on the niceties of law."[9] Later, he noted, "It was a short, modest book, but it made a strong impact because it was understated and because most of what it revealed [. . .] had not been known."[10] Understatement became a hallmark of al-Haq's work. Recalling his earlier fears, Shehadeh remembers being telephoned by the Israeli adviser on Arab affairs to the military government, who told him that "they had considered banning the book, but decided against it because 'that would make you a national hero.'"[11]

Not all of the reviews were as distanced from the political implications as was the book itself. A positive review in *Afrique-Asie* predicted that the publication "will mark a date in the history of international law" and "will be a weapon for other occupied peoples—Sahrawis, Namibians, Eritreans."[12] Closer to home, the Israeli press picked up on the mostly unspoken conclusion; a review in the *Jerusalem Post* observed that "it is not a better, more just, more humane occupation he is after, but the end of the occupation."[13] A publication of the Israeli left observed:

> Shehadeh's survey, though he does not say so, is meant to serve as a tool for lawyers, politicians and any other interested individuals who are in some way involved in the ideological-informational battle against the Israeli occupation and for Palestinian self-determination.[14]

Not all reactions were positive. A letter forwarded by a charitable organization shows a US lawyer writing that "from a legal standpoint the pamphlet strikes me as sheer nonsense." Shehadeh records the following encounter:

> I was asked to lunch with an Israeli law professor who has written quite scathing criticisms of the military legislation on the West Bank. I was invited together with a well-known international human rights figure. When our host greeted us—I had as usual lost my way in Tel Aviv trying to find his home—he was very gruff and cold, and I thought it was because we were late. We sat down to lunch and suddenly, without any warning, he turned to me and began shouting a barrage of insults about the book—how dare I—I don't know what I'm talking about—he would not give me a first-year pass mark in law school, such ignorance, lies, distortion. [...] It turned out (and this I still cannot quite believe, I don't know what to make of it) it turned out, he *had not read it either*.[15]

The response of the Israeli legal profession, endorsed by Justice Haim Cohn, was swift and had immediate effects. The ICJ secretary-general had opened his preface to *WBRL* by stressing that Israeli military orders "which have constituted the only form of legislation applicable to the area for over 13 years, are not published and are not to be found in any library," the orders mostly being "distributed to practising lawyers" and some being "sent to the people directly affected by them." In a much-quoted passage, MacDermot noted:

> There have been isolated cases, as in Chile, where one or two decrees of a military government have been treated as secret documents and not published. However, this is the first case to come to the attention of the International Commission of Jurists where the entire legislation of a territory is not published in an official gazette available to the general public.[16]

Shehadeh recalls that Israeli officialdom appeared particularly stung by comparative reference with the Chile of that time. In his 1994 article about al-Haq, Mouin Rabbani noted further:

> The frenzied Israeli reaction to the publication of the West Bank and the Rule of Law served to expose the Achilles' heel of the occupation and that which makes it unique among modern occupations: its dependence upon the perception of legality fostered by a constant attention to legalistic detail. To accuse Israel of repressing Palestinians was one thing, but to accuse it of doing so illegally quite another.[17]

A discernible impact became the more regular publication and distribution of military orders, although LSM was still investing considerable effort in collating and compiling collections for the first few years of its existence.[18] In 1983, Lieutenant Colonel Joel Singer of the Israeli army's International Law Branch wrote to Shehadeh and Kuttab that "for more than a year, two book stores are selling to the public copies of the military government orders" which he said was "in addition to the regular method of distribution of the orders."[19] In public, however, the Israeli establishment tended to simply deny the facts as presented. Perhaps nowhere was this more evident than in the response of the Israeli national section of the ICJ, titled *The Rule of Law in the Areas Administered by Israel* (1981) and without the ICJ as a copublisher. Haim Cohn contributed the foreword, referring to "the area of Judaea and Samaria," which along with the Gaza Strip and the Golan Heights "came under the control of Israel by virtue of belligerent occupation." He then noted that "no claim has been laid by the State of Israel so far to any of these 'administered areas'"—apart from "the city of Jerusalem which, including its eastern part, has always been regarded by the State of Israel, and under its laws, as an integral part of the territory of Israel." With no comment on the contradiction between Israel's action in Jerusalem and the prohibition on annexation under international law, Cohn described as "largely academic" the debate on the application of the laws of occupation because "it has from the very first been the declared policy of the State of Israel that its military and civil organs abide by the humanitarian provisions of the Hague Regulations and the Fourth Geneva Convention of 1949 as if they were binding and applicable."[20] Shehadeh pointed out with some alacrity that the report failed to examine the military orders affecting Israeli settlements as an example by which to test the lawfulness of Israel's conduct; in a later piece he observed:

> Not only did this position conceal the truth regarding the denial of the Palestinians as a national group with the inalienable right to self-determination, it also left Israel entirely free to pick and choose which international legal norms it wished to adhere to [. . .] because it did not at any point define what were these "humanitarian provisions," and it certainly never considered them to include the prohibition against the establishment of Jewish settlements in the Occupied Territories.[21]

Acknowledging that "Israel administers these territories as an uninvited ruler," the foreword explained:

> Rather than dissipating her resources on political polemics, Israel has preferred to concentrate her efforts on steadfastly ameliorating the administration of the territories and raising the living standards of the population—with the result, of course, that the voices of resentment have grown progressively stronger and have appeared to win the day by default.
>
> The political agitators have now, however, been joined by reputable legal scholars who have inscribed the motto "Law in the Service of Man" on their banner and who, thanks to their sincere motivation as co-fighters for the Rule of Law, have won affiliation with the International Commission of Jurists.[22]

Cohn observed that "the study of Messrs. Shehadeh and Kuttab can in no way be accepted as a correct statement either of the facts or of the law" while welcoming the challenge "to state both fact and law as they really are."[23] He then continued, in regard to the Israeli study:

> While this study is neither government-sponsored nor government-backed, it is mostly the work of lawyers who do their reserve duty in the Israel Defence Forces as legal advisers to the military commanders in the administered areas [. . .] keeping a constant and jealous watch for any infringement or diminution of the Rule of Law at the hands of military men and administrators not trained in the law. If they have not always succeeded, it is because security considerations, which are not within their competence or expertise, have been regarded as overriding—as indeed they are under the provisions of international law.

Most authors remained anonymous, but Cohn did pay particular tribute to Joel Singer, head of the army's International Law Branch. Cohn then dealt with the Israeli High Court of Justice and its assumption of jurisdiction—given his own role as a judge in that court—and concluded:

> It cannot in fairness be denied that, in the history of military occupations through-out the world, the Rule of Law has never been better served and implemented than by affording the rights and remedies that Israel has made available to the residents of her administered territories.[24]

Raising once again "the prevailing military concepts of security requirements," he indicated his own unhappiness at "certain aspects" but wrote that, given "terrorist influence and attacks, those concepts must prevail." In his final paragraph, Cohn addressed "the international legal community," anticipating that "the analytical mind of the lawyer" would

> easily differentiate between a *tractatus politicus* and a sober statement of law and fact. Not that a political pamphlet has no justification, especially if it is overtly presented as such and does not purport to pose as what it is not; but lawyers, as distinct from politicians, are hardly in the habit of contenting themselves too easily with what at best amounts to political argument, unsupported by evidence and authority.[25]

Cohn's assumptions demonstrated either real ignorance about the situation in the occupied territories or an inability to acknowledge such a dent in Israel's image as a rule-of-law state.[26]

The Israeli ICJ's publication provoked further reviews of the two reports. "Disagreements on the 'facts' abound," wrote one reviewer in *The Nation*. "The outsider lacking first-hand knowledge of life on the West Bank (as I do) cannot evaluate the truth or the falsity of the conflicting claims. . . . Whom does one believe?"[27] The authors of *WBRL* clearly spent considerable time responding to the reactions; a 1982 letter from Shehadeh to a coeditor of the US-based *Human Rights Internet Reporter*, responding to her review regarding the (then) availability of military orders,[28] noted that "perhaps because of the publicity which the ICJ and LSM report has caused, most of the Military Orders have now been printed and copies of them are now on sale at local book stores."[29]

This was "the beginning of the organisation in the public eye," says Shehadeh; "we began to have the feeling that we were 'called upon' and had to keep up with changes and alert the world." Different Arab radio stations and the local Palestinian press reported on the publication of *WBRL*,[30] which Shammas reports was "very influential for domestic perceptions." Shehadeh reports working lawyers discussing *WBRL* and recalls suggestions that Prince Hassan of Jordan had raised it with the Jordanian Bar Association (JBA). An Arabic translation was soon published in Jordan.[31] The organization began to recruit, widening its profile through informal networks. Shehadeh reports that they met with "scant interest" from lawyers when looking for recruits for the work;[32] the next lawyer to be drawn into LSM's activities on a long-term basis was Mona Rishmawi, who had grown up in the Gaza Strip, completed her law degree in Cairo, and joined the Shehadeh law office for her training.

The section in *WBRL* on "The Legal Profession" dealt entirely with the lawyers' strike, ending with the dismal consequences of the "lack of any organization of the profession."[33] Shehadeh recalled later, "I found no professional satisfaction in a ruined legal system."[34] Shammas describes Shehadeh as being "in shock at what he found back home." Shehadeh talks of "an emasculating experience" and of the "crippling use of negative power" on the part of Palestinian political forces, lest anything novel should lead to a new form of political force: "None of these factions [of the PLO] supported work that would improve the conditions of the judiciary. Such activity was seen as reformist and implied an acceptance of the status quo. Under these conditions, the fate of the lawyer was simply to endure."[35]

It was in the Shehadeh law office in Ramallah that a number of lawyers met in 1971 to "openly declare their position against the strike and call for its suspension"; the following day, Shehadeh's father and uncle were disbarred for life by the JBA, and his father's Jordanian passport was withdrawn.[36] Shehadeh describes the first case that drew his father back into practice after the occupation, involving a friend's young daughter who had been charged with offending the Israeli flag after an incident at the Allenby Bridge crossing from Jordan into the West Bank.[37] The case is typical of circumstances that brought lawyers back to the courts under the occupation: requests to defend those charged with hostile activity by the Israeli authorities in the military courts, land confiscation orders, ongoing cases in the civil courts, and the fact that in their absence, the occupation had allowed Israeli lawyers to practice not only in the military courts of the occupation but also in the civil courts, with no reciprocal recognition of Palestinian lawyers from the occupied territories. On the other hand, there were the arguments against recognizing the occupation by appearing in their courts and under their rule. George Bisharat, who came as a summer intern to LSM in 1982 while he was a law student at Harvard, describes conflicted feelings that gave rise to his subsequent scholarship on this issue.[38] In a socio-legal inquiry into cause lawyering published after Oslo, he reflects on the lawyers' dilemma:

> Should they accept invitation into the courts of the occupying power, to defend clients and press their claims? Or would they in doing so validate Israelis' assertion that theirs was a 'benign occupation' and so sap urgency from calls to end the occupation? [...] Has their advocacy ultimately legitimated the occupation or contributed to its prolongation?[39]

Accused of "collaboration" by a striking lawyer, Shehadeh acknowledges:

> This is a nightmare that haunts those of us who didn't go on strike. [...] I find myself suddenly thinking of us lawyers here on the West Bank as the daylight equivalents of the people dragged out in the middle of the night to whitewash over the slogans painted on the wall. It is as if by our very willingness to function under the distorted rules of "justice" that they have set up here we are providing the occupation—the theft of our land and liberties—with a clean bill of legalistic health.[40]

The choices for lawyers in the earlier years of the occupation were complex and often painful. Bisharat talks of the "palpable impact" of the discussions on the legitimacy and costs of lawyers' practice in the occupation's courts that led to the "fragmentation of the legal profession."[41] He wonders whether the activities of working lawyers on behalf of their clients "may have helped channel anger and resentment against the military government into relatively harmless forms."[42] This is examined further in the following chapters.

The benefit of legal advocacy under the occupation, besides relief for individual clients that might infrequently be won, Bisharat identifies as the appeal to the "court of public opinion." Insisting on "mini-trials" or "trials within trials" on allegations of torture and ill-treatment drove up the costs of the occupation. The premise for such activities, Bisharat notes, is Israel taking seriously the principles of democracy and the rule of law. Bisharat finds that "on balance, Palestinians' election to seek representation in Israeli courts, and lawyers' choice to assist them, has been justified" and that one result was in helping build a Palestinian human rights movement.[43] The broader issue, however, outlasted the West Bank lawyers' strike and continues to preoccupy at least some of those involved. Bisharat reports prominent Israeli rights lawyer Felicia Langer abandoning her practice in defense of Palestinians after 1990, due to her "fear that legitimation costs had exceeded the benefits of continued legal practice during the *intifada*."[44]

In his foreword to the Israeli ICJ's publication, Haim Cohn had argued that allowing Palestinians recourse against acts of the military authorities to the Israeli Supreme Court—acting as High Court of Justice—validated Israel's claims to respect the rule of law. Would recourse to the High Court "legitimate" Israel's rule? Some Palestinian defendants chose not to recognize the jurisdiction of Israel or the Israeli Court and declined to appeal. Others appealed. Bisharat observes:

> Given the understandable choice of Palestinian deportees, administrative detainees, expropriated landowners and others to fight military government actions against them, the question again was whether they would be represented by politically committed lawyers or other lawyers with other motivations and interests.[45]

In 1980, Shehadeh recorded in his journal the return of the two West Bank mayors (Fahd Qawasme and Muhammad Milhem) deported after the armed attack on settlers in Hebron; they were allowed back to appeal to the Israeli High Court against their deportation orders. Shehadeh's father Aziz was preparing one affidavit to the High Court on the Fourth Geneva Convention's prohibition of deportation and another on the illegality of deportation under the Jordanian constitution and the status of the British-issued Defence (Emergency) Regulations (1945) under which the orders had been made.[46] Shehadeh reported "wild hope amongst many" and wrote that "even the political die-hards who say we should never appeal to, or recognize, any Israeli institution are excited."[47] The hearings took place at the Allenby Bridge. At the end of his journal, Shehadeh records hopes crushed when the High Court declined to recommend the repeal of the deportation orders. Some Palestinians continued to have recourse to the High Court; others continued to refuse. In a study on deportation for al-Haq in 1986, Hiltermann reproduced extracts from the statement of two men who had refused to appeal at all, whether to the Military Advisory Committee or thereafter to the Israeli Supreme Court:

> We refuse to participate in measures which will give the deportation orders the appearance of legality, while they are contrary to international law, the rules of natural justice, and the law accepted by civilized nations, even in times of occupation . . . There is no reason to go through the legal measures when we are convinced that the [Advisory] Committee's hearing, like the hearing before the Supreme Court later, will only serve the State of Israel, which wishes to project a democratic image to the unjust and arbitrary deportation orders [. . .] The law is only the continuation of a policy, and as such we do not believe in it [. . .] We are not prepared to have the occupation authorities act as enemy and judge at one and the same time.[48]

In its early years, LSM had on occasion to educate foreign organizations who failed to recognize the stand behind such positions. One such, whom al-Haq asked in 1987 to intervene against the deportation of a Gaza resident who had decided not to appeal the order, telexed to say that it would be difficult for them to intervene if the man "wanted to be deported."[49] Despite the more general acceptance of recourse to the Supreme Court in later years, it remains the case that the Court's record has been mixed and not encouraging. Reviewing David Kretzmer's study of the Court's record in 2005, prominent Israeli human rights lawyer Michael Sfard reminds his readers that the court has refused to rule on the legality of Israel's settlement policy, although it has taken on individual cases; and it has also not decided whether the Fourth Geneva Convention applies.[50] Sfard addresses the "existential dilemma of the human rights lawyer" with his question: "From the perspective of human rights *and of those who seek a quick end to the occupation*, was (and is) the justiciability of the occupation a positive development?"[51] Given a lawyers' professional and moral obligations to their clients, Sfard suggests that this question should be answered by academics. "I reject the argument, which can be heard from time to time by human rights neutralists, according to which there must not be a linkage between objecting [to] human rights violations and objecting [to] the occupation."[52] Al-Haq's own voice on this is no longer "neutralist"—it is far more explicit about seeking an end to the occupation than was LSM in its early years.

Decades later, Shehadeh was to write: "I sometimes doubt whether our struggle will ever succeed in liberating us. What I've always been sure of is that, regardless of the cost, nothing proved more important in the fight against Israeli expansionist ambitions than our staying put on our land, our *summoud*."[53] Looking back at the Israeli response to *WBRL*, Shehadeh tracked the development of the interpretive arguments in the responses of the Israeli jurists Cohn and Singer forward to the positions enshrined in the Israeli-Palestinian Interim Agreement of 1995.[54] In particular, noting the agreement on "due regard to internationally accepted norms and principles of human rights and the rule of law" included in the text of the 1995 Interim Agreement, Shehadeh observes:

> If ever there was an empty gesture that exemplified hypocrisy and token adherence to principles of human rights, this was it. With this cynical assertion of the application of human rights, it was the Israeli position enunciated in 1982 by Justice Haim Cohn that won the day.[55]

It was clear after the publication of *WBRL* that the Israeli legal establishment would respond vigorously to Palestinian attempts to establish a narrative of the legal and human rights situation in the occupied territories, including an account of the applicable law, that differed from that of the official Israeli narrative. As Shehadeh put it, "The debate on the legal and human rights aspects of the Israeli occupation between Israelis and Palestinians had begun."[56] Whether the responses comprised denial of facts or denial of the legal classification of those facts as violations, they more than supported the insistence of all three cofounders that rigor had to be the basis of everything LSM did and said. Stanley Cohen, himself a significant actor in the Israeli human rights movement, classified the possibilities of denial according to "*what* exactly is being 'denied': literal, interpretative and implicatory." Literal denial "is the type of denial that fits the dictionary definition: the assertion that something did not happen or is not true"—hence, "the fact or knowledge of the fact is denied." In the second, interpretive denial, "the raw facts (something happened) are not being denied. Rather, they are given a different meaning from what seems apparent to others." And in the third, implicatory denial, "there is no attempt to deny either the facts or their conventional interpretation. What are denied or minimized are the psychological, political or moral implications that conventionally follow."[57]

There is more than a note of "implicatory denial" in the response by a senior Israeli legal figure to Kuttab and Shehadeh's next publication, a dry legal analysis of Military Order 947 (1981) establishing the Civilian Administration which the authors identify as "among the most important" of the "physical as well as legislative changes" being pursued through "energetic policies" by the Israeli authorities in line with the "autonomy plan agreed upon at Camp David."[58] Introducing their analysis, Kuttab and Shehadeh set out their understanding of what was going on in the occupied territories:

> A survey of the legislation promulgated by the military government legislation over the past fifteen years would lead one to conclude that this period was one of extensive and deliberate activity intended to fulfil the following policies:
>
> 1. The assumption of control over the local Arab population of the territories.
> 2. The close determination of the pace, extent, and manner of the development of key sectors of Palestinian society in the Area. The development of infrastructures and institutions that could serve as a basis for an independent Palestinian state has been inhibited. This control is achieved by prohibiting the exercise of a wide range of activities without permits and licenses which are within the total discretion of the military government to grant and which are withheld whenever the activity concerned conflicts with Israeli objectives in controlling Palestinian development.
> 3. The creation of a situation whereby many of the economic benefits which would accrue to the State of Israel from an annexation of the territory are obtained. Some of the ways through which this has been achieved are: the extension of elements of the Israeli taxation system to the West Bank; the incorporation of the West Bank into the Israeli customs cordon; the establishment of labour bureaus to channel West Bank labour resources; the regulation of employment of West Bank workers and the tying of other aspects of West Bank services and governances to those of Israel.
> 4. The facilitation of the creation of a strong, large and dominant Jewish civilian presence in the Area through the acquisition by the military Government of large areas which have been classified as "State land," the development of a communications network, the establishment of administrative, legal, defence, economic, and other structures for the Jewish settlements; and through the determination of the development of the Arab society in such a way as not to conflict with the proposed growth of the Jewish settlements.[59]

The particular areas of concern noted were not obviously "human rights" concerns as understood by the civil and political focus of the international movement at the time; it was very much a rule-of-law approach. LSM/al-Haq was subsequently to initiate projects and publish studies on planning and taxation and *Know Your Rights* publications on workers' rights which fitted more into the ICJ's growing thinking on economic and social rights and development.

Joel Singer responded in print again and forwarded copies of his article for Kuttab and Shehadeh with the "hope that this article will clarify some of the questions raised in your analysis of January 1982."[60] Shehadeh's 2008 reflection considers Singer's response as follows:

> Singer (1982) published a lengthy article defending this development and denying it had any prospective political objectives. He proposed that the newly established civilian administration intended to facilitate better rule of Palestinians in the areas he referred to as the "territories administered by Israel." Twelve years later when the Oslo Accords were drafted with Singer's help, the apartheid structure established in 1981 became more entrenched.[61]

By the start of the 1980s, then, with the publication of *WBRL* and the analysis of Military Order 947, LSM had provided evidence of what Israel was doing and how, and what it was planning for the future of the occupied territories following Camp David.

In al-Haq's archives is the text of Shehadeh's presentation to the First International NGO Meeting on the Question of Palestine, convened in Geneva in 1984 by the UN Division for Palestinian Rights, telling of the profile the young organization had already won. Shehadeh opened with the assertion that in the seventeenth year of occupation, "it is possible, with some authority, to speak very clearly about what seems to be already in place and what are the plans for the future and what is the vision that Israel sees for the population of the Jewish minority of less than 4 per cent and the Palestinian majority in the West Bank."[62] Starting with land confiscation and settlement, he moved to town planning and the proposed Road Plan No. 50, published that year by the Israeli authorities:

> The West Bank does have roads, these roads are adequate for its purposes and it is not a case of an area which did not have roads suddenly being brought civilization and better road systems. What is really intended behind this road plan is to tie the Jewish settlements to Israel and to do this by avoiding the Arab towns and villages."

Shehadeh informed his audience that the Israeli High Court of Justice had already reviewed and approved the Road Plan, and thus "we have come to a dead end as far as the possibilities of resorting to legal action within the existing legal framework that the occupation has provided us with." He suggested therefore that those present ask their governments to work for an advisory opinion from the International Court of Justice. An LSM publication later that year made the same recommendation in relation to the Road Plan, arguing that it was fundamental to Israel's plans for annexation of large parts of the West Bank and to its settlement policy.[63] MacDermot asked the UN Commission for Human Rights to propose to the General Assembly "that it seek an advisory opinion from the International Court of Justice on the [following] question":

> Is a military occupant entitled in international law to make major changes to the road system of an occupied territory in the supposed interest of the local population

(such as that in Road Plan Number 50 of February 1984) in the absence of any request or support from, or full consultation with, the inhabitants of the occupied territory and their elected representatives?[64]

In the West Bank, a committee was formed and hundreds of objections submitted against the plan; but neither the Shehadehs nor LSM built up the complex legal arguments or mobilized the necessary political support (local, regional, international) to seek the advisory opinion. Much later, Shehadeh wrote later that LSM had made sure the PLO received the study but received no response, and he doubted that the PLO was particularly interested.[65] Nevertheless, the analysis was prescient and two decades later, at the request of the UN General Assembly, the International Court of Justice issued its Advisory Opinion on the Legal Consequences of the Construction of a Wall in the Occupied Palestinian Territory.[66]

Shehadeh's scholarship in subsequent years demonstrated a continuing focus on the land. A different kind of publication, *Palestinian Walks*, was in 2008 awarded the Orwell Prize, which describes itself as "Britain's most prestigious prize for political writing"[67]—not the sort of accolade that Shehadeh could have been expected to seek or welcome back in his earlier life. In one passage in this book he describes walking in the hills around Ramallah with Jonathan Kuttab in the early 1980s, making exuberant plans for frustrating the "existential threat" of the settlements through use of the law and the energy of LSM; twenty-five years later, he wrote, "those times seem aeons away."[68]

JONATHAN KUTTAB

Jonathan Kuttab's family had left Jerusalem for the United States after he finished high school, and he took a degree in history followed by a JD. Qualifying at the New York Bar, he worked in corporate law in Wall Street to pay off his law school debts. With this done, he turned his attention back to Palestine, writing to the Shehadeh law office in Ramallah ("because they were the number one") to offer his services. He had the "specific purpose of doing something of service, of using the law as my contribution to helping the situation here in Palestine, helping the Palestinian cause." His letter found its way to Shehadeh, and Shammas met Kuttab in New York to explain the ongoing project to establish LSM and use the law in precisely the way that Kuttab was seeking; Shammas remembers that "wanting to be of service, that was exactly how Jonathan was presenting it." Kuttab came over late in 1979 on a volunteer status and subsistence wages with the Mennonite Central Committee: "I wrote my own job description, which was to learn Hebrew, understand Israeli law and work for justice, human rights and international law in the Palestinian community." Kuttab qualified at the Israeli Bar as a foreign attorney (taking advantage of the military order allowing Israeli lawyers to practice in the West Bank),[69] and then became a member of the Israeli Bar, later qualifying also at the West Bank Bar.

Kuttab's positioning distinguished him from both Shehadeh and Shammas, and his role in the organization built on his strengths. The following is an extract from a presentation he made in 1985 to the Foreign Affairs Committee of the US House of Representatives:

> My name is Jonathan Kuttab. I am a Palestinian attorney residing in Jerusalem. I studied at the University of Virginia Law School and am a member of the New York Bar Association, as well as the Israeli Bar. I am director of Law in the Service of Man, a human rights organization which is the West Bank affiliate of the International Commission of Jurists. I am addressing this Committee on behalf of the Palestine Human Rights Campaign, a non-profit, American organization which focuses exclusively on Palestinian human rights. PHRC's membership is comprised of church, peace, academic, Arab-American and Jewish communities who are concerned about peace in the Middle East. [...]
>
> I am quite familiar with the legal and human rights situation in Israel and the West Bank, and speak from the perspective of those in the US, in Israel, and among Palestinians who actively seek peace and justice, advocate human rights, and would like to see US aid and assistance become a constructive force leading to moderation, reconciliation, justice and peace in the Middle East. At the same time, as an American, I realize that governmental foreign aid is a limited resource that must be carefully distributed in accordance with well defined priorities; that it must be properly accounted for, and that it is an instrument of policy which needs to accommodate US interests while meeting the needs of others throughout the world.
>
> One of the several interests the US seeks to achieve through its foreign aid program is greater respect and observance for human rights and democratic principles by recipient nations. [Here Kuttab brings up the State Department country report for 1984 and other human rights reports about the situation.] The basic cause for most of the complaints is that Israel is attempting to pursue in the Occupied Territories policies of annexation and expansion contrary to international law, United Nations resolutions and to the vision of the US concerning the ultimate disposition of the territories. While the US believes the final status of the Occupied Territories should be determined in the context of a peaceful settlement whereby Israel exchanges territory for peace and recognition, Israel has been actively undermining that vision by attempting to Judaize the Occupied Territories (which it calls Judea and Samaria) and annexing them into the Jewish state. This course of behaviour necessarily leads to violations of the human rights of the indigenous Palestinians, including their right to self determination, their democratic rights, freedom of speech, freedom of assembly, and freedom of the press. It requires an oppressive military regime that denies them due process and imposes on them collective punishment. It also leads to systematically robbing Palestinians of their land and water resources, placing such resources in the hands of Jewish settlers for whom an entire infrastructure and separate regime is created. A classic de facto apartheid system has thus been created, with two separate and differing structures, courts, residences and rights— one for Palestinian Arabs and another for Israeli Jews.

> This behavior is not only violative of human rights generally, but is specifically contrary to US interests and is a major liability to the US policy in its relations with the Arab world.[70]

Kuttab speaks here "as an American," a US attorney, as well as a Palestinian, addressing US policy interests as a citizen. LSM's understanding of causes (Israel's annexationist agenda) and consequences (human rights violations) is clear in this presentation. Kuttab was an engaging public speaker, especially in the United States, often hosted by different church and peace groups that he drew into LSM's network. He was an active member of church groups and was engaged with the practice of nonviolence in resistance strategies.[71] To the founders, it seemed, LSM's organizational identity and rule-of-law framework rendered unnecessary any explicit reference to nonviolence in its own methodology. Nor, until later in its development, did the organization take a view on the use of violence in resistance to the occupation. Kuttab, however, was actively interested in the principle of nonviolent resistance, and in the early 1980s he helped set up the Palestinian Center for the Study of Non-Violence.[72] In an interview in 2001, Kuttab was discussing the need to involve US Christian churches in the campaign of nonviolent resistance to the occupation:

> Any challenge to the policy of domination is viewed as a threat against the survival of the state of Israel. We need to uncouple these two things before we can be effective in a nonviolence campaign. As a Palestinian Christian, I can be for the Palestinians, for the state of Israel, and for God—while at the same time be against the illegal occupation and the settlements.[73]

Kuttab's early public speaking commitments were much about building a network for LSM. "To survive under military occupation, we realized we needed a large network of people who knew about us and cared enough to fight for us if we got detained." Then there was the need to get information out, which under occupation and in the days before electronic communications was rarely straightforward. Al-Haq's archives hold copies of a large number of letters from Kuttab to lawyers, church leaders, people he had met on planes, etc. The letters enclosed publications and information about LSM. In 1982 Kuttab was at a meeting in Strasbourg: "My agenda was to go and collect as many cards as I could to build up our mailing list." He ended up—almost by accident, as he tells it—being proposed as the delegate for the Middle East group on the governing Council of the Human Rights Information and Documentation Systems (HURIDOCS), which was holding its founding assembly. This was probably LSM's first contact with the developing Arab human rights movement. HURIDOCS describes itself as "an NGO that helps human rights groups gather, organise and use information to create positive change in the world."[74] It was to be a long relationship; Kuttab worked with the organization until 2009. Observing that he was by no means a documentation systems specialist, he has the following to say on his role:

I was always bringing up the base of activists in the field, that we need proper tools to prepare proper documents for those activists. I always used to talk about the philosophy of documentation, how important it was for human rights work because the first line of defense for any oppressive regime is denial—what are you talking about, this doesn't happen. So if the documents are not of a high enough level of credibility, they can be dismissed. I was always drawing on our experience at al-Haq, in support of what HURIDOCS was trying to do.[75]

Kuttab became LSM's Steering Committee member responsible for the Fieldwork Unit, the quality of whose work is widely considered as behind the young organization's reputation and credibility. He shared a professional insistence on this with Shehadeh. It was Kuttab who leapt to the defense of the organization when its fieldwork-based credibility was directly and very publicly challenged in a key international forum by an Israeli official. The occasion was the joint LSM-ICJ publication of a report titled *Torture and Intimidation in the West Bank: The Case of Al-Fara'a Prison.*[76] In the report, LSM described "the conditions at al-Fara'a using the statements under oath of those with first hand experience."[77] The ICJ released it in Geneva. "Four days after publication of the LSM report," wrote Niall MacDermot, "the 41st session of the UN Commission on Human Rights opened in Geneva and its first item was the Israeli Occupied Territories. The discussions began with interventions by the representatives of Syria and the PLO, both of whom referred at some length to the Al-Fara'a report."[78] MacDermot also spoke, mostly on Israel's Road Plan No. 50, but noting that "the Al-Fara'a report was the first convincing report of the systematic use of torture by Israeli forces to reach the ICJ for over 10 years."[79] The Israeli ambassador responded the same day and also in a written statement a few days later, in which he referred to the report as "prepared by an ICJ's affiliate in the West Bank who intitulates itself bombastically 'Law in the Service of Men'" [sic] and to LSM as "a notorious front organization created by local PLO sympathisers."[80] Kuttab recalls his response to the Israeli Ministry of Foreign Affairs (with a copy to the ambassador) as "one of my best ever letters":

We fully understand the political and often polemical nature of statements made before that forum [the Commission on Human Rights], particularly by representatives of the different states, and we do not wish to engage in such debates, and will not address here most of the points raised by the statement of Ambassador Dowek. None the less, there were some very serious charges and innuendoes made in that statement which we cannot ignore, since they come from an official representative of the state under whose authority we are living in the occupied territories, and because they carry serious consequences for our organization.

Most serious of those is the charge that Law in the Service of Man is a " . . . front organisation, created by local PLO sympathisers . . . " Such a charge is very serious, and if proven, would render LSM illegal under the prevailing Military Orders in the West Bank and would subject members of LSM to prolonged prison sentences. Other statements published in the papers attributed to Israeli spokesmen have labelled LSM a "hostile" organisation. Mere contact with a "hostile" organisation under Military Order No. 284 subjects a resident of the West Bank to a prison term of up to ten years.

We therefore wish to state categorically that LSM is a fully independent body affiliated with the International Commission of Jurists, that it is not a "front" for any body or organisation, and that it is duly registered with the competent authorities of the Military government. Such false accusations concerning the character of the organisation and its independence, therefore, go beyond political discussions or even polemics and can have serious legal consequences for us.

Secondly: Ambassador Doweik states that LSM has the "open aim" to (1) discredit Israel, (2) stain its reputation of integrity and clean hands, (3) attract world attention, (4) blow up minor details out of all proportion and (5) give the semblance of credibility and respectability to unfounded allegations. LSM admits that one of its aims is attracting world attention (aim No. 3) but emphatically denies all of the four other aims attributed to it.

The true aims of the organisation are clearly stated in its articles of incorporation and reflected in its yearly activities. They are the promotion of the principles of the rule of law and of respect for human rights, and compliance with international norms. It is true that in pursuit of these goals LSM objectively monitors the human rights record of the Israeli military authorities and it is not surprising that the results of such investigation is not pleasing to the Israeli authorities. They should not be. However it is both false and dangerous to deduce from this that the "open aim" of LSM is to "discredit Israel and stain its reputation for integrity and clean hands, etc . . . " LSM endeavours to investigate these matters with integrity and objectivity, but it cannot be blamed for the substance of the violations it documents and the results it brings to light.

Thirdly: The statement of the Ambassador contained a direct attack on the credibility and truthfulness of LSM's documentation. Specifically it stated that "In the past, many affidavits, *including quite a few channelled through "Law in the Service of Men"* (sic), were proven, after proper investigation, as completely unfounded (my emphasis). Another spokesman referred to the Al-Fara'a report as an "unfounded web of lies."

LSM strenuously endeavours to maintain the highest possible standards of accuracy and truthfulness. Great care is taken in collecting information and sceptically investigating allegations of human rights violations. Evidence which does not meet our exacting standards of accuracy is never published. Our identity as a human rights organisation is closely linked to this careful approach to facts. That being the case, we would be most grateful to learn *which* of our affidavits have been proven to be unfounded. Even more, we hereby commit ourselves to amend, or retract any published material that is proven to be materially inaccurate and to publish such corrections or retractions as widely as possible. Such a commitment is not a concession by LSM but an essential ingredient of its nature as a serious human rights organisation on which it stakes its credibility. We therefore welcome a specific reply indicating which of our published material you believe you have proven to be false or inaccurate. Barring that we would appreciate it if official spokesmen for your ministry would refrain in future from making unsubstantiated attacks on LSM's credibility.[81]

The insistence on accuracy and "sceptically investigating allegations" was a cornerstone of the organization's methodology: "We'd drill it into everybody at al-Haq, field-workers and everyone else," says Kuttab, "that our credibility and accuracy was our greatest asset." Kuttab's preoccupations came through in his contribution to the first international law conference held in East Jerusalem, convened by al-Haq just as the first intifada moved into its second month in January 1988.[82] In "Avenues Open for Defence of Human Rights in the Israeli-Occupied Territories," Kuttab addressed Jordanian law and the Israeli High Court as "avenues that present themselves to the local practitioner." He noted "practical obstacles" to the International Court of Justice as an avenue of recourse, and then moved on to:

> the 'court of public opinion' and the engagement, through implication, of major segments of the international public, foreign governments, international human rights organizations, and even sectors and organizations in the Israeli public itself. Israel has shown itself as vulnerable, if not more vulnerable than other states, to international pressure but there have always been a number of serious and important qualifications surrounding this aspect. Individuals and organizations who attempt to work in this direction must keep in mind a number of factors that will determine the effectiveness of this method.[83]

The first of these factors was "specific, detailed, and accurate documentation of human rights violations and a detailed account of the responsibility of the Israeli government or the military authorities in causing or failing to curb such violations." Kuttab contrasted "generalized, exaggerated, and heartfelt but inaccurate descriptions of the human rights situation" with Al-Haq's "sober listing" based on "careful documentation through affidavits, medical and other records."[84] This resonates with Shehadeh's reference to "understatement" and goes also to other issues of methodology: according to Kuttab, "we never put out a 'condemnation' (*istinkar*), everyone else was doing that, we didn't want to start taking meaningless positions."[85] Shehadeh agrees that "the reason we survived was that we were very careful at every step, it was always careful legal language." This caution extended to the formalities expected of the cofounders; Shehadeh recalls feeling increasingly resentful at being the "someone who had to keep the balance and to be 'establishment,' always formally dressed and so on."

The second factor to which Kuttab turned was tone and political content:

> Proper work for human rights [. . .] requires an objective and dispassionate appeal to internationally recognized principles which apply to friend and foe alike [. . .] Appeals and attempts to defend human rights by working through the 'court of public opinion' require that the issue not be stated in political terms, but rather stated in terms of universal principles coupled with a willingness to apply these same principles to all parties in the dispute.[86]

For Kuttab, the universality principle was a key presumption shared by himself, Shehadeh, and Shammas when they came together to form LSM.[87] This meant that they expected to work, through LSM, on practices in Palestinian society as well. At the time, Kuttab says, "this wasn't a common presumption." However, al-Haq almost never commented on violations in other countries: it was not an international human rights organization.[88]

Kuttab then looked at the "use of publicity" and, against the background of the uprising, confirmed that "the mere presence of foreign observers and access to international media has an ameliorating effect on human rights violations."[89] Moving on to "implicating other groups," Kuttab drew on work initiated by Charles Shammas that was growing into the Enforcement Project, referring to third-party state obligations under the Fourth Geneva Convention and "the stake that every nation has in peace and in the value of adherence to human rights by every other nation." Here can also be read Kuttab's appeal to what Shammas has called "human rights as a high form of morality."[90] Finally Kuttab turned to the "Israeli court of public opinion":

> Some success can be achieved by appealing directly or indirectly to elements within the Israeli public itself or even the Israeli establishment. To do this, however, a human rights activist must obtain a full understanding of the structure and true goals and interests of Israeli society, and must avoid thinking of Israelis or even of the military government as a monolith, or a totally evil structure, and must be able to address it on its own terms, while being aware of the dangers inherent in this approach.[91]

By the time Kuttab was writing this paper, addressing interventions to the Israeli military or other authorities was well established as a methodology—and as he said, it "is often a necessary prerequisite to further intervention."[92] The passage reiterates the approach of taking seriously what the Israeli system—especially the legal system—said about itself in order to then face this system with its claims and with the facts that contradict them. Hiltermann was later to observe that:

> The genius of the method fashioned by al-Haq's founders was that al-Haq took Israel at its word (of being a democracy, as well as a self-declared reluctant, tolerant and benign occupier) and, playing fully by the rules of a democratic society, held it to its commitments, pressing it further and further as it retreated into a growing tangle of self-generated contradictions.[93]

This issue of legitimation of Israel's self-image and external projection, along with the impact of this on its conduct and reaction to challenge, has been widely theorized since, but it was clearly understood and consciously acted upon by the Palestinian practitioners who established al-Haq.[94] An early example of LSM/al-Haq's approach came in the wake of a raid on LSM's first office in a basement flat in Ramallah in November 1982. It was Kuttab who corresponded with Haim Cohn,[95] among others, describing the disruption of a regular evening meeting by a group of Israeli soldiers, which involved physical violence against LSM's first field-worker, Ali Jaradat, questioning, and the summoning of civilian Israeli police investigators to conduct a further search. An Amnesty International representative was a guest at the meeting. "The police seemed anxious to explain that what had prompted this action was that several cars with yellow Jerusalem plates were parked outside. The army wanted to know what was going on." After an initial response from Cohn, noting that he had written to the Judge Advocate General, a subsequent letter provoked Kuttab into pointing out a set of inconsistencies in the report that Cohn appeared to have received on the incident. These included apparent misreporting or selective reporting of Raja Shehadeh's testimony, a failure to interview Ali Jaradat (misrepresented as Jaradat's own failure to show) or to take up the offer of a statement from the Amnesty International representative. Kuttab concluded:

> The whole matter is hardly worth pursuing since more serious events occur regularly on the West Bank except for the fact that it illustrates the manner in which irregularities by the military government are insulated from the scrutiny of conscientious people like yourself who are genuinely concerned with the rule of law. In this case a worker from a recognized, and I trust credible, human rights organization is beaten in the presence of a representative of Amnesty International. And after going through the motions of a full and thorough investigation, I am surprised to receive your letter that implies you are now satisfied that there is no evidence that Mr. Jaradat was beaten or otherwise assaulted.[96]

Facing Justice Cohn with the possibility that he was not getting the full facts from the Israeli side, Kuttab presents this distortion and the practices it covered up as a matter of systemic practice, as well as reminding Cohn of the presence of a third party of potentially significant standing. In a sense, all these elements are key to the way LSM/al-Haq identified its priorities and pursued its objectives.

CHARLES SHAMMAS

In the 1982 raid on the office, some suspected that the soldiers had also been unsettled by the sight of Charles Shammas's "portable" computer. Shammas's engagement with new technology is discussed further below. Of the three founding Steering Committee members, he has worked most closely on the technical implications of the contractual obligations of third-party states with Israel (particularly EU states). Shammas insists that early on, "the most important thing in common was that we all wanted to effect change in situations we saw around us *from our practice*. [. . .] We were pragmatists, and law and human rights was a tool to use to reach out."

> The idea was there was no way [. . .] of getting any international support to restrain what Israel was doing without engaging the third states, the international environments under normative language that they themselves understood. That was

the attraction of it. None of us started out as human rights people. [. . .] The idea was we had to engage them in the language that they understood. And also the idea was to use law, but because law sets down what other actors have accepted. So we were starting from a starting point of the accepted discourse and norms that were not really being used as part of the struggle of people for their rights. The whole question was what was the nature of our struggle. What did the struggle consist of? I mean either we struggle alone—however we understand it and of course the scene was not very promising (that was the patronage and subsidies)—or we have to enlist others, we had to enlist other power. And the idea was not just they didn't understand what Israel was doing, which is the first step, but we had to figure out also how to make claims on them, on power, that ultimately led to the enforcement approach.

Al-Haq's Enforcement Project took institutional form in 1988 and departed amid some organizational controversy in 1992 (see chapter 5). In the period leading up to the establishment of LSM, Shammas, the only nonlawyer of the three, recalls that between himself and Shehadeh, "it wasn't talked about in terms of human rights but it was talked about in terms of the rest of the world is letting this happen and we're not fighting the larger battle." If Shehadeh's shock came from realizing what was going on with the legal system and the land, Shammas's came from observing the "culture of dependency." The letter to the ICJ quoted in the previous chapter that referred to a "society organized around [. . .] patronage and subsidy" set out Shammas's thinking at the time. Born and brought up in Brooklyn to Lebanese American parents, Shammas had spent some years in Lebanon after completing his degree in philosophy of knowledge at Yale, and had developed an interest in the "structural causes of economically driven migration":

> My interest in the economy was because I saw it as a fundamental problem in terms of the subjugation of the society and dependency. For me the issue was a culture of dependency that could only be alleviated or rectified if there were some structural economic changes. Dependency on foreign patronage, dependency on subsidies, dependency on cash flows. [. . .] We weren't generating wealth internally. I was struck by the fact that the economy was undocumented. I could see the patronage, I could see the dependency, I could see the fact that initiative was basically being squelched and neutralised, that if you wanted to survive, the way you accommodated to reality, was that you affiliated yourself with somebody and promoted their interest against their competitor's interest.

Here, Shammas reflects Bisharat's understanding of the dynamics of "over-control" in the West Bank at that time. In Shammas's case it was a question of

> looking at it from a standpoint of the economic foundations, basically how people earn their bread and butter, what they have to depend on makes all the difference in the world. [. . .] The economic issue was because of the general structure of Palestinian political life and how Palestinian efforts to cope with their Israeli adversary would be neutralised or made dysfunctional[. . .]—the economic side was that so much of the dysfunctionality was related to patronage, dependency, and the fact that

the first form of control is economic. I had never thought of economics before seeing that. [. . .] I'm not an economist, and I'm not a human rights person, by definition; for me those are all tools that are necessary to implement human rights but each one is a kind of an enterprise that is too limited [. . .]

It was struggle, it was the notion of struggle. I often use the word predatory, for me that was a very significant word, I saw it as a predatory process, and the question was how to overcome the dysfunctionality and the ineffectiveness and the inadequacy of the response to that predatory process. In principle it shouldn't be allowed to occur. Now, what to do about it?

In Lebanon, Shammas had developed some of his theories about patronage and the culture of dependency through observing the way the PLO was conducting itself. He inherited a clothing factory from the family business in Brooklyn and arrived in the West Bank in 1976 with the intention of setting up a "laboratory manufacturing venture" with an experimental structure. This was to be MAT-TIN, an Arabic acronym translating as the Centre for Applied Production Development.[97] Among other things, MATTIN began producing silk lingerie for the export market, inter alia to test the declared commitment of the (then) European Community to Palestinian development and to direct export from the occupied territories, in line with the Europeans' nonrecognition of Israeli control over the West Bank economy. Over the years, MATTIN was at the forefront of these efforts, sometimes working with other Palestinian producers, sometimes (as in the case of the lingerie) itself testing the practical viability of export routes and documenting Israeli obstruction of the same. Just before the outbreak of the first intifada, Shammas contributed the cover feature of an issue of al-Haq's Newsletter under the title "Restrictions on the Export of Goods from the Occupied Territories to the US," setting out the arguments in regard to Israeli settlement produce entering US markets labeled as "made in Israel" and the exclusion by law of West Bank/Gaza goods from that same market.[98] He framed the human rights argument in terms of the right to development and the prohibition of discrimination. This and other attempts to mainstream Shammas's particular interests at al-Haq did not at the time attract much of a following.

Alongside the substantive activities led by Shammas went a capacity-building approach to labor and management and workers' rights that sought to "work towards a collective, public interest, rather than private interest allying one group against another engaged in the same activity." Now considering himself "very naive at that time," Shammas nevertheless points to several successes in the MAT-TIN venture. As discussed in the next chapter, his colleagues in the first LSM Steering Committee had somewhat similar approaches, insisting on the individual investment of each worker in the substance of the work. In LSM/al-Haq, this became increasingly unwieldy as the organization grew. At MATTIN, the work—and Shammas's approach to economic development and hostility to the culture of dependency—drew some negative interest from leftist Palestinian groupings, particularly those associated with the PFLP. The Israeli authorities took a hostile interest and eventually the factory was forced to close, with Shammas and a few colleagues continuing to pursue project-based ventures involving Palestinian producers and the EU.[99]

Of the three members of the Steering Committee, Shammas was probably the least easy to place, and the MATTIN connection made some leftists at al-Haq uneasy. He also worried away at language all the time, working in both Arabic and English, whether written or spoken, to render in the most precise terms exactly what was intended—Shehadeh recalls Shammas revising and correcting letters to the ICJ word by word late into the night. Kuttab remembers that "Charles was always the thinker, and a large part of what Raja and I did was to try to understand him; when he talks, even in English, he's hard to understand." British researcher Candy Whittome summed up Shammas's distinctive contribution to al-Haq's collective leadership as that of a strategist focused on "how to get from A to B in a way that works, but that wasn't always massively straightforward."

With no formal legal training, Shammas argued international obligations and normative understandings with leading international jurists of the day, including senior ICRC mandate officials, relishing opportunities to pin down what law was supposed to do, and how to get it to do it. In London in 1989, at the first of several European symposia held through the efforts of al-Haq's Enforcement Project, Shammas presented his thinking on the "what":

> I work hard with an organization that is dedicated to defending human rights and promoting the rule of law. In highlighting the importance of enforcing international law to the process of dispute settlement, I do not mean to speak as a diplomat or politician. However, the fact that this Symposium has brought together human rights workers, jurists, politicians and civil servants is in large measure due to the fact that the defence of human rights, the enforcement of international humanitarian law and the process of dispute settlement are inextricably intertwined.
>
> The problem that we all must now confront is as follows: Twenty-two years of military rule in the West Bank and Gaza have occasioned extensive and systematic violations of basic human rights and a radical undermining of the rule of law within the occupied territories. Inevitably, the prosecution of this occupation has also further eroded respect for human rights and the rule of law within Israel itself.
>
> Palestinians and Israelis are, as a result, locked into an increasingly brutal conflict perpetuated by the fact that constraints and limits on coercive and conquestatorial options are necessary to inspire the will to seek accommodation. Such constraints and limits, starting with those clearly prescribed by international humanitarian law, have not been effectively applied or sufficiently felt.
>
> In the final analysis, any durable settlement is reliant on, or presupposes, a *de facto* situation in which international law is respected, international agreements are enforced, and third party guarantors can be relied upon to perform their role vigorously, objectively and effectively. The will to seek accommodation presupposes confidence that, having forsworn conquest and coercion, reparations and concessions

can establish peace. But this in turn presupposes confidence that international guarantees and the restoration of the rule of law can make peace durable. To satisfy this precondition, and to enhance the perceived feasibility of achieving a durable settlement, third party states and other prospective guarantors of a settlement must start by demonstrating their will and practical commitment to enforcing the body of humanitarian law that applies. They have not. [. . .]

The Fourth Geneva Convention is good law for Palestinians and Israelis alike. Innovative and serious efforts at enforcement can only have a positive impact on both parties to the dispute. Continued failure by the international community to enforce the most basic standards of humanitarian law in the occupied territories, on the other hand, can only create doubt in our two national societies about the possibility of utilising international guarantees, international law, enforceable treaties and guarantees, to finally put an end to a conflict which has afflicted us all for far too long.

If I were to outline an agenda for dispute settlement [. . .] my first point would be that some process must contain the dynamic of brutalisation and dispossession which continues to generate sentiment antithetical to accommodation within two political societies, the Palestinian as well as the Israeli. [. . .] My second point would be that an occupant who possesses overwhelming military superiority and all of the instruments of coercion must be checked in the scope and quality of his utilisation of those instruments of coercion. The political society of the occupant must have its assessment of the feasibility of prosecuting an agenda of conquest reduced, in order to be willing to entertain other political visions and options. Third, it is essential to build trust, through observing the minimal standards set forth in the Fourth Geneva Convention, in the will of the adversaries to be bound by law, regardless of the balance of power prevailing between them.[100]

Having learned IHL (and the intricacies of different areas of EU legislation) on the job, because he needed to understand it, Shammas has become a recognized authority and significant interlocutor in certain legal as well as technocratic and political circles.

In the early period, it was the MATTIN experiment that led to Shammas's investment in information technology: "We used computers to develop a system to manage and regulate and document the whole production process." This needs-based engagement with information technology meant that LSM/al-Haq was remarkably up-to-date on technical developments insofar as the circumstances of the occupation would allow (LSM managed to get a telephone line only in 1984, and Shammas introduced email communications at the organization a few years thereafter). Shammas also pioneered the development of the database. The idea "was to bridge between a critique of the institutional aspect of governance, the established facts in practice and the thematic violation. Cases of individuals had to be related to institutional governance issues. To do that effectively you needed a database." The following extract is from a draft document titled "Whence and Why the al-Haq Database?," undated and unattributed but probably from 1984–85 and authored (at least mainly) by Shammas:

In 1984, al-Haq, facing proliferating files and no adequate method of restoring and retrieving relevant information, began to explore ways in which it could organize its entire collection of materials into a manageable computerized database to facilitate storage and retrieval, and hence to improve its ability to make available al-Haq resources for research and other needs.

The purpose of the al-Haq database is quite clearly to serve the research and intervention capabilities of al-Haq staff in the first instance, and then secondarily also to provide public information collected by al-Haq in a useful format to concerned parties outside the organization. This particular purpose has dictated an idiosyncratic methodology of database development, reflecting as it does al-Haq's role as an activist human rights organization rather than as a public relations bureau serving the human rights bureaucracy in the western world. We have opted, for example, not for a bibliographic system of indexing information or for the latest in documentation technology, but for the type of structure and technology that (a) would respond adequately to al-Haq's objectives, and (b) is readily and cheaply available in the West Bank.

Al-Haq is not in the business of documenting any and all human rights violations that occur in the West Bank and transmitting the information in bibliographical format to other parties, thus allowing outsiders free and easy access to such information. There are other organizations who play that role, and who are better equipped than al-Haq to play such a role. Al-Haq rather aims primarily to document *certain patterns of violations* which are seen to exist and which may be of importance to al-Haq's work at any given time, in order to process the information thus obtained and act—usually locally—on the basis of our increased knowledge and understanding of the situation. We have therefore decided to focus on *events* as units of analysis, and to break these down into their constituent parts to discover or verify and test the patterns which al-Haq is interested in addressing.[101]

The issue of software, and which system would suit which kind of organization, became the subject of some disagreement as the possibilities of information technology—and the prospects of harmonization of information systems—advanced through the 1980s. Hiltermann later wrote an overview of the debates among human rights organizations on this, and the different priorities and needs that organizations in the Global South and international ones in the West had of their software.[102] Nina Atallah, who took over this work under Shammas's guidance and went on to head up the Database Unit and later the Monitoring and Documentation Directorate at al-Haq, recalls intense discussions within al-Haq's database committee at the time. Hiltermann reports that at a 1986 meeting with HURIDOCS and other conveners, an al-Haq representative criticized "the exclusive use of bibliographically-based programs"; a compromise was eventually worked out whereby al-Haq and other similarly minded organizations could be accommodated to link up to the central system without themselves having to fundamentally change the way they stored and retrieved data.[103] In 1988, al-Haq joined the HURIDOCS "taskforce to produce standard formats for recording human rights events."[104]

LSM STEERING COMMITTEE

Lori Allen found Shehadeh, Kuttab, and Shammas to have "an assertive faith in facts and logic, which fuelled their earnest optimism that they could confront the occupation successfully through law."[105] The three men constituted LSM's Steering Committee, its basic governance structure for many years. As noted above, Shammas had strong views and innovative ideas about how an organization might be run, views that were shared in different ways by Shehadeh and Kuttab, and that arguably shaped the organization in ways not entirely anticipated by its founders. The three men were in many ways quite disparate, with different personalities, interests, and focuses; Shammas recalls that in the early years, "we had a 'live and let live' approach, each had a specialised area and the others gave him their confidence." "We supported each other with shared values," says Kuttab. Candy Whittome recalls three men with "massively different personalities, massively different talents," who came together in an extraordinarily strong collective leadership. At the same time, Rabbani observes that "until the end of 1991 al-Haq was governed by only four (later three) individuals who came from nearly identical class, geographic, educational, confessional, and professional backgrounds."[106] Here Rabbani was including, as the fourth of the governing group, lawyer Mona Rishmawi, who joined the Executive Committee that replaced the three-man Steering Committee in 1985. She had finished her law degree in Cairo in 1981 and volunteered with LSM during her trainee period at the Shehadeh law firm, including writing most of the organization's Arabic publications for that period. She left in 1990 after two intense intifada years as al-Haq's first executive director.

Shehadeh, Kuttab, and Shammas set up and worked with LSM/al-Haq as volunteers, as did Rishmawi until she was employed as director. They all had other, full-time professional occupations, Shehadeh in his law practice with his family firm in Ramallah, Kuttab busy requalifying and then building his own legal practice, and Shammas heading up MATTIN. They were part of the professional elite, decidedly nonaffiliated politically, all from Christian families and all educated at least partially abroad. They were at something of a distance from the majority of Palestinian society by a "class and culture gap" that some of those interviewed for this study found significant. They themselves were aware of this, and of the potential limits it set to their goals for the work of LSM. How the three (and then the four) managed to get LSM/al-Haq up and working, what the young organization tried to do, and how it was perceived by staffers who joined it are examined in the next chapter.

4

Organization

LSM began the 1980s as the only organization in the occupied territories focused on legal and human rights issues in the West Bank. It recruited its first paid staff members in 1981 and was managed by a volunteer Steering Committee. By the end of 1987, when the first intifada began, it had developed into one of the biggest private employers in Ramallah. It had a substantial international profile, secure funding from western European and US nongovernmental foundations and agencies, new offices, a legal advice program, and a long and varied list of publications in English and in Arabic; and it was no longer the only Palestinian human rights organization in the area.[1]

The ambitions and aspirations of LSM's Steering Committee members were matched by their energy levels, but events outside the organization's control naturally affected the speed and direction of its development. In 1982 Israel invaded Lebanon and besieged Beirut. The armed PLO factions and the PLO leadership were evacuated to Tunis. The occupied territories, as well as other areas in the Arab world, saw widespread protests against the massacres at the Sabra and Shatila refugee camps and the other events of that summer. In 1985, Israeli planes bombed the PLO headquarters in Tunis, with substantial casualties, and Israeli commandos entered Tunis from the sea and assassinated Abu Jihad (Khalil al-Wazir), Arafat's second in command and a man closely engaged with pro-Fatah activists in the occupied territories.[2]

In the West Bank, with anger continuing at Camp David, the nationalist movement was regrouping after losing many of its original leaders to Israel's deportation policy in the 1970s. In the summer of 1985, then defense minister Yitzhak Rabin introduced the "new policy of intensified administrative punishments dubbed the 'Iron Fist,'" which is the background for Hiltermann's 1986 study on deportation for LSM/al-Haq.[3] Hiltermann contextualizes the reintroduction of deportation and intensification of administrative penalties (imposed without judicial process) such as administrative detention: "The Israeli military authorities presumably wish to

73

keep their hold on the Occupied Territories as tight as possible, so that in the event of negotiations over the territories' future disposition, no strong dissenting voice will emerge to thwart Israeli interests."[4] Hiltermann notes considerable pressure on the Israeli government at the time, with sustained protests by the settler movement following the May 1985 prisoner exchange which saw over a thousand Palestinian political prisoners released from Israeli prisons in exchange for the return of three Israeli soldiers held by the PFLP-GC in Lebanon. The final context was "that the brunt of resistance activity occurring during spring and summer of 1985 did not seem to have been ordered and directed by the Palestinian leadership outside, but consisted of attacks carried out by individuals operating autonomously" from inside the occupied territories.[5] The nationalist leadership (and Palestinian society more generally) in the West Bank and Gaza opposed Jordanian-Israeli talks, sanctioned by the PLO, to facilitate future negotiations between Israel and a joint Jordanian-PLO delegation.

This was the context in which LSM built its organizational structure and public profile in the 1980s, in accordance with its declared objective of promoting the principle of the rule of law in the occupied territories. The founders' focus on causes and the structural nature of Israel's policy-based violations, and their sensitivity to issues of documentation and credibility, led them to recruit not only legal researchers but field researchers with access to and the confidence of individuals and communities subject to the violations. LSM also expected to engage internal Palestinian processes, conduct, and expectations in its promotion of the rule of law. A consciously reflective practice is documented in public and internal documents, and the innovative structure of the organization reflected the founders' desire to develop "activists in the field of human rights rather than employees in a human rights organisation."[6] How this was attempted is the subject of this chapter.

WHO ARE WE? IN 1983

The first promotional document in al-Haq's archives is an introductory leaflet published in 1983, which presents the organization and its activities to the public locally and abroad, opening as follows:

> Law in the Service of Man (LSM) is the West Bank affiliate of the International Commission of Jurists, which is based in Geneva, Switzerland. LSM was founded in 1980 by a group of West Bank lawyers and other individuals concerned with the legal protection of individual and collective human rights, and with developing and promoting the rule of law in the area.[7] Its other objectives include providing services to the legal profession and extending legal aid and information to the non-legal community.

Here, the presentation of LSM has developed from the description given in *WBRL*, keeping a focus on the rule of law but including human rights, both individual and collective. The reference to collective human rights invokes the principle of self-determination, which was not explicit at this point in LSM's focus, probably to avoid drawing the attention of the Israeli authorities as being political or expressing nationalistic aspirations. It also reflects a growing awareness of international developments (specifically at ICJ meetings) on social and economic rights and the right to development. The reference to legal aid was to be realized with the opening of the Legal Advice Bureau in February 1985.[8]

The document then proceeds to describe the "projects" through which "LSM pursues its organisational objectives." These confirm Rabbani's 1994 observation that in its early years the organization

> from the outset has been at least as involved with understanding its environment as it has been in attempting to change it […] Legal research, as opposed to human rights monitoring and intervention as narrowly understood, assumed pride of place during al-Haq's formative period, and to this day the organization defines itself as both a legal research and human rights organization.[9]

The "projects" are divided between information, research and documentation, and the library.

The first item under the information subtitle is the preparation of "documented studies and reports in both English and Arabic assessing systematic practice and legislation enacted by the military authorities which appear to violate those internationally recognized principles." The broad reference to principles here is to normative concepts of human rights and the rule of law, and LSM's structural approach is emphasized in the focus on systematic practice by the occupation authorities. The second is:

> Preparing concise handbooks in Arabic advising local residents of such rights, protections and avenues of recourse that could be invoked in various situations where their interests are affected. These generally take the form of "what to do if . . . " or *Know Your Rights* monographs. LSM's members share the conviction that, even under conditions of belligerent occupation, an informed public is able to win certain important protections and benefits through assiduous recourse to the Law.

The *Know Your Rights* series was at this point authored by Mona Rishmawi and had already produced two important publications: *The Land: Legal Means of Defending It* (1982) and *The Citizen: Search, Arrest, Military Trial* (1983).[10] The order of these two publications can be seen as reflecting LSM's causes-before-consequences focus. Thus, the first was on how Palestinians might seek to protect their rights and access to their land against predatory action by the Israeli occupation authorities and its agents, action recognized by LSM as fundamentally about the prosecution of an annexationist agenda to the benefit of Israel's settlement policy. The second dealt with some of the measures taken by the military authorities against Palestinians resisting this predatory practice and other manifestations of the occupation's annexationist ambitions. In the last sentence of this paragraph, the capitalization of *Law* is in the original English version; the articulation of expectations invested in "Law" and the protective possibilities hoped for from it reflect LSM's thinking at the start of its journey. The reference to "LSM's members" invokes the innovative participatory governance arrangements that distinguished LSM in its early years, discussed below.

This section also refers to the Newsletter, which appeared for the first time in May 1984 in both English and Arabic and which is a mine of information on the activities, reflections, and aspirations of LSM/al-Haq over the four years from 1984 through 1987.[11] It was here that LSM informed its readers of its decision to phase out the name Law in the Service of Man. As lawyer Mona Rishmawi insists, "We weren't al-Haq then. The clue is in the name: it wasn't 'right' (*haqq*), it was 'law'; it was a law-based organization." However, from the beginning LSM deployed "al-Haq" as a logo on its letterhead and publications. By 1985, the Arabic Newsletter was routinely referring to "al-Haq" while the English version still used LSM; field-workers used both names.[12] At the start of 1986, the English version of the Newsletter explained:

> LSM has since its foundation come under criticism, some joking, some serious, because of the sexism inherent in the English version of its name.
>
> As a Palestinian organization, LSM decided on a name in Arabic, which was only later translated into English. The Arabic word 'insaan' means 'human being', and this was translated as 'man' with the intention of conveying the generic sense of the word. Members of LSM have repeatedly been called on to explain this, and they have found their explanations increasingly unconvincing. Although we enjoy receiving letters which have "Man" in quotation marks, we have now decided to phase out the name 'Law in the Service of Man' in favour of 'al-Haq', the name by which LSM has long been known locally.[13]

There is a self-deprecation here in setting out the discomfort generated by a deeper reflection on the implications of the English name. The company registration remained in the name of LSM.

In the second section, on research and documentation, the 1983 leaflet includes reference to its developing methodology: "collecting affidavits from witnesses to and victims of human rights violations; monitoring, confirming and recording alleged violations brought to LSM's attention." The choice of affidavit as the primary documentation tool is discussed further in chapter 6; the insertion of *alleged* is a reminder of al-Haq's legalistic approach. Then the leaflet refers to "systematic field investigation and documentation projects on selected practices, employing standardized information gathering and certification procedures," where the reference to selected practices underlines the fact that LSM did not intend to investigate all violations.

In the third section, on the library, the leaflet states that "LSM's library is the first public law library in the West Bank." This was a matter of considerable pride for the organization, and substantial investment was made over the years in developing the library's resources. Following Shehadeh and Kuttab's points about the unavailability of Israeli military orders, made to such impact in *WBRL*, these orders were available to lawyers and the public in the LSM library, along with other applicable laws and "reference sources on international law and human rights." The leaflet explained why:

> The library's resources are made available in the belief that people's knowledge of their basic human rights and imposed legal restrictions bestows an important measure of protection and constitutes a fundamental requirement for any progress towards achieving the rule of law in the long term.

This last sentence underlines an important element in LSM/al-Haq's public voice and commitments: that is, towards Palestinian society and, in the future, a Palestinian state, which LSM/al-Haq aspired to see characterized by law-based governance and a fully functioning judicial system. At this point, in 1983, LSM did not feel able to articulate this explicitly.

In 1983, the offices comprised a small first floor flat set back off Ramallah Main Street and recalled by Hiltermann:

> The receptionist (who doubled as administrative assistant) sat in an entrance space immediately off a small glassed-in veranda. The dining room served as meeting room-cum-library. Two small bedrooms offered working space for researchers. And the tiny bathroom accommodated copies of the organization's few but accumulating publications, stacked neatly on thin metal shelves.[14]

Communications were rudimentary, with no phone line till 1984;[15] the Newsletter and other reports were typed up in the office and photocopied, publications (such as occasional papers) were sent out to be printed, center-stapled, and card-covered. Distribution was by mail, and many of the Newsletters and other publications never made it to their intended recipients.[16] LSM called on the physical help of traveling staffers and allies to get them out. Censorship of materials in the local press by the Israeli military authorities is noted in the Newsletters and documented in correspondence to and from the office of the chief censor.[17]

Two subjects not mentioned in the 1983 brochure, LSM's funding sources and LSM's methodology of making "interventions" to the Israeli authorities, were covered in the first Newsletter in 1984. The English text explained that LSM was "funded by non-governmental organizations supporting human rights and developmental work—funders include OXFAM, ICCO, Humanitas International, the Ford Foundation, and various church organisations—together with the subscriptions of LSM associates."[18] The Arabic version omitted mention of the Ford Foundation and church organizations. The first Newsletter included a section on "Interventions and Responses," listing letters that LSM had sent to various Israeli officials (the minister of Defense, the attorney general, the legal adviser to the military government, the commissioner of prisons, and others) on subjects of pressing concern—including prison conditions, the right of appeal against decisions of the military courts in the West Bank, attacks on Palestinian schools with accompanying threats sprayed on walls that went inadequately investigated by the police, and the arrest of school students during the period of their final (*tawjihi*) examinations.

Whether to accept funding from the Ford Foundation had been debated at LSM's weekly meeting. Ford was subsequently to become one of al-Haq's most supportive funders, and two of al-Haq's senior staffers later became human rights program officers at Ford's Cairo office.[19] The second issue discussed was whether directly addressing the military government conferred some form of legitimacy upon it. Interventions to the military government and other Israeli officials were to become standard LSM procedure, as indicated by their inclusion in the Newsletter. But neither issue was obvious at the start. Resolution of these and other issues occurred within the context of the wider organization, in accordance with the structure set up with the conscious aim of involving every worker in every decision significantly affecting the organization.

This organizational vision prevailed in the 1980s. It is described in a 1988 draft document setting out proposed structural change. By 1988 an Executive Committee had replaced the initial Steering Committee and was comprised of Kuttab, Rishmawi, Shammas, and Shehadeh. The document, "Draft Study of al-Haq's Structure: Past, Present and Future," summarizes the organization's growth through to the late eighties. The thrust is the need for a full-time executive director, and it is perhaps remarkable that it took nearly ten years for al-Haq's leadership to come to this point. The following extract describes the early structure:

> When Law in the Service of Man was first formed, it was conceived as a group of lawyers and non lawyers dedicated to the protection of human rights who through coming together in a group can do more than what each individually can. Even after the establishment of the group, they continued to carry out human rights activities on their own, but much of what they did was done in the name of the organization. Slowly the organization was getting credibility and standing.
>
> Initially the preference was that all administrative aspects of the work will be kept at a minimum and that there would be complete sharing in everything. In this spirit, little money was sought from outside, members gave some of their own money to the group, the premises rented were humble, publications were produced in-house with the members and their friends doing all the work of printing, collating, stapling . . . . To unify everyone's thinking and keep up with the changes and developments which others were going through concerning the subject, there was a meeting once a week when information was exchanged and discussed and forms of action were decided upon and tasks assigned. At that time the administrative staff consisted of one, a secretary, who joined the weekly meeting.
>
> In order to learn more and to check what we picked up, a field worker was employed who covered the entire West Bank. The field worker was the first staff member [. . .] chosen because of his suitability for the job at hand. But still he was expected to develop his skills generally in order to assume a more integral work in

the organization. The attempt was, even since that time, to have everyone be able to share and assume all the responsibilities and risks which members of a human rights organization necessarily need to assume. It was hoped that through the general meeting, through working with others, through the opportunities provided for further education and reading, this will happen.

The expectation was that the group would, through its existence, its mode of operation and structure, develop a group of human rights activists who are dedicated and qualified and who would increase the initial core group of three.

As the organization grew, it needed more resources. [...]

The directors originally did not see themselves as directing a large institution but helping through discussion and exchange of experiences and opinions to give direction, leadership, to a group of self-directing, motivated, dedicated people. This was not an ideal hope. The work spent in discussing and working closely with everyone was expected to give this return and relieve the directors from having to assume the normal responsibilities which directors in a proper hierarchical structure would necessarily have to assume.[20]

This extract evokes how, over a sustained period, LSM's leadership sought to widen commitment to and participation in rule of law and human rights objectives. The following section considers the political context in which they tried to do this.

THE POLITICS OF LSM

In the early 1980s the term *human rights activist* was not a familiar one in the West Bank. *Activist* generally meant politically active. The core group had in mind the development of a different form of activism, explicitly outside the existing political factions and discourses. Interviewed for al-Haq's *Twenty Years* publication, Raja Shehadeh explained, "We were trying to create a politically independent and committed organization; al-Haq was the first of its kind, most other NGOs in the Occupied Territories were politically committed." Jonathan Kuttab invokes as a "new value" the aim of the core group of "avoiding factionalism: we fought to stay independent; it wasn't easy."

LSM was not created by supporters of a particular political group recruiting members of the same tendency and promoting the profile of the faction through the work done and services provided. Rather, the LSM founders insisted that staffers were to apply a rigorous impartiality. "Leave your politics at the door" was the mantra explicitly voiced by the core group as they recruited during this formative period and the only way they dealt directly with the issue of factional politics. As much as anything, this was a matter of methodology. Shawan Jabarin, general director of al-Haq since 2006 and originally recruited as a field-worker in 1987, recalls:

The founders put it across very clearly—it's no business of mine what your political thought is. My business is your conduct as related to the work of the organization.

> You have your convictions, but they may not affect your work with us. Your own political opinions, you leave them at the door, outside. When you come in here, you discuss on a different basis.

The critical and distinctive contribution field-workers made to the capacity and credibility of the organization is widely attested. As well as enabling the organization to monitor and investigate patterns of human rights violations, they were the face of the organization outside the Ramallah office. It is clear that the Steering Committee was well aware of its own limits in reaching different sectors of society, and consciously sought to recruit field researchers with their own networks, credibility, and reach within the community. Several of the first field-workers were social science graduates from Birzeit often associated with leftist factions, in several cases having spent time in prison on charges of membership in such groups. Shehadeh recalls:

> Most able young people, as we saw it, were committed (or at least could be counted as supporters [of particular factions]) and we couldn't say we only recruit people who don't "do politics." But the agreement was, you do your political activity as you like outside, but you don't bring it into the weekly meetings, into discussions or into the organization.

"Whether this could be done," mused Shehadeh, "was something else." He went on to say that there was a conscious effort to recruit people from different regions and classes: "I was still worried the organization was too elitist, still run by middle-class people and not getting entrenched."

The field researchers were recruited to work in their home areas where they had their own name and credibility. Ghazi Shashtari, recruited as a field researcher in Nablus in 1983, explains:

> I saw the work and saw something I was convinced of. But the idea wasn't very well known then; people in order to be convinced needed someone who knew them. If Lynn comes [to ask questions], they don't know Lynn, they know Ghazi. Socially I was good in the town and people knew me. It was important to us to expose the occupation, but we were extremely objective in our work. I didn't influence what people said. I was a certain color politically, but our point was not to go to people of the same color but to anyone who was a victim.

Shashtari's words remind us that the idea of human rights and the role of human rights monitoring and documentation were not familiar.[21] The role of the field researchers in explaining this idea was as important as their ability to gain access to victims and survivors of violations. Secondly, his reference to exposing the occupation goes to the employment of human rights methodology as a form of resistance, and to the critical criterion of objectivity in this work. Third is the principled irrelevance of personal politics to human rights methodology. Years later, Fateh Azzam, then program coordinator of al-Haq, was to address the issue in a piece for al-Haq's "Human Rights Corner" in the local Arabic press, two years after the Madrid Conference and just before the 1993 Declaration of Principles:

> The decision of the human rights defender must be an independent decision, not political, relying in its essence on the principles and laws that set out and defend human rights, regardless of the political positions of the person responsible for the violation and of the victim of the violation, in equal measure. Equality is the most important of human rights, and the non-governmental organisation must defend rights in equality, that is regardless of political, intellectual or sectarian tendencies of the concerned parties. The tools of the struggle for human rights [. . .] are based on equality and objectivity [. . .] The credibility of non-governmental organisations depends entirely on integrity in their work and unwavering commitment to these principles.[22]

In the 1980s, part of the struggle was to distinguish LSM—and the budding human rights project—from other civil society organizations in the occupied territories, affiliated with particular factions of the Palestinian (and specifically nationalist) body politic. The desire to be nonpolitical and to be seen as such, in the sense of being nonfactional, applied to the image of the organization with both Palestinian and non-Palestinian audiences. Zahi Jaradat, who also started as a field-worker in 1983 and later became field research coordinator, notes:

> I had my own political convictions, but I used to feel that al-Haq for me was completing these, not abrogating them. The organization respected me and my opinions, but al-Haq's policy of being far from politics was also political. It chose not to have politics, and this was a strange idea at the time. People would say al-Haq is leftist, I'd say no, there's so-and so, others would say it's Fatah because of so-and-so, and I'd say no [and so on].

The point about choosing not to be political being a political choice is well made, and goes to the broader issue of nationalist politics. Khaled Batrawi, fieldwork unit coordinator during the first intifada, observes that

> it was known that some people had contacts with the national movement, certain political commitments and contacts with factions, but this had no impact on the work. [. . .] The board was very clever, they brought in those with political commitment, strong clean people [. . .] There were people from different factions, not just one. But people still talked, and people's talk doesn't take you forwards or backwards. What's important is what al-Haq did. The idea of promoting human rights and rule of law was not known in society then, how to introduce it, this was not easy.

Even before the first intifada, several field-workers were subjected to arrest, administrative detention, and travel bans. In October 1985 the Newsletter informed its readers that "LSM has undergone major growth and development and also suffered disturbing setbacks." The growth included four new staff members at the office and the recruitment of new field researchers. The setbacks included "a severe blow" when two field-workers, Ghazi Shashtari and Zahi Jaradat, were placed under six months' administrative detention (imprisonment without charge or trial) within a day of each other. LSM reported that "even before the fieldworkers' arrests, the Israeli authorities appeared to be taking a close interest in LSM's work, and had questioned several of those working for LSM about their work and about the organization." The Newsletter dealt in detail with administrative detention, part of Israel's Iron Fist policy announced in August 1985 and the subject of LSM's first occasional paper.[23] Then the organization turned to the issue of its field researchers:

> Both Ghazi and Zahi have been doing fieldwork for LSM since 1983. Their work is of two kinds. They apprise LSM of possible violations of human rights which they learn about and make enquiries about other violations which have come to LSM's attention. If it appears to LSM that, prima facie, a violation has occurred, the fieldworkers are asked to document this in ways satisfactory to the organization. Their work inevitably brings them into frequent contact with those who are quite possibly under the close surveillance of the Israeli security services, but these contacts are required by their work for LSM and being made for that purpose are purely legal.
>
> It is true that no organization can take full responsibility for all the activities of its members. However LSM believes that had the two fieldworkers been personally involved in illegal activities without LSM's knowledge, charges would have been pressed against them and evidence would have been presented in open court to obtain a conviction [. . .] That this has not been done strengthens LSM's belief that the two are being victimised for their human rights work. Further evidence that there is no real suspicion that they have committed any offence is afforded by the fact that both Ghazi and Zahi confirm that they have not been questioned or interrogated about an alleged offence. Both however report that they had been questioned more than once during the course of their work about their human rights activities.[24]

This careful explanation shows the organization's concern in relation to both the defense of its workers and its own ability to function. A letter to Niall MacDermot two years later serves to illustrate the response that even al-Haq's closest allies might make to official Israeli explanations for the treatment of al-Haq workers. A senior al-Haq worker had been denied a document needed for travel to Geneva on al-Haq work. The ICJ intervened at the request of al-Haq and received a reply from the Israeli mission in Geneva, stating that this staffer's travel to the International Labour Organisation conference would "hamper public order" and that "the person is known as an activist of the terrorist organisation the Democratic Front and was arrested and detained several times during the period 1976–1983."[25] The ICJ subsequently wrote to al-Haq with a set of questions essentially concerning the al-Haq member's political affiliation and activism. Raja Shehadeh's response set out the facts on the record (including earlier convictions in Israeli military courts for membership, no arrest since 1981). He then continued, "It is never our practice, either at the time when we recruit people, nor during the course of their work with the organization, to ask them about their political views. I cannot therefore respond to the other questions in your letter under reference."[26]

This response seeks to educate the ICJ on what al-Haq considered was and was not its business. For al-Haq, the argument rested on the evidence of why particular staffers were harassed or detained in specific instances—that is, for their human rights work. A further concern for the organization was the need to rebut allegations about particular staff members being primarily political activists and the organization being some kind of "PLO front." This was a matter of protection: of individuals, of the organization's ability to function under the occupation, of the credibility of the organization with its international audience, and of the human rights message they wanted to put out to the Palestinian community: that human rights work was, in this sense, "nonpolitical." This challenge remains today, albeit in an altered political context and with the basic approach now widely accepted. US professor Iain Guest, who conducted a study on human rights work in Palestine in 2006–7, observed as follows:

> It is an article of faith that credible and effective human rights monitoring requires political neutrality and a strict separation from any political agenda. This was strongly affirmed by all those interviewed for this report. It is particularly important, said many, because the Palestinian factions—which evolved into political parties during the Oslo years—are widely seen as ideological, resistant to change and corrupt.
>
> In spite of this, it is not easy for human rights organizations to remain politically detached. Many emerged from left-wing political factions after the first intifada (1987–1991) and their members retain strong political ties to these factions. Palestine is a highly political society and individuals who go into human rights are committed and political.[27]

These challenges surfaced explicitly later in al-Haq's history. Mona Rishmawi reflects as follows on the presentation of human rights work as nonpolitical in the 1980s:

> You have to take it in context. The PLO was an illegal organization. Every Palestinian, even if not factional, had feelings one way or the other towards the PLO, and we couldn't have al-Haq being dismissed as an arm of the PLO, which a lot of organizations were—and they did try.

Besides the factional politics, there was the broader issue of being considered "nationalists." Rishmawi insists, "We were starting a new way of being nationalist. Nationalism was seen then as being part of the factions, the PLO; ours was a different way of doing it, and for many people it wasn't easy to think about."

It is clear that the initial core group of three had no confusion about the direction of their efforts. Shammas insisted on "the notion of struggle." Kuttab recalls an Israel Radio journalist asking whether al-Haq was a nationalist organization. After a moment's pause to weigh the possible consequences, "I said, 'I don't know what you mean. No, we have no connection with the PLO. But are we Palestinians? Yes. Are we part of society, do we care about society? Yes. That's a clear framework to be nationalist.'"[28] As for Shehadeh, he later reported that "Israeli security could not believe that there was a Palestinian activist who was not engaged in politics and, consequently, involved with the PLO" and decided that Shehadeh secretly belonged to the PLFP, while "the PLO thought that the Palestinian struggle against Israel was political and that human rights work was a distraction inspired by the CIA."[29] In a longer reflection on this phase of LSM's work, Shehadeh observes:

> The nonviolent activities of Al Haq did not impress the Organization [the PLO]. In their view, when Palestine was liberated, all illegal actions carried out by the occupying forces and their military government would be annulled as though they had never been. Why then bother to document and resist such interim measures? There was also the popularly held position that the struggle, in essence, was political and that concentrating on human rights could be distracting.[30]

In interview, Shehadeh acknowledged, "We were deaf by principle; we decided we'd just block our ears. If we responded to everything, we'd never get anything done." These particular issues seemed so straightforward to the founders that an impression comes across of impatience or even intolerance of mainstream political discourse and engagement. Someone who knew them at the time describes them as having "a strong sense of mission and not a lot of self-doubt." Shehadeh was later to say of himself, "I acted and operated as though there was no reality to this political context. I was incomprehensible to most people, and quite possibly insufferable."[31] In sum, three ideas involved in the issue of "nationalism" emerge: first, that those involved in the founding and running of the organization considered themselves engaged in the national struggle; secondly, how they were regarded by the Israeli authorities (and for personal security and the sustainability of the organization, the point was not to cross a line into recognizably political activity); and thirdly, how they were regarded by Palestinian society.

A number of Palestinian staffers from this period recall comments from their own circles about LSM/al-Haq's alleged CIA connections or otherwise dubious intent towards the national struggle. These staffers did not come with training in human rights or rule-of-law principles; one of al-Haq's activities during this period was to work on the development of the first local curricula for human rights courses.[32] But they did nearly all come, office-based staff and field-workers alike, with a general or particular nationalism that necessitated a conscious working through of the "nonpolitical" framework that applied at LSM and was part of the core group's vision of developing "human rights activists." Sami 'Ayad, who joined LSM as the organization's second field-worker in 1982, addresses this as follows:

> I didn't feel that the legal and human rights referential framework of the organization conflicted with the national discourse. It was new and strange in methods, and for me it was new, strange, and attractive. This objectivity depended on accuracy and accountability and responsibility of the person speaking [. . .] It was a methodology of struggle, especially in its first focuses—settlements, the Road Plan, collective rights . . .

Shawan Jabarin remembers wondering "who were these people behind it, maybe they're liberals," and continues:

Human rights as individual rights, this was a Western liberal school, tied up with capitalism, the right to private property, etc. I used to think, where are the collective rights? The right to self-determination is there, economic and social rights are there . . . So I began to read, I wanted to reconcile myself, as I can't live a contradiction—had I stopped being Marxist, progressive, and opted for a capitalist idea with its focus on the individual and on private property?[33]

Jabarin's concerns apparently receded when he read LSM's Arabic translation of the ICJ's 1966 text *The Rule of Law* and learned of the "different schools, different meanings, all the different rights" intended in this discourse.[34] "When I looked at it," he says, "it wasn't in conflict with my commitment to the bigger national cause of self-determination."

Field researcher Iyad Haddad recalls:

I remember in 1986, people had basically no idea of something called human rights. Secondly, the Palestinian intelligentsia treated these concepts as if they were a Western weapon aimed at undermining the Palestinian struggle. I didn't just feel or hear this; a leader in the Palestinian Communist Party at that time told me that the party didn't support these organizations; they were American organizations and possibly the CIA was behind them, but as he said, everybody had to earn a living [. . .] I thought that if I found a contradiction, I could effect change [. . .]. But when I joined the organization and saw that I had a role, I stayed on, especially when I realized that a good number of other employees working in the organization [. . .] were coming from the same position. The things that came up weren't in contradiction with the national struggle. Subsequently I understood more clearly that my own political affiliation was in support of peaceful struggle, and human rights is a form of peaceful struggle.

Field researcher Ghazi Shashtari agreed that the field researchers had a lot of awareness raising to do in their communities about the organization. "It became tangible for people when you got results," for example successfully challenging the military authorities' refusal to issue a driver's license to an individual; "so it became known," he says, "and even before the first intifada people were seeking us out as al-Haq to tell us what had happened." Nina Atallah remembers hearing that "society thought that LSM was CIA"; so she asked around and was told, "There's nothing serious, that's street talk." When she settled into the work, she remembers, "I felt no conflict with my political positions; this was purely about the occupation and its practices and it was only different in terms of method, not substance; there was the struggle in the street and there was the struggle with the law." Roger Heacock, a professor at Birzeit University who worked on a number of projects with LSM in the early 1980s, was "skeptical of human rights as ideology-free" but recalls that Shehadeh and Kuttab convinced him that "this was a worthy activity and had political purpose." Abdel Karim Kan'an, who joined LSM as a field-worker in 1985, remembers:

There were some political sides who considered we were working to tame the Palestinian people, move them away from the armed struggle to a legal, liberal struggle

> [. . .] Who is this Raja Shehadeh for example? This is all CIA stuff to make the Pal-
> estinians nonviolent. I heard that more than once, but mostly people were happy to
> sign [the affidavits]. I didn't have the same reservations. It was part of the struggle
> to show the world what was going on, very important; it was one form of struggle.

The concern that human rights work was a liberal project to "tame" or "defang" the
Palestinians as a national movement recalls the questions put by Bisharat and others as to whether the choices made by LSM to act in the courts of the occupier
worked in fact to sustain the occupation by drawing energy away from the "political" struggle and channeling anger into "relatively harmless forms."[35] For Hiltermann, al-Haq was a "methodology of struggle: in the end, we were fighting to
end the occupation." He nevertheless acknowledges a "major tension and a valid
debate" in the question as to whether doing human rights work was simply making the occupation look better.[36] While not agreeing, he concedes that, given the
limited real progress that has been made in the years since, "it is not a debate that
has been resolved."

Mouin Rabbani, a Palestinian brought up in the Netherlands, came to al-Haq
by default in 1988 (the universities he had applied to being all closed after the start
of the intifada), and remembers:

> I had no interest in al-Haq. I knew it was an organization which appealed to the
> Israeli authorities with respect to human rights, which is something that never quite
> made it through my logic processes [. . .] I couldn't comprehend the concept—
> occupation is based on denying human rights, so why apply to the occupier to re-
> spect them? This was in the 1980s, when the idea that you promote individual rights
> seemed in tension with simply pursuing the right to self-determination. I also didn't
> quite recognize that the strategy had more to do with building an international case
> against Israel's occupation regime than any illusions Israel's conduct would improve.

In his study of al-Haq written after he had left the organization, Rabbani revisited
this concern, observing that to "de-politicise the human rights debate also bore
its costs. If only subconsciously, it translated into [. . .]a reluctance to engage
the points of intersection between human and national rights."[37] Rabbini found the
clearest example of this to be al-Haq's failure to examine the right to self-
determination in the same way that it examined other rights.[38] In the early period,
while clearly upholding the right to self-determination, LSM invoked it without
analyzing it, and nor did it call for an end to the occupation, whether out of concerns for the organization's security or reluctance to join the dominant political
discourse. It was not until the Enforcement Project in 1988 that al-Haq articulated
the structural argument that linked rule of law with the end of occupation. At the
time, the project met opposition from within al-Haq as being political in its methods as in its arguments. In later times, in 2008, as al-Haq's director, Shawan Jabarin
criticized "certain local and international organisations in the human rights field
in Palestine who regrettably fail to address the occupation per se as a major cause

for the continuing degradation and infringement of human rights" and who "claim that demands to terminate occupation are political."[39]

Al-Haq did invoke the right to self-determination in several key publications in its early years, beginning its discussion of the Universal Declaration of Human Rights (UDHR) in an article published in 1985 with the statement that "We are denied the right to self-determination and the right to pursue our economic, social and cultural development."[40] The first sustained invocation came in the conclusion to the organization's first annual report, *Punishing a Nation*, on the tumultuous first year of the intifada. The last line reads, "The occupier's attack on this nation is—no more and no less—a punishment for its desire to be."[41] This position became more direct over the years as human rights discourse developed and the political situation in the West Bank and Gaza changed. Al-Haq's acceptance speech, when it was awarded the 1989 Carter-Menil Human Rights Award, declared, "The fundamental rights taken for granted by other nations have been denied to us, most importantly, the right to self-determination."[42] It is worth noting the disagreement in al-Haq over accepting this prize: Raqiya Abu Ghosh, who joined as a librarian in 1987, demanded in the general meeting to know whether "Carter, the architect of Camp David, which is against Palestinian self-determination, has changed his mind?" Despite strong arguments being made against accepting it, Hanan Rabbani recalls the majority being eventually convinced by the international exposure it would bring.

Another gap in LSM's legal research was the right to resistance. In her 2006 report, Hina Jilani, UN special rapporteur on human rights defenders, situated peaceful human rights work as a legitimate form of resistance to the occupation, and resistance itself as "a legitimate right of the Palestinian people."[43] The idea of human rights as intimately related to the political sphere is more widely accepted now than in LSM's formative period. Indeed, José Zalaquett, a prominent Chilean human rights defender invited by al-Haq to assist in its organizational review in 1994, identified one of the gains of the international human rights movement ("to which al-Haq belongs"):

> Human rights has emerged as the central notion of political ethics of our time. Despite persistent efforts at weakening or relativizing this notion there is no doubt that it has gained an increasingly prominent place (whether for sincere or opportunistic reasons) in ethical discourse as well as in the agenda of most States, political parties and a variety of other social actors.[44]

The academic debate is ongoing, and the backlash against the selective deployment of human rights discourse by powerful Western states in pursuit of evidently political goals includes cogent critiques. The acceptance of (at least some) human rights arguments made about the Israeli occupation appears to have had no impact on the action states are prepared to take to restrain Israel. In a comment echoed by several of those interviewed for this study, Charles Shammas speculates that

LSM's early insistence on the nonpolitical nature of human rights was "due to the youth of the human rights movement. We all said we're nonpolitical, but of course human rights *is* political." It was also, at the time, due to concern for the security of the young organization.

While those interviewed agreed with the nonpartisan approach for the organization as a whole, at least some took exception to the personal impatience of individuals in the core group towards prevailing nationalist politics and expressions of resistance. Jabarin insists that "politics is a discipline; in those days, the factions—unlike now—used to be schools, they built people [. . .] That political discipline could also teach you things, how to talk to people, reach the masses, how to get to an incident, how to get the information." Here Jabarin is clearly linking the personal political experience of certain al-Haq staffers to the successful fulfillment of their functions at the organization. Iain Guest, quoted above, agrees on the reduced role and significance of political factions in more recent times.[45] In early 1987, al-Haq conducted an in-house organizational reflection or "orientation" discussed further below. Among the written feedback from staffers was the following:

> I was not comfortable with the organisation's claim to its "objective" and "non-political" approach. In my view, the decision to not be a political party is itself a political decision. I also felt that there was some elitism vis-à-vis political organisations in that they were too easily dismissed. This attitude in my opinion only contributes to isolating LSM from the community and therefore making it difficult for LSM to achieve its ultimate objective of being a dynamic component in the process of our society's change and progress.[46]

Another interviewee observed that "not being politically affiliated themselves, the founders were rather unaccepting, rather judgmental about people who were." Also of interest is their perspective on al-Haq's "ultimate objective" with regard to Palestinian society: asked what they meant by the "rule of law" in relation to internal Palestinian processes, Shehadeh responded, "As in to improve society's consciousness of the importance of being governed by the rule of law, it would be fairer to everyone, there would be processes, different relationships between people, and we stressed that. We believed in it. I did."

At the end of 1985, these principles were set out in a long Newsletter that introduced LSM/al-Haq to an expanding audience (including new staffers perhaps) who "may not be aware of the principles and aims of the organization or of some of its activities." Against the background of Israel's Iron Fist policy the final two paragraphs, under the subheading "Philosophy of LSM," read:

> The unique situation of the West Bank being occupied territory under international law brings to the forefront issues of compliance by the occupying power with the standards and requirements of international law with respect to the protection of

civilians who fall under the authority of a country other than their own. Yet the issue of the rule of law is much broader than that. It requires dedication to a set of universal principles and standards which should be applicable in every country and in every situation and to which all authorities must be held accountable regardless of the political situation. LSM deliberately seeks to state its position with respect to events not based on the political leanings of its members or of their perceived interests, but rather on the same universal standards which it is willing to apply to friend and foe alike. LSM further believes that these standards are useful and necessary for the functioning of a new society and trusts that education in the field of human rights will yield favourable results to any society regardless of the political context.

In this respect LSM endeavours to carry out rigorous documentation that is objective and verifiable and which is based on universal principles generally accepted rather than on a narrow political vision. [. . .] Every attempt is made to appreciate extenuating circumstances and justifications that may be offered or presented by violators of human rights in order to ensure that the central message remains that of respect for human rights rather than partisan political views. This often means understating the case rather than exaggerating it. It also means that many politically offensive and injurious events which are contrary to the interest of Palestinians are totally outside the scope of LSM's work because they do not necessarily involve a specific violation of recognized human rights. Finally it means that LSM is concerned with education in human rights and with those violations which occur within Palestinian society as well as those relating to the occupation.[47]

This piece is addressing LSM's local profile and aspirations. The standards or values of the rule of law, human rights, and universality were those that the founders sought to transfer to the staffers of the growing organization, and more broadly to Palestinian society, in their effort to "build human rights activists." Staffers stress that different members of the Steering Committee established their own standing and credibility in the community, in particular the lawyers through their professional practice, with examples given of Shehadeh's work on land cases such as that of Sabri Gharib,[48] and the visits to detained al-Haq field researchers and others by Rishmawi and Kuttab. Looking back, some doubt that the organization was ever in fact as isolated as perhaps it felt. As the years passed and the political situation developed, the local profile and credibility of the organization increased; in the words of some staffers, it was "nationalized," in the sense of being recognized as a part of the national struggle, not apart from it. This was to become clear in the first intifada. Sami 'Ayad presents this as follows:

Were it not for the founders [. . .], this professional depth, this knowledge base, who gave the organization this message and vision [. . .] and on the other hand, were it not for the field researchers, with their credibility in their local community, and expertise and knowledge, and their readiness to transmit a new thought to our community, al-Haq couldn't have got as far as it did. It was complementary.

PARTICIPATION, VOLUNTARISM, AND WEDNESDAY EVENING MEETINGS

In his consideration of human rights activism in the Middle East and North Africa, Joe Stork describes two models of human rights organizations:

> One model involves a large and active membership that sets policies and priorities. Such organizations typically rely on members as volunteers to carry out their work. Another organizational model emphasizes a paid staff having professional skills in monitoring, advocacy, and provision of services like legal aid.[49]

The Tunisian League for Human Rights (LTDH), established just before LSM, was a membership organization, even if its membership was "carefully scrutinized" and not intended as a mass movement.[50] LSM was the first regional model of the second type, and its founders sought modest start-up funding for their projected activities and benefited also from in-kind assistance. It appears that substantial funding at the very beginning came from church groups, before broadening to development agencies and foundations; LSM did not seek funding from any government, on principle. The "highly divisive" foreign funding issue that was and is raised against other Arab human rights organizations was not raised in the same way in Palestine, where there was no national government whose sovereignty might be defended against external interference; these issues came after Oslo and the arrival of the Palestinian Authority (PA).[51]

Still, LSM's early focus went well beyond a paid staff and professional skills. The Steering Committee members worked as volunteers throughout their involvement with the organization, fitting their responsibilities around full-time commitments elsewhere. Others also played significant voluntary roles, including some who later became paid members of staff. Shehadeh explains the founders' thinking behind the structure they set up:

> We also had the conscious objective of creating a truly democratic organisation, an organisation completely owned and run by the team working in it. The spirit of voluntarism was also extremely important. Those who participated in creating and developing al-Haq had a singular and strong commitment.[52]

These principles—organizational democracy, staff participation, and voluntarism—continued to underpin LSM/al-Haq's culture even as it grew exponentially from the middle of the decade and into the first intifada. Kuttab recalls the Steering Committee struggling with "being a democratic organisation, and being a professional organisation":

> At the beginning, it was like a family, we'd get round for the Wednesday meeting, all decisions were taken by everybody, including whether to get [then secretary] Paulein curtains or a swivel chair. We wanted them involved, we wanted to instill a sense of ownership, and there were ideas that had to permeate the organization, not come top-down. It was very important that they internalize the values, and we'd do that by involving everyone in decision-making. But the flip side was that many began to

think that collective decision-making was part of human rights. We'd say no, there is nothing human rights-ish about collective decision-making.

The family motif is used by others recalling those early days; they also talked about the sense of "belonging" (*intima'*).[53] Ghazi Shashtari says, "I still have a sense of *intima'* to al-Haq. The old ones, the early ones, I felt we were a family." The emphasis on "belonging" came from the founders, says Nina Atallah. The Wednesday evening meetings were legendary. This was the highest policy and program decision-making body in the organization.[54] Attendance (and preferably participation) was mandatory for all office-based staff; field researchers were not obliged to attend, given that they were based out of the office in different parts of the West Bank. As Shammas says, "We didn't want to be bosses, we wanted participation. That's not a human rights issue, that's rather people trying to organize in a democratic way; you function better and make the most of staff resources."[55] "The whole thrust of the Wednesday meeting," says Shehadeh, "was that we all discuss, we all participate, it was collective responsibility. This was deliberate." Also:

> From the beginning I wanted to leave—I didn't want the burden of being in an organization as a manager—I wanted it and us to grow together so there would be no mysteries about why this or that happened . . . And human rights was not there as a profession, so the idea was to create the profession. It was very important to raise a generation of such people, and that could only happen if we discussed everything and grew together . . . We're all equal in our ignorance.[56]

Opinions vary of the general (Wednesday evening) meetings as a form of governance, although most staffers from the early days remain positive about it as a "great democratic tradition," in the words of one. Sami 'Ayad recalls:

> Things raised at the meetings would be policies, structure, issues, methodology, so this was how—to a certain extent—we learnt how to do the work. I was field research coordinator, we had part-time field researchers in different areas, and I'd report to the meeting on what we knew of what was going on in the occupied territories. We'd discuss how al-Haq would address these issues, everyone had a point, everyone had a role. Mostly things were agreed by consensus; if there was disagreement, there would be an attempt to agree so that as an organisation we had one perspective. If I had reservations, there had to be bases for them, not just a personal opinion; it had to be studied, not superficial, you had to come with evidence and arguments. It was professional, the *marja'iyya* was the rule of law and human rights.

The role of field research at LSM/al-Haq was key—the organization was very much driven by what was happening on the ground. The meeting was a key part of the knowledge transfer, "growing together" and taking responsibility at which the founders were aiming. Zahi Jaradat recalls:

> We'd vote on any decision for something al-Haq was going to work on, even if it was a big decision. This helped a lot in building the idea of belonging to the organisation. I used to feel that I was helping construct the organization and the future of human

rights by my participation in these decisions—if we ask for something, is this useful or not, you discuss and decide and vote. It wasn't always an easy discussion. It was a very good tradition.

Non-Palestinian LSM members agree on the positive dynamics of the general meeting at this time. Roger Heacock notes that "the relational dynamics at the meetings were exemplary: young and (relatively) old, local and international, intellectuals and nonintellectuals all participated on an equal footing." He credits this "relational issue" as being "very important to the organization's administration during its days of glory: that between the triumvirate and the administrators." The youth of the organization was matched by the relative youth of most of those involved; the founders were in their early thirties, the staff mostly in their early or mid-twenties.

But the meeting, along with the structure that it underpinned, was challenged within a few short years. Shammas recalls that by 1984–85, he was more critical of the Steering Committee's approach to governance. "Al-Haq's structure was an ideal, another utopian ideal." Something of a turning point—at least in expectations—appears to have been reached when the Steering Committee brought the issue of Ford Foundation funding to the Wednesday general meeting. According to Kuttab:

> Raja was determined, everyone had to be involved in the decision, at the meeting. It was political. Some said we can't take Ford money. Raja said everyone must decide on that. There was a vote. The meeting voted not to take a decision but to turn it back to us: we had to take the decision. They didn't want to take the political consequences of deciding to take money from Ford. Raja was very disappointed.

Whether or not Ford was particularly suspected of CIA connections, the prospect of defending a decision that entailed "taking money from the Americans," this close to Camp David, was not one that leftists at al-Haq might be expected to relish. While taking the Ford Foundation funding, the Steering Committee decided that no more than 20 percent of LSM's budget would be sought or accepted from a single source.[57] By late 1985, with the Iron Fist policy in full force and LSM/al-Haq expanding in focus, staff, and finances, the 1985 Programme Report announced a second relocation across the road on Main Street, Ramallah, and a change in organizational structure:

> LSM's decision-making structure was revised in 1985 in response to its increased workload and staff membership. All decisions of policy, budget approval, recruitment and entry into relationships with third parties are now decided upon by a new five member executive which includes, ex-officio, LSM's two directors and administrative director. All staff, members of the executive and invited consultants meet at LSM's weekly general meeting. The general meeting reviews the week's activities, makes decisions, discusses policy and initiates research ideas.[58]

The Executive Committee comprised Shehadeh, Kuttab, Shammas, Rishmawi, and a newly recruited administrator. The 1986 Programme Report, which is a much lengthier document addressed to associates, funders, and the local community, talks of a further period of growth with the weekly general meeting "at the heart of the organisation."[59] Judith Dueck, the administrative director, says the Wednesday meetings

> were the right thing at the time. They profoundly affected the major directions of the organization, the strategies that were developed, and the tactics executed. The meetings dealt with major aspects as well as some less significant items such as office furniture: some things could have been better dealt with in other organizational fora.

Dueck found the building of organizational culture and the transfer of knowledge and values to be very effective. When Steering Committee members and other staffers addressed visitors to al-Haq, others in the office, time permitting, would join to listen, and "everyone learned in these circumstances." The sustained participation of the founders in leadership, hands-on projects, and detailed tactical moves was essential as the young organization grew. Broadly, Shehadeh dealt with legal research, Kuttab with field research, and Shammas with the database (and later with the Enforcement Project), although there was always a degree of overlap. Shawan Jabarin speaks of how meetings "built a way of thinking, including self-criticism, and a high level of responsibility regarding the data, as well as organizational issues; the feeling of responsibility towards this was very important, it built a mindset (*dhihniyya*) in the organization." Zahi Jaradat similarly talks of the "al-Haq mentality" (*'aqliyya*). When it worked, this early approach helped the development of reflective practitioners in the human rights field.

By 1986, however, the strain of expansion was showing, embodied in the physical unwieldiness of the Pending File, a physical lever-arch file containing all correspondence of the week, placed in the library for LSM/al-Haq members to review and from which all matters needing follow-up were reported to the Wednesday meeting. The draft proposal for an executive director and consequent further changes in structure, quoted at the beginning of this chapter, and which went through several reviews by Shehadeh and Rishmawi, read in 1988:

> The reality has become that al-Haq is a group which is composed of individuals with a career commitment to human rights. All along, even during the most difficult times, the organisation has retained its distinctiveness: all members get together once a week and discuss everything. This should always be encouraged. The case remains, however, that the final responsibility for decisions and execution and policy is not assumed by all the members of staff. As the organisation is growing in a solid manner, the responsibilities put on the shoulders of its existing Executive Committee are growing as well. The risk to the continuity of the organisation now lies in the extremely heavy demands that its expanded scope of work makes on its Executive who are consequently unable and unwilling to give the time and effort needed

to discharge the responsibility of their directorship. This is what has necessitated this review.[60]

Emma Playfair refers to the "rapid and huge expansion of al-Haq" over the second half of the 1980s as "a continuing disaster for al-Haq: the new staffers didn't get a chance to absorb the ethics of the organization, they didn't have the same sense of close interaction with the directors, they missed that opportunity." Charles Shammas, intellectually and pragmatically interested in "how people react to new knowledge," talks of LSM/al-Haq's need to "find people already looking for something to challenge their understanding":

> We didn't know then that this was crucial, so we didn't look for it. The ethics of the organization didn't bring out the idea that you had to reach, strive for something that wasn't comprehensible to you but it was to someone else. I assumed too much readiness to learn . . . It's not "what I know." We are not "all the same," we needed people to struggle to find the sense that others see in things.

The following observations are from George Giacaman, a philosophy professor from Birzeit University who worked with al-Haq as research coordinator when the university was closed in the intifada:

> The work is crucial. People are not equal in terms of their abilities, their information, their judgement . . . They are equal in rights but that's a very different matter and it confuses things. There are rights that belong to everyone, but not everyone can share in the decision-making on issues if those people have neither the experience nor background nor training [. . .]. So to have a general meeting of everyone, I think, confuses roles. It's a form of populism and confuses things.

Several interviewees observed that the structure that the founders created could only work with a very small organization. As it grew in resources and profile, it was becoming unsustainable. According to Shehadeh:

> The organization was getting frustrated. We three all had other work, everything had to wait for us, there was frustration on both sides [. . .] I had to read everything, we couldn't risk something getting out that was against the "balance" [. . .] It was clear that it wasn't working, this strange structure of everyone having to be involved [. . .] People working day to day in the office were frustrated by the fact that we weren't working there, and for our part we had an idealistic view of how things should be— but the office was always a mess. [. . .] And in the general meetings, so much was unsaid, there were all these assumptions, people weren't speaking out, there would be these heavy silences when everyone was supposed to speak out.

This was the time of the build-up to the first intifada. At the turn of 1986–87, al-Haq presented to the public, in its Newsletter editorial titled "The Role of a Human Rights Organisation under Occupation," how it saw its role and internally organized a series of (re)orientation sessions for its staffers, old and new.

During its recent period of expansion, al-Haq has been evaluating its role and giving renewed thought to the role of a human rights organisation under occupation. Given the extreme circumstances of military rule, should [al-Haq] restrict itself to monitoring and censuring the occupying power's actions? Or should it also concern itself with the standards within its own society, and consider violations within that society? How should it play its part in preparing for the uncertain future of its society?

Al-Haq believes that a human rights organisation operating under these circumstances must play two roles [. . .] On the one hand it must do its best to act as a watchdog for the rights of the population, living under the rule of a foreign power. On the other hand, it should also work towards ensuring that the society of which it is a part maintains and develops its own standards of human rights, equipping it for the future as well as for the present.[. . .]

People living under occupation are living under alien rule. [. . .] Where there is a conflict of interest between the interests of the occupier's civilian population and the population of the occupied territories it is perhaps inevitable that the former will normally prevail. The latter have no state to represent their interests and restore the balance.

Human rights and other indigenous organisations must do their best to compensate the people for this lack. In the case of the human rights organisation, it must constantly represent the rights of the occupied population, ensuring that discrimination does not go unremarked for lack of representation and trying to halt and obtain redress for violations of human rights.

The usual tools of human rights organisations, such as the lobbying of politicians for change in the law, or use of the courts for testing issues, may be unavailable or inappropriate under occupation. Equally, the voice of a human rights organisation which is itself part of the occupied population may carry little weight with the occupier. Other ways of achieving progress must therefore be sought.

A human rights organisation is in a position to try to mobilise external support providing that it first establishes and maintains its reputation for veracity and reliability. By linking in to the network of human rights organisations, and other concerned bodies, and providing them with information on which they can rely, it can reach wider communities who will thus be better equipped to weigh, evaluate and act on the available information. At the same time it can apply pressure on states, directly and through other organisations, to fulfil their obligations in relation to conventions they have signed, in particular the Fourth Geneva Convention of 1949 which regulates occupations.

The legal framework within which a human rights organisation works differs under occupation from that applicable under normal circumstances. International law places specific limits on an occupier's actions. An effective human rights organisation must try to see that these laws are respected by the occupying power. If the occupying power refuses to acknowledge the applicability of such laws, or violates them notwithstanding, the organisation must seek to find means of enforcing the laws, in a situation where the domestic courts will not enforce the law and there is no state to take the occupying power to the international forum.

It must further explain to a public who may be quite unaware of their rights, that there are limitations to an occupier's power and what these limitations are. This may be particularly necessary with a prolonged occupation, since a people deprived of rights over a long period of time may come to accept this deprivation as a necessary evil of the situation and not contest it.

[. . .] Even if given a civilian face, an occupation is essentially maintained by the military, and in the case of the Israeli occupation the executive, legislative, and judicial arms of the occupying power are all in the hands of the military. The separation of these powers is one of the prime requirements of the rule of law, and the lack of separation is therefore a serious threat to the administration of justice. [. . .]

[. . .] It must clearly be high amongst the aims of any human rights organisation that, whatever the political situation, its own society should be one which respects both individual and collective, civil and political rights. [. . .] The population of occupied lands are not able to express their support for such concepts by instigating appropriate legislation, but much can be achieved by education and communication of the principles of human rights, to promote genuine acceptance of these concepts. [. . .]

Where the local legal structure has been fractured and the legal profession to some extent disempowered, the human rights organisation can perform some of the duties normally carried by a bar association. Subject to available means, it can make legal materials available, correlate, analyse, index and monitor current legislation and even provide legal education. At the same time it can seek the establishment of an independent bar association [. . .]

[. . . .] A non-discriminatory attitude towards the rights of women, minorities, and racial or religious groups and respect for the rights of workers and for civil and human rights in general is as essential for the health of a society under occupation as in any other situation. To ignore or postpone criticisms of violations within the society would not only undermine the validity and good faith of criticisms of violations perpetrated by others, but more importantly would endanger the nature of the society itself.

In al-Haq's evaluation of its work and planning for the future, it thus seeks to maintain a balance between its concern for the violation of the rights of Palestinians living under occupation by the Israeli authorities, and its efforts to promote respect for human rights within its own society.[61]

This piece of reflection sought to do a number of things, among them to situate the organization within the wider human rights movement, to link human rights to the rule of law, to present the particularity of occupation as a context for human rights work, and to insist on human rights as a framework for societal values and conduct. The organization had already recruited a retired schoolmaster to work on human rights education. Rishmawi's occasional paper on the legal position of Palestinian women under the British, Jordanian, and Israeli legal regimes in the West Bank had been published in Arabic that year and the rights of workers were under study, with two *Know Your Rights* booklets published.[62] The organization had resumed publication of its "Legal Corner" in *al-Quds* newspaper, and the same Newsletter included reports of al-Haq staffers giving talks at secondary schools and other public events. "All too often in the West Bank," commented the Newsletter, "the debate on human rights is reduced to a defence of the rights of Palestinians at the risk, in al-Haq's view, of ignoring the violations that take place within Palestinian society itself."[63] The editorial points to the thinking that was to develop into the Enforcement Project, including the invocation of state obligations under the Fourth Geneva Convention. The insistence on establishing and maintaining its "reputation for veracity and reliability"—primarily through the credibility of its primary data collected through field research—was, as ever, a primary focus. At the end of this Newsletter, for the first time and under the shadow of the Iron Fist, came a section titled "The Year 1986 in Statistics" giving lists of Palestinians subjected during the year to administrative punishments—deportation, town arrest, administrative detention, and house demolition.

In the meantime, recognizing the building frustrations, the organization's leadership was planning a series of directed discussion sessions "intended to lead to a thorough overhaul of the organization, its structure and its work." Originally envisaged in three stages, the first focused on "a critical evaluation of al-Haq's work and development since 1979, through the conflictual approach—why were things done in a certain way and not in another way." The document sets out the themes, including a number of questions that those leading the sessions might use "to elicit further information, provoke argument or call into question assumptions made."[64] Some of the questions clearly invoke issues bubbling under or spilling over in the organization at the time. Some elicit discussion around the substantive issues covered in the Newsletter. Others raise concerns preoccupying at least some in al-Haq: is human rights non-political, is al-Haq—and should it be—"representative," what is the nature of al-Haq's interventions with the Israeli authorities, what is the function of the Wednesday meeting, who do we take money from and why, and so on. A summary of the first session from the organizers lists a number of critical comments that had been made by participants; perhaps the al-Haq leadership were sensitive to particular criticisms, or were getting tired of explaining:

> If there is a genuine desire for reassessment and a willingness for change, there should be no need for defensiveness in responding to criticism.
>
> Concern was expressed at an impression given that our work is important and that that of some other organizations working in a different way is not.
>
> Are we really non-political and objective? Needs further discussion.
>
> Rule of law—needs further discussion.[65]

Another document in al-Haq's files lists suggestions that appear to have arisen from this exercise, including the training of al-Haq members as paralegals and the initiation of campaigns on single subjects, both of which were followed up in the coming years, as was a suggestion for an annual report, although this was to happen under the particular circumstances of the first year of the intifada. Under "matters postponed for discussion," this document includes some of the questions considered not to have been resolved in the orientation, including those regarding contact with the military authorities, what it meant to be a human rights activist, how to get more local associates, and "Is the balance in our work between individual and collective rights reasonable, or should we concentrate more on the right to self-determination etc?" As for the completion of the three-stage orientation, it appears that much got postponed in the buildup to and the outbreak of the first intifada.

MEMBERS AND STAFFERS

Some of the questions and comments above reflect the growing pains that any organization would suffer, let alone one that was substantively dependent upon the voluntary contributions of its Steering Committee. By the end of 1986, "the members of al-Haq now include fifteen local full-time employees, five volunteers seconded to al-Haq from several international organisations,[66] three field-workers and two professionals on substantial retainer."[67] It was to continue to expand into the first intifada, reaching at one point nearly forty staffers; it became the largest ICJ affiliate and had three times as many staff as the ICJ Secretariat in Geneva.[68]

Other issues raised are perhaps more specific to al-Haq or to a certain type of NGO in Palestine at that period. The question "Why do we have foreigners working with us?," suggested for discussion in the orientation document of 1987, was one that had already been given space in a 1985 training day, and that continued to need both reflection and clarification.[69] Mouin Rabbani, the first Palestinian from abroad to join the research staff, observed that "al-Haq has been slow and ineffectual at implementing its stated goal of attracting and developing local Palestinian skills to replace those of transient foreign volunteers upon whom it has relied."[70] Non-Palestinian staffers, and Palestinians from outside the oPt, found their way to LSM/al-Haq in a variety of ways. LSM/al-Haq relied heavily on these staffers in the production of its research publications, which were written first in English for distribution to the English-speaking West and Israeli society. They were subsequently translated into Arabic.[71] Publications written in Arabic for the local community—notably the *Know Your Rights* series—were not translated into English. There was little contact with allies in Arab countries, and, as already noted, apart from Kuttab's work with the Middle East group of HURIDOCS, sustained engagement with the Arab human rights movement came in the early 1990s.[72]

In al-Haq's research work, English language skills were one thing, research training and educational background another. Many of the "transient foreign volunteers" came with advanced research and writing skills, albeit not in human rights per se. The education system in the West Bank and Gaza did not provide as strong a training; the Palestinian universities were young, with study frequently interrupted by closures imposed by the military authorities, and there were very few advanced degrees on offer. A third factor was sheer time. The Palestinian staff put in long hours, but they had family and social obligations ("they had lives") that mostly did not apply (or at least, not to the same extent) to foreign staffers or Palestinians raised abroad. As far as the social scene was concerned, Ramallah was a very different place from the cultural hub packed with bars and events, film festivals and literature festivals, that it had become, for some, by the time of the Arab Spring. Looking back at long hours in the office in the mid-1980s, Hiltermann recalls:

> Even under occupation, a normal working day is something everyone's entitled to. We [foreign staffers] came as individuals, we mostly had no families there [. . .] Plus what else was there to do? There was nowhere to go out, some socializing at friends' homes perhaps, but it was mostly just work, work, work, and that made you happy and satisfied. There was a tension about that. After all, it was their struggle not ours. We'd come in and "do" much more the way they saw it—but of course they "did" more than us in another sense, as they had to live the consequences of the occupation [. . .] Some [foreign staffers] were sensitive to the need for Palestinian staff to feel sovereignty over the organisation's work—it was a Palestinian organisation, not a foreign implantation, we took direction from Palestinians, because it wasn't our organization.

The foreign staffers were not homogenous, and some were more aware than others of their place in the work and in the organization. Raja Shehadeh further recalls tensions "between foreigners with different perspectives and approaches." Hiltermann recognizes that it was easier for the foreign staff to travel and present al-Haq's work abroad: "We'd travel and meet people, and we'd get the kudos, the plaudits." In Ramallah, not all Palestinian staffers were able to address the many and varied foreign delegations and visitors who came to the office seeking briefings on the human rights situation. Inside and outside the organization, there were concerns about foreign staff "speaking for" Palestinians at al-Haq. For many years the Wednesday meeting was held in English, perhaps accidentally to start with, since there were foreign staff who did not speak enough Arabic to cope with the meeting. The Steering Committee members were perfectly comfortable in English, and office-based Palestinian staff and the fieldwork unit coordinator mostly had good English language skills. Judith Dueck observed that in her time, some fieldworkers were "not comfortable in English," and this was one reason that they did not attend some meetings, although there was also the practical challenge of getting back home in the evening.[73] Fieldwork unit coordinator Khaled Batrawi used to hold meetings of the unit on Wednesday afternoons, so that field-workers who were able to stay on would do so. Batrawi recalls that it was after a request from field researchers that the Wednesday meeting began to be conducted in Arabic, with informal translation provided to foreign researchers who needed it.

My interviews with field researchers raised a particular sensitivity—dating from slightly later—over "non-Palestinian researchers who'd come from abroad for two or three months, use all the information we had collected and publish a study with their name on it."[74] Zahi Jaradat observes that this division of labor was "no-one's fault, the field researcher stays in place, I can't say I'm going to stop doing fieldwork and write a study on my fieldwork in Jenin now please." He adds, however:

> There should be some fairness in this; perhaps the credit should be shared? All the work we do is an achievement of the field research. The field researcher is the one who takes the most risk, doing field research under occupation, with the settlers and the army.

In the office, sensitivities arose when work by Palestinian members of the legal research unit was not published as readily as that produced by non-Palestinian research staff; the first al-Haq annual report, *Punishing a Nation*, after the first year of the intifada, is given as an example. For Randa Siniora, it was clearly an issue:

> Those of us working in the research unit always felt that foreign staffers were given more attention by the organization's leadership, at the expense of more time and attention being invested with the Palestinian researchers. We felt we were marginalized.

For Charles Shammas, the issue was one of principle and pragmatism. He recalls repeated explicit discussions in al-Haq's Executive Committee about the organization's overreliance on foreign staff and the need to invest more in Palestinian staff, citing as a major regret that he and his colleagues did not in fact do that. During its early period, the organization did express explicit commitment to "stimulating professional development among its staff," a topic addressed in both the 1985 and 1986 Programme Reports. The Newsletter too carried reports of visits abroad made by Palestinian staff members to training courses, study sessions, conferences, and so on. In the spring of 1985, the Newsletter reported:

> For the second consecutive year, one of LSM's Palestinian researchers is attending a special teaching programme on 'Development, Law and Social Justice' at the Institute of Social Studies in The Hague [. . .] LSM believes that as a human rights organisation it should actively seek to advance its employees' understanding of the subject and the relevant law. Furthermore it believes that the broader perspectives, international contacts and knowledge of other areas gained on such a course are invaluable in widening interest beyond narrow and political concerns, while at the same time shedding new light on those concerns.[75]

The activities listed under "professional development" in the 1986 Programme Report included a human rights training course in Strasbourg (at the International Institute of Human Rights) attended by two al-Haq researchers; the report notes that as well as the theoretical introduction to human rights issues, this course provided a rare networking opportunity for the al-Haq staffers.[76] Other activities included a two-week internship with various international organizations in Geneva undertaken by the human rights educator, a member of the administrative staff doing an internship in Oslo on human rights documentation, conferences on feminist perspectives in law, communication and human rights (in Italy), and database techniques (Britain); local computer training courses and a specialist database training course; and monthly training seminars for the field researchers and regular translation workshops for the translators. Finally, the staff were "encouraged to study English or Arabic, sometimes with modest financial assistance from al-Haq."

Some of the field researchers nevertheless felt that they missed out on international exposure and learning opportunities that were more open to office-based staff. Later on, field researchers were sent to Tunis and to Strasbourg for human rights training, and the first al-Haq field-worker whose LLM study in the UK was facilitated by the organization was the Rafah field researcher Issam Younis, who joined the legal research unit on his return from the UK in 1993. Younis was encouraged in his plans by Said Zeedani, who came from Birzeit University to become program director at al-Haq in late 1990, and was to remain involved for many years, most notably as a board member. Zeedani was particularly focused on equipping Palestinian staff for the research and writing work at al-Haq—not just the research publications but also, for example, press releases in English. "It's an ownership issue," he says, "you can't keep relying on people coming from outside. You create a cadre who can take over and reduce reliance on foreign volunteers from the US/UK." A number of Palestinian staffers took their LLMs in quick succession, institutionalizing such arrangements as part of professional development; Zeedani considers this to have been a "turning point" in the organization.

INTO THE INTIFADA:
TWENTY YEARS OF OCCUPATION

With hindsight, the expanding al-Haq was caught up in the atmosphere as the occupied territories moved towards the first intifada in December 1987. Arguably it contributed to the buildup, providing a distinctive language and framing as Palestinians of the West Bank and Gaza grew in political awareness of their own space for action.[77] At the same time, al-Haq's founders and Steering Committee were finding the governance system they had set up unsustainable in terms of time, energy, and aspirations. The success of the organization's work brought its own challenges, including rapid recruitment and an organizational shift away from being a place where "everyone did everything" and becoming more process-oriented in its administrative structures.

The founders, conscious of the need to reduce reliance on their own voluntary and part-time input into program implementation, were looking to appoint a full-time in-house executive director. They nevertheless wanted to continue the vital element of staff participation that had distinguished their vision of the organization. A further version of the draft document (1989) setting out the need for an executive director proposed that the general meeting should ratify a new board of trustees (comprising the three founding members) with "legal responsibility for the organization, and the final authority to approve, review or change policy in accordance with its mandate and the organizational procedures described below." The document continued, "The new structure seeks to maintain and continue to refine the basic qualities and principles developed by al-Haq over time. The most important of these principles is wide staff participation in decision-making, while maintaining clear lines of responsibility."

> Because of the participatory nature of the organisation in its decision-making processes, the responsibility that falls on every employee goes beyond the terms of employment. This being the case, the ability of each responsible employee to exercise his or her privileges called for in the present situation must be taken into consideration before said employee is confirmed.

The draft also noted that it must "also serve as an institutional model to the community." The general meeting was to remain "the highest decision-making body on programme-related matters." A slightly later draft clarified that the general meeting was to decide on matters by consensus, and if unable to reach a consensus was to delegate the matter to the Steering Committee. The Steering Committee was to consist of the executive director, the administrative director, and three staff members to be selected by the board from five nominees elected by staff (with eligibility linked to length of service). There was to be a study group to include all researchers and field researchers to identify patterns of violations emerging and propose courses of action to the general meeting. There was also to be a staff council comprising the administrative director and a number of staffers elected by the staff body.

Mona Rishmawi was appointed as al-Haq's first executive director after she returned from completing her LLM at Columbia in 1989, in the middle of the first intifada; Shehadeh, Kuttab, and Shammas constituted the board of trustees. The handover from the board to their former colleague on the Executive/Steering Committee was not smooth, with both parties struggling to agree about the limits on authority. Rishmawi reflects now that "expectations were very high, we were all young and had limited experience. And this colored a lot of what happened afterwards; a lot of it was simply that—age and perspective—because we were focusing on something else, the pressures caused by the urgencies of the work." Of all the organizational crises that al-Haq has seen, this first is the one that people are least inclined to discuss: it was very hurtful for all involved. Perceptions now seem to fall between "it was bound to happen" (given the setup of the handover and the unavoidable turf war caused by the structure rather than by the individuals involved) and "it should never have happened" (given the commitments of all four to the organization and the swiftly reestablished professional relationship between al-Haq and Rishmawi). Rishmawi left the West Bank for the ICJ's Centre for the Independence of Judges and Lawyers in Geneva, where she stayed in regular contact and cooperation with al-Haq. The board stepped back in to cover the daily running until it could appoint another executive director—"we did so grudgingly" says Shehadeh, remembering a series of "rebellious" weekly meetings. It was a difficult time for management and staff alike, but by no means al-Haq's last management crisis.

A succession of executive directors (and boards) was to follow. Said Zeedani, who was appointed by the board following Rishmawi's departure, observes that "this whole issue of democracy in the organization—meetings deciding policy issues or financial issues—this was a lousy idea . . . It didn't work here, and I don't think it could work anywhere, as a model. If there is no hierarchy, you can't lead." On the other hand, Fateh Azzam observes:

> Even with all these other really difficult things, the weekly meeting was still going on, things were being decided, there was a sense of open discussion about the program, that was one of the main strengths of al-Haq . . . It was quite an extraordinary setup. Everyone complained, the meeting got longer and longer as everyone had to have a say, there were concerns about why should people who don't know the work have as much say as someone like Raja, for example. It was not an easy process, but a very useful and important one, I think.

Some staffers at al-Haq acknowledge that the troublesome relationships between board, director, and staff were at least in part a misapplication of the feelings of ownership and belonging that the founders had intentionally sought to inculcate. Looking back at the earlier years and also at subsequent crises in the organization, Nina Atallah recalls:

> At first it was lovely, we all did everything, there was no difference because of political opinion, everyone felt "al-Haq is mine and ours and we all work and help," the founders and the staff were involved in everything . . . Then, when new boards came, some didn't like it, the idea of belonging (*intima'*) can be a mistake, you start to think "this is my house and they're interfering," well, that's their job! This was the negative side of "belonging": "who are these people coming from outside?" [. . .] But if we invite them to do a job, we have to accept them!

Issam Younis, founder and director of the human rights NGO Al Mezan in Gaza, has a similar reflection. His experience of al-Haq's governance structures gave him what he considers invaluable experience in staff participation, adding however that "belonging (*intima'*) is not a problem, it's good, but not when it becomes 'who's this director, where are they from, we are the organization, we built it' and so on." With hindsight, certain appointments to management posts were unfortunate and there were, doubtless, board members who pushed their own agendas. However, many have suggested that the strength of al-Haq lies in the very fact of its institutionalization and its distance from a one-person organization model—it never was any individual's "shop." Getting the critical balance between staff empowerment and managerial authority and leadership was never going to be easy.

Meanwhile, back in 1987, al-Haq was intensively engaged in planning for the first international law conference to be held in the occupied territories. This was scheduled for January 1988, which turned out to be the very beginning of the first intifada. According to Emma Playfair, the idea "was conceived in 1986 in one of al-Haq's weekly meetings. Facing yet again a problem of law to which we found no answer, Raja Shehadeh suggested appealing to the world's experts in the law of war for their help in clarifying the international laws governing Israel's administration of the West Bank and Gaza."[78] Introducing the volume of papers she edited from the conference, Playfair talks of al-Haq's work in addressing violations of individual human rights but also of the importance it attached to "monitoring the treatment of the territories themselves and their infrastructure by the military authorities, since this is critical to the rights of the Palestinian people as a whole." She continues, "While there have been a number of situations of belligerent occupation since World War II, none has become institutionalised to the extent of Israel's occupation of the West Bank and Gaza. Consequently, many of the issues raised by this occupation have not been faced since the Fourth Geneva Convention came into force."[79] The conference was a pragmatic response, to engage with internationally recognized scholars who would help al-Haq work through the implications of key patterns of behavior on the part of the occupying power. In the interim, in summer 1987, al-Haq produced a substantive essay titled "Twenty Years of Occupation: A Time to Reflect," discussing Israel's occupation, the use(s) of law, and the organization's key and pressing concerns.

> [. . .] Twenty years have passed since Israel forcibly took control over the Territories in the June War of 1967 [. . .] What first looked like a temporary military occupation has been transformed into a long-term Israeli effort to colonise the Occupied Territories. Over the past two decades Palestinians living in the area have therefore had to readjust their expectations, and so also the way in which they live their lives under occupation, and deal with the occupier. This is true as well for Palestinian institutions that have emerged during the occupation, like al-Haq itself.
>
> [. . .] There was much talk in the beginning about an early withdrawal following some type of negotiated settlement of the conflict. With the increasing confiscation of Palestinian lands in the 1970s, however, and the establishment of Jewish settlements, Palestinians' analysis of the situation had to be modified. Today, after twenty years, few have doubts about what may be the occupier's primary aim in the West Bank and Gaza: to take the land and exploit human and material resources.
>
> To Palestinians, the Israeli enterprise is strongly reminiscent of events that took place during the height of the colonial era in the 19th and 20th centuries, when European nations conquered African and Asian land and mobilised indigenous resources by force [. . .] What is different is the Israelis' apparent long-term goal of population displacement, as well as the unique methods that they employ: they have given their colonising effort a legalistic veneer in the form of the military occupation.[. . .]

AL-HAQ'S GOALS

Operating under such circumstances, al-Haq, as an organisation dedicated to the protection of human rights and upholding the rule of law, devised its own methods of achieving its aims: it confronts the illegal acts of the occupier by documenting and contesting human rights violations, while at the same time it seeks to analyse, promote understanding of, and improve or alter existing legislation, in short, enforce adherence to the rule of law. Although al-Haq sees the effort to strengthen the rule of law as its primary goal, in the early years of its existence its activities were by necessity limited to the very basic tasks.

It is one of the unfortunate facts of life under occupation that the efforts of any organisation in the Territories are defined by the immediate needs of the situation prevailing at any time. Al-Haq, for example, has spent considered energies in pressuring the military authorities to publish and distribute the military orders and regulations they had been enacting since 1967, because lawyers continued to receive cases of individuals charged with violating an order of whose existence they were unaware.

Even after military orders had finally become available to the public, al-Haq faced the intimidating task of analysing this body of military laws and examining its legality in light of international conventions pertaining to occupied territories, primarily the Hague Regulations of 1907, and the IV Geneva Convention of 1949. One of the problems in this respect was to explain to a lay audience abroad how the occupier has used a complex legal structure at once to cover up and to justify its political and economic aims of colonising the Territories.

THE OCCUPIER'S USE OF THE LAW

The process of colonisation is very real for Palestinians who may wake up one morning to find that bulldozers have started to uproot the trees on their land to make room for an Israeli settlement. It may not be so visible to outsiders, however. This is so because colonising efforts, like the confiscation of Palestinian land, are justified by the occupying authorities either as required for Israeli military security needs or as desirable to promote the interests of the local population and—so it is argued—are effected within the bounds of the law, both local law and international conventions pertaining to occupied territories. According to the IV Geneva Convention, the occupying power cannot amend the laws in existence in the territories it occupies other than to serve its overriding security needs or the interests of the local population.

On the face of it the authorities' arguments might be convincing to a lay audience, especially if no violation of applicable laws can be seen to take place. There are, however, serious flaws in these arguments. Al-Haq has spent a disproportionate amount of time and energy during the past seven years . . . in attempting to set the record straight.

RESPONSE TO ISRAELI ARGUMENTS

[. . .] Security concerns are routinely cited for any measure which cannot otherwise be justified without incurring opposition [. . .] Even the Israeli High Court of Justice so far has not been able to pose a serious threat to the military authorities' own definition of their security needs [. . .]

The authorities have consequently been able to promote Israeli settlement of the Territories by defining some of its elements, like the construction of new roads, as beneficial to the local population. To them, however, "local population" is not only the Palestinians in the Territories, but is also the Israelis living in the settlements, even though the presence of the latter in the Territories is illegal by applicable international law, Article 49 of the IV Geneva Convention. [. . .]

Jordanian law, which applies in the West Bank, and the combination of British Mandatory and Egyptian law that is in force in Gaza, have been altered beyond recognition by the occupying authorities [. . .] What has emerged [. . .] in reality constitutes a radical departure from the law that nominally prevails, and which according to international law should prevail. [. . .] Partisan interpretations of terms such as "security needs" and "interests of the local population" ensure that the military authorities can deflect charges of violations of international law with relative ease.

The structure of military legislation serves to obscure the true nature of the massive Israeli colonisation effort that is underway in the Occupied Territories. With every military order enabling the confiscation of a patch of land for "security" reasons, the ultimate goal of the colonisation project has been brought one step closer. With every order limiting the economic activities of the Palestinian population, the occupiers have come closer to their goal of taking the land they have set out to conquer, without the population that lives on it today.

ROLE OF AL-HAQ UNDER OCCUPATION

As a human rights organisation, al-Haq endeavours to support the human rights of the Palestinian population under occupation. Al-Haq has documented in the past serious violations of such rights, including torture and maltreatment in prisons, administrative punishments like deportations and house demolitions, censorship of publications, and repression of trade union activities. In al-Haq's view, the fundamental problem which gives rise to these violations—a problem that is rarely voiced in discussions about the Palestinian-Israeli conflict—is the system of colonisation of the West Bank and Gaza: a consistent expropriation of Palestinian lands, exploitation of human and material resources, and undermining of social and physical infrastructure. This goes hand in hand with a refusal on the part of the occupier to maintain the status quo in the Occupied Territories, much less to allow the area's development in a manner beneficial to its population or to agree to negotiate seriously the Territories' final disposition.

Al-Haq has been forced by the situation to focus on exposing the occupier's goals by analysing the legal structure that has been built to justify them. This has taken much energy, and has inadvertently led to a reduced emphasis on the organisation's more long-term goals: to provide, through education and training, the legal resources of the Palestinian society of tomorrow, as well as to help give shape to the standards and principles that will serve as moral underpinnings of that society.

Twenty years of occupation having passed, including seven years of al-Haq's work during which the organisation succeeded in doing much of the basic ground work needed for its future activities, al-Haq now intends to dedicate more time and resources to the realisation of its long-term aims. In the first stage this means upgrading its human rights education program, and encouraging young

Palestinians to join its primary mission: the protection of human rights, and analysis, evaluation and improvement of prevailing law. This will facilitate the future task—a task shared by all Palestinians—of building those values and institutions which will be necessary in a future independent Palestinian state.[80]

This compelling piece speaks for itself in its urgency. The invocation of European colonialism is a departure for the organization, as is the criticism of Israel's refusal to "negotiate seriously" and the final reference to a future independent Palestinian state, both broadly political statements that the organization is now comfortable making. The reference to the occupier's goal of "taking the land without the population that lives on it" can be read as an implicit reference to the historical Zionist presentation of Palestine as "a land without a people for a people without a land." Key to al-Haq's reading is the link between the violations of human rights and Israel's systematic colonization of the occupied territories as a matter of policy. Al-Haq's determination to "devote more time and resources to the realisation of its long-term aims" was to be thwarted by the massive events of the first intifada and the brutality of Israel's reaction.

5

Interventions and Allies

During the 1980s, LSM/al-Haq developed and systematized its working methodologies and tightened its articulation of its priorities in response to developments in Israel's declared policy and documented practice. The basis, however, remained the understanding that serious violations of civil and political rights by the occupation authorities were committed in the service of pursuing a primary annexationist agenda. For legal analysis and underpinning of appeals to third parties, LSM/al-Haq moved from early invocations of the Universal Declaration of Human Rights (UDHR), on the one hand, and international humanitarian law (IHL) on the other (the Fourth Geneva Convention 1949 and the Hague Regulations 1907), and began looking also at international human rights instruments, at this stage for their moral and declaratory authority. The organization experimented with formats through which to publicize its findings, with the hope of prompting cessation or correction of the violations addressed. In the 1986 Programme Report—a lengthy document that demonstrates ongoing reflection on the work to date—al-Haq stated that the organization

> undertakes to detect, document and investigate human rights violations; to look for and identify patterns of violations and to investigate their antecedents and causes; to inform and educate individuals, groups, governments and international bodies regarding the facts, and their rights and obligations under law in the presence of those facts, as well as to consider their actions in the light of universal legal and human rights principles; and to challenge legislative acts and practices which contravene or prejudice the principles and rights which al-Haq seeks to uphold.

The critical question of "impact" currently being asked of all human rights organizations (by donors, by constituencies) may not have been phrased in quite the same way, but al-Haq's approach, both pragmatic and strategic, meant that the question of "what works" very much defined what it did with the information held through its fieldwork and legal research, as well as informing the direction and methodologies of this research. Field and legal research and interventions are identified in the 1986 report as the "core programme."

This chapter considers how the different elements of al-Haq's core program worked together. This includes how it developed and deployed what it termed interventions, how it sought to mobilize and work with allies, and the particular form and fate of its Enforcement Project.

INTERVENTIONS

As already noted, by 1984 LSM/al-Haq had an established practice of making interventions to identified persons with particular responsibilities for and authority over different aspects of life in the West Bank. Although this is now considered a standard form of human rights work, it was not then, nor was the decision to incorporate it as part of LSM's methodology straightforward or taken in one go. According to Emma Playfair:

> It seems obvious now, you write to those responsible and put the case and await a response, on the record. But then, it was really weird. [. . .] Any contact with the occupier was seen as immoral; it wasn't done then.

The first intervention was made in 1983.[1] Sami 'Ayad fieldwork coordinator at the time, recalls discussions about

> how to frame it, addressing the occupying power whose very presence you reject. You denounce the violation on the basis of evidence and give a list of demands for improvement, based on their obligations, military orders, etc. For example, the treatment of prisoners: you object to the prisons, but you demand action from the authorities. We were very careful who we addressed—the minister of defense, the military governor, for example. You have a relationship with the occupying power which you object to in the first place.

A draft document of Programme Objectives for 1987 defines both an "activist" and a "promotional" role for al-Haq, addressing both the local and the international communities. The first address under the activist heading is interventions with the Israeli government and military authorities, which the organization states it is undertaking in order "to redress and inhibit specific violations, provoke disclosure of information, elicit clarification of the criteria used by its personnel in actions taken vis-à-vis the local population and the implicit and explicit policies implemented in the Occupied Territories." An explanation of what goes into the making of an intervention begins with the organization's critical reliance on documentation:

> When satisfied that a particular action constitutes a violation of a legal principle and after all relevant facts have been established and properly documented, al-Haq addresses the appropriate authorities, and/or requests other organisations and

individuals to do so. Such interventions include a presentation of the evidence in al-Haq's possession; legal arguments asserting that there has been a violation of a recognised principle and that this must be remedied; and a petition to desist from the offending practice, to provide redress to the victim, to carry out an official investigation, or to provide other relief or action.[2]

By 1986, interventions were grouped into five broad subject areas:

(1) law and structure;

(2) deaths, injuries and harassment ("at the hands of all sections of the Israeli army, the police, Jewish settlers and Israeli-sponsored 'village leagues'");

(3) arrests and detention (including "cases of illegal arrest and detention, prison conditions and harassment of prisoners during and as a result of their detention");

(4) collective punishment (including house demolition and sealing and punitive curfews); and

(5) control measures preventing West Bank residents from "going about their normal business" (these included "restrictions on travel out of the West Bank, withholding of building permits or driving licences, restrictions on leaving a town or district within the West Bank, and closure of trade unions").[3]

An example of the process was al-Haq's intervention after the use of tear gas in Jnaid prison early in 1987. The organization had made interventions in a number of previous cases of the use of gas against political prisoners in the confined spaces of prisons. When the Jnaid incident happened, "al-Haq was then convinced that its unpublicised efforts to persuade the Israeli military authorities to stop this inhumane practice had failed" and it therefore "felt compelled to publicise its concern." Al-Haq issued a press release (which was censored by the Israeli authorities who barred the Arabic press from publishing it); this was attached to the Newsletter, which carried news of this intervention.[4]

In 1986 al-Haq reported nearly eighty interventions to date, which had met with "varying degrees of success."[5] The Draft Programme Objectives for 1987 noted that "despite al-Haq's disappointment at its past lack of success it plans to continue its efforts in this area, while at the same time seeking support from local and international partners who can assist." This had often been a feature of interventions—LSM would send a letter to the military authorities and a copy to the ICJ or to Amnesty, for example, or to ACRI, or would seek their direct intervention in a case or an issue within their mandate. The thinking around such appeals to allies was developing strategically in parallel with the organization's frustration or "disappointment." In his paper for the 1988 al-Haq conference, Jonathan Kuttab acknowledged the difference that an individual Israeli officer might make but noted that "such appeals are rarely effective, and have become even less so in recent times."

He also noted a change in practice on the part of "different constituent parts of the military government, and the civilian administration, to refer any complicated or controversial issue to the office of the legal adviser." He observed:

> To the extent that the holder of that office was conversant with international humanitarian law, and valued the concept of the rule of law, such appeals could be useful. At least a reasoned response would be forthcoming that is aware of the possibility of adverse publicity in case of a totally unintelligent response. For this reason it became an almost routine procedure for al-Haq, after carefully investigating and adequately documenting a human rights violation that came to its attention first to write a carefully worded intervention to the legal adviser, and await his response, both as to the factual accuracy of our statements, and for his legal response to the arguments we make.
>
> Unfortunately, the present staff of the legal adviser's office do not seem to be concerned about the rule of law, and protection of human rights. Their responses are very delayed, perfunctory, and lacking in substance. [. . .] We can no longer see in the legal adviser, even remotely, a possible avenue for redress.[6]

While continuing to place facts and petitions on record, al-Haq was developing its network of allies among Israeli lawyers and human rights activists and in the international community. It framed a theory of international protection or, more specifically, addresses to which appeals for third-party state intervention with the Israeli authorities might be made, on an international law basis, by members of the civilian Palestinian population of the occupied territories. In January 1988, at the beginning of the first intifada, al-Haq addressed its first such appeal directly to High Contracting Parties to the Fourth Geneva Convention.

Before this, the only communication with a third-party state made by LSM that could be classed as an intervention had been two responses to the chapter on Israel and the occupied territories in the Country Reports on Human Rights Practices prepared by the US State Department for the US Congress covering the years 1982 and 1984.[7] The idea of preparing the response seems to have come from groups in the United States,[8] and the drafter of the first observes:

> I do think there was some belief that the human rights reports were 'evidence-based' and by supplying evidence there was a possibility that future ones might better reflect reality. [. . .] As with the other projects, the aim was to produce objectively verifiable "facts" to establish a case—this was very much the LSM philosophy then.

The first LSM Newsletter reported that "we considered it necessary to correct the erroneous impression of the human rights situation as found by the American report, through critiquing and responding to it section by section."[9] The LSM response was sent via the US consul general in Jerusalem and included a letter to the US secretary of state noting that LSM had found "certain omissions and misrepresentations" and expressing the hope that "the information and observations contained in LSM's reply will be given careful consideration by you and your staff in the course of preparing the report for 1983, and that any necessary amendments to the 1982 Report be made for the record."[10] It was not to be long before LSM realized that this hope was overly ambitious, if not entirely misplaced: the US authorities had no intention of amending their own reports, particularly on Israel, simply in light of facts presented.

LSM's response to the 1982 US report opened with the "immense amount of US aid to Israel [. . .] which enables, for example, Israel to finance the expansion of its settlement programme in the occupied territories" and explains that the fact that "decisions on the granting of US aid are, by law, dependent on the human rights report" was the reason for LSM preparing its response.[11] Among the features that LSM particularly objected to were the absence of context, the "practice of recording Israeli opinions and government statements as facts, while referring to any information provided by Palestinians as 'allegations' and 'complaints,'" and the impression that actions by Israeli actors that violate Palestinian human rights are "in response to supposed acts of Palestinian terrorism and as such are understandable." The LSM response continues:

> The word terrorism is mentioned seven times in the Report, although a thorough review of the Israeli press during 1982 fails to find these acts of terrorism, unless the definition is to be greatly expanded to include groups of stone-throwing students, commercial strikes, and peaceful demonstrations.[12]

Skipping the State Department's Country Report for 1983, al-Haq published a second response on the report for 1984, a document in a rather different style. This time, the New York–based Lawyers' Committee for Human Rights (LCHR) had asked al-Haq to prepare a response, which LCHR then sent to the State Department endorsing al-Haq's conclusions, and met with the US assistant secretary of state for human rights; al-Haq also sent its response itself to the State Department.[13] In the preface to al-Haq's response, Hiltermann writes:

> In this reply [. . .] al-Haq concluded that, although the State Department had somewhat improved the content of its report compared with previous years by paying more attention to detail and correcting at least some of the errors al-Haq had pointed out in its earlier critique, a number of serious distortions and omissions of vital areas of the human rights situation in the Occupied Territories continued to undermine the Report's value. [. . .] Al-Haq's purpose in making public a written reply to the State Department's human rights report on this occasion was not so much to point out all individual errors committed by the Report's authors, as it had done in the 1983 reply, but to place the errors in their conceptual context: Why were such errors permitted to recur over and again? And why did al-Haq's previous critique, and critiques provided by other parties, have so little impact on the accuracy of subsequent State Department reports, or—in light of Israel's record in the area of human rights, described in these reports—on the continued high level of US economic and military aid to Israel in general?[14]

The context as presented by al-Haq included a proposed dramatic increase in economic and military aid to Israel, the creation of new settlements and "thickening" of existing ones, deterioration in prison conditions, an increase in settler aggression, and the entrenchment of the dual system of law "as exemplified by a military directive issued in 1984 which made it impossible for Palestinians to register complaints against Israeli citizens in the West Bank without a permit from the military authorities."[15] The response refers to "a political climate in Israel that is profoundly unfavourable to discussing Israeli practices in the West Bank and Gaza, let alone the Occupied Territories' final status. As a result the *status quo* is allowed to further evolve, bringing ever closer the day that the annexation of the West Bank and Gaza will be accomplished all but in name." The mode of reporting includes placing "Palestinians and Israelis on an equal level in terms of their conduct and/ or the violence to which they are exposed." The Report persists in referring to "information provided by Palestinians as 'claims,' 'allegations' or 'complaints' while the Israeli authorities 'state'"; there are serious problems with presenting the Israeli authorities' claims that they do not condone political killing, and a downplaying of the economic, social, and cultural situation in the occupied territories—here the response quotes then Israeli minister of defense Yitzhak Rabin as stating that "there will be no development [in the territories] initiated by the Israeli government, and no permits will be given for expanding agriculture or industry [there], which may compete with the State of Israel."[16] Omissions include the introduction of Jewish settlers in the occupied territories, and collective punishment imposed "in retaliation for individual acts of resistance by Palestinians." There is also the major contextual issue of Israel's military occupation which "combines repression with economic exploitation to deprive the Palestinian population of its most fundamental, inalienable rights":

> The report's orientation is in keeping with the traditional western definition of human rights as individual political rights, at the risk of ignoring such collective rights as the right to social and economic development, which the US government is "not prepared to recognize as a basic human right" (p. 7). This makes it possible for the report's authors to gloss over the impact of Israel's growing control of land and water resources, the building of new settlements, the denial of trade permits and licenses to set up industrial enterprises, and collective punishment— which are indeed key features of the violations of human rights suffered by the Palestinian population.[17]

The structural link to context and insistence on collective social and economic rights are key features of al-Haq's analysis, and the development in the nature of its response is evidence of an organization critically examining the impact of its past intervention. Al-Haq informs its readers that having pointed out "empirical and conceptual errors" in its two responses to the US Reports, and "in the absence of a substantive change in the State Department's reporting," the organization "has now decided that it would not be productive to compose a critical reply to the annual human rights report on a yearly basis."[18] This was an organization critically examining the impact of its past interventions and adopting a pragmatic response.

Al-Haq went on to issue three more public responses, against the changed and charged background of the first intifada, for the years 1989, 1990, and 1991. After this, it was to be more than fifteen years before al-Haq would publicly intervene again with the US State Department on the contents of its Country Report for Israel and the Occupied Territories, in the aftermath of the 2008–9 war on Gaza. This intervention was made in the form of a letter sent by al-Haq and sixteen other Palestinian and non-Palestinian organizations on the subject of the preparation of the US report for the year 2009.[19] In particular, this intervention invoked findings of "gross and massive violations of human rights constituting war crimes and possibly crimes against humanity" made public in the reporting period (2009), focusing especially on the Report of the UN Fact-Finding Mission to Gaza, mandated by the Human Rights Council (the "Goldstone report") after Israel's assault on Gaza in December 2008–January 2009.[20] The charge of war crimes and crimes against humanity are significant features of the current Palestinian NGO human rights discourse, and were arguably pioneered in Al-Haq's work on grave breaches of the Fourth Geneva Convention at the end of the 1980s.

There is another point to note about this intervention: the letter is addressed to Michael Posner, who for just over two months had been assistant secretary of state for democracy, human rights and labor in Barack Obama's government, but before that had for some thirty years been the first executive director of LCHR and then of its successor Human Rights First; it was under his leadership that LCHR had requested a critique of the 1984 State Department report from al-Haq, and it was Posner who played the leading role in LCHR's 1988 report on Israel's detention of four al-Haq field-workers along with two Gazan lawyers.[21] "We were gratified to learn," says the 2009 letter, "that someone with your human rights advocacy record has taken the helm of this important section of the State Department."

This kind of intervention was, however, the exception in al-Haq's earlier years. Most were addressed to the relevant military government authority responsible for the violation. The first Newsletter details interventions made to the Israeli minister of defense, with copies to the attorney general and the Knesset State Control Committee, regarding the fact that there was no system of judicial appeal against the decisions of Israeli military courts in the West Bank; and to the Minister of Defense, the attorney general and the coordinator of activities in the occupied territories seeking a full police investigation into the placing of "bombs or other explosive devices" at schools in the Ramallah district, coinciding with slogans and death threats on school walls "accompanied by the name 'Terror against Terror' and a number of Israeli flags."[22] It also reported a response to an intervention it had made in June 1983 and in March 1984 to other human rights organizations locally and internationally, as well as to the military authorities, on the subject of the arrest of secondary school students during the period of their *tawjihi* ("matriculation") exams concluding their high school education. LSM/al-Haq reported receipt of a copy of a letter sent by the office of the coordinator of activities in the occupied territories to the Israeli human rights group ACRI who had addressed him on the basis of the information sent by LSM. The official cited "security reasons" and insisted that it was "pure coincidence that the arrests occurred at the time of the *tawjihi* exams."[23]

Al-Haq was to continue following the issue of *tawjihi* arrests for the next few years, seeking inter alia to establish that they were anything but coincidental. Sami 'Ayad recalls the efforts made by LSM to establish systematic intent on the part of the Israeli authorities to cause these students to miss their final exams: "We collected lots of information, in different years and different places where the students were arrested. Sometimes there was no demonstration [going on at the time]. There were surprise detentions at exam time. It showed that there was a methodological intent in targeting them." The Introduction to a 1986 Newsletter, titled "Al-Haq's Action to Defend the Right to Education," reviewed al-Haq's efforts in regard to this practice from 1983, including communications by ACRI, the ICJ in Geneva, and Amnesty International.[24] Al-Haq had not received responses itself, but considered that it had achieved its objective of making this violation better known. It had been heartened by the decrease in numbers of reports of such arrests: "Despite the fact that it was clear from its enquiries that students are in fact still being arrested without either interrogation or charge, it still had reason to hope that its efforts and those of other human rights organizations locally and abroad had led to the end of this particular type of arrest." It had noted substantial decreases in the reported numbers and had had no reports for late 1985–86. In the meantime, al-Haq reported that in 1984 the organization "had a discussion with the Legal Advisor to the civilian Administration as to how it should deal with urgent matters. An agreement was reached whereby in urgent cases al-Haq could make quick contact by telephone or telegram so as to get immediate response to enable a violation to be halted before any permanent harm was done." When it learned, therefore, of further such arrests in 1986, the organization sent a telegram to the legal adviser in accordance with the agreement that had been reached, "but the response was by a letter received only when it was already too late for the students to sit their exams." It also then began to learn of other, unreported *tawjihi* arrests in previous years.[25] Al-Haq reflected on what might now be called a "small win" as follows:

> It is true that al-Haq was able through its efforts to reduce the number of students arrested from 38 in 1983 to 8 in this year. However, it had hoped that the violation would stop entirely, especially after it became well-known and documented. This hope was not realised. Despite a low number of student arrests this year in comparison with other years, this cannot be considered as a final resolution of the violation.
>
> This sequence of events has caused al-Haq to reflect on its expectations of progress in defending human rights in the Occupied Territories, and on its mode of operation.

Reflections such as the above are always necessary. The organization must continually reassess the manner in which it works, if it is to seek with all means available to find the best way to fulfill the objectives or tasks for which it was established, and refuse to accept the continuation of any violation, whatever its origin.[26]

The issue of the malicious arrest of *tawjihi* students was updated in the following Newsletter, but it was quite shortly to be overtaken by the closure of all educational institutions in the West Bank—and prohibiting of alternative arrangements for education—in response to the first intifada, described by al-Haq in 1988 as Israel's "war on education."[27] The interventions on the *tawjihi* arrests illustrate a number of features of al-Haq's intervention methods, including the difference that a change in personnel at particular Israeli officer posts (such as legal adviser) could bring. They also illustrate what Kuttab describes after the raid on the first LSM office in 1982; LSM wrote a letter of four paragraphs to the military authorities setting out their concerns (as recalled in chapter 3) and copied the letter to Haim Cohn, who wrote a letter of three paragraphs to inquire about the matter. "Some very high-level officers came, and they had very specific instructions to investigate and answer each of the three paragraphs; they didn't care what we wrote, but they cared what Haim Cohn wrote, they didn't even have a copy of our letter, it was his. It was a lesson for us: it matters who you write to."

Both ACRI and the Israeli section of the ICJ—or more specifically Haim Cohn—were early recipients of LSM's interventions, which were copied to these Israeli organizations that were more likely than LSM to get a response if they raised the issues with Israeli authorities. Less formally, Raja Shehadeh recalls regular meetings in the early 1980s with ACRI, the Jerusalem office of Quaker Peace and Service, and the ICRC. According to Shehadeh, it was during these meetings that ACRI became interested in the issue of settler violence and harassment against Palestinian civilians and property in the West Bank, and particularly on the issue of the apparent lack of proper investigation of such incidents by the police or military authorities. ACRI did not at that time work on the occupied territories, and at a retreat for human rights NGO leaders in Crete in 1989, a board member indicated the dilemmas the organization felt it still faced in choosing to get more involved, or on the other hand in choosing not to.[28] Back in 1981, the Israeli attorney general had appointed a commission of inquiry under the leadership of the deputy attorney general Yehudit Karp; her report, submitted in spring 1982 but not published until 1984, showed that of seventy cases of "murder, damage to property and vigilante activities allegedly by settlers," only fifteen had been investigated by police.[29] By 1985, Raja Shehadeh, who had given evidence to the State Control Committee of the Knesset on the West Bank legal system following publication of the Karp report, was recording still no action on its recommendations.[30] LSM/al-Haq continued to make interventions to the military authorities, for example a letter to the military commander of the Central Area in July 1987 following a raid by around two hundred armed Israeli settlers on the Palestinian refugee camp of Dheisha near Bethlehem.[31] The organization did not, however, publish separately on this subject until the annual reports of the first three years of the intifada, each of which contained a chapter on violence by Israeli settlers. Besides documenting the facts of different settler-related incidents, al-Haq's interventions stressed the issues of accountability and the development of two separate legal systems in the West Bank. In its intervention on the 1987 incident in Dheisha camp, for example, the organization asked the following questions:

1. What are the criteria used by the authorities in arming civilians in the West Bank, and what precautions are taken, if any, to ensure that they will not misuse their weapons?
2. Are the authorities investigating the reaction of the armed forces to the raid in order to establish whether or not they performed their duties according to international law?
3. Why was a 24-hour curfew imposed [on the camp], one camp entrance closed, and a high fence erected along one side of the camp following incidents which were provoked by the raid by Kiryat Arba settlers on the camp?
4. Why are the settlers who were arrested being tried in an Israeli court in Jerusalem, and not in the West Bank, despite the fact that the raid took place in the West Bank and the settlers are living in the West Bank?[32]

Other indications of LSM/al-Haq's rule-of-law focus include interventions in relation to the arrest or ill-treatment of lawyers, its monitoring and reporting on changes to the legal system, and its pursuit of the need for a professional body for lawyers in the West Bank. The first part of *The West Bank and the Rule of Law*, it will be recalled, was on "The Judiciary and the Legal Profession," and besides the professional engagement of both Shehadeh and Kuttab with the legal system, the organization had demonstrated a consistent commitment to the protection of an independent judicial profession under occupation. This included interventions on the discriminatory treatment of West Bank lawyers to which LSM objected as arising from Military Order 145, which allowed Israeli lawyers to practice in West Bank courts.[33] It also included a sustained interest in the establishment of an independent bar association for working West Bank lawyers who had been struck off or (if more recently qualified) were unable to join the Jordanian Bar Association. In this matter, there was a small win for the profession in the autumn of 1987. The Israeli High Court of Justice ruled on a 1984 petition from a group of West Bank lawyers asking that the military authorities be ordered to show cause why a bar association should not be permitted to establish itself in the West Bank. Al-Haq's Newsletter led with this judgment, providing a background of the petition, the strike, the provision under Jordanian law for a bar association, and the usurpation of the authorities of a bar association under Military Order 1164 in 1986 while the West Bank lawyers' petition was still pending at the High Court.

The order purported to establish a "Lawyers Council Bar Association under the direction of the Civilian Administration"; the latter would assume all powers of appointment and regulation of all financial matters internal to such an association.[34] Al-Haq had intervened with the minister of defense, while the West Bank petitioners maintained their petition to the High Court, arguing, among other things, that establishment of an independent bar association "did not harm any military interest" and was consistent with international legal obligations regulating an occupying power. According to al-Haq's presentation, the military commander responded:

> that elections to a professional association did pose a danger to security since in his view all elections in the West Bank are based on the political orientation of the candidates and as such expedite the attempt of "hostile" organisations to enhance their influence over the population.

Possibly because the issue involved a professional legal body, the Israeli High Court did not accept the security argument at face value. Referring to both the "right to organize," even under military occupation, and the need for "due regard to the social order and the security of the state," the ruling concluded:

> The Military Commander had not demonstrated that the independence of a bar association, with respect to the issue of the election of council members and control over the council's budget, would threaten security. Moreover, assuming that a "reasonable likelihood" of danger existed, the commander, on the evidence, had not properly weighed the factors involved. Neither had he considered alternative ways of dealing with the anticipated danger while at the same time maintaining, as far as possible, the independence of the new organisation.

Al-Haq gave a partial welcome: "in accordance with our belief in international human rights principles and norms and the rule of law, we see the independence and the proper functioning of the legal profession as an essential cornerstone of these standards" which would not be realized through an association set up under the terms of the military order. In particular, it welcomed the statement regarding the right of association, and the fact that the court had "looked into the issue of whether in exercising his authority and his discretion the Military Commander had weighed the relevant consideration" as a "fundamental principle of administrative justice." Al-Haq warned, however, that this decision was "by no means a victory" since it did not order the military commander to permit the West Bank lawyers to establish a bar association as provided for in Jordanian law. "The matter rests in the Military Commander's hands," concluded al-Haq, "and to date no action has been taken." The Newsletter carrying this article was published at the beginning of January 1988 and promised its readers that the next Newsletter would cover the events of the intifada, which had started on December 9, 1987. Events overtook the ruling on the bar association, and in 1997 the Palestine Bar Association was established under the Palestinian Authority.

LSM/al-Haq's focus on the legal profession was a key feature of its relationship with the ICJ. Of the international organizations upon whose solidarity al-Haq called in specific interventions, the ICJ was perhaps its most steadfast ally, given the institutional relationship with LSM/al-Haq and the robust attitude of the ICJ's Niall MacDermot. In 1985, an important principle of al-Haq's methodology of intervention—this time, intervention by publication—was to be clarified in acrimonious exchanges at the UN Commission on Human Rights around the report on torture in al-Fara'a prison, copublished by LSM and the ICJ.[35] One of the complaints made by the Israeli ambassador to the commission was that "prior notice of the report had not been given to the Israeli authorities, and that the ICJ Secretary-General had not disclosed its forthcoming publication to the Israeli Ambassador" when MacDermot had paid the ambassador a courtesy call some days before publication of the report.[36] Responding in an editorial in the ICJ's *Review*, MacDermot gave first reply to LSM:

> LSM comments "It is not LSM's practice to present its reports to the Israeli government for comment before making them public. We do however make interventions and request specific replies on human rights violations that come to our attention. We address such letters to the Minister of Defence in his capacity as minister with ultimate responsibility for the Military Government of the occupied territories. When a reply is received, which is not always the case, it is only after a long period of time and comes generally from the Legal Advisor to the Civilian Administration of the West Bank. . . . It is precisely because of the gravity of the circumstances related in the report that we are not willing to delay issuing the report while we wait for a response which experience has shown we are unlikely to receive."[37]

For his part, MacDermot explained that he had not felt "at liberty to disclose the forthcoming publication to the Ambassador without prior consultation with LSM" but that he had since told the ambassador that "he considers it would have been preferable to have advised LSM to give a summary of the report to the Israeli authorities before publication and invite their comments." Al-Haq did not alter its practice. Having taken the decision on the (limited) utility and the principle of corresponding with the military authorities to seek clarification of orders, directives, and practice, as well as in regard to the treatment of specific individuals or groups of individuals and events, and to set out its law-based concerns on such matters, al-Haq did not consider that it was in any way bound to follow the practice of other organizations, local or international, in submitting their publications for comment, in this case to the authorities of the occupying power. With the arrival of the Palestinian Authority in the summer of 1994, following the signing of the Israel-PLO Gaza-Jericho agreement, al-Haq was to revisit this practice in relation to the PA, though not in relation to the Israeli authorities. Its first report on PA directives and practice, *The Right to Freedom of Assembly*, appends the correspondence between al-Haq's coordinator Fateh Azzam and the director-general of the Palestinian Police, Brigadier-General Ghazi al-Jabali, to whom al-Haq had presented the draft report "in order to provide him with a further opportunity to express his opinion and address the issues discussed herein." No response was received to this particular request for comment.[38] The decision to submit the draft to the PA official had been taken after considerable discussion at al-Haq in the tense days of Oslo.

The 1985 report on al-Fara'a prison comprised a set of affidavits from former detainees. One section included three affidavits complaining of seriously inadequate medical care. LSM had in fact raised this before, as reported in its first Newsletter:

> LSM has also recently received reports of the involvement of Israeli medical personnel in the ill-treatment of detainees undergoing interrogation at West Bank detention centres. LSM has written to the Israeli Medical Association informing them of the allegations, pointing out the complete incompatibility of such involvement, if true, with all principles of medical ethics, and asking the Association to investigate the matter further.[39]

This straightforward paragraph had behind it a critical organizational challenge. The allegations against members of the professional Israeli medical authority (the IMA) were extremely serious; it was a huge professional issue, and the field-workers worked hard to collect and verify the information. Sami 'Ayad recalls the complexities, for example, of trying to identify as a doctor or nurse a person not known to the prisoner but who warned of the risks of their medical condition. The second Newsletter reported serious developments in the intervening two months. This time al-Haq was more open about specific allegations regarding the involvement of Israeli medical personnel in interrogating prisoners:

> The alleged involvement appears to take three forms: 1) Advising the interrogators on particular points of weakness in the detainee's body or health, following an initial medical examination; such points of weakness are then made use of in the interrogation. 2) Advising the interrogators as to the detainee's ability to sustain further interrogation. 3) Advising the detainee that unless he confesses and receives immediate medical attention his health could be permanently impaired. The methods of interrogation reported include beatings and other cruel and degrading treatment.[40]

Having sent its original letter to the IMA at the beginning of May, LSM was awaiting a reply when a press release was issued by the IMA on June 7 and reported in the Hebrew press, "accusing LSM of making malicious, unsubstantiated and libellous accusations against members of the Israeli medical profession" and naming Raja Shehadeh. The president of the IMA wrote back to LSM, in a letter mailed after the press release, and "repeated the allegation of 'slander.' But after stating that it was impossible to imagine an Israeli physician behaving in the way described he expressed readiness on the part of the IMA to investigate the reports if further details were given." By the time the IMA's letter arrived at LSM, the organization had already felt obliged to "respond publicly in order to defend the organisation's integrity and that of its co-director" in light of the IMA's press release. LSM issued its own press release attaching the original letter to the IMA and confirming that "LSM does hold prima facie evidence of the practices alleged which will be released if, on completion of its investigations LSM is satisfied that the allegations are well-founded." LSM also sought a public apology from the IMA, and noted in the Newsletter that "both the organisation and Mr Shehadeh are contemplating legal proceedings against the IMA if a full apology is not received." Neither the accusations to the IMA nor the grievance of LSM and Shehadeh resulted in legal proceedings, but it had been a tense time for LSM/al-Haq, which returned to its findings in regard to Israeli medical professionals in the 1985 al-Fara'a report.

In the early summer of 1985, LSM reported receipt of a letter from the IMA president (dated January 28, 1985) informing the organization that the general officer of the IDF Medical Corps had investigated and had found LSM's allegations to be groundless; but that "in future medical staff would be identifiable by their white coats."[41] While welcoming this undertaking, LSM's response focused on the reliance placed by the IMA president on the fact that to the best of his knowledge no prisoners' complaints on this subject had been raised by the ICRC. His conclusion was that "either the prisoners did not consider the complaints made to be very serious, or that the complaints had no serious basis." Al-Haq's concerns about how the ICRC's role was used by the Israeli authorities in such situations were to grow over the following years and are discussed further below. Its concerns about the role of Israeli medical personnel were taken up by others, including at the UN Committee against Torture during Israel's first appearance there in 1994, and in a dedicated Amnesty International report in 1996.[42]

Al-Haq continued to monitor the conduct of Israeli medical personnel, particularly in prisons and detention facilities. Early in the intifada, their role was raised in relation to access for the families to official Israeli investigations, including autopsy reports in cases where a family member had died in circumstances arousing suspicion that law enforcement personnel had been involved—notably, deaths in detention.[43] An overview of how al-Haq worked on what it described as "the main, precedent-setting case" illustrates the significance of its allies in different parts of the human rights movement.

ALLIES

The treatment of the case of Ibrahim al-Mtour illustrates the significance of the relations al-Haq was building. In this case, a Scottish forensic pathologist had been asked by the detainee's family (via al-Haq, after appeal to the Israeli High Court by the family's Israeli lawyer) to conduct a second autopsy some months after their son had been buried.[44] He held that a named prison doctor had committed "*prima facie*, a serious breach of medical ethics" by following an order from the commander of Dhahiriyya Military Detention Center to administer an injection of tranquilizers to the detainee who was at the time bound hand and foot "in an otherwise empty cell" where the commander had used tear gas on him.[45] Invoking the UN Principles of Medical Ethics (1982) and the Declaration of Tokyo of the World Medical Association (1975), Derrick Pounder recommended that "all the case information should be forwarded to the appropriate Israeli Medical Authorities with a view to initiating disciplinary proceedings" against the doctor and noting a suspicion that unethical practice by prison doctors was "a widespread problem."[46]

Pounder directed this and his other recommendations to four organizations: Amnesty International, Boston-based Physicians for Human Rights (PHR), the American Academy for the Advancement of Science (AAAS), and the Copenhagen-based Committee of Concerned Forensic Scientists (CCFS). PHR and AAAS had sponsored Pounder's visit, and CCFS was involved in sponsoring later interventions. Israeli lawyers (notably Leah Tsemel and Felicia Langer) acted for the family of the deceased in addressing the Israeli authorities and the High Court. Pounder's report was significant not only in itself but for the combined efforts of the Palestinian and Israeli human rights actors and international allies in the professional medical communities, and the courage and determination of the family of the deceased, Ibrahim al-Mtour. Deaths in Israeli detention centers had increased during the first year of the intifada; Joost Hiltermann, who worked on a number of these cases for al-Haq, wrote that it was the occurrence of five such deaths in one week in the summer of 1988 that prompted the development of an approach of seeking "small, step-by-step precedents" in response.[47] At the end of that year, in its first annual report, al-Haq reported:

> Independent investigation into the cause of these deaths has been made impossible by the authorities' refusal in many cases to make public the results of the official investigations (including autopsy reports), and by their refusal to allow independent forensic experts either to be present at the official autopsies or to conduct second autopsies on behalf of the families of the deceased.[48]

By the end of the second year of the intifada, al-Haq was able to report some—albeit mixed—results of the efforts to challenge the official Israeli narrative on these deaths and gain answers around deaths in detention, explaining these efforts as follows:[49]

> Al-Haq's aim has been, in the first instance, to gain the right for relatives of the deceased to send a representative of their choice to attend the autopsy and to obtain, within a reasonable amount of time, the results of both the autopsy and the investigation into the circumstances of death; and, in the second instance, to discourage excessive use of force by the army and GSS through threat of legal prosecution. Al-Haq's method in accomplishing these aims was to challenge the authorities' findings with expert opinions.[50]

Al-Haq had concluded in the second year of the uprising that there was a "state of lawlessness" in the occupied territories. The organization proceeded to methodically review Israeli law and practice and to seek to hold the occupation authorities to the terms they had set themselves. It also reviewed these terms under the standards of IHL, and drew on reports of the UN Special Rapporteur on extrajudicial summary or arbitrary executions. This examination (critical to Israel's claims to be following the rule of law) can in itself be described as "forensic."[51] Its review of events in 1989 included a detailed presentation of developments in the investigation into the death of al-Mtour and certain other deaths in detention, and with some reservations it is clear that al-Haq felt that "the consistent pressures of the past year have begun to pay off."[52] Nevertheless, its conclusions were somber. Felicia Langer's petition for a new investigation into the death of al-Mtour had been rejected by the High Court "despite overwhelming evidence, disclosed by Military Police investigators," that he had been severely abused in detention. Langer concluded that "not only was justice not seen to have been done, justice was not done at all."[53] Derrick Pounder had concluded that "the cause of death was asphyxiation due to ligature pressure on the neck" and continued:

> It is my opinion that more likely than not the mechanism of death was hanging. I consider that, for the three days prior to his death, the decedent was subjected to treatment which was prima facie, cruel, inhuman and degrading. I consider it possible that the decedent took his own life to escape this abuse. If such was the case, I would regard the death as an "aggravated suicide." On the information available, the possibility of homicide cannot be excluded. I consider the initial investigation of the death to have been inadequate and the information presently available to me to be incomplete.[54]

The increasing phenomenon of deaths in Israeli detention and al-Haq's efforts to determine cause and establish accountability had significant impact in the organization. Whether a detainee had died as result of torture or other illegal conduct or was thought to have taken his own life as a result of such treatment, the loneliness of such an end lingered in the mind, among the most compelling evidence of the lawlessness of the Israeli occupation, which was a central finding in the second year of the intifada. Al-Haq opened its report *A Nation under Siege* with an account of the death of Khaled al-Sheikh 'Ali, and closed it with that of Ibrahim al-Mtour, reproducing the organization's speech on accepting the 1989 Carter-Menil Human Rights Award:

> On 18 October 1988 Ibrahim al-Mtour was seen by other detainees at the Dhahiriyya military detention centre in the West Bank. Blood was flowing from his head and he was heard screaming: "I am Ibrahim al-Mtour. They are beating me to death. Detainees, witness!"
>
> Three days later, Ibrahim was dead. "Suicide," the prison authorities declared. It is our collective duty to answer Ibrahim's call, to witness, to act, so that in the future

> not only will the Ibrahims of this world be heard and not have to die but so that they
> will not have to scream at all.[55]

Al-Haq workers involved in following these investigations were deeply affected by the processes. Khaled Batrawi, then head of the fieldwork unit, commences a moving piece about al-Haq's work on autopsies and deaths in detention, written some two decades after Batrawi left al-Haq, with a tribute to all the martyrs of the uprising, "especially those whose skin was split by the autopsy razor. [. . .] At the time of the autopsy, they felt no pain, but I felt pain [then] and I still feel it."[56] Palestinians had, as already recognized in the Karp report, no faith in Israeli investigations (process or outcome), and had reason to fear repercussions should they seek to challenge them.[57] In addition, as Batrawi notes, it was not necessarily an avenue that Palestinian families would wish to pursue: "Palestinian society, like other Arab societies, did not accept autopsy for religious and social reasons, and the overriding concern for the family of martyrs was to bury them, given [the saying that] 'to honour the dead is to bury them [swiftly].'" And suicide was difficult to accept even where the efforts of human rights actors established "aggravated suicide" at the hands of their captors. The families of the detainees traveled a very difficult road, and their human rights contacts were bound to accompany them.

By the mid-1980s, al-Haq was also cooperating with other Palestinian human rights organizations in the occupied territories. LSM/al-Haq had actively assisted in the establishment (as an ICJ affiliate) of the Gaza Centre for Rights and Law in 1985, including copublishing a study of the military court system written by a shared researcher.[58] When the GCRL became mired in internal difficulties, the Gaza affiliate of the ICJ became and remains the Palestinian Centre for Human Rights (PCHR), established in 1995 under the directorship of lawyer Raji Sourani. Al-Haq also cooperated with the second human rights organization to be set up in the West Bank, the Palestine Human Rights Information Center (PHRIC), which operated out of Jerusalem. PHRIC was established in 1986 by the Arab Studies Society and published large amounts of data on human rights violations, particularly after the start of the intifada. In a 1988 comparison, Penny Johnson attributed "a more activist agenda" to PHRIC and less of a focus on legal research than al-Haq: "Director Jan Abu Shakra emphasizes that the Center sees its primary constituency as local, because 'rights must be claimed.'"[59]

Despite their cooperation, Rabbani has pointed to certain tensions between PHRIC and al-Haq because of the latter's sometimes perhaps overly painstaking approach and its "predictable refusal to comment on events in the Gaza Strip during 1987–1988 because it did not have its own sources of information."[60] Tensions also arose with the first Israeli group to initiate systematic human rights work in the occupied territories. A new type of relationship was required when in 1989 B'Tselem was established. Rabbani's comment here is telling:

> It was not unexpected that, as an Israeli organisation [. . .] it would immediately
> acquire the exposure, credibility, and funding which had eluded al-Haq for 10 years.

But when several B'Tselem staff began to conduct themselves as if it was they who had been in the field for a decade, relations began to deteriorate, reaching their low point in November 1989 when B'Tselem [. . .] was named as al-Haq's co-recipient of the 1989 Carter-Menil Human Rights Award for transparently political motives.[61]

It is surely clear that political reasons did indeed underlie the prize givers' decision to divide the honors due the ten-year-old al-Haq with an Israeli organization of one year's standing. Rabbani's piece conveys something of the rancor of that time and points to difficulties in working out peer relationships (rather than "relations of paternalism") between citizens of an occupying power and members of the occupied population. An explicit recognition of the power relationships involved, and a determination to address them, are among the requisites of such relationships as outlined in postcolonial literature. At the retreat organized in Crete in 1989 for "active and creative leaders in non-governmental human rights organisations," a question was raised as to "the degree to which NGOs within the state of an occupying power and within the occupied territory" were able to cooperate. Among the participants were Raja Shehadeh and an ACRI board member. No discussion is recorded, only the summary that "there were clear risks for both parties in such cooperation, but also strong potential benefits."[62] Rabbani for his part noted a marked subsequent improvement in relations between al-Haq, B'Tselem, and PHRIC, "in an admirable show of common purpose"—given the real exigencies of the situation—and by dint of a "functional division of labour" which he described as follows:

> Al-Haq's comparative advantage is in its legal knowledge, fieldwork, and its excellent contacts with the diplomatic corps and foreign elites; the PHRIC's in comprehensive documentation and reporting, rapid intervention, and an extremely professional international distribution network; and B'Tselem's—in addition to the quality of its own research—in its access to the media and official sources, and the crucial contribution of an Israeli Jewish certificate of authenticity to reports of Israeli human rights abuses.[63]

Until the intifada, al-Haq's international interventions were directed at peers in the "community of human rights organizations"; the Draft Program Objectives for 1987 observed that al-Haq had "come some way towards having them mobilise their resources in exposing and challenging human rights violations in the Occupied Territories." According to the report of the Crete retreat, "Al-Haq's primary strategy is to publicize violations through international channels, and to work with International NGOs investigating violations in the occupied territories."[64] Johnson quotes Mona Rishmawi on al-Haq's concentration on information work in the international NGO community at that time and continues: "Al-Haq has pursued this route perhaps more systematically than any other organisation in the occupied territories to date. Its publications are geared to this audience."[65] While both the Steiner report and Johnson's piece note al-Haq's outreach work in the local Palestinian community (especially its human rights education program), the focus on international allies is striking. It was, as someone from the time put it, "the first experiment where a local Palestinian organisation has a completely international law reference point and there are organisations outside backing it up; as soon as something happens you resort to your network—that's very common now but it wasn't then." It was physically also very labor-intensive work in the era before electronic communications ("countless hours sending faxes").

LSM/al-Haq's first institutional relationship was with the ICJ under the leadership of Niall MacDermot, and it benefited enormously from this relationship and different activities that developed. As did the ICJ; al-Haq was one of the most—if not *the* most—active of the ICJ affiliates with an international reputation of its own and eventually a size that exceeded that of its parent organization. LSM's affiliation with the ICJ was sought for a combination of motives but primarily for the possibility of protection that the founders felt might come if they established under the ICJ umbrella. Solidarity—in the form of interventions on issues within their mandates, including the harassment of LSM/al-Haq workers—was also sought from other international human rights organizations. Amnesty International was among LSM's early visitors. Al-Haq/LSM—and staffers whose cases were addressed—benefited from Amnesty's existing position in regard to membership of the PLO and the status of "prisoner of conscience." In a 1991 response to the Israeli Ministry of Justice, the organization acknowledged:

> Amnesty International has a long-standing disagreement with the Israeli government over the relevance of issues such as the membership of the Palestine Liberation Organisation (PLO) in determining whether someone is a prisoner of conscience. The Israeli Government maintains that such membership of itself automatically amounts at least to advocacy of violence against Israel. Amnesty International disagrees.[66]

This was not a new position, nor one that Amnesty had newly adopted in response to the situation in the occupied territories. The status of prisoner of conscience, a cornerstone of Amnesty's mandate and advocacy, was reserved for those imprisoned solely on the grounds of their nonviolent expression of their political or religious beliefs. Adoption by Amnesty as a prisoner of conscience meant personal advocacy by individual Amnesty members as well as significant moral recognition.[67] Amnesty's explanation to the Israeli Ministry of Justice stated that it

> recognizes that the PLO remains committed to the legitimacy of the use of violent means in its opposition to Israel, that factions of the PLO have carried out acts of violence against Israelis, and that obviously a large number of PLO members approve of or sympathize with that. However, it also understands that the PLO is an organization composed of several factions and bodies involved in political, social and cultural activities as well as military or violent activities. The vast majority of Palestinians view the PLO as their sole representative and the only vehicle for organized expression of their national aspirations. Palestinians may join or be otherwise associated with the PLO because they share its overall political objectives without necessarily agreeing with all its policies, including those relating to the use of violence.

> Amnesty International does not consider that membership of or association with the PLO or one of its factions is in itself conclusive evidence that a certain individual has used or advocated violence. In determining whether an individual is a prisoner of conscience, Amnesty International looks into whether the individual personally used or advocated violence in the circumstances relating to his or her arrest.[68]

Amnesty applied these criteria inter alia to the status of a number of al-Haq field-workers arrested in the early years of the intifada. Amnesty's first substantial report on administrative detention (1989) examined their cases in some detail, as indeed did a report by the LCHR.[69] A detailed exposition was made in a letter from Amnesty's secretary-general to the Israeli minister of defense in 1990 in relation to the administrative detention of Shawan Jabarin.[70] Amnesty's seven-page intervention went methodically through Jabarin's arrest and detention record, including a relatively reduced prison sentence in December 1985 because the Israeli military judge acknowledged that "relations between Shawan Jabarin and the PFLP had undoubtedly been broken at a certain stage." It raised one of the most notorious parts of Jabarin's detention history, when his lawyer won disclosure of part of the secret material on the basis of which he had been administratively detained, only for it to be revealed that the alleged incident had taken place while Jabarin was already in custody.[71] The Amnesty letter also included a report of a conversation between an Amnesty researcher who visited Ketziot (Ansar 3 prison camp) with Jabarin's lawyer and very unusually managed a conversation "in private and without time limits." The letter sets out a summary of Jabarin's answers to the researcher's requests for clarification of various aspects of the Israeli allegations relating to his current administrative detention order, including stone-throwing and inciting disturbances (including during his detention). A letter from the Ministry of Justice had described Jabarin as a "hardened terrorist"; it is possibly this, as well as Jabarin's standing as a field-worker with al-Haq (and confiscation of human rights–related materials during a search of his house) that prompted the in-depth response from Amnesty to the Israeli authorities. After spending a further page-and-a-half analyzing the available evidence in regard to Israel's allegations, including the use of secret evidence, Amnesty's letter concluded that

> bearing in mind the pattern of use of administrative detention by the Israeli authorities and the circumstances of this case so far as information is available to us, Amnesty International believes that it is reasonable to conclude that Sha'wan Jabarin is a prisoner of conscience, held on account of his non-violent political beliefs and/or his human rights activities, and that he was unable to exercise effectively his right to challenge his detention order.

As it happened, Amnesty's intervention was sent just three days before Jabarin was scheduled for release, but its significance is in illustrating Amnesty's application of its policy on prisoners of conscience to Palestinian detainees and the organization's questioning of the assertions by Israel's military judicial system and government of Israel's security exigencies.

The letter also reiterated Amnesty's then position on administrative detention, outlined in the organization's 1989 report, recommending that all those held in administrative detention "on account of their non-violent political opinions or activities be immediately and unconditionally released and all others to be provided the opportunity to exercise effectively their right to challenge their detention"; and since administrative detention should not be used to avoid the safeguards of the criminal justice system, the Israeli authorities should "review the appropriateness and necessity" of maintaining the practice. Although Amnesty did not at this point work under the framework of IHL, the fact that "internment" was contemplated (albeit in extreme circumstances) by the Fourth Geneva Convention meant that the organization did not take a position on human rights grounds calling unequivocally for the end of Israel's use of administrative detention.[72] The change in this position came at Amnesty's Yokohama meeting in 1991; Amnesty's International Council "decided to oppose as a matter of principle the detention of administrative detainees unless they are to be given a fair trial within a reasonable time."[73] Other changes directly relating to Amnesty's work on Israel and the occupied territories were also made at the 1991 meeting, which decided that Amnesty "will oppose the forcible exile of people on account of their non-violent beliefs" and "in principle to oppose the demolition or sealing of houses as a punishment imposed for political reasons."[74] Part of the background to the changes in Amnesty's mandate was pressure from certain southern sections of Amnesty for a position shift in favor of substantive opposition to these administrative penalties. Another part of the context, however, was Amnesty staffers' discussions with al-Haq and other Palestinian human rights organizations. Claudio Cordone, then Israel / occupied territories researcher at Amnesty, recalls intensive discussion with al-Haq staffers on IHL (given Amnesty's then reliance on IHRL) and notes that "certainly work on the Occupied Territories and with al-Haq contributed to our thinking." Cordone himself began to argue whether "IHL is more or less protective of human rights" and to consider IHL more systematically over the next few years.

An issue that took longer for Amnesty to address, that was fundamental to al-Haq and other Palestinian human rights groups, and that to their minds lay at the root of Israel's other security justifications and resulting violations of civil and political rights was settlement policy and practice. Human Rights Watch took even longer. In this one can see a reflection of the disagreement reported by Steiner from the 1989 retreat, with the southern groups criticizing Westerns INGOs for too narrow a focus on individual civil and political rights and a failure to address in any depth the causes of human rights violations.[75] Peter Rosenblum recalls "great internal struggles" in the late eighties at HRW and LCHR, in particular "over the extent of their advocacy on Israel and the Occupied Territories."[76] Rabbani offers several illustrations in support of his statement that "the activities of LCHR in particular have been hostage to a political agenda."[77] Neier describes HRW's work on Israel/Palestine as "the work that attracted by far the greatest controversy" for the organization's Middle East division, referring to "widespread denunciations" of "findings critical of Israeli government practices." In 2009 he found himself obliged to respond to a *New York Times* op-ed by HRW's founding chair, Robert Bernstein, criticizing HRW's coverage of Israeli violations during Israel's assault on Gaza in 2008–2009.[78]

Al-Haq was engaged in collaborative work with its INGO colleagues on facts and fact-finding. As Steiner's report of the discussions at the Crete retreat continued:

> Gathering information is the principal occasion for cooperation between NGOs and INGOs. Local groups have greater access to the facts and can provide better documentation. But no simple division of functions exists. National NGOs do not "find the facts" which INGOs then incorporate into their reports.[79]

In the late 1980s it is clear that a certain amount of tension existed around the issue. For al-Haq, it was crucial to get the information on what was going on out to international allies with wider reach in terms of public and advocacy; but there was a considerable time and effort cost, especially for field-workers, who would often accompany researchers from INGOs in their field investigations, introducing them to a range of contacts.[80] The relationship differed between different organizations and indeed their different representatives; Claudio Cordone of Amnesty recalls of al-Haq in the late 1980s:

> I was very impressed by the number of people involved, the quality of their thinking. It wasn't just "give me information," that was even too much, it was the discussions [. . .] I mean al-Haq was doing affidavits and getting the information, but it was the discussions of strategy, what do we do with them that were even more valuable.

From al-Haq's perspective, assisting research visits by international actors was a matter of methodology and principle, and of hard work. In the case of special international delegations not familiar with the context, it also represented a considerable degree of risk, beyond risks taken by the field-workers, which was sometimes not appreciated by delegation members. Foreign delegates variously fell asleep in meetings with Palestinian interlocutors, failed to pay attention, canceled meetings at short notice and for no apparent or acceptable reason, and on at least one occasion saw no problem in accepting lifts with an Israeli army jeep on a strike day when their transport could not be organized on time.[81] Al-Haq's international allies, it turned out, brought potential liabilities not foreseen by the organization.

Al-Haq files contain a confidential letter from Raja Shehadeh written in the late 1980s to an international organization that had dispatched a delegation to the territories. Al-Haq was hosting the delegation and as the visit unfolded became more and more concerned at its direction and the conduct of individual members. Shehadeh's letter referred to al-Haq's "dashed hopes" and attached a detailed confidential report as a record, in the hope that this might "facilitate planning for future missions." The details in the report are embarrassing. For its part, the letter talks of a unilateral narrowing of the scope of the mandate—on the basis of which al-Haq had agreed to host it—by members of the mission, with the result, in al-Haq's view, that the problems encountered were not necessarily understood in their proper context; of a doubt on al-Haq's part about the desire of the mission to fulfill an investigative function, of a lack of preparedness and a lack of probing. Shehadeh concluded with an explanation of how such matters affected not only al-Haq's own credibility and reputation, but potentially the effectiveness of the delegation:

> Al-Haq's position as a Palestinian human rights organisation, arranging a programme which involved meetings with Palestinians, Israelis and the Israeli authorities was a sensitive one. The mission failed to appreciate the difficulties and jeopardised the effectiveness of their mission by inappropriate and insensitive behaviour which caused disquiet among the Palestinian community. This could have led to a refusal to cooperate with the mission on the part of Palestinians in the Territories.

Field-workers interviewed for this study stressed the effort that went into assisting and accompanying international delegations. Candy Whittome, a UK lawyer who acted as coordinator in the office for many of the international delegations or partners, remembers that "normally I was pretty annoyed with them."[82] She spent considerable time reminding these visitors that it was a two-way relationship; there was "such a journey" to be traveled in the relationship between international human rights groups and their local counterparts; there was no joint planning, the field-workers were "running around and barely getting any thanks, grace was lacking." Pondering on this later, she reflects:

> I'm not sure I was brave enough to use the word at the time but exploitation is the word that springs to mind. I felt very strongly that people came with models of how things should be and they were simply thinking about it in their terms, we need this information you've got, then we—the great, the good, the powerful—we can publish it and then we'll make everything all right for you [. . .] Obviously I'm exaggerating the point, but there was a strong feeling that this was not a partnership or a collaboration, it was "we need this from you, we need the information, where is it?" Obviously some were better than others and you saw that quite clearly.[83]

Whittome stresses the importance of these episodes in building the relationship and getting out al-Haq's information, and reports productive discussions when the human costs and complexities of al-Haq's contribution to their visit were explained to members of different delegations. Increasing confidence and improvements in communications technology have changed much. For one thing, as Donatella Rovera of Amnesty International says, the local-international NGO dynamic has changed: "The days are gone when international NGOs would squeeze local ones for their data—now the local NGOs can publish it themselves, why should they give it to internationals?" In some cases, international organizations now publish joint reports with local ones. Palestinian (and indeed other

Arab) human rights groups expect peer relationships with their international counterparts, particularly given increasing recognition of the formers' foundational role in the global movement.

THE ICRC

One of the most significant disagreements that al-Haq had with an international partner was with the ICRC. ICRC delegates arrived in Israel a few days before the 1967 war, alerted by growing tensions in the region to the likelihood of a need for its presence.[84] The 1967 war was a turning point for the working methods of the ICRC, with a "fundamental shift in the behaviour of the institution as it now *anticipated* its possible interventions."[85] Another distinguishing feature is pointed out by Moorehead, writing in 1998 that, despite fluctuations in the number of delegates and offices over the years, "it [Israel] is the only country which the Committee has never judged sufficiently peaceable to enable it to withdraw all its delegates."[86] A posting in Tel Aviv or Jerusalem was a formative experience for ICRC personnel.[87] The many complex contextual issues include the ICRC's notoriously dismal record in regard to Jewish and other victims of Nazi Germany in the Second World War, when the ICRC by all accounts (including subsequently its own) "lost its normative compass."[88] Moorehead's history of the ICRC invokes a "famous meeting" when it was agreed that "it was not in the best interests of the International Committee or of the victims of war they had been set up to protect to speak out about the concentration camps."[89] This goes most immediately to the ICRC's deployment of its confidentiality policy and the decisions it takes on when to speak out. In regard to ICRC delegates in Israel, Moorehead says, "in no other country does the Committee's war time past surface so relentlessly."[90]

The Swiss organization's status and mandate is distinct from human rights NGOs, lawyers' groups, and other international allies. It is a humanitarian agency specifically focused on IHL, the "guardian" of the Geneva Conventions. ICRC delegates—in LSM's early days a role restricted to Swiss nationals—were in regular contact and dialogue with LSM from the start. Under the Fourth Geneva Convention, the occupying power is obliged to request or accept "the offer of the services of a humanitarian organisation, such as the International Committee of the Red Cross, to assume the humanitarian functions performed by Protecting Powers"[91] should the system of protecting powers fail and the protected population of the occupied territories be left without a neutral state to act as representative of all the state parties to the convention in safeguarding their rights and interests as protected under the convention. Early in the occupation, and "in spite of the ICRC's persistent representations," the Israeli government "declared that it wished 'to leave in abeyance for the time being' the question of the applicability of the Fourth Convention in the occupied territories, preferring to act on a pragmatic basis by granting delegates practical facilities."[92] Holding that the convention applied de jure, in

1972 ICRC made a formal offer to act as an official substitute for the protecting power, which Israel declined; by now unequivocally holding that the convention did not apply as a matter of law, the Israeli authorities claimed that they would abide by its "humanitarian provisions" but not its "political provisions"—a distinction not recognized in the convention itself, nor by the ICRC and state parties.[93]

This was the position advanced by Haim Cohn in his introduction to the Israeli ICJ's response to LSM's *The West Bank and the Rule of Law*. In 1977, the ICRC had made a public statement to the effect that a number of problems it had been raising regularly with the Israeli authorities remained unresolved, and they were still not allowed to see detainees under interrogation.[94] Negotiations continued, and in 1978 the ICRC and the Israeli Government concluded a formal agreement to govern the ICRC's action in the occupied territories.[95] The Israeli government undertook to inform the ICRC twelve days after any arrest of Palestinians from the occupied territories and to grant delegates access to the detainee within fourteen days of the arrest; during a visit, the ICRC delegate could speak to the detainee "only about his personal situation and the state of his health" and was "prohibited from transmitting any information whatsoever to an outside body or to the family of the detainee other than the date of arrest, the place and date of visit and the detainee's state of health."[96]

As Shehadeh acknowledged, the argument in support of this arrangement was that such visits were better than no visits at all.[97] When mass arrests began in the first intifada, al-Haq itself was only able to find out the whereabouts of some of its detained field-workers through the ICRC. However, frustration was growing with the limits—both contractual and self-imposed—of the ICRC's activities in the occupied territories. Shehadeh noted that the fourteen days before ICRC visits provided the military authorities with ample time to isolate and interrogate and mistreat detainees, and that "in the opinion of many ex-prisoners, the visits of the ICRC were of little, if any, significance or practical help."[98] With its work on al-Fara'a prison in the forefront, al-Haq was beginning to feel like a voice in the wilderness, as one interviewee recalled, and clearly they felt that the ICRC should be speaking out. A 1985 Newsletter set out concerns about the use made by the Israeli authorities of the fact that the ICRC did not (could not) share its information or its reports with "anyone other than the Israeli authorities"; this was in relation to LSM/al-Haq's investigation of complaints against Israeli medical personnel, described above. Al-Haq noted, "It is the Israeli authorities' practice to refer to the Red Cross visits whenever allegations are made about prison conditions, as though the silence of the Red Cross disproves the allegations."[99]

Al-Haq was becoming frustrated with the confidentiality policy of the ICRC—not a policy specific to the occupied territories—and its reluctance to go public even with broader concerns that would not violate its agreement with the Israeli authorities. In its second report in the uprising, al-Haq noted the ICRC's public statements on the Iran-Iraq war in 1983–84 in regard to the duty of all state parties to ensure respect for the Geneva Conventions:

> It is therefore surprising, although irrelevant from a legal point of view, that the ICRC has made no such public appeal to state signatories in response to Israel's 22-year-old occupation of the West Bank and Gaza Strip. The danger clearly inherent in such a policy is that the ICRC's silence may be interpreted as tacit approval of Israel's policy. In such an event the continued presence of the ICRC might become counterproductive.[100]

Al-Haq's relations with the ICRC were becoming fraught. As the first intifada wore on, the ICRC did make a number of public statements about Israel's treatment of Palestinian detainees, stating in 1992, for example, that through private interviews with those under interrogation "it has reached the conclusion that to obtain information and confessions from detainees, means of physical and psychological pressure are being used" in violation of the Fourth Geneva Convention and that ICRC representations to the Israeli authorities had had no effect.[101] It might have been this public intervention that was the cause of a return to "icy formality, and a very literal interpretation of our mandate" by the Israeli authorities, described by a former ICRC delegate.[102] On the practical level, the ICRC's medical, health, and other services to the West Bank and Gaza increased in range and in focus as the occupation dragged on.[103]

It is now clear that a further distinguishing feature of the ICRC's relationship with Israel and the occupied territories arose directly from Israel's sustained refusal to acknowledge the de jure applicability of the Fourth Geneva Convention and its equally persistent structural violations manifested most obviously in settlement policy. At the start of 2012, an interview with Raja Shehadeh was published in the *International Review of the Red Cross* as part of a special thematic edition on occupation. Selected for interview as "someone who has lived and practised law in an occupied territory,"[104] Shehadeh was asked what his expectations had been of the ICRC. Shehadeh first paid tribute to the "help given on a small scale" to detainees otherwise in isolation, which was "not to be underrated." However, looking back, he observed, "Maybe my expectations were simply too high. [. . .] Maybe that's always a problem when you start out with high hopes—the hopes are dashed." He then went on to regret what he had perceived as

> reluctance on the part of the ICRC to take up issues in an effective way, to speak out openly against the settlements or the civil administration, and to use every possible power the organization has to help put a stop to these detrimental violations. Sometimes I detected more fear of speaking out against Israel than I had witnessed in Israel itself.

He had himself challenged ICRC delegates on many occasions. He agreed with the importance of "being economical in the frequency of public statements"—after all, this had also been the practice at al-Haq. However, he was of the opinion that "the ICRC did not speak out when it should have."

The same volume of the *Review*, published on the 150th anniversary of the founding of the ICRC, included a paper by the then ICRC president, Peter Maurer, on "Israel's occupation policy," presented as a decision by the ICRC "to engage in a public debate over these issues."[105] Maurer tells his readers that "the particular challenges of humanitarian action" in Israel and the occupied territories cannot be tackled without "an honest look at certain Israeli policies that have become key features of the occupation."[106]

> The ICRC has been unable to engage in any meaningful dialogue with the Israeli government on the impact for Palestinians of Israel's annexation of East Jerusalem, the routing of the West Bank Barrier, and the presence and further expansion of Israeli settlements. The ICRC has therefore opted to engage with civil society, academia, and the Israeli public directly in explaining its position regarding the discrepancies between IHL and the Israeli Government's policy in the Occupied Palestinian Territory.[107]

If this initiative was a departure for the ICRC in method, it was not a change in position. The ICRC had, in previous public communications over the years, made clear its position on the IHL rules governing Israel's occupation of the Palestinian territories (including East Jerusalem).[108] Introducing the reader to the 150th anniversary issue of the *Review*, the editor-in-chief stated that "over the years the ICRC has chosen to develop direct and confidential dialogue as its privileged method of engagement with its interlocutors"—this approach was "at the core of its identity."[109] At stake was access to those the ICRC was committed to assisting, which meant building and maintaining the trust and confidence of its interlocutors. Bernard insisted on the effectiveness of the confidentiality approach "from the humanitarian point of view" while stressing that it was not unconditional, that progress must be made, and that the quality of the dialogue was important.

As part of engaging in public debate, the *Review* solicited and published a response to Maurer's piece by Alan Baker, who had served as legal adviser to the Israeli Ministry of Foreign Affairs and as a military legal adviser in the Israeli army, among other positions.[110] It is hard to read into Baker's response any positive movement towards the ICRC's suggestion of a public debate and dialogue. Baker repeated the official Israeli positions on all the issues of law and policy raised by Maurer as core concerns for the ICRC, repeating the standard assertion that in any case the convention did not apply.[111] He did not take up the issue of the confidentiality dilemma posed by Maurer for discussion, but rather took the ICRC to task on another of its core principles, the "fundamental principle of neutrality." Baker tackled Maurer for his use of the designation "occupied Palestinian territory," which Baker rejected as "inaccurate historically and legally, and [. . .] inherently and clearly politically slanted."[112] Turning at the end to the ICRC's idea of a public debate on Israel's occupation policies, Baker told the ICRC president:

Engaging the public, whether through public speeches and statements, the public use of politically-generated terminology, reliance on biased and inaccurate information, and the adoption of formal policy positions based in political assumptions that have the potential to influence, undermine or prejudice ongoing processes of negotiation and reconciliation, would all appear to run contrary to the fundamental principle of neutrality.[113]

For Baker, insisting on IHL principles risked disrupting rather than underpinning political negotiations. These arguments are similar to those that blocked development of law-based political positions by European states in deference to a US political agenda following the first intifada.

THE ENFORCEMENT PROJECT

Notwithstanding al-Haq's criticism of the ICRC in the 1980s, a dialogue had been opened up with delegates in Jerusalem and through them with officials in the Geneva-based Department of Principles, Law and Relations with the Movement. From al-Haq's side, this effort was led by Charles Shammas and focused on the rights and duties of Israel's coparties to the Fourth Geneva Convention in affording protection to the Palestinian population. Al-Haq Draft Program Objectives for 1987 noted that it was

> imperative for al-Haq to seek to activate alternative mechanisms of enforcement and accountability within the international community of law. Towards this end, al-Haq plans to address governmental and non-governmental members of the system who proclaim adherence to the body of human rights and humanitarian law with the intention of enforcing on them their obligation to investigate and intervene against violations, and to participate in enforcement.[114]

The first direct "Appeal to State Signatories to the IV Geneva Convention" was issued as a press release (its tenth ever) by al-Haq five days into the first intifada, calling on states "to intervene urgently with the Israeli authorities to halt the killing and wounding of Palestinians in the occupied West Bank and Gaza."[115] Describing its repeated interventions with the Israeli authorities over the previous three years regarding instances of death and wounding caused by the use of live ammunition, and noting the authorities' "tacit approval of the 'shoot-to-kill' practices of the military," the organization explained:

> Al-Haq is calling upon the state signatories to the Fourth Geneva Convention to carry out their legal and moral obligations under the Convention. Under Article 1 of the Convention, signatory countries have undertaken not only to respect the Convention themselves, but also to ensure respect for the Convention. The underlying principle on which the Convention rests, namely respect for human life, is being violated.[116]

The next month, as the European Parliament was considering the ratification of new trade protocols with Israel, the Israeli authorities issued nine deportation orders as their violent reaction to the intifada continued. A memorandum by al-Haq explained the organization's standing to make a direct claim on state parties to the Fourth Geneva Convention:

> Al-Haq has addressed the enclosed memorandum to the European Community, its President, Parliament and member states, in its capacity as part of the protected population recognised by the Convention, and on behalf of that population. We present it as a Palestinian petitioner with standing under the Convention, with a right to claim the protection of the Member States and of the European Community. In so doing, we affirm our obligation to help activate the body of humanitarian law, the respect for which we believe unites us.[117]

The memorandum reminded state parties of their "duty under Article 1 to 'ensure respect' by third parties" and argued:

> To renew preferential trading privileges in the face of Israel's continuing serious violations of the Fourth Geneva Convention, and in the face of Israel's proclaimed intent to persist in committing such violations, would be an act of acquiescence to Israeli lawlessness.[118]

It followed that, before ratification of the EEC trade agreement with Israel, states should request, "as a condition precedent, an undertaking by Israel to comply with its obligations under the Fourth Geneva Convention." It was a departure for al-Haq to directly address elected parliamentarians in this manner. In the autumn of 1988, the Enforcement Project was formally established with the recruitment of a full-time worker (myself), based in London and going between Europe and Ramallah, and the participation of staffers in Ramallah. The end of 1988 saw al-Haq publish its first annual report, a development driven entirely by the continuing escalation of the intifada and Israel's reactions to it, rather than by forward planning. The conclusion invokes Article 1 of the Fourth Geneva Convention as a basis for "active international intervention to safeguard the lives and rights of the Palestinians as protected persons."[119] Its more planned-for successor, *A Nation under Siege*, gave sustained attention to the arguments being developed by the enforcement team.

During 1989, the second year of the intifada, al-Haq delivered interventions to governments through their consulates in East Jerusalem, calling for in situ monitoring and intervention by consular officials and the conduct of consular investigations, notably after a massive raid and multiple casualties in the West Bank village of Nahhalin and after "tax raids" in Beit Sahour.[120] The first of these protested "the failure of State Signatories to the Fourth Geneva Convention to provide any effective measure of international protection to the Palestinian population of the Occupied Territories" and appears to have been the first intervention in which al-Haq specifically drew attention to the category of grave breaches of the convention. The second urged consuls (in the absence of a protecting power) to "visit Beit Sahour and intervene with the Israeli military and tax authorities there, in order to provide a measure of physical protection for the inhabitants of the town in line with your duties under Article 1 of the Fourth Geneva Convention 1949." Consuls-general of seven European states set out on a fact-finding visit, only to be turned back at a roadblock by an Israeli officer who stated that the town had been closed "for operational reasons."[121] The British consul-general also visited Nablus and called for an investigation into a killing by the Israeli army.[122] Following a formal complaint made against the British consul-general by the Israeli ambassador in London, a parliamentary question prompted a Foreign Office minister to confirm that the consul-general had "done nothing without instructions from the British Government" and "nothing outside his proper role."[123]

In the meantime, the Enforcement Project was also developing its Europe-focused advocacy and allies. In the summer the first of four "enforcement symposia" was held, each with the participation of legal and political actors. These were the result of steady efforts in making contacts, presenting arguments, drafting parliamentary questions, sending letters to ministers, and other interventions. Other advocacy groups use similar methods, but al-Haq's efforts were distinguished at the time by its focus on IHL and third-party states' law-based rights and responsibilities. Besides setting out to a wider audience al-Haq's thinking on the law-based role of third parties, the symposia provided related opportunities; in London in 1989, for example, to draw out the ICRC. In response to a letter sent to its president by the two British MPs convening the enforcement symposium, the director of the ICRC's Principles, Law and Relations with the Movement Department wrote back confirming that:

> The ICRC considers it vital that the States party to the Geneva Conventions take all possible steps to ensure respect for that body of law, the purpose of which is to lessen the suffering of people affected by armed conflict. It is moreover a legal obligation for them to do so because, in becoming party to the Geneva Conventions, those States have undertaken not only to respect the said Conventions themselves, but also to ensure respect for them by other States in all circumstances. This is the tenor of Article 1 common to the four Conventions.[124]

The ICRC response had taken a while to be drafted (the MPs' letter was sent over three months before), but it arrived in time to be included in the publication arising from the symposium.[125] Back in Ramallah, al-Haq was preparing its second annual report, *A Nation under Siege*, which was to show the impact of the developing enforcement thinking. A chapter titled "The Role of the International Community" set out how different law-based options and roles came together in this context, and the report's exposition of violations committed over the course of the year identified those constituting "grave breaches" of the Fourth Geneva Convention. As a category of violations, grave breaches are the only instance where other state parties are required to take specific action, promulgating legislation allowing them to prosecute those against whom there is relevant evidence wherever the violation occurred.[126] In Ramallah, fieldwork coordinator Khaled Batrawi opened "grave breaches" files in an early attempt to collect documentation for use in criminal cases against alleged perpetrators, albeit the organization's understanding of evidential and other requirements was, at that time, rudimentary.[127]

The Enforcement Project was thus from the start distinguished from al-Haq's treatment of the law, and documentation of violations, by its focus on how to get third states acting in support of the law.[128] The exigencies of the intifada and the Israeli authorities' response thereto gave enormous impetus to the work and secured an audience for the arguments. As Shammas has put it, "largely untutored in the workings of international law, the Project's approach was based on logical necessity: we needed the law to work, and logically it had to work: we had to work out how."[129] With the ICRC, he recalls, "we [the Project] were recognised as a kind of very operational provocateur in terms of questions of doctrine." In 1990, Shammas was invited as a panelist—along with members of the international legal community—at the Fifteenth Roundtable of the International Institute of Humanitarian Law in San Remo, an annual event convened by the ICRC and other nongovernmental and intergovernmental actors, to contribute to the discussion on Article 1's requirement of state parties to "ensure respect for" the convention. The summary of proceedings reports that the majority in the working group took the view that "although the majority of the participants in the Diplomatic Conference of 1949 [which adopted the texts of the Conventions] did not intend the phrase 'ensure respect for' to engage the responsibility of third States, it had now become clear that Article 1 created both a right and an obligation for third States to ensure respect for IHL."[130]

The ICRC's interpretation is not accepted by all IHL scholars and experts, but it is a measure of the reach of this advocacy that those who disagreed nevertheless paid attention to the arguments made by al-Haq and its allies. Prominent Dutch jurist Frits Kalshoven explained as follows the arguments of those he referred to as "the Palestinians and their supporters":

> Their argument: by virtue of common Article 1, all states, and particularly those with close relations with Israel, are under an obligation to ensure that Israel respects all the rules of the Fourth Convention relative to military occupation. In support of their contention, they rely squarely on the ICRC Commentaries to the Conventions. Their interest was, and is, of course, to see that Israel remains under constant international pressure to relinquish the territory it keeps occupied. Given that interest, they may be forgiven for accepting the ICRC stance as gospel truth.[131]

That same year, 1990, also saw significant action by regional and intergovernmental bodies in regard to the application of IHL to the occupied territories—and, critically, the role of third-party states. The context included key events in the ongoing intifada as well as developments in Israel and internationally. The then Soviet Union was exercised about reports that large numbers of Jewish Soviet citizens emigrating to Israel under recently agreed arrangements were being settled in the occupied territories, including East Jerusalem, and sought to have the issue of settlements addressed in the Security Council. The United States, while generally avoiding asserting its previous position of the illegality of Israel's settlement policy in favor of insisting that settlements were an obstacle to peace, held up a significant US loan guarantee to Israel for the housing of Soviet immigrants when Israel declined to give assurance that the funds would not be used directly or indirectly to support settlement activity in the occupied territories and particularly East Jerusalem. In the meantime, the killing of seven Palestinian workers inside Israel in May and the killing of fifteen and wounding of some two thousand others during ensuing protests in the occupied territories prompted the drafting of what became known as the "protection resolution" at the UN Security Council. This envisaged a Security Council Commission being dispatched to recommend "ways and means for ensuring the safety and protection of the Palestinian civilians under Israeli occupation." At the end of May, the United States vetoed the draft resolution, but the issue returned in October, particularly after mass killings and injuries at al-Haram al-Sharif in East Jerusalem. With Israel still refusing to receive a team from the UN secretary-general, a report was written without a visit, giving specific focus to the obligations of Israel and also of third-party states under the Fourth Geneva Convention. Negotiations began at the Security Council on the text of a resolution.

These negotiations were still in progress when in December Israel announced deportation orders against four Palestinians from Gaza. The UNSC adopted Resolution 681 (1990), which called upon state parties to the Fourth Geneva Convention "to ensure respect by Israel of its obligations in accordance with Article 1." Dormann and Serralvo give this resolution as an example of states actively seeking to prevent violations of IHL in furtherance of their duty under Article 1 "to ensure respect" for the convention, acting as they did on Israel's announcement of its intent to commit the violations.[132] These developments were analyzed by al-Haq in its third annual report, *Protection Denied*. Al-Haq described the adoption of Resolution 681 as "a milestone." It was the first time the organization had reviewed UN developments in this way.[133] Elsewhere in the region, in August Iraq invaded Kuwait, and in January 1991 US-led forces engaged Iraqi troops in Kuwait in Operation Desert Storm. The aftermath of this included fresh efforts by the US administration to broker Israeli-Palestinian talks that were to lead to the Madrid talks later in 1991. In *Protection Denied*, al-Haq inter alia drew attention to the fact that the Security Council had been quick to explicitly allege grave breaches of the Geneva Convention by Iraq during its occupation of Kuwait, while remaining unable to agree on a text that would refer to Israel's policy-based grave breaches in the occupied territories.[134]

In June 1990, after the United States had vetoed the draft "protection resolution" at the Security Council, al-Haq and the PHRIC in Jerusalem issued a statement titled "Representation to State Signatories of the Fourth Geneva Convention" that addressed a set of possible measures to be taken, firstly through the United Nations and secondly by individual states. The accompanying supplement was titled "The Need for International Protection."[135] This representation is the most indicative statement of the thinking of al-Haq on enforcement in the circumstances of that period. It began with the possibility for protection to be afforded by the action of third-party states through the United Nations in accordance with the Uniting for Peace Resolution (1950) and the stationing of an observer force in the occupied territories. In the end, it was not until 1997 that the UN General Assembly employed the Uniting for Peace mechanism to establish the Tenth Emergency Session (on "illegal Israeli actions in occupied East Jerusalem and the rest of the occupied Palestinian territory").[136] This forum reconvened over the years and gave rise to three conferences of High Contracting Parties on "measures to enforce the Fourth Geneva Convention in the Occupied Palestinian Territories" (in 1999, after further vetoing by the United States at the UN; in 2001 after Ariel Sharon's visit to al-Haram al-Sharif and the eruption of the second intifada; and in 2014, after Israel's summer assault on Gaza). These conferences produced no discussions on mechanisms to operationalize the law.[137] The introduction of "refugee protection officers" by the United Nations Relief and Works Agency (UNRWA), following Security Council Resolution 681 (1990), was to prove important in many individual cases, although the public reporting mechanism quickly ceased to operate. The other observation/monitoring mechanism instituted by international actors in the occupied territories, the Temporary International Presence in Hebron (TIPH), was established after the massacre at the Ibrahimi mosque by Israeli settler Baruch Goldstein at the end of 1994. The TIPH was created outside the framework of IHL and given no public reporting mandate or authority to intervene; it remained in the city of Hebron until expelled by Israeli prime minister Netanyahu at the end of January 2019.[138]

As for action by states "jointly and severally," the 1990 representation suggested how states might instruct their consular officials and asked states to confirm that monitoring Israel's compliance with the convention was a principal duty of these officials and in their own national interest, given their obligations under Article 1. The eliciting of statements from "like-minded states"—which would acknowledge a common interest in upholding the norms and protections of IHL—was an initial focus of the Enforcement Project, supported by its advocacy efforts in the countries and institutions of the then EEC. The reaction of PLO representatives and officials in different European countries at the time was varied, sometimes supportive and excited, mostly rather disinterested; direct contact at the time would have posed a risk to al-Haq, but the arguments were presented through intermediaries.

The circumstances of the time allowed a measure of success to these efforts. At the end of June 1990, the Dublin Declaration, issued by the European Council at the end of the Irish presidency, included an unprecedented reference to the obligation of parties to the Fourth Geneva Convention to respect and ensure respect for the convention in the occupied territories.[139] In December the adoption of UN Security Council Resolution 681 (1990) also provided space for efforts to encourage "like-minded states" to consider ways of operationalizing the law through efforts to act in cooperation (in accordance with United Nations principles) in defense of the law. The secretary-general was asked to solicit the opinions of member states on ways and means to ensure the safety and protection of the Palestinian population, specifically seeking their input on the idea of convening a meeting of the High Contracting Parties to the Fourth Geneva Convention. In May 1991, a common response from the then twelve member states of the European Community supported the idea of a meeting at a "favourable time." In the meantime, they would be considering the establishment of a "consultative committee" which could seek ways of ensuring respect for the convention in the occupied territories.

The final part of al-Haq's 1990 representation to the signatory states concerned the duties of third-party states in regard to grave breaches of the convention by the occupying power. The exercise of universal jurisdiction over grave breaches had been an early focus for the Enforcement Project, being the only measure of enforcement that state parties to the convention are under an obligation to take. At the time, there was considerably less interest, knowledge, and activity around the issue of universal criminal jurisdiction than is the case now; the International Criminal Court was nearly a decade away. The only available criminal court recourse, failing that of the occupying power, remained the national courts of third state parties, which had no history of being put to such use. The initial research and contacts made by al-Haq's Enforcement Project, although valuable, could not take such hugely complicated efforts forward. It was not until many years later that moves towards prosecutions in third states for grave breaches began in earnest.[140]

In 1990, the scale of violations taking place during the intifada and the quite desperate situation of the civilian Palestinian population, combined with a growing international perception of Israel's intransigence and a relatively facilitative international climate, had made it possible to secure some developments towards a law-based approach, in particular on the part of EU states and their diplomatic personnel. This was short-lived. As of the spring of 1991, against the background of the first Iraq war, these developments and initiatives were shelved in deference to the US-led political initiative in the region. The Madrid talks, the Oslo processes, and the establishment of the Palestinian Authority transformed the context yet again.[141] Hajjar notes in relation to the political process that "the biggest blow for the human rights movement was the direction the negotiations took, namely the emphasis on security and territory rather than rights."[142] The United States began to consider IHL as an unacceptably tight constraint on its political interventions, and European states had no political will to challenge the US on this. From being the law that was designed to facilitate an end to conflict, IHL came to be viewed, by powerful third parties, as itself an obstacle to peace.[143]

By the time of the 1993 Declaration of Principles, the institutional home of the Enforcement Project had moved away from al-Haq and was now hosted next door in the office of MATTIN as the ambitiously named Centre for International Human Rights Enforcement (CIHRE). By the late 1990s, the work had developed into MATTIN's core program, and Shammas and his colleagues worked with European and Palestinian allies (as well as advising Palestinian officials) in an increasingly technocratic focus on "passive enforcement" in sustained engagement with European Union states and bodies.[144] The articulation of the established state duty of nonrecognition as the legal obligation incurred in the Article 1 text "to ensure respect" was a key development that has also been taken up by other Palestinian human rights organizations and allied advocacy. Shammas has termed this approach noncontentious, while noting that "more unusual was its application, in technical detail, to areas of state practice such as community law, rules of origin and other texts of trade agreements."[145] In 2013, Shammas's sustained work with MATTIN colleagues on the responsibility of EU member states in this regard was credited in an al-Haq position paper in further illustration, perhaps, of how work once regarded as controversial in the human rights field has been mainstreamed.[146] In the summer of 2013, in a major breakthrough, the European Commission issued a notice implementing a previous position that "all agreements between the State of Israel and the EU must unequivocally and explicitly indicate their inapplicability to the territories occupied by Israel in 1967."[147] Al-Haq posted on its website a notice welcoming this development in the name of the Palestinian Human Rights Organisations Council (PHROC), with the logos of eleven council members attached.[148] In a further breakthrough, in 2015 the Commission gave "interpretive notice" on the identification of the origins of goods from the "territories occupied by Israel since June 1967"—as PHROC hailed it, "EU labelling of settlement products" to ensure they do not enter EU markets as "produce of / made in Israel."

However, at al-Haq in the early nineties, the Enforcement Project was increasingly being seen as problematic. As the work took a higher profile both locally and internationally, a number of doctrinal and political challenges were posed. Perhaps the most significant was—and is—whether there is a conflict, or contradiction, between working to achieve the implementation of IHL in the occupied territories and working to achieve an end to the Israeli occupation. This objection was made by local and international interlocutors at the beginning of al-Haq's Enforcement Project; and it has been, and continues to be, voiced explicitly by individuals with an interest in the law, including legal practitioners and academics, as well as by actors engaged in the broader political debates and—implicitly—by those tired of the rhetoric of international law in the face of its manifest failure to protect.

Against the background of massive violations of IHL during the first intifada and unprecedented media coverage of the same, this anxiety reflected concerns that for external actors to oblige Israel into an attitude of compliance with its obligations as an occupying power would be to return to the previous image of Israel as a benign occupier. If Israel were obliged to correct its conduct, would the international attention given to addressing the situation, prompted and fueled by the ferocity and visibility of ongoing violations of IHL, be reduced and the political impetus to bring Israel into negotiations about ending the occupation falter?

Al-Haq's Enforcement Project—and its successors—argued that the logic of the law is otherwise.[149] IHL does not "preserve" a situation of occupation, but does regulate it. It should serve as a holding mechanism for the status of the occupied territories and the rights of the population, but also facilitate ending the occupation. Fundamentally, the law establishes protections for an occupied population and prohibits the occupying power from pursuing an annexationist agenda. Properly implemented, the law protects the prospects for political settlement from being derailed by the rancor caused by serious human rights abuses, and from impasses created by policies of conquest and annexation, in pursuit of which abuses are committed. By rendering such policies and their results illegal in and of themselves, the law is supposed to remove potentially intractable obstacles from the negotiating process, and to offer the occupying power, prohibited from acquiring any significant advantage from the land or resources, little prospect of gain in prolonging its occupation. Conversely, reluctance by powerful third parties to act in defense of the law when challenged by the occupying power can undermine both the will to negotiate and support for those charged with negotiating. In the case of Israel, after years of failure to ensure Israel's compliance with IHL, its violations of international law became the basis upon which negotiations, once started, were premised. Failure to respect or ensure respect for the law thus had (and continues to have) tangible consequences for both human rights protection and dispute resolution. In the case of the occupied territories, de facto toleration of its non-implementation has led to the "creation of facts" in violation of the convention—most notably settlements and the annexation of East Jerusalem—that continue to constitute some of the most difficult and apparently intractable issues on the negotiating agenda, such as it is.

Doubts about the political utility of seeking law-based conduct by the occupying power had been posed to al-Haq's founders and field-workers since the establishment of the organization. Nevertheless, Rabbani's 1994 understanding of the Enforcement Project was that it occasioned a "gradual politicization" in al-Haq, whether through those whom the project was engaging ("politicians as a primary audience") or the associated "necessity to develop appealing political arguments"[150]—what might be described as utilitarian arguments linking law-based action with political goals desirable to European political interlocutors. Some al-Haqqers apparently worried that the enforcement approach might undermine the political battle to end the occupation and realize the right to self-determination.

This argument became pertinent again alongside internal developments. The talks in Madrid and Washington began to bring out political differences among al-Haq staffers that were not easily submerged by the considerable ongoing work-load. The Madrid talks of 1991 also provided the immediate cause for Raja Sheha-deh's decision to leave al-Haq's board when invited to join the Palestinian delegation to Madrid and then the United States as a legal adviser. Jonathan Kuttab left at the same time—he and Shehadeh, as well as Shammas to a certain extent, had wearied of the heavy responsibilities and the increasing wrangling among al-Haq staffers. And all had other professional engagements to which they wished to devote more time than their al-Haq duties permitted. Staff-board differences included remaining anger on the part of some staffers over Mona Rishmawi's departure and at the depar-ture of two members of the founding board, as well as the eventual failure to forge a working relationship with the new board. The Enforcement Project was probably as much a victim of these turbulent developments as of its own weaknesses.

Among al-Haq workers, there were other reservations about the project. Inter-viewed for this study, staffers from the time recalled finding the Enforcement Project—variously—new, unclear, badly communicated, "parachuted in," highly complex, esoteric, the "fourth generation of human rights work," "a very strange project for us," and scary—"we weren't sure where was it taking us."[151] Khaled Batrawi, an enthusiastic member of the Enforcement Team, says that the work was "not among the known alphabets" of human rights work at the time.[152] Internally, it was al-Haq's most controversial project. A number of factors appear to have com-bined to generate discomfort, starting with the direct engagement with elements of foreign political systems. Seeking action from powerful third-party states to correct conduct by the occupying power did not hold the same costs for Palestin-ians in the occupied territories as it would for those working in national systems with sovereign governments; nevertheless, for rather different reasons, some at al-Haq felt that talking to governments was the prerogative of the PLO, as the Pales-tinians' political representative. Here, even with Jerusalem-based consuls-general, Mona Rishmawi recalls that "it was a big political issue when we started talking to them." The ideas and the work developed apace, and Charles Shammas was not at his best in explaining them to the rapidly increasing numbers of staffers assembled at the general meeting. Despite the building of an Enforcement Team at al-Haq that drew on members from different units, the project was seen as "particular to Charles" (whose role at MATTIN was also not always understood) and otherwise dependent on non-Palestinian staff. Despite its impact on the substance of the second and third annual reports and in interventions, the project did not manage to integrate its work into the organization as a whole; it was always somehow iso-lated. Neither Shehadeh nor Kuttab was engaged with the project, and some had doubts that these two were really in support but also felt unable to tell Shammas of their concerns. It was expensive, with the UK field representative based in London and high travel costs for the advocacy schedule in Europe. European donors were particularly enthusiastic about the project and earmarked funds for its support at al-Haq;[153] but there was a perception of foreign travel, privilege, and prestige associated with the project that, together with this high level of funding, generated questions and risked resentment. Even the project's then innovative use of email for communications gave rise to comment, whether for using dial-up modems that tied up al-Haq's phone line, which was needed for the field-workers to call in, or because it was one more thing not familiar (and not adequately explained) to fellow workers. It was also in the nature of the work that the European advocacy and research side suffered from a lack of direct or daily oversight from the al-Haq office in Ramallah, although the project was also accused of "overreporting" on its activities, taking too much of staffers' time to explain itself and—from a management perspective—filling up filing cabinet drawers with lengthy reporting documents that nobody had time to read.

Finally, the board that succeeded Shehadeh, Kuttab, and Shammas felt there was risk of a conflict of interest. Charles Shammas had himself stayed on the new board with a view to providing some institutional memory and aiding the transition to the new governing body. He did not see a conflict of interest through his holding an (unpaid) operational role in the organization's work, although he offered to withdraw. Discussions with members of the new board became increasingly acrimonious, however, and in June 1992 the board decided to terminate the project by the end of the year. The reasons given were "the high financial cost of the project" and "the administrative complications arising mainly from Charles' double role as a board member and project coordinator. [. . .] We are sorry," wrote al-Haq's then program coordinator to me (al-Haq's field representative in London), "for the unhappy ending of al-Haq's enforcement project."[154]

As it happened, by the end of the summer, Fateh Azzam—an active supporter of the Enforcement Project—returned from completing his LLM in the UK and took over as program coordinator, in which role he sought to review this decision and to revive discussions with al-Haq's board. But other challenges were also presenting themselves in the organization, and the new board resigned when the staff refused to accept its proposals for a new structure examined in chapter 7.[155] Azzam organized a vote among staff on whether the Enforcement Project should stay with al-Haq; the vote, according to Azzam, was for keeping the project, but only by a very narrow margin. After five years, support for the project among the staff was seriously divided, and Shammas and I left al-Haq.[156] Institutional communications were maintained through Azzam's involvement in the advisory board of CIHRE.

Reflecting on the "unhappy ending" of the project at al-Haq, Nina Atallah's observation sums up the thoughts also of others from the time who remain engaged in human rights work: "Maybe it wasn't its time for us at the organization, because now we all think it's important," she says, "but in its time it was obscure, and things that are obscure are usually uncomfortable. I myself couldn't make up my mind." Issam Younis, a member of the Enforcement Team and subsequently founder and director of Al Mezan human rights organization in Gaza, agrees that "perhaps al-Haq didn't appreciate the value of the Project, but the team's work was important; today that's what we organizations do."[157] The invocation of third-party state responsibilities through targeted direct interventions and communications to a range of third-party (state and nonstate) actors—often by a group of Palestinian organizations—is now standard. In more recent years, al-Haq employed an EU advocacy officer based in its Netherlands and Brussels office and has currently a section on its website dedicated to this work.

As for the al-Haq Enforcement Project, despite the complicating factors set out above, it was, strangely, very much of its time. It sprang from a growing realization of the impossibility of accessing local remedies or protections, and the insistence that, logically, the law couldn't let things stop there. In the late 1990s al-Haq, having passed through the turbulent years of Oslo and its aftermath and lost nearly all of its staff in an organizational crisis, returned to the legacy of its project. In 1998 it formed a working group for enforcement of the Fourth Geneva Convention with four other NGOs. The next year, in a Newsletter article about the Conference of High Contracting Parties convened in July 1999, al-Haq laid claim, possibly for the first time, to the organization's contribution to this work: "al-Haq pioneered the movement to raise the issue of Israel's refusal to apply the Fourth Geneva Convention at the level of the international community."[158] The annual report issued by al-Haq (by then under the leadership of Randa Siniora) on the first year of the second intifada, *In Need of Protection* (2002), in its final section developed the arguments and implications of the provisions on grave breaches and the Article 1 obligation, and formally thanked Shammas, "whose work greatly informed our own."

6

———

Field and Legal Research

LSM's first paid worker was a field researcher, and by the early years of the intifada the organization was employing some fifteen field-workers in different governorates of the West Bank and Gaza. The Fieldwork Unit and those who worked with it are widely considered the cornerstone of the organization's work. The rigor of the fieldwork methodology was key to the organization's reputation and credibility with Israeli and international human rights and other actors. For their part, as discussed in chapter 4, the field-workers introduced the organization to different parts of the Palestinian community. They informed victims of violations and the wider society about their rights, principles of the rule of law, and the wider human rights discourse; as their role developed, a number of field-workers were assigned as paralegals in towns in the West Bank, with a formal brief to advise on a range of issues. The information collected by the field-workers and their close knowledge of events in their localities fed directly into the organization's work program, on structural and policy developments.

FIELDWORK METHODOLOGY

It is hard to overstate the stress that LSM/al-Haq founders and staffers, including the field-workers themselves, place on the rigor brought to the fieldwork and thence the analysis and presentation of LSM/al-Haq's work as a whole. "Documentation" (*tawthiq*) was the basis of everything. New field-workers would accompany established colleagues to the field to observe how to conduct interviews, how to take affidavits and complete questionnaires, and how to pursue follow-up; the unit coordinator would at times accompany the field-worker to observe the work. LSM/al-Haq provided training on types of violations and the rights involved.

The office end of the system was focused around what Fateh Azzam refers to as "the all-important meeting of the field-workers."[1] Every Wednesday the coordinator would meet separately with each field-worker and go over piece by piece the information the field-worker had documented. This was followed by a meeting of all the field-workers together, to discuss the overall patterns in violations that had occurred in each area. Others recall that this part of the meeting might also involve field-workers presenting their work as a learning exercise for the group as a whole. The unit would then present a written "weekly report on events in the field" to the general meeting, where it would be discussed.[2] Discussion in the general meeting would be aimed at evaluation and analysis, and decision-taking on al-Haq's program in light of the information from the fieldwork unit—"do we take this up?" Fateh Azzam recalls finding the organization "absolutely driven by developments on the ground."[3]

In the 1980s, one of LSM/al-Haq's main objectives was to establish the facts of Israel's violation of international law, before press coverage of the first intifada brought many of these to international attention. After the furor that greeted the LSM/ICJ 1985 publication of the report on al-Fara'a prison, Jonathan Kuttab's commitment (in his letter to the Israeli Ministry of Foreign Affairs) to "retract any published material that is proven to be materially inaccurate" was "not a concession [...] but an essential ingredient of [LSM's] nature as a serious human rights organisation on which it stakes its credibility." The first time that al-Haq had to amend material inaccuracy in its published material was in 1990. Seventeen Palestinian civilians were shot and killed by members of the Israeli Border Police ("at least" another 150 were wounded) at al-Haram al-Sharif in Jerusalem, the compound that contains al-Aqsa mosque and the Dome of the Rock.[4] A significant number of al-Haq staffers (field-workers and others, including researchers) decamped to Jerusalem, setting up temporary office in the National Palace Hotel to facilitate, over an intense few days, "an in-depth investigation including detailed interviews with over 50 eyewitnesses to the events."[5] Field-worker Ahmad Jaradat recalled that "we worked on the grounds of the al-Aqsa mosque night and day."[6] In its first public statement, the organization named one person twice, increasing the number of fatalities by one, due to the presentation of the person's name in two different ways. Batrawi (who notes that this error did not originate with the field-work unit) recalls the wide distribution of the statement of correction as soon as the error was identified. Al-Haq's speedy response meant that its first public error did not damage its credibility; its revised "Reconstruction of Events" was (along with the report of B'Tselem) appended to the report of the UN secretary-general to the UN Security Council as the international community continued to wrangle over protection of the Palestinian population.[7]

This mistake does not appear to have been repeated during these most intense years of the first intifada. The insistence on accuracy (*diqqa*) in its fieldwork remains a matter of pride and professional honor, for the field-workers involved at the time as well as for other staffers.[8] LSM/al-Haq's awareness of the likely challenge by Israel to its fact-based claims and public interventions, along with the professional background of Shehadeh and Kuttab, probably led to the choice of the affidavit, or sworn statement, as the "pillar of documentation" at the organization, and to the long hours that staffers recall being spent in going over them in the office.[9] Like other things, however, it developed over time. Shehadeh recalls going to see farmer Sabri Gharib and taking what was probably the first affidavit for LSM, in January 1982. The affidavit set out Israeli attempts to take over Gharib's land. It was to be a long struggle for the affiant; in defiance of harassment from settlers and the military authorities he took every legal step he could (including appealing to the Military Objection Committee and the Israeli High Court) but lost most of his farmland to the settlement, although he saved his house.[10] Sabri Gharib died in April 2012. Shehadeh, who had kept up with Gharib's struggle over the years, wrote, "For me, Sabri's death marks the end of an era when it was possible to believe that law could save Palestinian land from Jewish settlers."[11]

Back in the early eighties when Shehadeh still believed in the power of the law, LSM began to collect a growing number of affidavits from victims of and witnesses to a range of violations. Its first Newsletter set out its motivation for this methodology. "Although often such violations do not become the subject of legal proceedings, it is felt that they should not go unrecorded and LSM has found that such personal testimonies are in many cases more effective in documenting human rights violations than the use of questionnaires and other methods."[12] The emphasis on sworn statements was not shared by human rights organizations elsewhere at the time; interviews might be carried out rigorously and accompanied by cross-checking and verification of other evidence, but the victim/witness was not asked to sign under oath.[13] However, the tone of LSM's explanation—that these events should be recorded through testimony—recalls Shehadeh's account in his journal of "the shooting of Hani," his teenage neighbor shot in the leg by a soldier in 1980, and the intimidation of the boy's mother to stop her from filing charges (when that was possible) against the military authorities. He was struck by Hani's mother's reaction when Shehadeh suggested legal action: "What difference does it make? [. . .] Just keep those monsters out of my life." Shehadeh reflected at the time:

> In her, I see how anger has gradually, through the years of occupation, given way to despair. Anger fuels memory, keeps it alive. Without this fuel, you give up even the right to assert the truth. You let others write your history for you, and this is the ultimate capitulation. We *samidin* cannot fight the Israelis' brute physical force but we must keep the anger burning—steel our wills to fight the lies. It is up to us to remember and record.[14]

A decade later, George Giacaman, a Birzeit professor of philosophy and for a time research coordinator at al-Haq, found that "reading the affidavits was very moving." Affidavits would be taken on a printed form, which after recording personal details confirmed that this was a "statement under oath" with the affiant confirming the truth of the contents, after having been "warned of the legal implications of making false statements under oath."[15] In its first publication of a collection of such statements in 1983, LSM explained how affidavits were taken:

They were collected by trained fieldworkers employed by LSM, who took great care to assure accuracy and precision. In each instance, information was taken down as dictated by the affiant. Questions were asked on points of which he or she might have been unsure. The rule against hearsay was followed, as well as other rules relating to evidence that are observed in judicial inquiries. Finally, the written version was read to the affiant, who was asked to sign it. Only those affidavits that were signed are presented here. In a number of cases, after the affidavit was prepared and approved the person who had given it refused to sign for fear of further harassment.[16]

A further distinction was made between those who signed affidavits and were content to have their names published with their testimony, and those who signed but asked for their names to be withheld, trusting the organization not to use their names without permission. Field-worker Ghazi Shashtari recalls that "the main challenge was people's fear . . . We had to convince them, the people experiencing the violation. Here, the trust in the field-worker was important." Iyad Haddad similarly remembers that, besides people's hesitation in the face of this new kind of document, "mostly what I'd hear was 'if your foe is the judge, who are you going to complain to?' meaning there was no trust in the Israeli system, so in the end what was the point of al-Haq submitting complaints, etc."[17] Other field-workers from pre-intifada days likewise recall some interviewees declining in the end to sign the affidavit.[18] "Some people didn't necessarily want to give affidavits," remembers Zahi Jaradat, "but they wanted to talk about what had happened to them." LSM/al-Haq insisted on certain wording, certain forms and formats of documentation, in a manner that appeared to some as almost an obsession with how an affidavit should be presented or produced. The LSM team decided early on against using notaries to take the affidavits, deploying and training field-workers for this purpose.

There was clearly a desire to put out there the voices of Palestinians directly affected by human rights violations. Scholarship has paid considerable attention to the use of first-person testimonials/narratives in the context of human rights reporting.[19] Al-Haq published sets of affidavits on particular themes and also extracted sections from affidavits to insert in other reports. Al-Haq's production of this form of record shows how the information was marshaled, and how much narrative of significance to the affiant may have been found not relevant to documenting the empirical facts that establish a human rights violation.[20] In the office, the discussion was on how to use the affidavits, how to present them, where they could be stored so that they could be cross-checked if necessary for evidence, and how to keep the names of affiants safe in case the office was raided by the authorities.

By the time LSM issued its first Newsletter, it had also developed other tools for documenting violations. "The idea of documenting a range of violations," says Shehadeh, "only came to us gradually." Zahi Jaradat recalls drafting the first LSM questionnaire with Sami 'Ayad on house demolition. By 1984, LSM's field-workers were using questionnaires to document all those subject (currently or in the past) to travel restriction orders and all cases of punitive house demolitions and sealings, as well as what the English Newsletter referred to as all killings of Palestinians by Israeli soldiers or settlers, or members of the Village Leagues.[21] The Arabic Newsletter, and the printed form of the questionnaire developed at al-Haq for the purpose of documentation, used martyrdom (*istishhad*), rather than killing, as the standard expression in the community; the first time the organization used the term *martyrdom* in English for those killed by the occupation forces appears to have been in the dedication of *A Nation under Siege* (1989). Not to use the term *martyrdom* in such contexts, recalled Fateh Azzam, would be almost to pretend not to be a Palestinian organization, in the interests of appearing neutral to a Western audience.

Other questionnaire forms in the archives from the mid-eighties include one directed at juvenile detainees, which might have been developed in reaction to reports of practice at al-Fara'a prison; wounding (including the means of wounding—"bullets, beating with clubs, beating with gun-butts, other"); treatment under interrogation (this questionnaire sought to establish inter alia whether certain patterns of torture and ill-treatment had been used—"position abuse [*shabah*] and which form; showers; beating; sleep deprivation, food deprivation, insults and humiliation, other"); medical care in prison; and one following up the situation of Palestinians liberated in the prisoner exchange of May 1985.

The questionnaires illustrate the organization's interest in documenting the violation of rights not only accurately, but within the framework of a structure or policy; questions were posed as to follow-up in terms of hospital referrals, complaints, investigations. In examining cases of killing and wounding, they sought to determine the degree of deliberation and the immediate surrounding circumstances. Accompanying documentation would include medical reports, copies of military orders, spent cartridges or rubber bullets, photographs, sketches of the site by the field-worker, and an "incident report" from the field-worker setting out his (or—later on—her) efforts to document the violation. The emphasis on accuracy meant that field-workers would have to return for follow-up if their documentation was found to be incomplete or "weak" for reasons not apparently to do with the incident itself; in the case of affidavits, they might be turned into or incorporated within a report should the contents be found to be not suitable for a sworn statement. Affidavits were particularly difficult: "they had to be written in such a way that any question someone had on reading it would already be answered."[22] The questioning of victims and of witnesses had to be thorough. Kuttab says, "We taught our field-workers to be very skeptical. It was difficult to do; they had to ask the questions that a hostile interrogator would ask." Azzam recalls, "One of the reasons people at al-Haq tended to think the local community thought us elitist was that the work was in a way so technical, such tiring detail, even to the point that you almost have to interrogate people when you're doing fieldwork." Affidavits were a very constructed form of story-telling, and field-workers experienced what Paul Gready has referred to as the "tension between the duty to treat testifying victims with sensitivity and respect, and the duty to ensure that their claims about abuses are factually true: the tension between 'validating the victim' and 'validating the story.'"[23]

The strategy according to Batrawi was that "al-Haq was looking for the truth, and no more than that."[24] Kan'an recalls, "Raja and Jonathan used to tell us, credibility is everything, there are human rights violations here night and day, we don't have to make them up." Like good human rights investigators the world around, field-workers developed a sense for when something was not quite right. In his "Memories" of the al-Haq fieldwork unit written for this study, Batrawi cites examples where good fieldwork (and good instinct) revealed "alleged violations which upon investigation had nothing to do with the occupation." These were exceptions, but the motivations for making the allegation were not difficult to discern. The death of a family member as a martyr, a *shahid*, having been killed by the occupation forces, was more honorable than if the person had been killed as an alleged collaborator or by accident involving illegal firearms, and a pension (from funds from outside) could be paid to the family of a *shahid*. If al-Haq had documented one such case in error, says Batrawi, "I would have resigned."[25]

The field-workers laid great emphasis on the credibility and standing they had in their own parts of the West Bank (and later Gaza), where they worked for LSM/al-Haq, and on the need for the field-workers to be "in and of" the community in order to put their interlocutors at ease rather than add to their discomfort in distressing times. Particular personal skills were needed. They had to judge when to push with more questions and when to decide to come back another day; they had to ensure they conducted appropriate follow-up. Other demands on the field-workers of a more social nature are also clear. "We told people about their rights," says Kan'an, "and us taking an interest was important. Okay, we had no material aid to give them, but having someone listen, document, follow up your case [. . .] people felt that someone cared about what happened to them." Very focused on the outreach side of his work with al-Haq, Kan'an adds that "a human rights organization shouldn't be an 'organization' as such . . . The field researchers are its arms into the community." If the quality of al-Haq's field research and documentation made the organization's credibility internationally, the field-workers made it locally.

THE RISKS OF FIELDWORK

Other major challenges came from the Israeli occupation authorities. Being a field-worker was demanding and not infrequently dangerous work. Field-workers had to travel throughout the governorates in which they worked and beyond when called upon; not all had personal transport. There were no mobile phones, and regular landlines were not plentiful. Besides the immediate risks of the work taking them out and about in hot spots, their efforts drew the attention of the Israeli authorities to their activities. Already in September 1985, as noted in chapter 4, LSM field-workers Ghazi Shashtari and Zahi Jaradat had been arrested and placed under administrative detention for six months, shortly after the Israeli cabinet had announced the reintroduction of administrative detention, deportation, and other measures under Israel's Iron Fist policy.[26] LSM used its next Newsletter to explain administrative detention to its readers, having spent much of the preceding three months working on this issue.[27] The organization also reported to its readers on an intervention it had made to its networks suggesting that observers attend the appeal hearings. LSM's careful presentation of the context of the arrests and detention of its field-workers and the organization's reasons for concluding they were held because of their human rights work have been set out in chapter 4.[28]

The risk of arrest for field-workers increased substantially with the outbreak of the first intifada in December 1987. Al-Haq's report on the first year of the uprising, *Punishing a Nation*, is dedicated to five al-Haq field-workers who had spent most of that year under administrative detention, along with Riziq Shuqair, former coordinator of the fieldwork unit who had moved to the research unit. His status— some three weeks after his arrest—was still unknown by the time the report was issued.[29] Three of the field-workers were named as "prisoners of conscience" by Amnesty International.[30]

Among the memories that field-workers relate of the time they spent in prison are the way in which their human rights work exposed them to arrest, the way the authorities reacted to their mention of LSM/al-Haq, and the physical circumstances of their arrest and detention. They tell of the support provided to them by the organization, often including LSM's lawyers (Shehadeh, Kuttab, Rishmawi) representing them at different stages of the process of their incarceration. They also recall the support they received from Israeli human rights lawyers and from visitors and letters from lawyers and human rights activists further abroad.[31] They tell of human rights work they conducted inside prison, from taking a law-based stand with the prison authorities, for example refusing to do work for the army, to explaining the Fourth Geneva Convention and detainees' rights to fellow detainees. Several found ways of smuggling out to al-Haq affidavits they had taken in prison, and reports on prison conditions.[32] And then there are more personal memories. Zahi Jaradat, for example, recalls having been only recently married when he was arrested again in September 1985 at the start of the Iron Fist policy; not questioned or charged, when released he was placed under house arrest, required to go from his village, Sa'ir, to the city of Hebron once a day to sign in at the police station. He spent his months of house arrest reading up on international law; colleagues from the office visited, and Batrawi came once a month to deliver his salary.

Kan'an says it was "bitter" to miss out on his children, recalling the reaction of one of his young sons when he got out: "In the evening I put on my pajamas and I was sitting there, and he said, 'Aren't you going home?' I said 'Yes, this is our home.' He said, 'This isn't your home, your home is in prison.'" Kan'an was detained in November 1988, together with Riziq Shuqair:

> We'd been to Raja [Shehadeh]'s wedding, me and Riziq. We left and it was so cold, it was raining [. . .] As we drove through Beit Hanina, we got a stone through the window, so Riziq said I should stay with him that night. In the middle of the night, the army came for Riziq, and they told me to get in as well.

In *A Nation under Siege*, al-Haq gave the instances of Kan'an and Jabarin as "two cases [that] merit particular attention, illustrating, as they do, both the brutality and lack of due process which have characterized Israel's response to the uprising."[33] Jabarin's case involved, on his arrest in October 1989, a severe beating in the vehicle taking him to the Hebron lockup and then further mistreatment when he arrived and after he had complained of the initial beating. Hiltermann considers Jabarin to have had several lucky breaks during this process, failing which he might have been "another Ibrahim al-Mtour": he was seen by other detainees in the Hebron lockup where he was beaten and subjected to other mistreatment, and these prisoners were released the same day and informed his family. An army doctor in the same facility "refused to take responsibility for his condition," and a Druze soldier was concerned and compassionate enough to drive Jabarin to an Israeli hospital, where a Palestinian who was working there saw him. Informed of the incident, al-Haq intervened with the military authorities and also with international human rights organizations, which resulted in further interventions, including by Jimmy Carter.[34] Defense Minister Yitzhak Rabin wrote back to Carter. The case drew "unprecedented international attention," including in the US press. The Israeli embassy in Washington released a statement stating that Jabarin had "resisted arrest" and that therefore it had been "necessary to use reasonable force to put him in jail."[35] Al-Haq responded as follows:

1. Mr Jabarin was blindfolded and according to eyewitnesses was not resisting arrest when taken from his house to the car. In addition, he was blindfolded and handcuffed at the time he was beaten.
2. More importantly, in al-Haq's view, jumping on a person for ten minutes, burning him with a cigarette, and squeezing his testicles cannot be considered "reasonable force." In a letter to former US President Jimmy Carter, Defence Minister Yitzhak Rabin reviewed Mr Jabarin's case and concluded:
3. "As to the beating of the man, it was only moderate enough to convince him to accept detention."[36]

Despite the various interventions, press columns in the *New York Times*, and a resolution in the European parliament, Jabarin's one-year administrative detention order was confirmed.[37] His wife Lamia gave birth to their first child three weeks after his arrest. Jabarin learned of the birth of their son when he was in Ansar III, where there were no visitors, from a photograph in a newspaper brought in one day by the ICRC, a picture of his son in the arms of Jimmy Carter; "that was the first time I saw him."[38] Al-Haq's third annual report of human rights violations during the intifada reproduces a translation of a lengthy affidavit in the form of his "detention memoirs" which describe conditions in Ansar III and the treatment of detainees.[39] The memoir is a good illustration of what an al-Haq field-worker might consider of relevance to a human rights affidavit—it focuses on empirical narrative and does not venture into personal reflection.

INTIFADA EXPANSION

The arrest of the majority of al-Haq's field-workers in the first year of the uprising, combined with the huge increase in the number and range of violations that were occurring, led to the recruitment of new members of the unit and a geographical expansion, for the first time, into Gaza. Previously, besides close work with Gaza lawyers setting up the GCRL and work with Gaza trades unions under its project on workers' rights, LSM/al-Haq had not carried out its own substantive documentation work in or on the Gaza Strip. Its initial focus had been the way in which Israeli military orders were changing the local law in the West Bank, and the legal history of the Gaza Strip since 1948 had been significantly different, as was the judicial system, albeit that the content of the military orders issued for the Gaza Strip (by the army's Southern Command) was substantively the same.

When the intifada broke out, however, it became awkward when the organization, continuing its practice of not publishing or commenting on information that it had not verified through its own work, found itself unable to include the massive violations taking place in Gaza. This position had caused friction with PHRIC. A considered but practical response was in order. In *Punishing a Nation*, the organization announced that despite al-Haq not having its own field-workers there, "because human rights violations in Gaza are even worse than those in the West Bank, documentation which could be confirmed without actual fieldwork is included in this report."[40] In 1989, new recruits to the fieldwork unit included Palestinians from the Gaza Strip. They also included female field-workers. Batrawi recalls proposing that there should be at least one female field-worker each in the West Bank and the Gaza Strip, with a specific geographical remit and a thematic one that focused on violations that particularly affected women, such as the effects of tear gas on pregnancies. Male field-workers, he adds, found it hard to ask the questions that had to be asked of released women detainees.[41] In the summer of 1987, al-Haq had recruited Randa Siniora to develop a women's rights project at al-Haq, and it was in the second annual report that al-Haq included a separate chapter on violations of women's rights during the intifada.[42] A woman field-worker recruited at the time observed that the division of fieldwork was not usually gendered.

The expansion in the numbers of field-workers and in the violations they had to cover occasioned some practical decisions. By way of example, when administrative detention was reintroduced in 1985, the organization, as we have seen, focused considerable energy on researching the legal background, issuing its first occasional paper on this subject. At the end of 1986, the organization published a list of 37 Palestinians from the West Bank and Gaza placed under administrative detention during the course of the year. At the end of 1987, after the start of the intifada and the huge increase in violations, the Newsletter gave a number of 189 Palestinians from the West Bank placed under administrative detention By the time *Punishing a Nation* was published, the organization was focusing on the implementation of the policy, with case examples, and on conditions in detention centers, reporting that "three to four thousand people had been placed under administrative detention since the beginning of the uprising."[43]

LSM/al-Haq never set itself the goal of documenting and reporting on all violations occurring in the occupied territories. Well before the first intifada, decisions had to be made on what to investigate and what to cover: "The way of thinking," says Jabarin, "was that nothing was separate from the bigger picture. Is there a policy behind this, where's it going? [. . .] It means you don't see the incident in isolation." It was a question of documenting "certain patterns of violations" rather than every violative incident. Batrawi presents the field-workers' focus during his time at al-Haq in the first intifada as documentation of all cases of killing, deportation, house demolition or sealing, town arrest, and the closure of educational institutions (as a collective penalty); and some but not all of other issues such as cases of administrative detention, wounding, curfew, the uprooting of trees, and the closure of village or camp entrances. Some specific briefs were developed in response to the documentation requirements of the research unit or for campaigns against particular violations that the organization was to start launching in the early 1990s: here, Batrawi lists refusal to grant family reunification (al-Haq's first campaign was on this subject), house demolition on the pretext of no building permit (in connection with the work on town planning), the closure of educational institutions, torture, and tax raids.

FROM AFFIDAVITS TO
PUBLICATIONS AND CAMPAIGNS

There was early on a feeling that the substantial amount of information being collected had to "go somewhere." In 1984, al-Haq's database was introduced as one response to "proliferating files." A particular commitment seems to have been felt towards the accumulating affidavits, and this was certainly one of the spurs behind the publication of the organization's first collection. *In Their Own Words* was published by the World Council of Churches in 1983 with the subtitle "Affidavits Collected by LSM." The affidavits were presented by theme, with sections titled "Settlers," "Village Leagues" (in this section the names of the affiants were withheld), "House Demolitions and Sealings," "Universities," and "Town Arrest."

Tim Hiller, who wrote the introduction to each section, recalls that "the aim was to let the affidavits speak for themselves and to provide a fairly dry, 'objective' introduction to each section." At the same time, the themes indicate the political environment at that time. Israel had invaded Lebanon in the summer of 1982, and focus remained on that conflict; support for Israel in different constituencies abroad had been affected. The introduction by the director of the Commission of Churches on International Affairs stressed concern lest the experience of the West Bank and Gaza indicate what was to come should Israel engage in a long-term occupation.[44] And the preface by LSM struck a note of hope for the intended impact of the publication, at a time when certainly Shehadeh believed that alerting Israeli public opinion to what was going on would bring pressure from Israel's domestic constituency to desist:

> LSM hopes this publication will provide focus for those interested in preventing the repetition of the events described here and in putting an end to dangerous trends to which allusion is made—especially for Israelis and friends of Israel abroad. By emphasizing the human element it provides the opportunity for the meeting of minds of people of differing political persuasions in a common concern for justice, dignity and respect for human rights.[45]

The publication, according to LSM, was widely distributed, and within a few months the International Jewish Committee on Interreligious Consultations had published a reply, titled *The Other Side*. This was more akin to the Israeli Section of the ICJ's response to *The West Bank and the Rule of Law*. In its first Newsletter, LSM reported that the organization "had cooperated with the WCC in answering the criticisms made in the reply. The IJCIC have since dropped their demand that the WCC distribute *The Other Side* together with *In Their Own Words*."[46]

The next collection of affidavits to be published was the 1985 al-Fara'a report, which arose directly from the work of the fieldwork unit; the report is unusually attributed to "the staff of LSM." After that, extensive use was made of affidavits in LSM/al-Haq publications, including publishing extracts and appending full texts in the first two annual reports during the uprising, but as Rabbani notes, it is perhaps "surprising" that more themed collections were not published in their own right.[47] This did not happen again until a set of fifteen affidavits was published in *Application Denied* (1991), a booklet prepared in support of al-Haq's first international campaign, "Stop Separating Palestinian Families!"[48] The idea of a campaign was new; while the organization had published studies—mostly occasional papers—on particular issues, these were not in the context of a wider consolidated campaign; there were no recommendations for action or specific demands on the Israeli authorities. The 1991 campaign, like those that followed, combined publications with other communications—posters, stickers, leaflets, and an international speaking tour. Allies were invited to organize meetings and awareness raising activities with al-Haq providing material and speakers, to establish networks with like-minded groups and organizations, to write to the press and to the Israeli authorities or to national governments.[49] The issue in focus—the denial of family reunification applications by the Israeli authorities—was described by Adama Dieng, then secretary-general of the ICJ, as among other measures of "cruel, inhuman and degrading treatment suffered by the Palestinian population" which are "less prominent and remain in the shadows."[50] In her 1990 study, which Dieng's words prefaced, Whittome opened as follows:

> The right to live together with your spouse and children, in your homeland, is fundamental. But for Palestinians in the West Bank, the Gaza Strip and East Jerusalem, there is no such right. At best, Palestinians are granted permanent residence in the Occupied Territories as a privilege, but not as a right. At worst, they are compelled either to live illegally with their families in the Occupied Territories, to live apart from their spouse, or to leave the country of their birth and childhood.
>
> This is no accident. On the contrary, it is the result of a calculated policy, systematically implemented by the Israeli authorities.[51]

In preparation for the campaign and in support of the study, al-Haq field-workers completed 1,609 questionnaires from Palestinians whose application for family reunification had been refused. These included husbands/wives applying for permission for their spouse to join them in the occupied territories, parents applying for reunification with their children, and other relatives applying to join families in the territories. As Whittome explained, separated Palestinian families would be obliged to apply to the Israeli authorities for family reunification in cases where residents had fled during the 1967 war and were then prevented from returning, where Palestinian residents of the occupied territories married a nonresident and wished to live together in the territories, and where "former residents of the Occupied Territories lost their rights to residency under laws and regulations issued by the Israeli authorities since 1967." Al-Haq had been unable to access reliable and up-to-date statistics on the full number of applications made, granted, and refused by the Israeli authorities since 1967, but believed the field-workers' 1,609 questionnaires documented only a "relatively small sample" of those rejected.[52] Whittome pointed out that, at the time of her study, the issue of separated Palestinian families was a "relatively unknown and unpublicised subject." The campaign was designed to change that. The subject was low-profile in terms of the attention it attracted, but it was devastating—immediately and in the longer term—for the individuals and family units affected. As Whittome's study showed, and as has been shown further down the decades, it was part of a systematic policy aimed at forcing as many Palestinians as possible out of the occupied territories while taking control of the land. The affidavits in the campaign publication vividly illustrate the terrible choices that people were being forced to make, the dreadful situations in which they lived, and what this was doing to their families.

The campaign was new, but al-Haq's attention to this subject was long-standing. The all-important issue of the "right to residence" and the possession of an identity card (ID) issued by the Israeli military authorities after the 1967 occupation—and how these cards were used by the authorities—were a focus for the organization in the early 1980s.[53] Cases had been brought to its Legal Advice Programme since its establishment at the beginning of 1985.[54] Whittome's 1990 study was a revision and expansion of a 1987 al-Haq briefing paper on family reunification. After the early intense years of the intifada, with both the fact and the extent of violations more visible to the international community, the organization sought to turn the focus onto the policy underlying the more visible violations. There was a distinct local impact. Even given the organization's increased profile in the first intifada, Zahi Jaradat recalls that "the welcome was different" after the campaigns; there was a "good impact locally," says Batrawi. Azzam recalls that al-Haq staffers enjoyed this new form of initiative, which was followed the next year by a campaign against house demolition and sealing and then (1993–94, after the arrival of the Palestinian Authority) one on "women, justice and the law."[55]

AFFIDAVITS AND THE PALESTINIAN AUDIENCE

The next publication of affidavits was a collection titled *Palestinian Victims of Torture Speak Out* and was published first in Arabic, an indication possibly of al-Haq's increasing attention to distributing the results of its research locally as the area prepared to receive the Palestinian Authority.[56] Another collection, in 1995, appears to have been published only in Arabic, although this does not mean that there was never an intention to have it translated. This was a set of documents and affidavits published a year after the killing by Israeli settler Baruch Goldstein at the Ibrahimi mosque in Hebron of twenty-nine Palestinian worshippers on Friday, February 24, 1994. A press release issued by al-Haq two days later stated that protests in different towns and refugee camps in the West Bank and Gaza Strip had raised the death toll to forty-nine and some two hundred injured. The US/Russia–sponsored peace talks were suspended and the UN Security Council argued for three weeks over the text of a resolution (904 of 1994); subsequently, an "Agreement on Security Arrangements in Hebron" was signed between the heads of the PLO and Israeli delegations to the talks, which led to the installation of the Temporary International Presence in Hebron (TIPH) and the resumption of the Gaza-Jericho talks.

Al-Haq's frustration with this state of affairs was part of the context for the publication of this collection of affidavits one year after the massacre.[57] The 1995 publication is attributed to researcher Khamis Shalabi and, unusually, to field researcher Zahi Jaradat.[58] It is presented in three parts: a report and related affidavits on continuing human rights violations in Hebron during the year 1994; affidavits from the February massacre, al-Haq's press release and a comment by the organization on the results of the official Israeli inquiry into events; a record of violations of human rights after the massacre by soldiers and settlers, together with a list of sixty-one

Palestinians killed by Israeli security forces or settlers in Hebron during the year 1994. The publication of this report seems to reflect a feeling of responsibility on the part of the organization towards its local constituency;[59] in the absence of any progress on the situation in Hebron, the enormity of the massacre at the Ibrahimi mosque demanded a public intervention by way of this publication. Also, contacts with the Arab human rights movement had been established and were growing since the organization became closely involved with preparation for the 1993 UN World Conference on Human Rights in Vienna, so there was a growing regional, Arabic-reading audience that had not previously been a routine address for al-Haq publications.

FIELDWORK AND THE DATABASE

One significant destination for the enormous amount of material collected by the field researchers was al-Haq's database unit. The early development of this system has been discussed in chapter 3; in its later development, its software was the product of remarkable effort by al-Haq staffer Umar Ayyoub.[60] Judith Dueck, who became closely involved with the work of HURIDOCS in subsequent years, recalls that she accompanied Jonathan Kuttab to a Rome meeting of the organization and that "al-Haq was further along in establishing the priorities of the database, so it was able to assist HURIDOCS when they were looking to establish a database that would serve a number of organizations from elsewhere in the world." Nina Atallah, subsequently head of the database directorate in al-Haq, recalls her experience in sharing al-Haq's systems with other human rights activists in international fora down the years. However, internally, the work was not always attractive to other al-Haq workers; she even notes wryly that at times "it was up and down whether the director got the point."

The early choice and implementation of an Arabic-English transliteration system was tedious for some, but critical to the standardization of a retrieval system. The database was—and is—key to al-Haq's documentation strategy: documentation was for a purpose, not for its own sake. Joanna Oyediran, who joined al-Haq as a researcher in 1994, notes the tensions that could arise here:

> The field-workers are going out there and there are so many awful things happening, they're taking affidavits and questionnaires, all this information is to show the consistency of a pattern, but it can be frustrating. Sometimes it must have felt like the researchers were just sitting on it. At least at al-Haq it was going into the database and going out as statistics.

Oyediran was one of a number of staffers who suggested that the work would have benefited from a greater integration of the field and legal research work. Nevertheless, standing by itself, the fieldwork unit was an extraordinary accomplishment for the organization. Coordinator Khaled Batrawi gave training courses on fact-finding in different international fora.[61] When other Palestinian human rights organizations became established, al-Haq field-workers helped with their fact-finding and documentation strategies; they gave talks at schools and universities, and they distributed al-Haq's *Know Your Rights* series of information booklets discussed further below, which were published only in Arabic and dealt with a mixture of internal human rights issues and rights related to the occupation authorities.[62] By the early 1990s, field-workers were also trained as paralegals, joining with al-Haq's legal services unit to provide legal advice on recurrent issues (such as family reunification) in offices in Hebron and Nablus for those for whom travel to al-Haq's Ramallah office was becoming increasingly difficult and expensive. Fateh Azzam notes the change in the field-workers' role in this regard: "At first, they were out in the field to get information and bring it back to al-Haq; now, we thought of them as extensions of al-Haq in the different areas, distributing *Know Your Rights* and other publications, working as paralegals in the offices outside Ramallah, a dissemination point."

In the end, Rabbani credits al-Haq's field research efforts and methodology as the most important factor in building the organization's credibility. "At the end of the day, it was because al-Haq got all its information from the source, the field, and did it in a very professional way. If anyone wanted to check out the validity of the affidavits they'd come back with the same information." The position of (almost) never intervening before documenting an event itself, he notes, "while seemingly paranoid, [. . .] was not an inappropriate response to the accurate fear that one careless mistake by a Palestinian human rights organisation would undermine its entire record and severely compromise its reputation."[63] Rabbani reports personally retaining "a morbid fear of inaccuracy drilled into me at al-Haq."

Jonathan Kuttab is particularly proud, not only of LSM/al-Haq's reputation for accuracy, but also of a wider diffusion of the values of accuracy and documentation in Palestinian society and a greater readiness on the part of foreign actors to accept Palestinian statements as true. Developments in the first intifada also forced the fact of violations by the Israeli occupation forces into the consciousness of the international media and their audiences. It provoked a development in al-Haq's research and publication strategy discussed further below.

PUBLISHING ON PRISONS

One of the methodological consequences of al-Haq's approach was an overall caution in drawing conclusions once the facts had been investigated; understatement, according to Kuttab, was the order of the day. Shehadeh relates this caution to the sustainability of the organization: "We were so careful; we weighed at every stage, what could we say at any certain point in time." This shows in the tone of al-Haq's publications, and one example often given by those who worked with LSM in the early and mid-1980s was how long it took the organization to use the word *torture*.

In particular, using *torture* in the title of the 1985 report on al-Fara'a prison was a huge step for the young organization: as Shehaheh remembered, "Could we get away with it? If not, they'd close us down." This particular milestone was passed at the prompting of Niall MacDermot of the ICJ, which copublished the report. MacDermot had been on the drafting committee of the Declaration against Torture, adopted by the UN General Assembly in 1975, and the ICJ under his leadership had assisted in the drafting of the Convention against Torture.[64] The CAT opened for signature and ratification in December 1984, just over a month before the ICJ/LSM report was published. The timing was significant; "the word *torture* was being defined and criminalized at an international level, it was an international story," remembers Mona Rishmawi. Kuttab recalls MacDermot "taking me to task for al-Haq being so careful about being neutral" and observing that "yes, we have to be objective, but I don't think we have to be neutral; there is a point when torture is torture, and you're not neutral when you're dealing with either the torturer or the victim." Some years later, al-Haq was still struggling with this balance in its presentation of its material to Palestinian constituency. After a 1987 press conference, al-Haq took issue with one press report that suggested al-Haq "suffers from objectivity to the extent that they have started to consider themselves as any neutral and outside party, and not a Palestinian party concerned with Palestinian human rights."[65]

LSM had in fact published an earlier report on al-Fara'a in April 1984, a nine-sided paper titled "A Report on the Treatment of Security Prisoners at the West Bank Prison of al-Fara'a." The former British army camp had been brought into use by the Israeli occupation authorities to detain some of the many Palestinians arrested during widespread protest against the dismissal of West Bank mayors in 1982; those taken to al-Fara'a "would be kept, without interrogation, for the eighteen days allowed by Military Order 378 and then released."[66] This was part of a policy introduced under the Israeli chief of staff in April 1982, "to act with force against the agitators and to imprison them at every opportunity."[67] Arresting them, imprisoning them for the period allowed under military orders, releasing them, and rearresting them was, along with other measures, part of a policy of *tertur*.[68] In the autumn of 1983, interrogation rooms were constructed, and the prison began to be used for investigation and interrogation. Another reason for concern was that the majority of the 250 prisoners being held there then were aged fifteen to eighteen.[69] LSM's concern had been shared by elements in Israeli society; ACRI held a press conference in March 1984, and there had been a petition to the High Court of Justice asking for "an injunction against the military commander of the area to order him to show cause why those working on his behalf will not be prevented from applying a system of beatings and torture in al-Fara'a, and why those responsible for torture should not be brought to trial."[70] By the summer of 1984, two Israeli army officers—one the head of the prison named in extracts from affidavits in al-Haq's report—had been charged and sentenced in military court.[71] Israeli journalists had been interested, reporting ACRI's allegations of "torture, brutality and inhuman conditions" to break the detainees.[72] For its part, LSM had for the first time held a press conference in its office, bringing young former detainees from the prison to present their experiences or, as Shehadeh put it, "to tell their stories in addition to our affidavits." In this first report, however, LSM did not itself describe the treatment as torture, ascribing this description of their treatment to the words of the detainees themselves.

As discussed in chapter 3, the furor over the release of the 1985 report seems to have stemmed from the timing and direct international exposure that Israeli diplomatic officials experienced in Geneva at the Human Rights Commission; perhaps it owed some of its impact precisely to the fact that, although still understated in its introduction and explanations of the different sections, the prevailing voice was that of the detainees, directly and forcefully presented to the public. The motive behind publication of this report in collaboration with the ICJ was explained by LSM as follows:

> The evidence demonstrates that al-Fara'a is intended to operate as an intimidation centre to which groups—mainly of young people—are taken for a certain period, given harsh treatment and later tried on the basis of confessions that appear in many cases to be extracted against their will, then released. This being the case, it is the function which al-Fara'a is intended to serve which constitutes the violation that must be stopped.[73]

This passage illustrates LSM/Al-Haq's methodological focus on the "why" as the context for the "what" of human rights violations that came to its attention. The aim of the practices at al-Fara'a appeared to be not "the obtaining of information relating to specific events" but rather "humiliation and intimidation." Therefore, "detention at al-Far'a should be understood, we believe, in the context of other measures aimed at controlling the West Bank population, such as curfews, house demolitions and the withdrawal of basic services from whole neighbourhoods."[74]

A second report on the conditions in which political prisoners were held was issued in October 1984, this time in the newly opened Jnaid prison near Nablus that the authorities had presented as a response to overcrowding in other West Bank prisons when they opened it in June 1984.[75] In this case, the prisoners were mostly under forty years of age and serving sentences of ten years or more. The prisoners had made attempts to improve their conditions, including interventions with the director, Israeli prison authorities, and the minister of the interior. They had declared a hunger strike, which lasted for twelve days and drew support from prisoners in other facilities and from members of the wider population, who variously held sit-ins and general strikes in solidarity. The LSM report included the list of the prisoners' demands and the response from the prison director. The twelve-page paper publication, similar in physical form to the 1984 al-Fara'a report, reviewed each area of concern: overcrowding; deprivation of exercise, medical services, and food; use of gas, punishment, and control; restrictions on religious worship; and isolation from the outside world and the prevention of social contact. It did not extract or reproduce affidavits, but referred instead to reports from prisoners; LSM members had also visited the prison. As with its previous report, LSM did not make specific demands or recommendations; it set out the facts and compared them with existing legal standards.

One development in the Jnaid report was the reference to international legal standards. The 1984 al-Fara'a report had reviewed the organization's concerns at al-Fara'a in reference to Israeli military orders regulating prison and arrest and detention procedures in the West Bank.[76] The Jnaid report, a few months later, reviewed each area of concern not only in relation to Israeli military orders, but also in light of international standards; these included, in relation to the medical treatment given to prisoners, the Fourth Geneva Convention and the UN Principles of Medical Ethics (1982), and more systematically, the relevant provisions of the UN Standard Minimum Rules for the Treatment of Prisoners. In explaining its reliance on these rules, LSM explained that "they do not constitute binding law, but are internationally recognised principles."[77] The 1985 al-Fara'a report was almost entirely free of legal references, letting the affidavits speak for themselves.[78] The structural intent (control and intimidation of wider Palestinian society) was clear.

Al-Haq's next reports on prisons were to be produced in the first year of the intifada, as thousands were arrested and new facilities opened by the Israeli authorities; the organization later reported that between December 1987 and May 1992, Israel had detained more than eighty thousand Palestinians.[79] In May 1988, al-Haq produced "Dhahiriyyeh: Centre for Punishment," a thirteen-page paper about another former British army camp near Hebron used to hold thousands of detainees and where the conditions and treatment amounted, according to LSM, to "collective punishment and other degrading and cruel treatment." Al-Haq invoked not only the Standard Minimum Rules and the Fourth Geneva Convention but also the UDHR and the ICCPR, in relation to the prohibition on torture. Israel had signed the ICCPR but had not yet ratified it. Unlike in its previous prison reports, Al-Haq provided a conclusion. Noting that the already notorious conditions and the treatment at the detention center were clearly intended to be punitive, it concluded: "It appears that the Israeli authorities believe that by so treating detainees it can break their spirit. The prison is thus one of the means used in an attempt to force the Palestinians into submission."[80]

It was in the next prison report in August 1988 that al-Haq made its first explicit demand in a publication. The demand was in the title: "Ansar 3: A Case for Closure." This prison, in an Israeli military camp in the Negev desert near the border with Egypt, was at the time of the report holding twenty-five hundred Palestinians, mostly in administrative detention. Officially called Ketziot, it was known to Palestinians as Ansar 3 in invocation of the Ansar prison camp set up by the Israeli occupying authorities in South Lebanon in 1982. Explaining why the analogy was appropriate despite the fact that torture was not a feature at Ansar 3, al-Haq drew attention to the physical isolation of the camp, to the rationale—the rounding up of huge numbers of Palestinians, the attempt to break their spirit and the spirit of wider society—and to the treatment dealt the detainees aimed at humiliating and degrading them. Four of al-Haq's field-workers were held here under administrative detention, and the thirty-three-page report was dedicated to them. The legal standards it invoked were similar to those referred to in the Dhahiriyyeh report, with the important addition of the fact that holding Palestinians from the occupied territories inside Israel was in direct violation of the Fourth Geneva Convention. Al-Haq concluded that conditions at the prison constituted "inhuman and degrading treatment" and called for its immediate closure.

STRUCTURAL WORK

The Ansar 3 report was to be al-Haq's last effort in this direction; for the next few years, prison conditions were dealt with in chapters in the annual reports of human rights violations during the uprising. The prison reports had arisen from fieldwork, and while LSM/al-Haq had placed them in an overall contextual (and structural) framework, they were something of an exception to its more usual work. Al-Haq's briefing papers issued on the occasion of the twentieth anniversary of the Israeli occupation are illustrative of its dominant focus and cover the following topics: the West Bank legal system and structure, the military court system, administrative measures of punishment and control, trade unions under Israeli occupation, and the suppression of academic, political, and cultural life. Some of these resulted in publications.[81]

Al-Haq's primary focus can also be seen in the structure of its 1988 conference titled "International Law and the Administration of Occupied Territories," mentioned in Chapter 4. The "administration" focus explored issues such as financial administration and taxation, economic policies, the exploitation of land and water resources, trade unions, and the provision of services by mass-based Palestinian organizations. The conference also explored the international law implications of prolonged military occupation, and strategies of enforcement, through Israeli fora and UN-based mechanisms.[82] The object of the conference was to bring experts to discuss matters that were not, at that time, resolved or even particularly under discussion. It was the first international law conference to be held in the territories, and Emma Playfair spent a couple of years contacting different experts, meeting with them, and explaining the challenges and the objectives of the conference. She had some tough meetings, and at least some considered it a political minefield. Those who did come found themselves in East Jerusalem at the start of the first intifada, confronted with daily news of human rights violations while considering their brief on the underlying structure of the occupation. Abdel Karim Kan'an remembers driving people back and forth to present testimony: "We really wanted this conference to be successful, we worked so hard for it." For Shehadeh, the event was a breakthrough. A decade after the event, Playfair pointed to an impact wider than the particular situation in the occupied territories: "The published views of legal experts are an important source of international and customary law, so the expert contributions to this conference will directly contribute to the development and explanation of humanitarian law."[83] So many outstanding people did come, she explains, "all due to al-Haq's fact-finding—exposing the violations and the wrongfulness of the Israeli view on the law—that was al-Haq's contribution."

LSM/al-Haq's focus from its early years on structural violations and on collective and economic and social rights was a very different start than was the case, for example, with the Israeli human rights organization B'Tselem, established in 1989 in the middle of the intifada. Former B'Tselem staffer and director Eitan Felner notes that "like many traditional human rights groups around the world, its work initially focused on civil and political rights."[84] Al-Haq, in contrast, was not a "traditional human rights group."[85] Its work started and ended with the structural context of the violations it addressed. Rishmawi recalls that LSM's turn to a more explicitly human rights focus in these and other matters was prompted by Shehadeh's participation in what Tolley has referred to as "a major 1981 conference at The Hague, [where] the ICJ connected development to the rule of law."[86] From these ideas, says Rishmawi, "we started thinking in terms of rights as collective and individual." According to Tolley, "ICJ advocacy of development as a human right sought to bridge a major North-South divide."[87]

Prime examples of LSM's early publications include the study on *Civilian Administration* in the West Bank, the study on Israel's Road Plan No. 50 for the West Bank, and an LSM occasional paper by Rishmawi on planning and land use. In 1985, Shehadeh published what he described as a sequel to *The West Bank and the Rule of Law*: "It is the thesis of this study," he told his readers, "that the policy which Israel has been pursing in the West Bank is intended to drive out the Palestinians, to take over their land, and eventually to annex the occupied territories."[88] *Occupier's Law* was published by the Institute for Palestine Studies in Washington, although the title rubric indicated that it had been prepared for al-Haq.

The book deals in section one with "the various methods by which the alienation of 40% of the land of the West Bank has been brought about" and how Palestinian use of the remaining land was restricted. The second section looks at the administrative structures and the three judicial systems in operation—the local courts, which were by now precluded from hearing any cases against any Israelis, soldiers or settlers; the military courts and tribunals; and Israeli (settler) civilian courts in the West Bank—all of which underpinned Shehadeh's conclusion that "the status which Israel has accorded to the Palestinians in the West Bank is that of permanent alien residents."[89] The last section looks at the "extensive powers of granting to Palestinians permits necessary for running the day-to-day business of society," justified by Israel's concept of "security," but used to "stifle the growth of the Palestinian population" in any number of economic, social, and cultural ways. An overview of human rights violations is also included in this last section. The second edition of *Occupier's Law* included a new introduction covering international legal instruments applicable in the territories and describing the "four legislative stages of the occupation" to date. In relation to the fourth and then current one, which he dated from 1981, Shehadeh observed that this stage had "primarily involved planning regulations pertaining to the use of the extensive areas of land that were and are being acquired for Jewish settlement" as well as amendments to tax laws that were increasing revenues to Israel from the occupied territories.[90]

These findings described not only what was, but indeed what was to come. In 2008 Shehadeh gave perhaps his most concise and lucid account connecting Israel's colonial plans, as perceived in the eighties by Shehadeh and his colleagues, to the dismal results of the Oslo peace process and beyond. In particular reference to the Road Plan proposed in 1984, to be implemented to connect settlement blocs and urban centers inside Israel, bypassing Palestinian towns, he notes: "Oslo confirmed all this."[91] The information was already there; and Shehadeh's bitterness at the Oslo process included the lack of attention paid to his own legal input by the Palestinian team ignoring the warnings of Israel's colonial aspirations that had been voiced so conscientiously and energetically over the previous years.

Back in 1986, LSM/al-Haq had published its own in-house study on planning and land use,[92] and was to follow this up with the unusual step of commissioning a UK academic expert, Anthony Coon, to produce a study on town planning in the West Bank. Coon conducted substantial fieldwork, meeting "planners, architects, lawyers, surveyors and engineers" as well as "ordinary citizens" of the West Bank; al-Haq staff who worked with him recall this as a hugely significant project and a major investment by al-Haq.[93] Introducing the book to his readers, Coon conceded that the subject "might seem like an irrelevant distraction from the more substantial issues which arise in a prolonged military occupation." As he explained, however:

> Town planning has a more direct and a more intense impact on the quality of the lives of Palestinians than it has on the inhabitants of almost any other territory. For Palestinians the planning system is of vital concern because it affects not only their prospects of future prosperity, but their prospects of nationhood.[94]

Published the year before the Oslo process was to begin with the 1993 Declaration of Principles, Coon's study identified as "the principal requirement" the reestablishment of "planning institutions which are representative of and responsive to the needs of Palestinians, for these to be adequately funded, and for them to have access to information (in particular the Land Registry)." He also called for "international pressure" to be brought on Israel and argued that "'legal' restrictions preventing access to and use by non-Jews of seized land and settlements should be abolished."[95] If such measures were not "taken soon," Coon concluded, "the world should expect the Palestinian human rights tragedy in the West Bank to be ever intensified—a tragedy in which the conduct of town planning has long been instrumental."[96]

Coon's book was published in the United Kingdom by an academic publishing company, although copyright was retained by al-Haq. This particular experiment appears not to have been repeated, although the interest in having substantial studies taken on by established publishers abroad, with their own distribution possibilities, is also demonstrated by Shehadeh's work with the Institute for Palestine Studies. In the early 1980s, al-Haq's directors were also publishing shorter pieces abroad, some of which were made available (as "LSM publications") as reprints from LSM/al-Haq. These were published variously in the *Review* of the ICJ, the *Journal of Palestine Studies, Le Monde Diplomatique, Hawliat Siyasiyah*, and in volumes of collected articles. They focused on structural issues: settlements, the juridical status of the occupied territories, land law, and (in Kuttab's case) the acquisition of property.[97] The first research paper on a specific legal topic by a researcher other than LSM's directors came about through a request from the UK-based *Index on Censorship*. A US volunteer at al-Haq prepared the article on military censorship in the West Bank, published by *Index* in 1984 and reprinted by LSM in 1985. A series of columns and correspondence in the London-based *Jewish Chronicle* criticizing the article and *Index*'s decision to publish it, and responses to these critiques, were appended to al-Haq's printing of the article in late 1986, together with letters sent by Raja Shehadeh to both; this appended material exceeded the length of the original article.[98]

LSM/al-Haq was not a research institute, and it was sometimes at pains to stress that it did not consider theory for theory's sake, but by 1986 the organization had found a format for its own research publications. The early occasional papers examined particular legal issues developing in Israeli policy and practice. The exception in the early years was the paper by Rishmawi mentioned previously, which provided a historical examination of the legal status of Palestinian women, and—also exceptionally—was published in Arabic.[99]

Playfair's 1987 paper on house demolition and sealing, the fifth in the series, evolved from a "full report" that had been sent by al-Haq to various organizations abroad in August 1986.[100] Al-Haq had

> noted with alarm a dramatic increase since 1985 in the number of houses demolished or sealed by the Israeli authorities as a punitive or allegedly deterrent measure, following the arrest of one of the inhabitants of the house. [. . .]
>
> Amongst houses demolished by the Israeli authorities in 1986 were those in the West Bank village of Burqa reported in Newsletter 12. These demolitions followed the rejection by the Israeli High Court of Justice on 24 March 1986 of petitions made by the owners and inhabitants of the three houses. [. . .] On reading the High Court decision in the Burqa case, al-Haq came to the conclusion that neither the efforts it has exerted in the past [. . .] to oppose this practice, nor the appeals to the High

Court, have been to any effect. It concluded that the greatest hope of ending the practice lay in the efforts of members of the international community concerned with human rights and justice.

In the light of these developments, al-Haq decided to prepare a thorough brief about this practice for human rights organisations and individuals locally and worldwide, and to ask them, if they concur with al-Haq's view that this is an illegal, arbitrary and oppressive measure, to intervene in whatever way they consider most likely to achieve the cessation of the practice.[101]

Al-Haq's cautious and understated mode of addressing its local and international allies is evident here, as is its emphasis on the steps it had taken prior to this "intervention by study" and why it felt it necessary to proceed in this manner. Playfair's paper proceeded methodically through the justifications for the practice presented by the Israeli authorities and the High Court, responding with reference to "local law"—in this case the Defence (Emergency) Regulations (DERs) 1945, issued by the British Mandate authorities, on which demolition orders were based—the Hague Regulations of 1907, the Fourth Geneva Convention of 1949, statements by the High Court of Justice, the writings of eminent experts on the laws of war, and principles of natural justice and other international law (UDHR). The commentary draws on al-Haq's fieldwork to present cases contradicting the statements under examination and to emphasize the impact of the measure. It appends a particularly notorious ruling from the High Court of Justice and two sample demolition and sealing orders. The final part of the commentary takes up a paragraph in the HCJ's Burqa decision that clearly contributed to al-Haq's conclusion that the Court "does not provide an effective forum for review against demolitions."[102] The Court held:

> There is no basis to the petitioners' complaint that house demolition is a form of collective punishment. In their opinion, only the terrorists and criminals themselves should be punished, and house demolition punishes additional family members. Such an interpretation, if accepted by us, would leave the above regulation and its orders void of content, leaving only the possibility of punishing a terrorist who lives alone.[103]

This is an extraordinary example of Cohen's "interpretative denial."[104] Al-Haq's (and Playfair's) response was that "a law can be interpreted by reference to the fact that it must have been intended to have some effect; but it cannot be deduced, from the fact that the apparent intention is forbidden by international law, that some other purpose must have been intended."[105]

As demolitions and sealings increased exponentially in number and in method through the intifada, al-Haq published two further occasional papers on the subject and launched an international campaign against house demolition in 1992.[106] All drew substantially on al-Haq's field research. A detailed consideration of Israel's use of the British DERs (1945) in deportations, house demolitions, and sealings was issued during the first years of the intifada, along with a rather ambitiously titled research study into the *Enforcement of International Law in the Israeli-Occupied Territories*. This latter, linked with the Enforcement Project, aimed to show "that states have a legal obligation to ensure that the Fourth Geneva Convention [. . .] is applied by Israel within the Occupied Territories."[107] Rabbani identifies this—and a later publication on taxation—as al-Haq venturing into new legal areas including the law-based intervention of third-party states.

LSM/al-Haq continually sought to increase the effectiveness of its interventions. Some projects appear not to have resulted in a publication, as with a 1985 project on what it termed "institutional discrimination," and on which it corresponded with the World Council of Churches' unit on racism.[108] The 1986 program report refers to a substantial fieldwork effort on this, on the basis of which it sought to determine "whether a practice is a result of individual or mass conduct, or official policy"—the latter category being the one of interest to the organization. Three areas of Israeli policy were under examination:

> disposition of land, the allocation of resources, and the use of labour. In each area field data have been collected and examined with a view to determining the degree to which racist policies are being practised against Palestinians in the Occupied Territories, and the short and long-term objectives such policies may be designed to serve.[109]

Evident again are the question "why" as well as "what" and the need to understand the policy behind the practice. These were early days to be researching this angle.

LEGAL ADVICE AND *KNOW YOUR RIGHTS*

One of the criticisms directed at LSM/al-Haq—certainly before it began its campaigns—was that its focus tended to be directed towards mostly external actors and public opinion, and more particularly lawyers, human rights organizations, and activists in Israel, Europe, and the United States. The organization did make a concerted effort to develop an "internal" agenda promoting rule-of-law and human rights awareness in Palestinian society. Besides the development of what was to become a "massive library" on law and human rights for public use,[110] other elements included public lectures and talks, employment of a human rights educator to develop material for schools, and articles in the local Arabic press. There were two themes in this work: firstly, educating members of Palestinian society about their rights, such as they were, vis-à-vis the occupying authorities, and secondly, promoting ideas of the rule of law and human rights in relation to Palestinians' conduct towards each other. The challenges of the first were set out in the draft program objectives for 1987 as follows:

> The promotion of an awareness of the individual and collective rights of Palestinians is a particularly pressing task in a society where a history of social and political

domination has nurtured a sceptical attitude towards the prospect of achieving these rights. Moreover, widespread ignorance of the rights and protections that are, in theory, available to them renders the population ill-equipped to use the law to defend its vital individual and collective interests.

LSM/al-Haq opened its legal advice program in early 1985. By the end of 1986, Mona Rishmawi was sitting twice a week "to offer legal advice to residents in any matter related to law; to follow up cases concerning violations of basic human rights principles; [and] to adopt cases which do not require court procedures."[111] The subjects on which advice was being provided included "travel restrictions, disappearances of residents or relatives of residents outside the West Bank and on the bridges, family reunification, issuance of driving permits [and] registration of charitable associations." Some successes had been registered in challenging refusal of permission to travel abroad, but family reunification was an area "where it has been very difficult to obtain a significant outcome." Therefore, the organization would resort to "employing tactics which may not lead directly to a desired final result, but which may nonetheless contribute"—in this case, trying to have the authorities release the criteria on which it was denying applications for family reunification. The organization set out the incremental development of its positions: "One of al-Haq's goals in intervening with the authorities should be—and is—to clarify the legal situation under occupation, so as to create a more solid legal basis on which to intervene with the authorities and to provide legal advice to those whose human rights are violated."[112]

As demands on the legal advice program grew, al-Haq made a decision to work with an in-house lawyer to train staff as paralegals to implement the majority of the work. Jacqueline Shahinian first took on the paralegal role, using materials produced by the ICJ for paralegals and drawing on assistance from practitioners in the United Kingdom; Shahinian was sent to London to look at the Citizens' Advice Bureau and the Citizens' Law Centres as models. Field-workers were later trained as paralegals, and by 1993 the Legal Services Unit was intensifying its activities in its new offices in Hebron, Nablus, and Ramallah. The Legal Advice/Legal Services Unit was to continue its work even through the organizational crisis that caused the near collapse of al-Haq in 1997. Shahinian was kept on by the board when it fired nearly all of the other employees, to open the office and follow up on cases at the unit. The unit was finally closed by Randa Siniora on the basis of a strategic review she carried out in 2005 as al-Haq's director; there were other organizations providing legal aid, she explained, and at that point Al-Haq's distinctive strengths lay elsewhere.

Beginning in late 1983, for its first three years the "Legal Corner," a weekly column in *al-Fajr* Arabic newspaper, was written by Mona Rishmawi and covered an extraordinary range of subjects that included developments in the law and practice of the occupation authorities, the concepts of human rights and the rule of law, the international human rights movement, and other, more internal issues such as tenancy laws, the law of tort (focusing on negligence), "revenge" killings, bounced checks, and "the woman lawyer and the legal profession."[113] According to a draft report on the impact of LSM's publications, the column was "very widely read and often provokes discussion and interest in other aspects of al-Haq's work." The individual pieces were never collected for publication despite an apparent intention to do so. Revived in 1993 when the organization was staff run, the column was renamed the "Human Rights Corner" and published in *al-Quds* newspaper, with staff members from across al-Haq's units writing pieces along with a few invited guest contributors. A first set of these columns was republished by al-Haq in a 1995 collection.[114]

Finally, we come to the *Know Your Rights* series of locally directed pamphlets aimed at educating and equipping the community in regard to its legal rights. On this, Shahinian comments:

> The Know Your Rights concept was a brilliant method to reach the grassroots to allow people to change their way of thinking, that even though the occupation will still go on making our lives miserable, this should not stop us from both complaining and asking why.

Shahinian's experience at the Legal Services Unit clearly influenced her enthusiasm for the *Know Your Rights* series; in the early nineties, the unit was to produce a number of leaflets addressing issues commonly raised by those coming for advice.[115] The *Know Your Rights* series, produced in Arabic and written by Palestinian staffers, reflected ongoing priorities at the organization. Joost Hiltermann was later to state that the series was "one of al-Haq's most important undertakings during its first decade,"[116] although other workers were less sure of the series' impact. In part, Hiltermann reflects, the series was a response to the early suspicion that "nobody knew what we were about"; the *Know Your Rights* series showed that "this was not just an elite debate that we were fighting in Washington—although that's important—but this is also useful for the community." The inspiration behind the series was not, however, utilitarian, but arose directly from the early aspirations of LSM's leadership that the Palestinian public should have recourse to the law. The first three publications in this series were written by Mona Rishmawi, one a year from 1982, and it was perhaps inevitable that the very first would deal with "The Land," with the subtitle "Legal Means of Protecting It." On the inside front cover, the rubric reads as follows:

> These pages have been prepared to help citizens in the West Bank in the legal means to which recourse may be had when their land is at risk of attack. They have been written in simple legal language to help the ordinary citizen in understanding them and benefitting from them.

This publication urges immediate recourse in the event of "an attack on your land" to the Israeli Military Objections Committee, "and not the Israeli High Court of Justice as is the prevailing belief among the people." An "attack" is explained as such actions as "ploughing, planting, grazing livestock, building etc" by "ordinary persons or companies," in which case recourse might be had to the local courts and police; and measures such as confiscation, a declaration of the land being "state land" or "absentee property" or other of the means through which the occupation authorities were taking control of Palestinian land. The booklet advises the reader to retain a lawyer, but provides indications of the documents the affected Palestinians would need for their submission to the Military Objections Committee, and includes the forms for the submission of an objection. This first *Know Your Rights* publication is focused on local law.

The second, titled "al-Muwatin" (with a subtitle: "Search, Arrest and Military Trial"), contains introductory quotes from the UDHR, which the booklet says that Israel—as a signatory and a member of the UN—should "respect in its entirety."[117] The publication "explains the procedures followed during detention and military trial as based on Military Orders, especially Order no. 378, without commenting on the extent to which these procedures conform to human rights principles." It appends the full text of the UDHR "to emphasise the importance of human rights and in the belief that our compatriots will benefit greatly from knowledge thereof."[118] The third in the series (1984) dealt with "town arrest" (or residence restriction orders) in light of an increase in resort to this form of administrative control and punishment. In this one, Rishmawi dealt with the relevant provisions of Military Order 378 applicable in the West Bank apart from Jerusalem, and the relevant provisions of the 1945 DERs on the basis of which orders were imposed on East Jerusalem Palestinians. She appended both sets of provisions, along with Article 87 of the Fourth Geneva Convention (which, it is explained, constrains the occupier's authority) "in the belief that citizens of the Occupied Territories should be aware of the international law principles that govern their situation."

The next booklet in the series turned to internal human rights promotion. "For us," says Kuttab, "human rights wasn't just about the occupation," but "the whole universal human rights thing wasn't shared by everyone, it wasn't on the political scene." In 1986, the organization had observed:

> Al-Haq has undertaken to intervene with indigenous institutional structures that appear to violate individual and collective human rights, particularly in the areas of labour rights and women's rights. Al-Haq will attempt to confront practices which violate existing laws and, more importantly, to press for the application of internationally recognised principles and covenants on which local legislation is inarticulate. This task is particularly challenging for al-Haq, operating as it does in a social and political context where the absence of a competent and impartial judiciary and system of law enforcement renders the local population relatively powerless and unprotected vis-à-vis established local institutions and centres of power. Current work on labour and women's issues will continue in 1987 and it is hoped that al-Haq will be able to play a more activist role in addressing selected violations of human rights in Palestinian society.[119]

The Labour Rights Project produced the next two *Know Your Rights* publications. The first was directed to Palestinians working in the West Bank and the second to those working for Israeli employers. The latter sought to brief the thousands from the occupied territories who went to work in Israel ("behind the Green Line"), examining Israeli law from which these workers might "even if only in a modest way" benefit, despite "the clear discrimination between Israeli and Palestinian workers." The first sought to build awareness among Palestinians working in the West Bank of their rights under Jordanian labor law vis-à-vis their Palestinian employers.[120] Both began by situating workers' rights as human rights. Both invoked international labor standards as articulated by the International Labour Organization (ILO). The second, for those working for Israeli employers, highlighted the right to belong to a trade union and to be protected from arbitrary discrimination; the first invoked a set of workers' rights affirmed by the ILO. Al-Haq had first begun reporting on its concerns on trade union rights in 1986, and the Newsletter explained its interest:

> The right of association and the right to trade union activity are universally acknowledged to be fundamental to the development of a just and democratic social order. Al-Haq has recently focused its attention on the treatment of trade unions and unionists in the West Bank by the Israeli authorities, and has intervened on a number of occasions in connection with arrests, restrictions, closures and other measures. Al-Haq has [. . .] addressed the Israeli authorities on these matters in light of Israel's proclaimed support for the trade union environment.[121]

Mervat Rishmawi, whose first paid work with al-Haq was on the Labour Rights Project, notes that the project was "focused on provision of legal advice and services to workers and trade unions." In 1986 the organization provided input and advice to a group of West Bank trade unions in their submission of a representation to the ILO regarding Israel's arrest and detention without trial of a number of trade unionists and the deportation of two others. The ILO replied that "the representation was not receivable" because, firstly, "the occupation by Israel of Arab territories in 1967 cannot be considered as having extended to the Occupied Territories Israel's obligations under Conventions it has ratified," and secondly (and subsequently), because "actions taken by Israel in the Occupied Territories cannot be considered as having taken place 'within its jurisdiction.'"[122] These were arguments similar to those that the Palestinian human rights movement was later to face from Israeli officials refusing the application of human rights treaties it had ratified to its actions in the occupied territories. Al-Haq engaged in a detailed correspondence with the ILO, and the following year, together with the Gaza Centre for Rights and Law, the organization assisted two Gazan trade unions in preparing a complaint to the ILO's Freedom of Association Committee after the military authorities had banned them from holding their elections and then, when they went ahead anyway, refused to recognize the results.[123] The complaint was delivered to the Freedom of Association Committee by al-Haq members who joined an ICJ delegation to the ILO's annual international conference in Geneva.[124]

The Labour Rights Project was thus the context of al-Haq's first exposure (albeit not as a direct party) to a UN mechanism of "enforcement" that employed international normative instruments based outside IHL. Project staffers recall that al-Haq played a facilitating role between the faction-based unions, "because we were seen as being neutral." Intensive briefing work was carried out with visiting international and regional trade union delegations particularly, after the intifada began. At the same time, Rishmawi notes, the project engaged in intensive "national work," helping with trainings particularly on local labor law and ILO standards. The Legal Advice Unit was briefed on services to workers, "although we were careful not to take the place of the unions." Marty Rosenbluth for his part recalls "a tension between the unions as a nationalist movement and the unions as a workers' rights movement" which they came across in this work.

The women's rights project was the second dealing explicitly with "local institutions and centres of power"[125] and had begun in informal fashion in 1985. At the time there were a number of women's committees politically affiliated with the different nationalist factions.[126] Mona Rishmawi's participation in the Nairobi NGO Forum at the end of the UN Decade for Women (1975–85) provided a framework for LSM to launch its own work from a nonfactional base. Rishmawi published articles in the *Legal Corner* series, joined the West Bank Planning Committee to prepare for the forum, and coconvened a study day on the conference's themes of equality, peace, and development. Rishmawi's occasional paper on Palestinian women's legal status was published in Arabic in 1986, and the following year Randa Siniora was recruited to establish and coordinate a Women's Rights Project. Siniora begins her reflections on the project in a piece written for al-Haq's *Twenty Years* publication with a quotation from the head of a charitable women's organization who suggested, when Siniora met her to introduce al-Haq's project, that Siniora and the organization should rather "go and do something with your partner Amnesty International" (about torture and other violations) and "leave women's problems to be resolved privately and discreetly by the extended family."[127] Human rights violations by the occupation were considered the proper focus for a human rights organization at the time.

Siniora says that al-Haq's legal and rights focus meant "we weren't duplicating" the existing work of the women's committees. Not long after she joined, however, the first intifada "turned everything upside down," and staffers on the Women's Rights Project, like those on the Labour Rights Project, were pulled into the organization's response to the massive violations from the occupying forces (including against women). Sustained work on the internal aspects of these projects was in practical terms suspended.[128] "It wasn't until a couple of years later," says Siniora, "that we realised that the *intifada* was a matter of everyday life within the Palestinian society, and that we needed to focus on some problematic human rights issues that are not necessarily related to Israeli violations."[129] The project began to look at gender-based violence in the Palestinian family and at personal status laws, as well as the impact on women of Israeli violations such as house demolition and denial of family reunification. The project reached its peak, according to Siniora, with the work on "Women, Justice and the Law: Towards the Empowerment of Palestinian Women," a project which involved a range of women's leaders in conceptualizing and convening workshops around the occupied territories on a set of issues comprising health, personal status law, protection against violence, labor and social security issues, civil and political rights, and education and professional training. This work culminated in a major conference in East Jerusalem in the summer of 1994, which closed with a mock tribunal hearing cases of violence against women and other violations of women's rights.[130]

Siniora brought the idea of the conference and particularly the tribunal back from her experiences representing al-Haq at the 1993 Vienna World Conference on Human Rights and the Bangkok preparatory meeting for the Asia-Pacific region that had preceded it. Al-Haq had agreed to become coordinator of the West Asia grouping of NGOs. In a packed few months (March–May 1993), Fateh Azzam had also attended the first meeting of its kind of Arab human rights organizations preparing for the Vienna conference, while Mervat Rishmawi went to Geneva for a further preparatory meeting.[131] The preparatory meetings, the conference itself, and follow-up to the Programme of Action adopted at Vienna exposed al-Haq intensively to human rights activists and organizations from the Global South, including the Arab world. Seeing itself as part of the Arab human rights movement was something new, and establishing those links was particularly important: "We'd been pretty isolated before," says Azzam. "I was surprised by the welcome we got from the Arab groups; I hadn't realized our work was so well known in the region." A range of impressive activists and organizations from South Asia brought to al-Haq new ideas for strategy and advocacy. Mervat Rishmawi says she "learned about proper campaigning" from "amazing colleagues from Asia." For Siniora, "it was a huge thing, my first real exposure; I came back asking: How can we use law as a tool? How can we refer to international human rights instruments? I met so many women from Asia working on women, law and development." Mona Rishmawi, by then at the ICJ in Geneva, identifies this as the point that al-Haq and other national NGOs began to assert their significance as part of the global human rights movement and to reevaluate their relationship with the international NGOs.[132]

The timing of this process was also critical. The Madrid talks between Israel and representatives of Palestinians from the occupied territories had begun in December 1991; they were superseded by the Israel-PLO Declaration of Principles in September 1993 and the lead-up to the Oslo agreements establishing the Palestinian Authority. Earlier that year, the Israeli authorities had closed off from each other the northern and southern parts of the West Bank, East Jerusalem, and the Gaza Strip, restricting movement of people and goods between them and further preparing the ground—physically—for the fragmentation that exists today. By 1994 the Palestinian Authority was partially in place, and al-Haq, alongside other groups and society at large, was looking to the internal processes to be expected of a national authority alongside the occupying forces. Some of the impact at al-Haq of these developments is reflected in the series of *Know Your Rights* publications.

Following publication of the second of the labor rights booklets in 1986, there was a break of nearly three years before al-Haq returned to the *Know Your Rights* format. The next four publications addressed Israeli policies and practices that the organization was also taking up in other ways. The booklet titled *Willful Killing* set out the elements of this crime under the Fourth Geneva Convention and addressed issues of evidence (including autopsy) that would establish such killings as grave breaches.[133] Succeeding *Know Your Rights* publications examined Israel's policy on family reunification, coinciding with al-Haq's campaign on this, and torture, the latter running alongside al-Haq's major documentation exercise and setting out steps by detainees, their families, lawyers, and NGOs to assist the effort to document and seek redress.[134]

In September 1993, the organization published *A Code of Conduct for Law Enforcement Officials*, reproducing the 1979 UN text, with commentaries on its articles.[135] The publication was presented as "a contribution from al-Haq to current efforts to re-build Palestinian society." An extensive introduction by then coordinator Fateh Azzam set this publication squarely in the context of the 1993 Declaration of Principles, particularly the reference to the "strong police force" that was to be established by the Palestinian Council.[136] "Palestinian society has for decades suffered from the different security agencies under whose authority it lived," pointed out Azzam, "so what is a 'strong police force'?" He drew out the rule of law, the role of legislation and the need for just laws, the achievement of a balance between the rights and responsibilities of citizens and law enforcement officers, and the need there would be for solid training of members of the Palestinian police "so that these principles become a part of each one."[137] Al-Haq's role in police training became an area of organizational disagreement as the Palestinian Authority arrived in Jericho and Gaza in 1994. Al-Haq updated Rishmawi's *The Citizen* in view of the changes to Israeli military legislation since the 1983 original and given that "we are still going to be living under these laws," since "it is expected that they will remain applicable at least in the interim period."[138] In August 1994 al-Haq published the *Body of Principles for the Protection of All Persons under Any Form of Detention or Imprisonment*, a 1988 UN document, with a forthright introduction by Azzam that urged the incoming Palestinian authorities to ensure respect for these norms and to "provide for legal means to punish every responsible person who deviates from respect for these principles in their entirety, letter and spirit [. . .] We must start now, not tomorrow." The introduction concluded:

> Finally, let us repeat here that society always reaps what it sows. If we sow oppression and violation, we will reap rebellion and instability. If we sow respect for human rights, we will surely reap respect for duties, and respect for the Authority itself.[139]

Two further *Know Your Rights* booklets, before a break of over a decade, focused on building human rights awareness within Palestinian society. The first of these was on violence against women, particularly violence in the family, and included contact details of two organizations to which women might turn for help.[140] The second, by senior researcher Riziq Shuqair, addresses arguments about the cultural relativity of human rights as used against proponents of universality.[141] The debate had been very much in focus at Bangkok and Vienna, and the piece draws on documents from these conferences, stressing universality and indivisibility: "in order to refute these [relativist] claims." Hanny Megally noted in the aftermath of Vienna that in the Arab region "one cannot discuss human rights without being confronted with everyday issues of religion and culture."[142] Shuqair's piece is, however, probably the first time that al-Haq addressed this issue in print. Unlike its sister organizations elsewhere in the Arab world, LSM/al-Haq had not dealt with challenges from religion or culture when it started with its work on the occupation. Things were changing with a greater focus on society and with the advent of the PA, which was soon to deploy arguments of "foreign funding" and "agents of the West" against Palestinian human rights NGOs. Shuqair's piece makes only the sparsest of references to the "accumulated gains of divine religions and human experience" as the source of the concept of human rights. But in taking on and responding to the arguments one by one, the piece reads as an intervention to Palestinian society that staunchly confronts any portrayal of human rights as fundamentally a child of the West, a West by which the Palestinian people had long been betrayed, and which Shuqair and his colleagues at al-Haq could not allow to be represented as the "owners" of the principles on which they based their work. As a *Know Your Rights* publication, it is an unusual intervention, but very much of its time.

INVOKING THE LAW

LSM/Al-Haq's relationship to and invocation of different bodies of law reflected developments both in those bodies of law and in al-Haq's understandings of their implications. In its very early years, as seen, the organization was engaged in an effort to understand its legal environment and the implications of changes made by the occupation authorities.[143] Its rule-of-law arguments, focused on Israeli changes to local law and quotidian practices of the occupying power that appeared systematic and policy based, were bolstered initially with reference to the Fourth Geneva Convention and the Hague Regulations, but also invoked the UDHR in support of fundamental norms binding—morally if not by treaty obligation—on Israel.

In 1986, for example, an intervention informed the legal adviser of the military governor that the harassment of prisoners released in the 1985 exchange violated

> sections 3, 5, 6, 7, 9, 12 and 13a of the Universal Declaration of Human Rights which guarantee the rights of freedom from cruel and inhuman punishment and arbitrary arrest, freedom from arbitrary interference in a person's privacy, freedom of movement, and the right to life, liberty and personal security.[144]

At the end of 1987, al-Haq reported a more substantial consideration of human rights norms in an intervention on the closure of a print shop in a refugee camp. Al-Haq considered this a violation of article 19 of the UDHR and article 19 of the ICCPR, and invoked country reports and related jurisprudence at the UN Human Rights Committee, the *Travaux Preparatoires* of the ICCPR, and a case from the European Court of Human Rights, holding that:

> In al-Haq's opinion Israel is morally obliged to abide by the provisions of the UDHR and the ICCPR. While the provisions of the UDHR and the ICCPR are not explicitly binding on Israel, which is a signatory to both but has not ratified the ICCPR, the relevant provisions of these conventions are generally accepted as customary law.[145]

A year later, al-Haq's first annual report dealt mainly with IHL as well as Israeli military orders and Israel's use of the DERs (1945), but referred also to the UDHR and the ICCPR. Based primarily on al-Haq's documentation (affidavits, questionnaires and reports), the report described Israel's response to the uprising as "more of the same, but much more"—the scale of repression had changed and so had Israel's response:

> Whereas in the past the authorities were reluctant to admit to abuses, let alone condone them in public, and would at most seek to rationalise them, the exposure given world-wide to Israel's reaction to the uprising has forced the authorities to go on record defending particular policies which even the most casual observer could understand as blatantly illegal.[146]

Al-Haq's task had thus changed; no longer having to prove that violations were taking place, the purpose had become "to indicate the scope of the practices that occur."[147] Al-Haq's archives record directors and staffers debating whether to publish a three-month or a six-month report as the intifada gathered momentum, each of these moments passing as the uprising intensified to include widespread civil disobedience as well as street protests, a tax revolt, and other resistance. The publication was thus not originally intended as an annual report. Rabbani recalls that its impact was massive: "nothing like it had been attempted before" in documenting human rights in the occupied territories. The uprising, said al-Haq in this report, "has primarily been an act of collective anger" and "a collective attempt by Palestinians to protect themselves against the predatory behaviour of the Israeli state."[148] Shehadeh observed that the report "was a huge thing, a whole new stage for al-Haq"—and indeed for Shehadeh, who was beginning to find the workload unsustainable. The second intifada report, *A Nation under Siege*, told al-Haq's readers:

> This year, al-Haq concludes that the systematic human rights violations in the Occupied Territories, in many cases amounting to "grave breaches" of the Fourth Geneva Convention, demonstrate that Palestinians live under a state of lawlessness. The total absence of effective local remedy, discussed at length in this report, has led al-Haq to reiterate its call for international protection.[149]

A Nation under Siege included an expanded thematic focus and also paid close attention to accountability and monitoring. Its final chapter was on mechanisms of international protection. For the first time, violations categorized as grave breaches of the Fourth Geneva Convention were identified in each relevant chapter. Rabbani finds a "new agenda" reflected in this second intifada report, which came in at 672 pages in the hardback publication.

Within a couple of years, al-Haq's spread of legal focus and organizational interest was to increase substantively. Al-Haq's work on IHL (and particularly on grave breaches and the third-party state obligations to which these give rise) and IHRL (including the treaty mechanisms that were established to monitor compliance by state parties) came together in Melissa Phillips's *Torture for Security: The Systematic Torture And Ill-Treatment of Palestinians by Israel*.[150] This was the result of a marathon fieldwork and research effort that involved detailed interviews with over seven hundred former detainees in the West Bank and Gaza, first selected randomly and then targeting persons known to have been interrogated while in Israeli custody.[151] The findings, together with the analysis of policy and statements by Israeli government officials, pointed to "a systematic and, indeed, institutionalized use of torture both to intimidate and to extract information."[152] The study exemplifies al-Haq's work spanning the later years of the intifada and the arrival of the PA in Gaza and Jericho; it was felt to be a major achievement by al-Haq staffers. Different units were closely engaged with the study: the field-workers, the database, and the researchers. Khaled Batrawi recalls the many and specific challenges of investigating and documenting torture, given that there were usually no witnesses for corroboration, detainees were held incommunicado, they were often hooded for long periods and thus unable to identify their torturers, who used code names, there was a failure to investigate complaints of torture on the part of the authorities, and techniques were used that did not leave marks on the body.[153] The unit put great effort into the documentation. Oyediran describes the result as "a very sophisticated study that demonstrated the richness of al-Haq staffers' approaches to social research."

The collection by the field-workers of the documentation had started in 1990; its material basis covered the treatment of Palestinians in Israeli custody over the first four years of the intifada, 1988–92.[154] As the study pointed out, torture was not new in Israeli prisons, nor was this the first study on the subject. However, "what is new is that an overwhelming majority of Palestinians detained have been tortured."[155] Just before the intifada began, the report of the Landau Commission (but not its attached interrogation guidelines) had been published. The commission had found that "Shin Bet agents had followed an unwritten but systematic policy of committing perjury to conceal the use of physical force and other pressure to extract confessions."[156] Preferring not to use the word *torture*, the report "absolve[d] political echelons of all knowledge and the Shin Bet of any evil intention in interrogation and court testimony."[157] Landau found that "the future use of 'moderate physical and psychological pressure' was permissible on the basis of legal arguments of 'necessity' and 'justification.'"[158] These pronouncements were the target of sustained advocacy from human rights organizations.

There were two further significant elements in the context for al-Haq's work on torture. In 1991, Israel ratified the CAT.[159] When Israel submitted its first report to the Committee against Torture in 1994, al-Haq submitted a brief to the same, presenting documented cases of torture. Israel had not reported to the committee on its actions in the occupied territories or in regard to Palestinians from the occupied territories detained inside Israel; its arguments that its obligations under international human rights law did not apply to the West Bank and Gaza were to be maintained for years. The committee disagreed, holding that Israel was in breach of the convention in a number of policy areas, including in the use of "moderate physical pressure" as recommended by the Landau Commission.[160]

This appears to have been the first time that al-Haq made a formal submission to a UN human rights treaty mechanism, the year after the Vienna conference. It marked a development both in the context in which it found itself working and in its own thinking, as well as a new international focus for activity. The relationship between IHL and international human rights law (IHRL), and in particular the situation of occupied territories under these treaties, was one with which al-Haq was already engaged. That same year, 1994, al-Haq published a study on the applicability of human rights law to occupied territories,[161] and its submission to the Committee against Torture drew on these arguments to assert the committee's responsibility to investigate Israel's actions in the West Bank and Gaza.[162] Fateh Azzam explains that the organization's developing research interest in IHRL—having previously focused on IHL—was prompted both by Israel's 1991 ratifications and by the declaration by Yasser Arafat that "the PLO was committed to respect and incorporate into Palestinian legislation all internationally recognized human rights standards," a statement made to Amnesty International representatives in Tunis in October 1993, and followed by other similar indications.[163] The fact that key Palestinian staffers had recently taken master's degrees in IHRL gave added energy to the endeavors. The 1994 study examined the applicability of both conventional and customary human rights law to occupied territory and theories about how conventional human rights instruments would interact with international humanitarian law. It also looked at the responsibilities of the Palestinian "governing entity" in the event that various authorities were transferred to it from the occupying power. In the preface, Fateh Azzam, as program coordinator, stressed that "al-Haq's interest is not in the theories of law for their own sake" but to locate the standards through which the governing authority could be obligated to protect human rights in the occupied Palestinian territory.[164]

By the time the *Torture* report was published in 1995, the Palestinian Authority's own human rights–related conduct was under criticism by al-Haq and other human rights groups; the organization's first publication in this regard, *Freedom of Assembly*, was published in Arabic the same year. The PA was in place in Jericho and Gaza, and negotiations were ongoing for it to take over other designated urban areas of the West Bank. Azzam's preface to the torture report is squarely placed in this context, and foreshadows al-Haq's approach to the challenges of Oslo and the interim period:

> In the quest for long-lasting peace, justice must be perceived to have been achieved. That justice can only be predicated on a truthful account of past abuses. The major documentation effort contained in this study remains an important historical record and a contribution, albeit partial, to that account.
>
> Moreover, the analysis of the systematic nature of Israeli torture techniques provides a curious case study of premeditated governmental circumvention of the absolute prohibition of torture in international treaty and customary law. A thorough understanding of existing rules and methods of torture in Israeli interrogation facilities will also help to accurately define any changes or forewarning to the Palestinian authorities themselves of the pitfalls and dangers of legitimizing fundamentally illegal practices.
>
> Most importantly, the needs and timelines of this study will never be lost to the victims of torture themselves. It is testimony to the fact that their suffering has been seen, understood, and protested. This, in our view, is no small achievement.[165]

7

——

Fallouts

In January 1994, the distinguished Chilean human rights leader José Zalaquett arrived at al-Haq to conduct an intensive evaluation of the organization against the background of rapidly unfolding political developments and internal organizational pressures. The previous year, the Israeli authorities had closed off the northern and southern parts of the West Bank, East Jerusalem, and the Gaza Strip from each other.[1] The political negotiations that had been underway in Washington following the 1991 Madrid Peace Conference between a delegation of Palestinians from the occupied territories (in a joint delegation with Jordan) and an Israel delegation had been superseded in September 1993 with the signing of the Declaration of Principles (DoP) in Washington between Israel and the PLO. The DoP was the result of a secret parallel political process that had been facilitated by the Norwegians and that set the scene for the establishment of the Palestinian Authority.[2] The first intifada had largely lost momentum by the time that the Madrid conference was jointly convened by the United States and the Soviet Union after the end of the Gulf War;[3] the limited law-based moves that had been adopted notably by Europe in response to Israel's brutal repression of the intifada were overtaken by the US-led drive to get a peace process going. The Declaration of the Palestinian State (in the territories occupied in 1967) made by the Palestine National Council in Algiers on November 15, 1988, seemed a long time ago.

An expanded mandate and the beginnings of internal fractures had put pressure on al-Haq even as it rallied to respond to internal and external challenges through the intifada years. Zalaquett's intervention came midway between the first real cracks appearing in al-Haq (around Madrid in 1991) and the 1997 crisis and near-collapse of the organization. Zalaquett was invited urgently by Fateh Azzam to help think strategically about al-Haq's challenges and role in the transitional period as Palestinian government became a reality. Al-Haq was now a staff-owned and staff-governed organization. This was a novel experience that saw considerable output but also consumed much energy. The nineties were a difficult decade for al-Haq; as Mouin Rabbani said, "Oslo gave al-Haq an identity crisis." In this the organization was no different from human rights organizations elsewhere in situations of major political transition.[4] Bell and Keenan identify how "patterns of conflict, the human rights mechanisms available, and the human rights 'players'" mutate following agreements on political transition.[5] Looking at the situation in the occupied Palestinian territory (oPt, as the West Bank—including East Jerusalem—and Gaza were now called), Zalaquett identified for al-Haq some of the "main variables" that might arise and that "may, in the time to come, impinge on the situation of human rights and on the work of human rights organizations in the West Bank and Gaza":[6]

1. The Israeli-Palestinian agreements
   The nature of the agreements that may be concluded, the pace of such process, and the possibilities of major difficulties or failure, both in concluding satisfactory agreements or in implementing them [. . .]
2. Tensions that might develop within the Palestinian community
   Some of the foreseeable tensions are: a) strains between resident Palestinians, Palestinians returning from abroad and those remaining abroad; b) conflicts between groups advocating competing ideological/political models for the organization of the now Occupied Territories [. . .] c) a possibility of growing armamentism and the development of militias within Palestinian society [. . .]
3. Possible changes in patterns of violations and abuses and in the participation of different perpetrators[7]
   [. . . Al-Haq] may be called upon to pronounce itself with regard to any of the following practices:
   → Violations committed by Israeli occupation authorities, whether along the previously-known patterns or new ones.
   → Abuses committed by Israeli settlers or other non-governmental Israeli actors. [. . .]
   → Possible abuses committed by a hypothetical Palestinian authority or its agents.
   → Acts of violence and other abuses committed by Palestinian non-governmental groups, whether they are in opposition to a local Palestinian authority or in favour of it.
   → Permanent or endemic human rights problems which cannot be attributed to policy or actions of a given government, but constitute failings or insufficient development of the society or its institutions (discrimination against certain groups, non politically-motivated police abuses, insufficient protection of labour rights etc).
4. Possible developments in the NGO community
   [. . .] There may be a proliferation of organizations which claim to work on a human rights agenda. [. . .] One of the main risks is the politicization of the human rights debate [. . .]

> It is also to be expected that many human rights activists will emigrate to other
> fields of activity such as politics, government or the academia [. . .][8]
>
> Finally, it is to be expected that the human rights agenda may elicit less
> interest from the international public opinion and even from the local popula-
> tion, because of competing issues.

Many of Zalaquett's variables did in fact manifest in the oPt. Perhaps most significant is his identification of the challenges that would be posed by the nature
and pace of the political agreements being negotiated after the signing of the
DoP. The severe limitations placed on the authorities of the incoming Palestinian Authority established in Gaza and Jericho (a "quasi-government" according
to Mona Rishmawi) were the subject of much human rights concern, including
from al-Haq.[9] But there was also criticism of the postponement until final status negotiations (scheduled to start three years into the interim period) of key
issues including Israeli settlements, the status of Jerusalem, refugees, borders, and
external relations; Edward Said wrote of "the truly astonishing proportion of the
Palestinian capitulation."[10]

For its part, al-Haq entered the transitional period in a somewhat weakened
state. Like others, al-Haq may not have immediately recognized the intifada for
what it was, but it had risen to the occasion with an energy that saw it through
the first intense years, recruiting significant numbers of new staff, widening its
coverage geographically, and adapting its focus and to a certain extent its output to
meet the demands of the new situation. Besides the daily violations by the Israeli
authorities, curfews, and strikes, not to mention the arrest of many al-Haq field-
workers, the political developments put their own stresses on the organization:
Oslo made it very difficult to leave your politics at the door.

The intifada years had exacerbated burgeoning internal differences, many
of them viewed as politically affiliated positions towards the ongoing political
processes with little to do with human rights per se. Earlier in the intifada, there
had been disagreement on a substantive issue—the killing of collaborators—that
was considered as not based on factional politics, but rather on the difference
between on the one hand a straight human rights approach and on the other a
perspective that took into account context and community, or perhaps was not
willing to isolate itself from "the street," for professional as well as personal reasons. Al-Haq had from its earliest years documented patterns of violations committed by Israeli armed forces, settlers, and most relevantly here, by Palestinian
collaborators—notably members of the Village Leagues.[11] Although by the late
1980s the Village Leagues were of little significance, Israel maintained a network
of collaborators in the oPt which al-Haq in *A Nation under Siege* divided into
three categories: informers inside and outside the prison system (often coer-
cively recruited by the Israeli authorities); "middlemen who make a living acting

as go-betweens" for Palestinians trying to access the many permits needed for routine life in the territories; and "armed collaborators, who often sell land and wield control through intimidation and violence in their places of residence, in many cases receiving instructions directly from the [Israeli] military or the intelligence services."[12] The chapter titled "Collaborators" dealt with the last group and detailed acts of violence committed by such persons in the second year of the intifada. Its first section, on applicable legal standards, described such collaborators as "agents of the state"[13] and invoked Article 29 of the Fourth Geneva Convention to argue that the Israeli authorities were "under a positive obligation to investigate and prosecute" violations of the convention by such collaborators, who as Azzam put it "exhibited extreme gangster-like violence and brutality towards the community."[14] This was the first sustained treatment that al-Haq had published on collaborator violence.

If for al-Haq this was the human rights story of collaborators, that year (1989) another story was attracting more attention. The United National Leadership of the Uprising (UNLU) called on Palestinians working with the police, Israeli-appointed village and town councils, and the tax offices to resign from their positions. Many collaborators also recanted, requiring Israel to rebuild its networks.[15] Local popular committees (soon outlawed) took over law-and-order functions on the street in a resort to self-help mechanisms familiar elsewhere when central authority withdraws.[16] The Israeli authorities stepped up their hunt for wanted activists; "death squads" of armed Israelis targeted intifada activists.[17] Palestinian attacks against alleged collaborators increased, and according to Hammami:

> By the end of the *intifada's* third year, the collective weight of Israel's anti-insurgency strategies had succeeded in turning the mass-based civilian uprising into a militarized underground movement of armed youth primarily interested in rooting out alleged collaborators.[18]

By October 1989, Amnesty International reported that 130 suspected collaborators had been killed in the intifada.[19] Al-Haq cited the Amnesty figure in its own report for 1989, because the organization did not document such killings, for reasons it felt obliged to set out. Technically at this point killings by nonstate actors (not then a routine subject of IHRL) were not in the official mandate of Amnesty either,[20] but the fact that Amnesty ran a newsletter story on the subject is indicative of the intense interest shown by international human rights groups and media, as well as the Israeli media, in this upsurge in Palestinian-on-Palestinian violence. One staffer recalled unspecified international organizations asking for information from al-Haq on this subject "so they could look even-handed." Rabbani reports that "it was informally suggested that this [al-Haq's failure to join other public condemnations of the killings] stemmed from a mixture of political bias and a fear of the consequences."[21]

Inside al-Haq, Azzam recalls "very hot debates" on the killing of collaborators and whether, when, and how the organization should take a public position.[22]

During the intifada, al-Haq's reputation had soared internationally and locally, and this was important to many staffers who welcomed the name-recognition (now positive) that the intifada brought: "We felt and we were felt like a Palestinian organization, the intifada took us to the street." Professionally, as Azzam explains, "if you want to get information about a particular event, you need to have access and contacts, and if they don't trust you, you don't get the contacts." He continues:

> If you come out of the fold on an issue like the killing of collaborators, you "come out of your skin" [. . .] jeopardizing access is part of it and how the staff felt about it—the staff are part of the community too, they're not outside it, you're part of the community and at the end of the day you go back to them [. . .] The debates going on in the streets were going on in al-Haq too. It's not always easy to maintain a strong and proper human rights perspective on everything.

Some would argue that in the end al-Haq took a correct legal stand but failed to take a strong enough position in human rights terms against intra-Palestinian violence.[23] Al-Haq had previously documented violations by Palestinian nonstate actors and was already working on internal issues such as labor rights and women's rights, where elements of Palestinian society could be the major abusers; it was soon to face debates on how to address violations by the Palestinian authorities and their agents and other armed groups in the territories. But at this initial stage, al-Haq was torn. "Do we talk from a nationalist discourse, or pure human rights?" asked Khaled Batrawi, recalling the discussions at al-Haq in 1989. "If it's pure human rights then no-one has the right to deprive anyone of their life [. . .] There was discussion on this in the organization, and inside each one of us." People at al-Haq were enormously frustrated at the attention given this issue by international media—it felt at times like this was the only story anyone from outside was interested in, that they provided no context, that they had almost stopped looking at Israeli actions in the oPt, and that in the end it was all about getting back to the more (internationally) familiar role of Palestinians as villains, not victims. However, beyond the issue of hostile media coverage lay the substance. Staffer Hanan Rabbani recalls "difficult discussions":

> If al-Haq had decided to work on the killings of collaborators it would have affected its credibility nationally; but then if you're setting standards for human rights respect, you need to take that risk. I'm thinking in retrospect here, I don't think I'd have had the courage to think this way then. Now, after years of experience, I think that was the most difficult issue to tackle, but organizations should be setting the example that human life is not something that we decide to end.

General director Shawan Jabarin concedes that "at that time, it was too embarrassing for us to come out and denounce publicly. We were nervous, the board was nervous. [. . .] Now, no, we're more mature, as an organization, as people, we speak on nationalist issues from a position of strength." The questions around the applicable law and accountability were real; as Playfair observed, "It took a lot of time, how to deal with it [. . .] But it was happening under our noses, we could have dealt with it, even if international law wasn't at a stage to deal with it really, that shouldn't have stopped al-Haq. But it was politically charged."

In the end, after months of external questioning and internal agonizing, al-Haq set out in two paragraphs in *A Nation under Siege* (1990) its position on the killing of alleged collaborators:

> Al-Haq does not condone the killing of collaborators and, as a human rights organization, opposes the death penalty, with or without due process, under all circumstances and considers the right to life to be paramount. At the same time, actions taken by or against collaborators in the Occupied Territories must be judged on the basis of the laws of belligerent occupation, in particular Additional Protocol 1 to the Geneva Conventions. In al-Haq's view, both Israel as an occupying power and the Palestine Liberation Organization (PLO) as a resistance movement are expected to respect the Protocol.[24]
>
> Since the Israeli authorities exercise *de facto* control over the West Bank and Gaza Strip, however, they are solely accountable for law enforcement in these territories. The PLO, although considered by virtually all Palestinians to be their sole legitimate representative, does not exercise control over local legal institutions such as courts, prisons, and police. There is, therefore, no legal mechanism available to either the PLO, or the Palestinian civilian population, to control and hold to account collaborators and those who attack them. In al-Haq's view, only an entity (governmental or otherwise) which exercises effective law enforcement in territory under its control can be held accountable for human rights violations. The military government has in fact exercised its prerogative as the sole law enforcement power in the Occupied Territories; individuals and groups involved or suspected of involvement in activities against collaborators are arrested and severely punished. For these reasons, al-Haq does not document killings of collaborators.[25]

These paragraphs appear in the substantive chapter on collaborators and in the introduction to the report, the latter being the only concession al-Haq appears to have made to foreground its position on the issue.[26] It was, says Azzam, "a soft correct position, not a strong one, but correct." At the launch of *A Nation under Siege*, a "confused delivery" of the position in response to questions from journalists resulted in "negative press coverage," but Rabbani observes that in the end the issue "was basically put to rest."[27] Alongside its public position, al-Haq pursued what Azzam calls "quiet diplomacy" with militant activists, "correctly delineating the responsibilities of the PLO and its organs under international humanitarian law despite the lack of legal mechanism or recourse available to them for bringing collaborators to justice."[28] A later, substantive report by B'Tselem on collaborators notes internal Palestinian opposition to the killings growing from 1989 onwards and particularly after the Gulf War, when senior political figures in the oPt and the PLO leadership in Tunis joined the growing criticism of this form of vigilante justice that, as Azzam observes, "threatened to sanction and 'normalise' in some way the 'unofficial' use of force within the Palestinian community."[29]

Jumping ahead briefly, somewhat similar debates took place at al-Haq later in the nineties, in the lead-up to the second intifada, in relation to armed attacks—notably suicide bombings—against civilian Israeli targets. Staffers recall substantial debates about the issuing of a statement by al-Haq (one remembered "a long discussion which seems extraordinary now") focusing around how to treat Palestinian nonstate actors, the authors of these acts. Writing in 2005, against the background of more suicide attacks in the first three years of the second intifada, Fateh Azzam calls al-Haq's failure to take a clear public position a "serious gap to date in al-Haq's honourable human rights record."[30] Acknowledging the frustration in the oPt with the outcomes of Oslo, he argues that "the debate around 'martyrdom operations,' as they are often called in Arabic, is framed wrongly"—it is not the perpetrator that defines the act but the target:, and "targeting civilians for any reason is a crime under international law."[31] The opposing argument in the 1990s, he recalls, was not a legal one. Jabarin again attributes the initial failure to speak out to weakness in the organization as compared to "when you feel strong in your position, when the organization is strong." The strong position, articulated more clearly in later years, is the distinction between the lawful right to resist (within the limits of IHL) and targeting civilians (which is outside those limits).

This underlines a fundamental point: that al-Haq did not and does not take a principled position against political violence per se.[32] Its absolute opposition to the death penalty articulated in *A Nation under Siege* is a specific position. The most immediate international legal framework in occupied territory does not prohibit killing but rather regulates it, including by "organised resistance movements" whose actions comply with the laws of war.[33] At the time LSM was founded, most Palestinian political factions recognized armed struggle as one form of resistance to Israel's occupation, even if after the PLO left Lebanon in 1982, according to Erakat, for the most part "armed struggle fell into abeyance."[34] A principled position on nonviolence was not publicly espoused by the organization, nor does it seem there was a discussion as to whether nonviolence should be a part of its identity, at least not beyond the founders. It was the armed attacks against civilian Israeli targets that raised issues of al-Haq speaking out institutionally in the nineties and the second intifada.

In this, al-Haq differed from other domestic human rights organizations faced with similar questions. Steiner's 1991 report notes that up till a decade or so before, violent actions by nongovernmental armed groups were the concern of domestic criminal law and not a human rights law matter, a consensus that had now disappeared.[35] Joe Stork notes human rights groups working on the Kurdish issue in southeastern Turkey having to address issues of IHL as the internal armed conflict developed and describes as "controversial in the membership" one organization's decision in 1992 to hold all parties (armed groups as well as state forces) accountable under common Article 3 of the Geneva Conventions.[36] Felner's exploration of the debate in the Committee on the Administration of Justice (CAJ) in Belfast points up interesting comparisons with the debate in al-Haq (although Felner's own comparison is made with B'Tselem).[37] CAJ, as one of its three core principles, "disavowed the use of political violence as a tool for political ends."[38] With its basis in IHRL, CAJ focused from its beginnings on violations by the British state, and as discussions increased on whether and how to expand its work to include paramilitary violence, undertook a formal debate on the issue over 1991–92 which according to Felner was "probably one of the most intense debates in the organization's history."[39] Christine Bell, who worked at and with CAJ for many years, observes that "the commitment not to support political violence [. . .] was a deliberate choice, not directly constrained by human rights standards" but implicitly making choices about "the applicability of human rights law, and the non-application of humanitarian law which might have justified forms of state and non-state violence."[40] The distinction between military and civilian targets was not found helpful in this context, and Maggie Beirne reminds readers that CAJ "had its roots in pacifism and was opposed to the use of violence."[41]

Back at al-Haq, the arguments and agonizing and gradual polarization of debates continued as the first intifada wore on. A relatively minor disagreement arose when in the summer of 1990 Iraq invaded Kuwait. Hanafi and Taber here note that across different Palestinian human rights organizations, "national and patriotic motives" (rather than legal ones) led some activists to display a lack of conviction that the Fourth Geneva Convention should apply.[42] In the end, al-Haq did not make a public statement—indeed, it would have been unusual for it to comment on a situation beyond its own mandate and against the organization's practice of not making reactive statements. As the United States and its allies were building up momentum to send in troops against the Iraqis, Said Zeedani, who joined al-Haq as program director in November 1990, recalls: "The spectre of the Gulf War was hovering. The first week I'm there, we're talking about gas masks; if Saddam Hussein attacks Israel with biological or chemical weapons, does the occupying power have the obligation to provide masks for the civilian population of the occupied territories?" When the war started, Ramallah was under curfew for weeks, and staffers found other places to work from, such as Kuttab's office in Jerusalem, and sneaked out to borrow neighbors' phone lines in Ramallah to send out public documents through the European field representative (myself, in London) using the new dial-up tool of email.

Besides the routine and heavy workload, al-Haq staffers were coming under strain from internal disagreements and external developments as the intifada progressed into its fourth year. Politically, the cooperation between different nationalist factions that had flourished at the start of the intifada disintegrated, and new political challenges arose from Islamist groups (notably Hamas).[43] Sectarian division between the different factions was to crystallize around the imminent peace agreements. In 1991, international attention came back to Israel-Palestine after the end of the Gulf War, and political pressure built towards some kind of resolution. Factional tensions made their way into al-Haq. Hajjar refers to the original optimism of the intifada being replaced by "an embattled determination that things would not return to the status quo ante."[44] Al-Haq had recruited widely during the intifada, and the first real organizational crisis, the rupture between the founding board and its first executive director, Mona Rishmawi, had shaken the organization and left bitterness in its wake.

As international developments played out, major changes occurred in the roles played by al-Haq's founding group of three. If the staffers were feeling fractious, so were the founders, who had stepped back in after Rishmawi's departure in 1990 and who, to varying degrees, were ready to quit their engagement with al-Haq. They began the process of constituting a new board. In 1991, Shehadeh formally left on the grounds that his engagement with the Palestinian delegation to the Madrid peace conference (and then the Washington talks) was overtly political and incompatible with his al-Haq responsibilities. He had been asked by the Palestinian delegation head, Haidar Abdel Shafi, to advise on how the Palestinian team might bring the issue of Israeli settlements into the negotiations, given the existing terms of reference. Shehadeh was to prepare extensive arguments for an initial review of existing arrangements, and an outline of preliminary proposals was identified by the Palestinian team (and approved by the PLO in Tunis in the spring of 1992). These included the rescinding of "discriminatory and extra-territorial legislation" and the cessation of new Israeli military orders, as well as framing by the Fourth Geneva Convention and Hague Regulations governing the conduct of Israel as an occupying power.[45] Shehadeh attended talks in Washington as legal adviser to the team, but was not allowed into the negotiations room due to Israeli objections to the inclusion of any Palestinian with a Jerusalem ID or from outside the oPt. In September 1992 Shehadeh ceased his engagement after "instructions arrived from Tunis [. . .] that there was no meaning for the review of the military orders since this can only give those orders recognition and legitimacy."[46]

Kuttab left al-Haq's board at the same time as Shehadeh, the two transferring their shares (as the owners of the company) to the new board; Kuttab subsequently headed the Legal Committee negotiating the 1994 Israel-PLO Gaza-Jericho Agreement.[47] Shammas stayed on for a while to provide some continuity, and also continued his work with the Enforcement Project. It was a febrile atmosphere; Zeedani recalls that "Madrid was coming, and everyone wanted al-Haq to take it up. The issue was how to separate things. We could say so much, but we couldn't take a political stand for or against political action by Palestinian leaders." A few days before the opening of the Madrid Conference, al-Haq sent a memorandum to the Palestinian delegation, opening with a reference to the "established international law governing Israel's conduct in the territories occupied in 1967" (particularly the Fourth Geneva Convention, and invoking also Security Council Resolution 681 of 1990) and declaring that "al-Haq takes no position with regard to the merits of the political process in question."[48] The organization was, however, "deeply concerned" that, given Israel's refusal to recognize the applicability of the convention and the failure of other states to persuade the United States to support the convention, "the process will be allowed to proceed in a manner which circumvents or compromises provisions of international humanitarian law." The memorandum then set out Israel's serious and ongoing violations (settlements, deportation, annexation, and others) and recalled al-Haq's own record and standing:

> We have spoken out both as an institution committed to defending the established norms and standards of human rights and the rule of law against politically motivated encroachment, and as Palestinians determined to realise our internationally recognised rights as "protected persons" under the Fourth Convention.

The organization reminded the Palestinian representatives that in accordance with Article 47 of the Fourth Geneva Convention, they might not concede rights and protections guaranteed to "protected persons" under the convention:

> In conclusion, until such time as an internationally recognised sovereign authority replaces the regime of belligerent occupation in the occupied territories, the present opportunity to negotiate interim arrangements can only be utilized to:
>
> 1) achieve implementation of the Convention, and
> 2) resolve other matters and concerns in accordance with the principles of mutuality and reciprocity, without prejudicing the protections established in international humanitarian law.

The memorandum set out the legal limits to what could be conceded by any Palestinian representative of the protected civilian population under the established terms of IHL which all the states concerned—except Israel in regard to the Fourth Geneva Convention—agreed applied de jure to the occupation of the territories.

Al-Haq had done what it could in seeking to uphold the applicable law. As Shehadeh was to argue, however, the letter of invitation to the Madrid conference had already set parameters that were to govern all future negotiations, in particular by keeping Israeli settlements out of the remit despite efforts to have them included. Certainly, future Palestinian negotiators found the legal approach to be not only straitening but inconvenient. From the perspective of Shehadeh and many in al-Haq, a mechanism envisaged to prevent an occupying power from gaining territory and resources from its occupation (the convention, and especially Article 47) was dismissed in favor of belief in a political process in which the main gain was recognition (by Israel and by the United States) of the PLO as the representative of the Palestinian people.[49] As the local Palestinian delegation continued its efforts, with the talks transferred to Washington, al-Haq made a further intervention by way of an "Open Letter to Palestinian Public Opinion" stating that any just, comprehensive, and durable peace must be based on respect for human rights and the rule of law and invoking the right to self-determination of the Palestinian people.[50]

The letter warned the delegation against negotiating on respect for human rights and the application of international law "or waiving them in whole or part in return for partial gains." Al-Haq's report on the letter concluded that:

> Adhering to principles of human rights and the rule of law, and starting from them in the struggle for protecting human rights and fundamental freedoms, is not an interim or tactical matter tied to the phase our people is passing through under occupation, but is a strategic long-term choice.

Erakat clearly agrees with Shehadeh on the PLO's approach:

> The intifada provided the PLO with a legal opportunity to leverage international law and norms, including those it had helped to establish, in its pursuit of Palestinian self-determination. It could have used those legal instruments to demand better negotiating terms and/or as a defensive tool to resist Israeli demands; it did neither.[51]

Erakat attributes this to "a lack of appreciation for the law's utility and risk, as well as a general political miscalculation."[52] Meanwhile, this whole period witnessed considerable turmoil in al-Haq. There was amongst some longer-standing members a sense of ownership that in hindsight fed into a reluctance to accord authority to the externally recruited incoming management or to the new board, made up largely of academics from Birzeit University, lacking, in the eyes of these staffers, both human rights and NGO experience. Some date the beginning of the problems to the resignations of Shehadeh and Kuttab; for Kan'an, the three founders and Rishmawi had been the "safety valve" for al-Haq. With the staff burned out from the intifada years and increasingly riven by factional divisions and personal recriminations, there was, according to Said Zeedani, "more talk about benefits and raises than about work and the quality of the work."[53] Bell and Keenan list such elements as manifesting in organizational crises—or dysfunctionality—in established and successful human rights NGOs during political transitions even when a peace process is going well.[54] That sort of perspective, however, to be offered by Zalaquett in 1994, was not yet available to al-Haq workers or management. Already in summer 1992, the files show a hand-written letter from the visiting program officer of one long-standing funder, addressed to the staff and board members of al-Haq:

> During the last few days it became clear to me that your present crisis is a very dangerous one. Apparently your board collapses and your senior staff is extremely discouraged. For many other staff members it is only because of their own motivation for human rights work that they continue.

Concerned at the time and energy lost in infighting, he set out what he saw to be at stake in al-Haq's "life-threatening crisis," explaining what he perceived al-Haq's role to have been in the oPt and its impact abroad. Although al-Haq was no longer the only Palestinian human rights organization, it would be "a major blow to the Palestinian people if al-Haq were to collapse."

As it was, al-Haq did not collapse. Later in the year, the board resigned en masse when the staff objected to a restructuring plan; the staff argued that they had not been involved in drawing it up, that it was overly bureaucratic and did not meet the needs of the work.[55] Al-Haq needed a body with legal responsibility for LSM under company law; the previous board wanted rid of the shares (and of responsibility), but Shehadeh and Kuttab were unwilling to take them back. At a general meeting, the staff elected six of their number (two men and four women) to hold the shares on behalf of all. They voted in an Executive Committee and Fateh Azzam as coordinator, taking as their motto "collective responsibility for decision-making, personal responsibility for implementation."

This was the context into which Zalaquett stepped in January 1994, called on by al-Haq "to help the organisation consider the immediate and more distant future, and how its own role may change to meet the new needs."[56] The months following issuance of the Declaration of Principles had been hectic, with workshops and meetings to discuss the implications of the DoP for the judicial system and broader human rights issues. Al-Haq reported that its contribution had been to stress the "universality of human rights" and the duty of every ruling authority to respect and guarantee them.[57] In a logical move following its interventions to the Palestinian delegation to the negotiations, al-Haq quickly published a *Human Rights Assessment* of the DoP, consisting of a comment and analysis together with the declaration, in Arabic and English texts together in one small book.[58] It was telling that al-Haq had been unable to access the official final text of this most significant political agreement and had to work from "final drafts" accessed through two different sources on the Palestinian side. The al-Haq comment did not include the caveat that had opened its memorandum to the Palestinian team going to Madrid, distancing itself from judgment of the political process per se. It did, however, open its analysis with the potential impact of the DoP—in al-Haq's reading—on the right of the Palestinians to self-determination, its widest consideration of the principle that it had often invoked but not yet studied. The organization voiced concern that this right could be impaired in the "interim period" by "substantial changes" that interpretation of the DoP might allow to happen,[59] concern at "the absence of any human rights provisions and the failure to agree expressly to the amendment of Israeli military legislation and practice" and consequently at the prospects for human rights protection during the interim phase, and concern at the obscurity over the jurisdictions of the Israeli and Palestinian authorities and the threats this held for human rights accountability in the coming interim period.[60] These "three basic human rights issues" were elaborated in the assessment in some detail, including that "the legal status of the West Bank and Gaza Strip continues to be that of occupied territories, and Israel the Occupying Power" and therefore "legally responsible for upholding humanitarian standards in all areas of authority that have not been transferred in full to the Palestinian authority."[61] Al-Haq also invoked for the first time the right of Palestinian refugees "to decide to return or receive compensation" in the context of the DoP, and welcomed the prospect of direct, free, and general political elections, another issue that preempted the many variables soon to be raised by Zalaquett.[62]

As for the incoming Palestinian authorities, al-Haq called on them to incorporate the Geneva Conventions and their Additional Protocols and the two International Covenants into domestic legislation and to "respect the provisions of Protocol II in the event of any internal armed conflict arising in the future."[63] Shortly after the DoP was signed, al-Haq announced that it "views positively" statements made by Yassir Arafat to the effect that the PLO was "determined to respect human rights standards as internationally recognised and to apply them entirely in Palestinian legislation."[64] In its press release, al-Haq made two key points that were preoccupying the organization: the importance of the independence of the work of non-governmental human rights organizations and its hope to establish cooperative relations and exchange information with the Authority "without this leading to constraints on the rights of NGOs in future human rights work."

These concerns were to be heightened in the coming period, but for the moment the growing Palestinian human rights movement was joined by what was to become the National Human Rights Institution for the territories.[65] Initially called the Palestinian Independent Commission for Citizens' Rights (later changed to the Independent Commission on Human Rights), the PICCR was established by decree by Arafat in Tunis before his entry to the oPt through an initiative led by Hanan Ashrawi, a Birzeit University professor and high-profile member of the Palestinian delegations to Madrid and Washington.[66]

Despite these initially hopeful moves, al-Haq was in considerable turmoil. The *Human Rights Assessment* had been produced through discussions where often, Azzam remembers, "the debates were fundamentally political," insisting nonetheless that "the legal position always won." In his 2005 overview of al-Haq's history, Azzam summarizes as follows the "rancorous debates" in wider society about Oslo and the PA, which "al-Haq was not spared":

> whether the gradual approach of incremental agreements could possibly work, whether the Declaration of Principles did in effect give up Palestinian rights, especially the refugees' right of return; whether the PLO as a liberation movement can indeed become a state in formation and transform the individualized authoritarian leadership style into accountable institutions of governance.[67]

During the early Oslo years, Azzam notes that these wider issues "resurfaced every time a violation or programme or event was brought up for discussion, and truth be told, it was an exhausting process for the over-worked staff of al-Haq."[68] Being staff-owned and staff-run probably allowed more space for these arguments than might have happened in a more vertical institutional structure. Focusing on human rights implications gave coherence to al-Haq's public response, but the debates were ongoing and were clearly picked up by Zalaquett. For his part, Zalaquett's input clearly framed discussions at the organization around its different roles. Many interviewees for this study either referred explicitly to Zalaquett's input or invoked the choices he had set out for the work ahead; some ruefully observed that they should have paid more attention to his warnings about the risks of transitional moments. The arguments within al-Haq generated by the arrival of the PA (and its security/police forces) focused on two or three particular issues: foremost perhaps was how to deal with the PA, how to treat it, what the relationship should be, and what tone al-Haq should adopt. Those interviewed recalled that the question was not about whether al-Haq would monitor the actions of the PA from a human rights perspective, but how this should be conducted: how to play the watchdog role and how—or indeed whether—to play the "propositional" or advisory role. "Some wanted al-Haq to play the same [watchdog] role combating the PA as we did on the occupation," said Iyad Haddad, "and this political position, coming from outside al-Haq in that sense, impacted on the work inside the organisation." Mustafa Mar'i explained it as "some said it doesn't matter where they come from, the PA is the power in the country and we deal with it accordingly; others said we needed to go more softly, bear in mind this is a different situation."

Mar'i, who came to al-Haq in 1992 to direct the Legal Services Unit, stressed the tensions between these different approaches: "I think the right approach was somewhere in the middle, but we couldn't engage in constructive discussion without having already made up our minds about where we wanted it to end—it wasn't a real discussion, in a way." Nina Atallah agreed: "It was never a real discussion. People were for and against Oslo, but we'd mix things up and go back and forth [. . .] Nobody gave a clear idea." For Atallah, this was particularly frustrating: "I needed to know for the database, the lines weren't clear, there was no agreement on methodology, nobody had a clear picture of how to deal with [reports of violations by the PA and its agents]." There were legal issues to be clarified, including the "central concept of accountability"—al-Haq had noted the confusion in its *Human Rights Assessment*.[69] But fundamentally, these arguments seem to have been fueled as much by political positions as by confusion over the nature of the PA as a legal address. Azzam recalls that, while al-Haq agreed that the occupation was not over just because the PA had been created, "the more extreme view in the organization held that the PA was just an agent of the occupation."

Al-Haq staffers made an early visit to the newly arrived PA in Jericho and met with a senior official, a visit which Abdel Karim Kan'an explained as follows: "We wanted to clarify that we were an objective, independent, neutral human rights organization—neutral in the sense that if there's a violation we document it, no matter who the perpetrator." Azzam remembers explaining what al-Haq was and being met with a gracious but paternalistic response ("let me know if you need anything"); "we had to explain, there may be things that we'll disagree on, we'll have to go on the record, that's how we work. He said we'll take care of it, we're here now."[70] Azzam summarizes the organization's strategy: "In the early post-Oslo years it was to engage the PNA in a constructive dialogue, combined with training. This was perceived to be a 'must' strategy in the beginning, to assure the PNA that no political aims lay behind human rights advocacy." But this was not to be pursued "at the expense of public discussion of unacceptable practices and the strategy of 'shaming.'"[71] Bell and Keenan express this as the challenge for human rights NGOs "to learn how to co-operate without being co-opted."[72]

But it was within the wider idea of the "propositional" role as identified by Zalaquett that more heated debates arose. The issue of training—particularly of the PA police force—prompted particularly fierce disagreements—or, as Azzam puts it, "quite heated debates" in and out of general meetings.[73] Al-Haq did in fact engage in organizing human rights training courses for the Palestinian police and security forces early on, and Mar'i remembers this as a "big issue" and one of two that probably contributed to "speeding up the 'split' in al-Haq or making it more visible"; those against taking up this role "argued that we'll be seen as responsible for their actions post-training, or it might be used as a cover." Batrawi, a vigorous supporter of this step, shows some of the tensions when he describes the argument arising from Zalaquett's report over what al-Haq's role as watchdog or advisory might be:

> The organization was split over the training. I said I'm doing it [. . .] A Palestinian Authority is a million times better than an occupation, and our role now is to play watchdog and advisory. Advisory means promoting human rights in society. The people [Palestinians returning] from outside had a military mentality, some you'll never change [. . .] but there's a new generation, these *shabab* of the police are the intifada *shabab*, the prison *shabab* [. . .] Others said, if we train them, we'll be held responsible. I said, medical colleges graduate doctors but aren't responsible for the doctors' mistakes, and doctors don't grant life. I said, if only one Palestinian law enforcement officer gets the idea from doing this training, it's still a good thing to do, better than sitting drinking coffee and doing nothing.

It was also suggested that contacts made through training of security personnel could lead to informal avenues of access and (occasionally) time-sensitive tip-offs in cases of torture and ill-treatment. Others at al-Haq also supported the training but were less than sanguine about the results. One remembers being confronted at the end of a course with "a young guy who said to me, 'Okay, this is all very nice, but if my boss tells me go teach this guy a lesson, what am I going to do: I'll teach the guy a lesson.' [. . .] It was all a bit different in reality." Another alleged that at some point, "certain individuals" at al-Haq were drafting responses to the organization's interventions for the Palestinian security forces to use: "the point here being that these guys weren't even learning." Issam Younis generally recalls:

> Mostly the attitude was, how can we help the PA? I went to Jericho, many of us went to do training for police officers [. . .] This was the vision and I think it was correct. Others said you don't get human rights respect by training, it's a waste of time. But it was still important. So the result was that al-Haq came out of the situation with the idea that the occupation is continuing, the PA is ongoing, and al-Haq saw a role in building [capacity] and assistance and also monitoring.

The "building capacity and assistance" included not only providing training but also, to a lesser degree apparently, providing advice to the PA on human rights issues in the context of its ongoing negotiations. This was also controversial in al-Haq—Mar'i lists it as the second issue that precipitated the split in the organization. Mar'i was involved in one such exercise in the context of al-Haq's large family reunification campaign, which included building an informal coalition of Palestinian and Israeli human rights organizations to work on a joint position. He recalls being sent as unnamed legal adviser to the Palestinian delegation, sitting around till the early hours in Arafat's Jericho compound in order to provide the briefing for discussion with the Israeli side about Palestinians displaced in 1967. Al-Haq had agreed that Mar'i could go, unnamed, and if he wished to say something to the Palestinian team he would call the negotiators out of the meeting, say it, and then they would return to the meeting. Mar'i's reflections on the experience resonate with Shehadeh's disappointment in Arafat's lack of interest in legal arguments, and stress his sudden, tangible grasp of the difference between how IHL was intended to protect the rights of the occupied population and what was going on with Israel:

> We're not actually negotiating with them, we're rather at their mercy, it's what they are willing to give. Look at how they treated us from the time we got to the Green Line, you have to wait, get a permit, they want you to know, leave no doubt who's in control. This leads you to really understand the Geneva Convention rules on negotiations between the occupying power and the occupied population, I really felt that then, because you have to think as well, "What happens to me after this?"

In the end, says Mar'i, "I only did it once, I told the organization it probably didn't have a lot of value."

Issues also arose over organizing prison visits and the need to ensure access through the PA. And if everyone agreed that al-Haq would be monitoring PA conduct, there remained the issue of approach. Haddad recalls that some in al-Haq argued that the organization should address the responsible PA officials privately, rather than going public right away. By the summer of 1994, al-Haq's Newsletter, reporting a year after the DoP, noted that al-Haq had decided (as standard practice) to adopt an approach of "quiet diplomacy" and gave examples. There had been violations by the police, but "it is too early to jump to conclusions and it is not yet clear whether these violations were of isolated nature or resemble somehow a systematic approach by the PNA."[74] The organization's first press release on a human rights violation by PA police and security agents came in July 1994 after a death in Palestinian police custody. It accompanied a letter to the Palestinian minister of justice and the interior. The violation of detainees' rights in PA custody was relatively quickly a significant concern for Palestinian human rights groups.

Similarly, as noted, Mar'i's publication on freedom of expression under the PA (the first such report issued by al-Haq on PA violations) was first sent to the Palestinian authorities for comment before being released; no comments were received. There was also the more routine matter of language, which as ever preoccupied al-Haq. Oyediran recalls being asked to draft a press release on the establishment of the State Security Court and the news of unfair trials being held in the middle of the night; she titled it "Al-Haq Condemns President Arafat's State Security Court" and took it to Azzam, who changed the wording to something like "Al-Haq Objects to . . .": "I made all the changes but they didn't get saved [. . .] so the version that was translated into Arabic and sent out was my original draft." At the next weekly meeting, Oyediran recalls an intense discussion: "Some were saying that we should never use 'condemn' in a press release—this was agreed at the meeting," but apparently some factions inside al-Haq really liked the original and "photocopied it and distributed it in huge numbers."[75]

Al-Haq's website (in its 'Brief History of al-Haq') refers to the events of this period coyly as "internal disagreement over how to approach the new situation created by Oslo." But for all the disagreements, this was a very productive time with the Newsletters recording a veritable whirl of activity. There was a huge amount going on to which the organization felt obliged to respond. Fateh Azzam stresses the huge impetus to al-Haq's work provided by the political agreements, the prospect of formal Palestinian political authority and governance (however limited), and the arrival of the PA. Then there were the closures imposed by the Israeli authorities, construction of the bypass roads, increasing settlement activities, and administrative punishments to quell resistance. Azzam attributes the fact that the organization pulled through this period to the new focus on human rights law: "The only thing that kept us together, that made it possible to think about this stuff, was human rights law. The commitment to human rights was what helped us get through." It was also one of the reasons that Azzam invited in Zalaquett, a recognized expert on human rights in periods of transition.

Zalaquett's report identified al-Haq as among the "core" human rights organizations in the international movement: "It is generally perceived in the West Bank and Gaza, as well as abroad, that al-Haq is the premier human rights organisation in the region."[76] It had created awareness of human rights values and the rule of law. Its main work had been "to oppose the practices of Israeli Occupation that contradict individual and national rights of Palestinians," doing this by "professionally documenting patterns of abuses and specifying how they contradicted international norms." The organization's "primary target (until recently) was a foreign audience that could use al-Haq's material and multiply its message" with the impact on the occupying power (as well as on parts of Palestinian society), getting back "mostly as a reverberation of this internationally-aimed message."[77] Zalaquett concluded this section as follows:

> From a professional viewpoint, al-Haq sought to uphold the high standards set
> up by the main human rights organizations. This meant: a) to use as its normative

> framework uncontested international norms; b) to base its conclusions on rigorous fact-finding; c) to adopt a style of objectivity and accuracy in reporting; and d) to refrain from taking positions on issues which are alien to a human rights agenda.[78]

By functioning in this way, Zalaquett observed, "al-Haq laid a cornerstone in the Occupied Territories for the subsequent development of the local human rights movement." The field now, he noted, had "become more crowded and varied" with more organizations being set up and some of the challenges recognizable from other contexts being raised. His main critique was of a rather reactive response to various major political changes of recent times (the intifada and current political transformations), although he suggested that the organization's engagement in this review process was one way of seeking to overcome this tendency and to think things through systematically.[79]

Zalaquett's exploration of possible human rights agendas for al-Haq in the changing context acknowledged that the organization was in fact already engaged, albeit not systematically, in many of the new fields of work, as well as pursuing its core "oppositional" agenda of documenting human rights violations related to the Israeli occupation. Just after his report was delivered came the massacre in Hebron's Ibrahimi mosque by Israeli settler Baruch Goldstein, and in June al-Haq was calling for the disbanding of Israeli "death squads"—special units carrying out summary executions in the oPt—as well as working on the closure of the oPt.[80] New fields of work included for Zalaquett "contributing from a human rights perspective to the establishment of Palestinian institutions and policies," a "propositional" human rights agenda "by nature more controversial than an 'oppositional' one."[81] Al-Haq's internally contested involvement in human rights training for the security forces was specifically noted by Zalaquett as a possible area of work. Al-Haq had also already made interventions to the Palestinian delegation to the Washington talks as well as publishing a human rights analysis of the DoP; it had convened a seminar on the independence of the judiciary in Jericho and, in the summer of 1994, announced that with campaign partners (PHRIC and the Palestine Amnesty groups) it had secured funding for the first year of a major human rights education campaign.[82] It also published some "first thoughts on human rights criteria" for the elections that were foreseen in the political agreements with Israel (Oslo) and that used as its main law reference the ICCPR.[83] This piece did not, however, deal with the link between human rights, democracy, and the rule of law, which Zalaquett had raised in his evaluation as one of the things that al-Haq might need to articulate: "Most prominent human rights organisations do not make explicit connections between human rights and a particular political system," he observed, but particularly since the mid-1980s there had been "wide explicit acceptance that human rights, the rule of law and democratic institutions are intimately connected."[84] He proposed that al-Haq might need to elaborate more on what it understood by the "rule of law" and the relationship between the rule of law and the democratic system:

> This may entail a certain declaration of principles about the connection between human rights and democracy. No doubt, the matter may be contentious, but it might prove necessary if al-Haq decides in the future to get involved in issues of political participation, fair elections etc as human rights issues.[85]

This would include the results of "a more conscious effort at systematizing the international norms/values [al-Haq] will use as a reference" in its future human rights work. These principles would form part of its organizational culture and set of beliefs, be included in training of staff (new and old), and be presented as brief texts that could be reproduced in the opening pages of al-Haq's publications. This recommendation surely sprang from Zalaquett's perception of the divisions growing among al-Haq staff and was intended to encourage the organization to have things out in a manner that focused on the tools that human rights offered. The result would be an explicit consensus on internal principles that al-Haq had never really articulated. It was after the organizational crisis of 1997 that the organization seems to have paid serious attention to organizational consensus on its mandate, its human rights framework, and its values. Recalling Zalaquett's visit to al-Haq, Randa Siniora mused: "He warned us about the dangers of transitions, how it had gone in South America and many organizations had collapsed. And although he warned us, we did not learn from this lesson, I think."

The specific issue of democracy and elections had not so far been in al-Haq's vocabulary, as it had been addressing the occupying power; however, it did become involved in monitoring the first elections for the Palestinian Legislative Council, an activity that Zalaquett noted some international human rights organizations now engaged in "as a human rights activity." On the constitutional law side, al-Haq was soon to publish on the draft basic law and was deeply engaged in legislative critique in the following years, often in coalition with other organizations. Probably the best-known effort in this regard was the intense and ultimately successful work by the Palestinian Network of NGOs, established in 1994, on the draft NGO regulation law that the PA adapted from an Egyptian model.[86] Hajjar puts this in the context of the PA's desire to have control over funds coming in to the oPt (after the World Bank launched a substantial NGO trust fund for the oPt in 1995) and its dismissal of (and growing antipathy to) the "operational autonomy" of Palestinian civil society that had developed during the decades of Israeli occupation.[87] The draft NGO law can be seen as the beginning of the deterioration of the relationship between the PA and Palestinian human rights organizations.

Zalaquett's third area of possible future work was "political legacy and overcoming the legacy of past human rights violations," a major preoccupation in other countries including, of course, Chile. In his comment, he noted that al-Haq appeared to see no role for itself in this now.[88] This was not the time for a reconciliation process with Israel; the internal conflicts of other societies posed some significantly different challenges from those experienced by the Palestinians under occupation. The turn to international criminal law after the second intifada (by PCHR followed by al-Haq and other Palestinian organizations) was a response to Israel's sustained success in denying any access to remedy by the occupied population, but it was not an attempt to tackle the political legacy of the ongoing occupation.

Zalaquett then moved on to the human rights agenda that involved monitoring the performance of the PA and other Palestinian groups, in which al-Haq's early efforts have already been discussed. Aware of the exceptional situation of the Palestinian groups, Zalaquett simply observed: "This human rights agenda is the one most typically undertaken by local human rights groups all over the world, but in the presently Occupied Territories it will be a novel one, when the time comes."[89] Similarly, considering work on "third generation" or "collective" rights, he noted that for Palestinian human rights organizations "the specific issue of national rights, as [an] expression of 'collective rights,' is of course constantly present."

Then he turned to "fighting 'internal' or 'endemic' violations and protecting and promoting 'civil rights.'" Zalaquett's presentation to al-Haq of what he meant by "civil rights" is interesting:

> Civil rights are of course a part of the set of internationally recognized human rights. Here we use the expression "civil rights" with the connotation given in certain English-speaking countries—a campaign for the improvement in the protection of the rights of individuals, which does not presuppose that such rights are being primarily violated by a deliberate governmental policy, and which sometimes seeks to refine or enlarge the content of the rights being protected, beyond what is stipulated in international norms.[90]

Al-Haq was already involved in a major year-long campaign on women, justice, and the law, a society-focused effort directed by a steering committee under the auspices of al-Haq that culminated in a major conference in September 1994.[91] Among other initiatives, interviewees also picked out work on disability rights, including the rights of persons disabled by injuries in the intifada and those whose disabilities were neither intifada nor occupation related. The study considered the obligations of the occupying power but also addressed Palestinians with disabilities, their friends and carers, offering a reference for future Palestinian formulations of disability legislation.[92]

The final part of Zalaquett's report to be recalled here is his consideration of structure and organizational culture. On the positive side, he noted that staff had an adherence to human rights values, and to staff development. Less positively, "there is a lack of awareness of or regard for managerial skills" and "it may be said that managerial capabilities are somewhat lacking at all levels of al-Haq."[93] This was when al-Haq was staff owned and staff run, but it is likely that many at the organization would have felt the comment generally applicable to the organization's set-up. It was to be a number of years before improvement was to be seen and felt. Zalaquett continues:

Within the organization, certain key notions have developed, which seem to reflect dominant political internal values. They include the concepts of internal democracy, collective decision making and participation, as well as the above-mentioned notion of staff development. It is to be remarked, however, that the counterpart notion of staff responsibility and accountability does not seem to form part, in any comparable degree, of the same set of internal values. (This is not to say that al-Haq staff does not appreciate responsibility, but rather that the notion of internal democracy within al-Haq means more the rejection of the idea of a one-person-show than a clearly articulated notion of an alternative model, in which participation and delegation has a counterpart in accountability.)[94]

Some al-Haq staffers remember the two-year staff-run experiment with affection: "These were perfect years," according to Haddad, marked by greater transparency and feelings of belonging (and ownership) and "not counting the hours you worked"—although, he added, "some got very relaxed, perhaps it went too far." But as time wore on and the challenges of Oslo and the new political situation grew, the time needed every week for discussion also grew. Some staffers felt the absence of a decision maker of last resort and raised the point made by Zalaquett in this regard, that the accountability part of the equation was not working.

Zalaquett conducted a workshop with al-Haq staffers to discuss the prospect of reestablishing a board. He reported that some had doubts as to whether suitably qualified persons could be found; that some felt that a board should reflect different political tendencies while others wanted members who were politically independent; and yet others wanted board members who were "close to al-Haq's culture."[95] At the end of 1994 and after nearly two years of the staff-run experiment, al-Haq's staff agreed it was no longer sustainable. "It was almost like we'd discovered the limits of too much democracy" said Azzam, while Atallah recalled "feeling the lack of something outside, when you're working in the organization and you're [also] taking the decisions, it's hard to be objective. People are people."[96] Al-Haq proceeded to recruit for a new board from outside the organization and very soon, as Azzam departed for a Ford Foundation consultancy, new program and administrative directors.

The organization proved difficult to manage, however. Al-Haq staffers (current and former) interviewed for this study almost invariably wanted to talk about the crisis (*azma*) that happened within a couple of years, when the organization was all but closed down by its board. As some pointed out, this could only be because al-Haq meant so much to those involved—it was "such a massive thing"—and the implosions were so destructive for the organization "partly because people cared so much." Staff, management, and board stress different elements of what went wrong. It should go without saying that there is no one truth in this narrative, no way of presenting this particular part of al-Haq's history in a way that can satisfy those who were there and that does justice to the complexities of the engagement with the organization of so many highly motivated and strongly committed individuals working things through in a hugely charged political context. What follows should be read with that in mind.

There is some agreement that many staffers (particularly those of longer standing) had difficulty in accepting the authority of new board members (even though they had agreed they needed a board) and an externally recruited management with no familiarity with al-Haq's rather particular culture. The organization was for years, according to various interviewees, verging on the unmanageable. There was dissatisfaction or resentment over new appointments, promotions made, or preferments shown. Strong personalities were involved, and the staff began to fall increasingly into two camps: those who fell politically into the PF-aligned camp and those who did not, although there was a smaller third set trying to stay out of it. This did not necessarily make the second group "anti-PF"; indeed, some of them had traditionally been closer to that political tendency than to other Palestinian factions. Rather, their concerns were framed as a defense of more political (factional) pluralism among staffers and board and an anxiety that the organization itself was at risk of developing a factionally partisan public profile. Significant differences among political groupings outside the organization began to be reproduced inside, in substantive discussions and approaches. George Giacaman agrees that even earlier there were attempts to "get your own people in," stressing however that this was by no means peculiar to al-Haq but rather was happening across the range of NGOs; Palestinian political factions, but particularly the left, had been weakened after Oslo, and this was one of the fallouts.[97] However, many other organizations were already more politically homogenous (and didn't require their employees to leave their politics at the door). This may be why al-Haq was disproportionately affected by the incursion of factional politics during the Oslo period. The factional disagreements centered at least in theory around the political context. The fact that there had still been no real agreement on organizational approaches to the PA, as had been recommended by Zalaquett, was identified by some as being at the heart of the problem. Sectarian politics permeated work discussions and affected personal working relationships. Staffers complained of polarization in the staff body, serious underproductivity, some individuals "playing dirty" to get ahead, others intimidated into keeping quiet in case what they said was later used against them. Al-Haq became an increasingly unhappy place to work.

As for the board and in-house management, managerial styles were starkly different from the staff-run days. The individuals were not familiar with al-Haq's in-house culture and were felt by some staffers to be taking sides in the increasingly split staff body, lining up with the "PF camp." Administrative requirements were perceived as overly hierarchical: "I began to feel like an 'employee,' not an active member in an association to which I belonged," recalled Haddad, in a comment that underlines the regret felt by some staffers at the loss of the egalitarian ethos of the staff-run years. Some staff refused to comply, some stopped talking to colleagues in increasingly poisoned relationships, some found difficulty in cooperating with line managers from the other camp. In the late summer of 1996, the staff union addressed an "Appeal to Save al-Haq" to the members of the board of trustees. This followed one-on-one interviews conducted by union delegates with the Ramallah-based staff to elicit views on what was holding back al-Haq's work and how the identified issues might be resolved.[98] The appeal acknowledged that responsibility for the dire situation in the organization was shared between staff, board, and management, but had a list of demands for the board. These included allowing the general director to get on with the job (an acknowledgment of the tension between general director and board) and completing its own task of designing and implementing a full restructure and related review of job descriptions and salary scales (an implicit criticism of board processes). Significant numbers of staffers complained of an absence of evaluations and a lack of clear lines of responsibility and leadership.[99] Further, the union appeal stressed that the board should "show sensitivity to things that affect or challenge the independence and neutrality of the organisation," as al-Haq's work requires "maintaining complete neutrality in regard to political issues" and "loyalty [. . .] to the cause of human rights." This invocation of al-Haq's founding principles was to be repeated, but it did not manage to galvanize the board or management or to reduce the intensity of increasingly acrimonious relations with and between staff members.

At the end of 1996 the head of the research unit, one of the most senior and long-standing of al-Haq workers, who had become increasingly vocal in his criticism of management and board, was temporarily suspended and then issued a warning. In the first months of 1997, things seem to have come to a head with hints from certain staff (aligned with the board) that dismissals of other colleagues were imminent. This sealed a long list of complaints, some repeating the concerns from the earlier appeal. A memorandum titled "Where the Board Has Crossed the Line" was drawn up by a group of staffers with concerns over the conduct of board members and the direction in which they were seen as taking the organization.[100] This document seems to have been the justification for the action taken in March 1997 by four of the six staff members to whom the LSM company shares had been transferred when the organization became staff run and staff owned in 1993. The six company shares had not yet been transferred to the new board of trustees appointed in 1995. In March 1997, two of the six employee-owners were not available in Ramallah; one was abroad on a temporary leave of absence for a consultancy, and one was in administrative detention. The four present at al-Haq at that time, disturbed by events at the organization, went to the bank to freeze the accounts, changed the locks at al-Haq, and announced that "as owners" (legally) of al-Haq (that is, of the LSM Company) they were taking over: the board was to resign and its decisions would be nullified. The public justification for the action given was the perceived politicization of the board and the resulting threat to al-Haq's reputation and ability to continue its work. They carried nearly half the permanent staffers with them. Staffers who disagreed with them concede some genuine concerns and underlying good faith ("they had a point, but it wasn't the right way to do things") given the parlous state of the organization. Nevertheless, for this opposing group, as expressed in a letter to human rights NGOs in the oPt, what had happened was a "betrayal of trust" and a dangerous precedent that impugned the legitimacy of al-Haq as an organization.[101]

For the next month or so, al-Haq staffers were expected to turn up to work, but very little got done. Those who opposed the takeover (for them, the "coup") insist that they were in the majority among the employees, albeit by a narrow margin. Al-Haq was split down the middle. The employee-owners formed themselves into a management council and wrote to the donors. Those opposed asked the board to stay and also wrote to the donors. The board declined to resign. The fifth shareholder returned from abroad and joined her name to those opposed to the takeover. People remember the fax machine being locked down, stories of one colleague physically attacking another (found "farcical" or "exaggerated" in retrospect), and extremely hurtful personal abuse and recrimination. Oyediran recalls representatives of donors seeking her out to ask what was "really" going on: "I refused to answer. I'm not neutral just because I'm a foreigner; it was really inappropriate." Palestinian staffers on both sides of the divide assert that there were attempts at external political interference in the organization at this time. Closer to home, some insist that Raja Shehadeh was fully aware of (and was at the least not opposed to) the group of four's intent to assert the prerogatives of share ownership and dismiss the board in an attempt, as it were, to save the organization from itself; Shehadeh's support would certainly have given them considerable confidence. And particular censure is reserved for a key human rights player in the West Bank who was approached to help with the crisis at al-Haq but who, according to different reports, played an extremely negative role and appeared to prefer the prospect of the collapse of a rival NGO to the opportunity to pull a peer back from the brink. The crisis at al-Haq perhaps pointed up weaknesses in the wider movement and its allies.

Negotiations continued between the two sides among the staffers, the board, and the management. In May an agreement was reached between the board of trustees, the governing council of the LSM company (the six staff shareholders, "employee-owners"), and the staff, to the effect that the six governing council members would relinquish their shares to a new board of trustees. Pending this new board being constituted and becoming operational, the shares would be transferred to the trusteeship of two trusted parties external to the organization, one of these being Raja Shehadeh. Names of persons to approach for a new board were agreed on, and the existing board undertook to follow up and transfer its authority. A final clause assented to a two-man team to "review the situation of the organisation" in cooperation with and under the direction of the new board of trustees when constituted.[102]

Said Zeedani became chair of the new board, finding the organization in a "disastrous situation [. . .] It was appalling to go to the office, they were fighting all the time and no work was getting done, there were no reports, the library was in disarray, the database . . . " and himself at least initially in a minority on the new board in fighting to keep al-Haq alive as an organization. The review team reported in August.[103] The report found that the most serious organizational problem was "a fractious, insubordinate and entrenched organizational culture [. . .] that is inconsistent with efficient and effective operation."[104] Describing as difficult or impossible "work-related cooperation across the divide" of the two factions, and of some employees with the administration, the report declared:

> This divisive, uncooperative atmosphere results most immediately from the employee-shareholder takeover of al-Haq and forced resignation of the then board of directors in February/March 1997, an event that was seen as absolutely necessary by some employees but as absolutely improper by others. But the roots of the division and of al-Haq's dysfunctional institutional culture in general lie much farther back in the past. The number of remarkably different governing structures that al-Haq has experienced in its eighteen-year history [. . .] is probably best seen as the fundamental cause.[105]

After reviewing briefly the different forms of governance that al-Haq had seen in the years since its establishment, the report came back to the idea of staff investment in the organization, that feeling of ownership that the founders had sought so consciously to build at the beginning:

> Overall, there is a strong sense of what might be called "personal sovereignty," or "staff sovereignty" among long-term employees of the organization, a sense that, as is frequently said, "we are al-Haq." To the extent that this indicates a strong commitment to the organization and a belief in its principles, this is an admirable sentiment. However, to the extent that this implies that staff are not subject to supervision and may not be held accountable to anyone else inside or outside the organization, it is destructive.[106]

Here, the report invoked Zalaquett's 1994 evaluation, and in particular his finding of the relative absence of the "counterpart notion of staff responsibility and accountability," a lack which the 1997 review team now found "even more evident at al-Haq." Zalaquett was referenced again in their finding of a noticeable deterioration in the quality of al-Haq outputs since the events of February/March 1997, some of which they considered "very damaging" to al-Haq. They warned that Zalaquett's finding that al-Haq was widely considered a professional standard-setter was a perception that "may have slipped already."[107] And in their discussion on institutional strategy, they stressed the importance of the current period and the significance (from a human rights perspective) of the establishment of the PA, invoking Zalaquett's recommendation that a human rights approach to the PA should include not only monitoring but also "programs that contribute from a human rights perspective to the establishment of Palestinian institutions and policies." They noted that in their interviews, many staffers had raised the point that al-Haq's approach to the PA was still ad hoc and lacking a systematic strategy, and concluded:

> It should also be noted that the failure over the last two years to evolve a comprehensive strategy *vis à vis* the Palestinian authority is a significant factor in the current polarization among al-Haq staff. The absence of a clear strategy has led to differences, or perhaps exacerbated other existing differences, among the staff.[108]

The report ended with an assessment of the advantages and disadvantages of five options for al-Haq's future to be considered by the board of trustees. The options ranged from the most severe (dissolution of the organization) to the least (reorganization). Said Zeedani and like-minded colleagues on the board fought for the middle option, reconstruction, which according to the report

> would entail the early termination of all current employees, followed by a board-directed period of planning and redesign of the organization. The planning period would lead in three to six months to a competitive recruitment process to hire staff required to carry out the new program of the reconstructed organization.[109]

In the autumn, after meetings to explain and discuss, the board proceeded to terminate all staff contracts. Jacqueline Shahinian was asked to come in to keep the legal advice office operational.[110] The rest of the staff went off in different directions. It was a shock. Zahi Jaradat remembers, "I felt dismissed, it's not good to work for fourteen years and get thrown out, it was a big thing for me," although with hindsight, Atallah reflects that "in the end it was a wise decision." The whole thing had been a painful ordeal. Some of the wounds from that time are not completely healed, although there have been personal reconciliations. One of the group of four reflected:

> The day after we took the decision [to take over the organization], I knew it was a mistake. Not that there wasn't a real issue, but we tried to solve it the wrong way [. . .] It was a lack of respect to the history of the organization. If I had my time again I wouldn't do it.[111]

Zeedani was honored by al-Haq at its thirty-year celebration for the efforts he put in; for himself, he says that he is "really very proud to have contributed something to save the organization at that time." Al-Haq was not going be a casualty of Oslo; Zeedani and other board members (all volunteers) spent months engaged in intensive structure and program design, recruitment processes, and fundraising. In recreating the organization in the new situation ("a new al-Haq"), the issue, Zeedani said, was not so much the PA, but an increasingly crowded field with new and specialized human rights organizations in addition to the well-established and high-profile PCHR in Gaza and LAW in Beit Hanina. Zeedani also emphasizes one very important thing that had *not* gone wrong with al-Haq: the financial systems were tight and transparent, despite everything else going on, there were no issues of financial mismanagement or corruption such as those that were later implicated in the collapse of LAW.[112]

After some months, a new director and some key new staffers were recruited. In the late summer of 1998, al-Haq's Newsletter reappeared in both English and Arabic, although with some differences in detail for the different audiences; in both editions the cover feature was the first death penalty sentences carried out by the PA.[113] The Arabic edition, where the piece about al-Haq was placed at the beginning, under a title referring to the reorganizing and restructuring of al-Haq, started with an acknowledgement that "it is no secret that al-Haq has been through a tough period of internal crisis." It thanked its board of trustees and those local and international individuals and organizations that had helped it through for the sake of the continuing benefit to Palestinian society represented by al-Haq's existence. The English version thanked former al-Haq staffers for their work; that came as the last item. Both texts then addressed the issue of al-Haq's mandate in a manner that suggested an attempt to clarify its normative referential frameworks and especially the organization's work in regard to the PA, as Zalaquett had suggested might be necessary:

> Al-Haq has long been known for its character as a "Legal and Human Rights Research Organization." As such, added emphasis will be placed on the research conducted. Its research will be concentrated in two main areas: 1) investigating Israeli violations of Palestinian human rights and examining those issues which will be discussed during final status negotiations (settlements, status of Jerusalem, etc.); and 2) monitoring and reporting the human rights situation in the areas administered by the Palestinian Authority and assisting in the creation of sound civil society structures.
>
> In analyzing Israeli practices, the organization will continue to rely as it has done in the past on international humanitarian law, given the continuing occupation. We will also refer to human rights commitments made by Israel, as defined by the treaties and conventions into which Israel has entered. Moreover, Israel's membership in the United Nations also imposes certain legal obligations upon it which al-Haq will continue to point to and seek enforcement of.
>
> Al-Haq believes in the universality of human rights and that they should be applied to friend and foe alike. The Palestinian National Authority cannot be exempted from the applicability of the same principles Al-Haq demanded to be respected by the Israeli occupation. Yet the nature of relationship between Al Haq and the Palestinian authorities is necessarily different. We have greater access to Palestinian decision-makers, and a greater ability to influence and convince them to act in accordance with human rights principles. Furthermore, we have a unique opportunity to participate in training the new authority and its personnel in respect for human rights, and to use our credit and credibility in the past and current fight against Israeli violations to demand and insist on proper behavior by our own National Authority. Therefore, al-Haq will continue to offer assistance in the institutionalization of the principles of the rule of law within the work of the Palestinian National Authority. Al-Haq's concern for this issue is at the heart of its mandate and is the key element in

the protection of human rights. Al-Haq will offer all it can to inform the authorities of the requirements of the rule of law, to encourage them to adopt legislation, mechanisms and procedures that will assure the institutionalization of these concepts that restrain the abuse of power.[114]

Thus, in relation to the PA, the organization intended to act both as watchdog and as adviser. Its approach to Israel was explicitly expanded to included treaty-based human rights as well as other areas of UN-related advocacy in which al-Haq was to become very involved. The legal advice services were to continue, but with the emphasis on legal research went a much reduced focus on and capacity for field research and monitoring.

The new director resigned in 2000, and the board recruited former staffer Randa Siniora as director. Other key and long-standing members rejoined, including Shawan Jabarin, Nina Atallah, and Zahi Jaradat. Under Siniora's leadership, al-Haq began to come back into its own, a process at least partly enabled by the values and commitment instilled in the early years of the organization under the "triumvirate" of Kuttab, Shammas, and Shehadeh, albeit tempered by some distressing lessons. When Siniora left at the end of 2005, Jabarin was appointed as her successor at al-Haq, where at the time of writing he remains, the longest-serving general director the organization has had since its establishment in 1979.

Epilogue

Al-Haq these days is rather more of a conventional organization than when it started. After close engagement with the coalition working on the development of the Palestinian NGO law, al-Haq finally departed from its company framework and in early 2004 registered under the Palestinian law.[1] It has a board of directors, the members of which are elected for three-year terms by and from within the membership of a General Assembly. The General Assembly consists of "working members" of al-Haq. These members are approved by the board, the applications accepted on a set of conditions including that they be "active and [...] have interests that are attested in the field of defending human rights and freedoms and to be an expert or academic personality with advanced academic degrees in the field of human rights and freedoms," and be over the age of thirty.[2] The board of directors, inter alia, is charged with hiring and firing, approving terms and conditions, and approving the budget. Al-Haq's website makes it clear that decision making in the organization lies with the general director, who consults with the heads of al-Haq's three departments: Finance and Administration, Legal Research and Advocacy, Monitoring and Documentation. These four make up the Steering Committee, which meets weekly. There is still a regular general meeting of the whole staff, but it convenes on a monthly basis and there is no suggestion it carries organizational authority: al-Haq "encourages teamwork but also has clear lines of responsibility and accountability."

Al-Haq confronts extraordinary times and extreme challenges that currently present bleak prospects for the achievement of the organization's vision of seeing "the rule of law and standards of international human rights and humanitarian law implemented and adhered to, so that Palestinians can enjoy equal treatment with respect to their human dignity, free from occupation and with the full realisation of their right to self-determination."[3] The year 2017 witnessed a number of significant anniversaries: a hundred years since the 1917 Balfour

Declaration, seventy years since the 1947 Partition Resolution at the UN, fifty years since the 1967 Israeli occupation of the West Bank (including East Jerusalem) and Gaza Strip, and thirty years since the outbreak in 1987 of the first intifada. The following year, 2018, marked seventy years since the *Nakba* in 1948. In June 2017, al-Haq published a statement marking fifty years of occupation (issued jointly with six other groups) and noting two further "grim milestones" falling that same week: fifteen years since the occupation authorities starting working on the Wall, and ten years of the closure and naval blockade of Gaza.[4] The years since 2000 also saw the eruption of the second intifada, during which al-Haq's offices on Main Street, Ramallah, along with those of many other NGOs, were broken into by Israeli soldiers who destroyed equipment and wreaked havoc with the files; many areas under PA jurisdiction were reoccupied and—as Hajjar puts it—the PA infrastructure eviscerated.[5] Suicide bombings inside Israel began to follow Israel's "targeted assassinations" of leaders of the Palestinian resistance.[6] In 2004 President Arafat died in France after three years confined to his compound in Ramallah, with allegations of poisoning quickly following his death. Widespread security breakdown preoccupied al-Haq and other parts of civil society. The victory by Hamas in the legislative elections of 2006 was resisted by Fatah, and the subsequent battle between the two factions in 2007 (referred to by Erakat as a "US-supported attempted coup")[7] left Hamas in control of Gaza, Fatah in power in the West Bank, a suspended Legislative Council unable to act, an increasingly divided judicial system, security forces with little accountability, competition between the different ruling authorities, factional retaliations against individuals and agencies, and serious lack of public funds following retaliatory actions by Israel (e.g., withholding tax credits) and Western donors to the PA.

The human rights implications of this division were enormous. In a 2007 consultancy paper on the challenges and opportunities of defending human rights in the oPt, Iain Guest noted:

> After a year of Israeli incursions, targeted assassinations, poverty and international isolation, Palestinians are increasingly sceptical about the value and purpose of human rights. The decision by Western governments to insist on elections and then reject the result has created further cynicism.[8]

Al-Haq has issued and joined calls for national unity and reconciliation.[9] It cooperated with allies in documenting and seeking redress for violations of the laws of armed conflict in the three sustained Israeli attacks on Gaza, as discussed briefly below.[10] It documented Israel's continuing seizure and expansion of its control over Palestinian land and resources and the violations of IHL and of human rights law to which Israel has continued to resort in order to quell opposition to this primary agenda, including the Wall and policies designed to strip East Jerusalem's

Palestinians of their residency rights in favor of Israeli settlers and further isolate Arab Jerusalem from its Palestinian hinterland.

Al-Haq has continued to take on a wide set of the functions identified by José Zalaquett as possible approaches to the Palestinian authorities. In regard to Palestinian society more broadly, as well as cooperation with Palestinian schools and universities (including law clinics), al-Haq has engaged with a range of partners to develop programs and analytical and educational materials; for example, it partnered with the Israel/Palestine section of the Global IHL Resource Centre of Diakonia to provide highly regarded training on IHL. The organization also has a growing sense of its place in the regional and international human rights movement, notably through the vehicle of its Center for Applied International Law. The center contains al-Haq's public library as well as hosting seminars, training, and other events focused on the practical application of international law. Among the goals is the "transfer [of] al-Haq's practical experience in the areas of international humanitarian and human rights law to activists and students from Arab countries."[11] The year 2011 saw the center partner with the Tunis-based Arab Human Rights Institute to provide its first regional human rights seminar (in Tunis);[12] and since 2015 it has run applied international law summer schools in Ramallah for postgraduate law students and researchers invited from around the world. This growing sense of regional and indeed global leadership is shown in publications that seek to disseminate the methodological lessons learned by al-Haq field researchers and database workers down the decades. First among these is an Arabic-language *Guide to the Documentation of Human Rights Violations* aimed at "placing the experience of the first human rights organisation in the Arab world, al-Haq, in monitoring and documenting human rights violations into the hands of human rights activists in the Arab region, so that they can take from it whatever is appropriate for their own field of work."[13]

A second, related publication is in English and not drawn from al-Haq's direct experience but rather authored by a former Royal Artillery instructor in the British army who subsequently worked with NGOs including Human Rights Watch and Amnesty International in field investigations. In his introduction, Shawan Jabarin explains that he first encountered the author when investigating incidents in Nablus during the second intifada, and that "expert reports in different areas are considered important documents for supporting any file related to the criminal prosecution of Israeli war criminals."[14] By this time, it had become clear that the international community was not going to hold Israel accountable for alleged war crimes and other laws of war violations committed during the massive assault on Gaza in 2008–9. The UN-commissioned fact-finding mission into violations by both Israel and Hamas was boycotted by Israel but attracted huge efforts from the Palestinian human rights community, including al-Haq. The substantial report that resulted (the "Goldstone report")[15] noted inter alia:

> The Mission was struck by the repeated comment of Palestinian victims, human rights defenders, civil society interlocutors and officials that they hoped that this would be the last investigative mission of its kind, because action for justice would follow from it. It was struck, as well, by the comment that every time a report is published and no action follows, this "emboldens Israel and her conviction of being untouchable." To deny modes of accountability reinforces impunity, and tarnishes the credibility of the United Nations and of the international community. The Mission believes these comments ought to be at the forefront in the consideration by Members States and United Nations bodies of its findings and recommendations and action consequent upon them.[16]

No action was taken by the Security Council on the recommendations in the report, which included referral of the situation in Gaza to the prosecutor of the International Criminal Court by the Security Council acting under Chapter Seven of the UN Charter, should the Gazan and the Israeli authorities not at least commence good-faith investigations within a six-month period. Pressure was applied by the Obama administration on the Palestinian delegation not to push for its proposed resolution to the Human Rights Council, and the Palestinian side gave in, only to reverse its agreement to defer once the magnitude of the reaction to its decision among its Palestinian constituency manifested itself.[17] The bitter story of the Goldstone report gave substantial impetus to the efforts by al-Haq and other Palestinian human rights organizations to activate more direct Palestinian access to the ICC, as discussed below, and thus to equip themselves with the tools required to deal with not only IHL and international human rights law but also, now, with international criminal law.[18]

As for its work in regard to the conduct of the Palestinian Authority, noted in the previous chapter, al-Haq did get involved in election monitoring after the arrival of the PA, but does not seem to have had the conversation about human rights and democracy that Zalaquett proposed should take place in such circumstances.[19] In more conventional human rights work, it has published legal critiques and analyses of draft laws and the implementation of enacted legislation, and institutional challenges (the establishment of the State Security Court for example); and taken positions of principle, notably against the death penalty since its implementation in the West Bank and Gaza. It has engaged widely in human rights training, and it has intervened on countless occasions by letter and memo to Palestinian officials about a range of issues within its mandate of defending rights and freedoms and promoting the rule of law.[20] The organization—or rather, certain individuals at the organization—is also informally consulted or otherwise contacted by individuals working with different branches of the Palestinian Authority to pass on time-sensitive information about situations of concern, sometimes enabling timely intervention.

Al-Haq's appeals to the PA invoke Palestinian law as well as human rights and rule-of-law principles. The State of Palestine had its status upgraded at the UN in 2012,[21] and two years later acceded to seven of the core international human rights treaties (as well as the Geneva Conventions).[22] There is now a range of more specific obligations that may be invoked and a variety of new institutional mechanisms and considerations at work in the PA in relation to human rights and international law. For example, al-Haq took a leadership role in challenging the PA's Cybercrimes Decree Law of 2017 and the subsequent draft decree law amending it. A comment by al-Haq describes the complex layers of communications and interactions involving Palestinian governmental institutions (ministries, legal advisors, committees, the office of the Public Prosecution) and nongovernmental actors (al-Haq and other civil society organizations), the Independent Commission for Human Rights, the UN Special Rapporteur on the promotion and protection of the right to freedom of opinion and expression, and the UN OHCHR. Towards the end of 2017, the PA's Committee on the Alignment of Legislation with International Conventions (on which al-Haq was sitting, with DCI-Palestine, as nonvoting civil society participants to discuss the Cybercrimes Law) rejected the amendments proposed by al-Haq and others. Al-Haq's comment on this affair notes:

> Consequently, questions arise about the significance of this Committee, the role it plays, and the continued role of civil society organisations in debating regulations upheld by the official authorities in spite of explicitly contravening the provisions of the Palestinian Basic Law, international conventions, and relevant international standards.[23]

Lori Allen's 2013 critique of PA and security figures acting "as if" human rights mattered beyond the rounds of training and going through the motions, might seem to apply here, although not to the Palestinian NGO actors and indeed not, it seems from this narrative, to all the Palestinian officials. But Allen's analysis does give some idea of the different levels at which Palestine, as a weak state, "performs" human rights.[24] At the same time it sheds light on how al-Haq, along with other Palestinian human rights organizations, is responding to the use of decrees by the Ramallah-based Palestinian executive to issue legislation in the sustained absence of the Palestinian Legislative Council since the Fateh-Hamas split. In a January 2018 meeting that it hosted about the Law by Decree on the High Criminal Court, al-Haq joined forces with over two hundred civil society organizations to call for the decree law to be repealed and for lawyers to decline to appear before the Court; constitutionally, the decree law did not "satisfy the prerequisite of necessity" that was required by the Basic Law for executive approval of such legislation in the absence of the PLC.[25]

Much of al-Haq's immediate public-facing work, whether regarding violations by Israel or addressing the PA, is now carried out in established or ad hoc coalition with other groups. Al-Haq works in a much more populated human rights field than when it began. In 2007, Iain Guest noted over twenty-five hundred NGOs registered with the PA, estimating the number of those fitting "the conventional profile of professional human rights monitors" as just under forty.[26] Al-Haq remains the largest and most established in the West Bank. Along with Al Mezan and PCHR in Gaza, it is one of the three preeminent core or "generalist" Palestinian human rights organizations; a fourth, LAW,[27] had expanded during al-Haq's difficult years to take the latter's place as the leading West Bank human rights organization, but LAW came to an ignominious end in the early 2000s in a financial scandal that did much to increase public skepticism about human rights NGOs.[28] The organizations that cosigned al-Haq's statement on fifty years of occupation are more specialized, and include one community action group based in al-Quds University, a Jerusalem civic coalition, and others focusing on refugees and prisoners' rights.

Al-Haq engages with other Palestinian human rights NGOs and rights-based groups in the West Bank (including East Jerusalem), the Gaza Strip (most closely with Al Mezan, directed by former al-Haq researcher Issam Younis, but also with PCHR, directed by Raji Sourani), inside Israel's 1948 borders (Adalah), and in the Israeli-occupied Syrian Golan, where al-Haq encouraged Syrian colleagues as they established the Al-Marsad Arab Human Rights Centre in 2003. Formalized coalitions in which al-Haq participates include the Palestinian Human Rights Organizations Council (PHROC) and the Palestinian NGO Network (PNGO). Single-organization public statements about particular developments are less frequent. On the other hand, al-Haq has been criticized for electing not to publicly associate itself with the Palestinian civil society initiative calling for boycott, divestment, and sanctions (BDS) which was launched in 2005: one long-standing friend of the organization attributed this to an "organizational mystique of being apolitical," but it may also be linked to institutional survival.[29]

One of the most prominent examples of outward-facing cooperation with other oPt human rights NGOs in recent years has been conducted in parallel with extremely internal, confidential cooperation, investigation, and development of argumentation by the organizations involved. This has been the sustained cooperation firstly in lobbying the Palestinian authorities to sign on to the statute of the ICC despite explicit threats and/or inducements designed to prevent such a move by Israel, the United States, the United Kingdom, and others; and secondly in gathering evidence from the field of alleged crimes by Israeli individuals that come under the jurisdiction of the Court. An interview from 2016 with Raji Sourani of PCHR and Shawan Jabarin of al-Haq is deftly presented as a forum where "two of the most prominent Palestinian human rights defenders [. . .] discuss their commitment to the legal process despite the political realities that limit its promise to deliver justice."[30] In it, Sourani provides some background on PCHR's work on grave breaches of the Fourth Geneva Convention, previous Palestinian attempts to persuade the first ICC prosecutor to intervene in regard to violations during Israeli attacks on Gaza, and US and EU pressure applied to dissuade the Palestinian leadership from signing on to the ICC Statute once it became clearly eligible after its status was upgraded at the UN.[31] The PA refrained from signing the ICC Statute when it ratified other international treaties in April 2014. Sourani describes intense lobbying of the Palestinian authorities after Israel's 2014 assault on Gaza, not only by human rights organizations and other civil society groups, but by all of the various political factions (including Islamist groups) to have President Abbas sign on, arguing, among other points, that the very legitimacy of the PA required it to defend (and be seen as defending) Palestinian lives. In the end, the Palestinian leadership signed the Rome Statute at the very end of 2014, the day after the UN Security Council "failed to adopt a draft resolution that would have affirmed the 'urgent need' to reach within 12 months a peaceful solution to the situation in the Middle East and would have paved the way to a Palestinian state with East Jerusalem as its capital."[32] The ICC prosecutor opened a preliminary investigation to examine the situation in the acceding state party. The PA did not itself at that time submit files relating to alleged crimes on its territory. Erakat observes that "the Palestinian leadership has pursued ICC jurisdiction formulaically, without any appreciation for its political nature."[33] But the Palestinian human rights community was not waiting for the PA to act in this regard, and, as Sourani put it in the interview, the PA had learned from the "tragic and strategic mistake made on the Goldstone file" and was not standing in the way of the NGOs.[34]

By the end of 2017, al-Haq, PCHR, Al Mezan, and Al-Dameer had submitted five substantive communications to the ICC prosecutor in The Hague supporting allegations of particular war crimes and crimes against humanity attributable to identified Israeli military and civilian individuals with high levels of authority and responsibility. The first contained evidence from Israel's 2014 offensive against Gaza, with "illustrative instances of murder, persecution, torture and other inhumane acts as well as intentional attacks on civilian persons and objects and extensive destruction not justified by military necessity." The second focused on crimes committed in Rafah by the Israeli military in a specific four-day concentrated assault in August 2014, following Israel's invocation of the so-called "Hannibal doctrine" when an Israeli soldier went missing and was presumed kidnapped; this file focused on "unlawful attacks against Palestinian civilian population and their infrastructure and property." The third dossier presented evidence to argue that Israel's extended closure of the Gaza Strip constituted the crime against humanity of "persecution" under the Rome Statute. The fourth concentrated on the West Bank (including East Jerusalem) to present evidence for "the crimes of persecution and apartheid" against the occupied Palestinian population, "forcible transfer" of the occupied population and the "implantation of Israeli settlers in their stead," the "extensive appropriation and destruction as well as pillaging of Palestinian property," and three hundred cases of "wilful killing and murder." The fifth communication argued that Israel was "unable and unwilling to conduct effective investigations into international crimes committed during the July–August 2014 Israeli military offensive," as a matter of policy and structure. "Justice for Palestinian victims must be obtained as a prerequisite for genuine and lasting peace," said Jabarin.[35] In late 2019, the ICC prosecutor finally moved on the "situation of Palestine" and submitted "the question of territorial jurisdiction" to the Court's Pre-Trial Chamber. Al-Haq and its allies gave a qualified welcome to the move, producing a lengthy intervention that concluded that "the PTC examination [. . .] is a redundant and moot point, amounting to an unnecessary delay in the progression of the situation to full investigation."[36] Subsequently the organizations submitted their observations to the PTC, and the International Commission of Jurists argued similarly in an amicus brief that failure to accept jurisdiction "would run counter to the [Rome] Statute's object and purpose of combatting impunity for serious crimes under international law."[37]

It is in giving the lie to official Israeli self-images of justice and the rule of law as the basis of its governance (as well as in holding the Palestinian authorities to account) that current Palestinian human rights work, albeit in much more complex circumstances, most closely evokes the impetus that established al-Haq in the late 1970s. The level of violations and the extraordinary degree of impunity built into the Israeli systems as Palestinian lives, homes, and livelihoods are destroyed in front of the world's media time and again have combined to provoke searches for new avenues of redress. At the same time, the situation has provoked a refusal to participate in redress systems designed for form alone. In a high-profile move in 2016, B'Tselem announced that after twenty-five years of investigating and submitting complaints for Palestinian victims and survivors of abuse of force by the Israeli military, it had come to the conclusion that "cooperation with the military investigation and enforcement systems has not promoted accountability, but helped lend legitimacy to the occupation regime and whitewash it." It has decided to "stop playing a part in the system's charade."[38]

Accountability is a central pillar of the work of many Palestinian human rights groups. Attempts have been made to have individual third-party states investigate and prosecute alleged grave breaches of the Fourth Geneva Convention committed against members of the protected Palestinian population by high-level Israeli officials, as originally explored by al-Haq's Enforcement Team. Al-Haq's current accountability focus developed from a "war crimes project" instituted in 2006 and then expanded to include other venues, processes, and actors.[39] The universal jurisdiction work was led from the mid-2000s on the Palestinian side by PCHR, taking off after the second intifada when, as Hajjar puts it, Israel became "the first state in the world to publicly proclaim the legality of 'pre-emptive targeted killing'" after a post-Oslo "doing-and-denying phase."[40] Al-Haq has also worked with allies to mobilize third-party legal systems in defense of international law, for example in the United Kingdom in a petition for judicial review of UK conduct on arms sales to Israel in regard to Israel's breaches of international law in its 2008–9 assault on Gaza.[41] Michael Kearny traces the development of these litigation initiatives to the ICJ's 2004 advisory opinion on the Wall and its confirmation of state responsibility and individual criminal accountability in the oPt.[42] And al-Haq has directed efforts towards investigating, publicizing, and sometimes seeking to litigate in third countries on foreign businesses with co-ventures, partnerships, and other contractual relationships with Israeli settlement-based enterprises, contending that "the presence of companies in illegal Israeli settlements and the exploitation of Palestinian natural resources by such companies [. . .] constitute manifest violations of international law."[43] This work is done in close cooperation with allies outside the oPt and draws momentum from the preparation by the UN OHCHR of a "database of all business enterprises engaged in certain specified activities related to the Israeli settlements in the Occupied Palestinian Territory" pursuant to a 2016 Human Rights Council resolution. Publication of the database was delayed for some years, but a first release was made early in 2020.[44] The organization was the 2019 recipient of the Human Rights and Business Award from the UN Forum on Business and Human Rights, which called al-Haq "a recognised leader" in the development of this area of human rights work in the region.

After returning from the brink of dissolution in the late 1990s, al-Haq has consolidated its position within the regional human rights movement, through joint interventions (notably with CIHRS), issue-specific coalitions such as that on the death penalty,[45] and membership (sometimes in elected leadership roles) of regional networks—notably EuroMed Rights[46]—and international alliances including FIDH, OMCT, and Habitat International Coalition.[47] Al-Haq remains the West Bank affiliate of the ICJ.[48] To some extent, these networks continue, in a world of communications unimagined in al-Haq's early years, to play their role in the "boomerang" effect described by Keck and Sikkink, amplifying al-Haq's messages and projecting them internationally whence they reverberate back, to Israel and nowadays to the PA.[49] They also play a vital solidarity role as al-Haq becomes increasingly targeted by Israel. In 2017, for example, OMCT wrote an open letter to the UN secretary-general, Antonio Guterres, regarding "slandering statements" made to the press by Israel's permanent representative about al-Haq and Al Mezan. The language used by the Israeli ambassador recalls that used against LSM in its early days:

> Ambassador Danon said that *"Al Mezan is an organisation which cooperates with Hamas, an internationally recognised terror group,"* and linked *"Al Haq (. . .), led by Shawan Jabareen"* to the so-called *"PFLP terrorist organisation."* Ambassador Danon went on falsely characterising both human rights groups as *"supporters of terrorism,"* and *"inciters of violence."*[50]

But this is not just more of the same. In March 2016 al-Haq issued a statement putting on record the increasingly vicious harassment of the organization (false communications to donors and staff members, smear campaigns, etc. through social media) that the organization noted as "coinciding with, and as a result of, the progress achieved at the level of the International Criminal Court and decisions at the

EU level regarding the labelling of settlement products." The reason for the statement was that this campaign had now risen to the level of death threats made in anonymous phone calls to Shawan Jabarin and another staff member.[51] The complex context of the so-called war on terror, the 2003 invasion of Iraq and US and European interventions in other wars in the region since the uprisings of 2011, together with Israel's critical identity as a key US ally (if not indeed its vanguard) in regional power and resource struggles, embolden extremists in a divided Israel and mute those attempts that European states might make to defend the principles of international law. European states' interventions and their narrowing security-lens view of the region have weakened key third-party states as potential allies in seeking Israel's respect for its international law obligations in relation to the Palestinian population of the oPt.[52]

The concept of "lawfare" links two areas of official Israeli policy and discourse that have been identified by scholars as marking twenty-first-century developments, along with the global "war on terror" paradigm and the related war model (as compared to a policing model) within which the Israeli state engages with Palestinians in the oPt post-Oslo.[53] Lawfare, according to Kearney, is a "critique of human rights activism and advocacy [that] emerged in response to human rights litigation during the 'war on terror' [...] . Its primary goals are to delegitimize human rights activists and discredit international law."[54] Neve Gordon argues that human rights organizations are themselves "increasingly being constituted as a security threat" in order "to enable primarily Israel and the US to carry out military campaigns unhindered."[55] Nongovernmental projects and commentators hostile to Palestinian attempts to invoke international law in defense of their rights have deployed the lawfare narrative "to present Palestinian engagement with the law as being the latest and most invidious manifestation of the terrorist threat."[56]

Gordon and Kearney agree that Israeli official discourse took up the lawfare narrative "to limit the content and application of IHL in Israel's wars" after the publication of the Goldstone report and the arrest warrant issued in London in late 2009 against then Israeli foreign minister Tzipi Livni;[57] for Gordon, "the report itself was reconstituted in the Israeli public domain as a national threat."[58] Israeli prime minister Benjamin Netanyahu told an Israeli security institute (against the background of the Goldstone report) that "organisations that claimed to support the principles of human rights and international law [were] the third strategic threat to Israel's security"—that is, "third after Iran and Hizbullah."[59] Israeli human rights groups that had cooperated with or provided information to the UN fact-finding mission were rounded on with substantial official and public vitriol, as was Richard Goldstone; the single largest donor to Israeli human rights groups announced it would not provide funding to Israeli groups supporting the exercise of universal jurisdiction against Israeli officials.[60] Draft laws to restrict sources of foreign funding for groups supporting the universal jurisdiction work or associating themselves with the BDS movement reached different stages of the legislature.[61] In June 2018 the Israeli Ministry of Strategic Affairs and Public Diplomacy issued a report "calling on the European Union and EU states to halt their direct and indirect financial support and funding to Palestinian and international human rights organisations that 'have ties to terror and promote boycotts against Israel.'" Al-Haq and its NGO partners considered that this "reveals the State of Israel's direct official involvement in smear campaigns against Palestinian human rights organisations and their European partners."[62]

The other area is what Hajjar terms "state lawfare."[63] If the first form of lawfare involves the Israeli state (and others) impugning Palestinian attempts to mobilize the law as something to be resisted in the (global) war on terror, then this second form concerns the Israeli state's arguments for and application of doctrines of IHL that seek to render "lawful" serious violations of IHL rules. Hajjar's focus is on both Israeli and US policy arguments for the legality of their publicly declared targeted killing policies. Erakat considers this "legal work" by Israel, supported in large part by the United States, to constitute "two fundamental and interlocking shifts. The first was to unsettle the applicable legal framework regulating the Israeli state's relationship to Palestinians. The second was to change the laws of war that regulated a belligerent's right to use force more generally."[64] Hajjar notes the documented (but denied) history of Israel's extrajudicial executions in the oPt from the first intifada, with an increase in the 1990s following the redeployment of Israeli troops from Palestinian Area A and suicide bombings of Israeli targets (including civilian targets) from 1993. She dates the public adoption of "targeted killings" as a "lawful" policy within the war model of engagement from early in the second intifada. Concluding on the policies in both Israel and the US, she notes:

> These attempts exemplify state lawfare because they deviate from and defy international consensus about what is lawful in the conduct of war and armed conflict. In the case of Israel, the asserted right to engage in targeted killing in Gaza and the West Bank hinges on the (internationally rejected) proposition that they are no longer occupied and therefore are legitimate sites of warfare, and that extra-judicial execution of people who ostensibly cannot be arrested is a legitimate form of national self-defense.[65]

Hajjar quite rightly points out that as a manifestation of "state lawfare" this is not a departure for the Israeli state, which in the first months of the occupation changed its mind about the de jure applicability of the Fourth Geneva Convention and since then has declined to recognize the restraints it places on the conduct of an occupying power. The annexation of East Jerusalem, Israel's policies of land expropriation and settlement, and its "pioneering legacy of 'legalizing' torture (in 1987)" are other cases in point, away from the conduct of military action.[66]

Another important change to the way al-Haq works now lies in its relations with human rights organizations in and from Arab states. It was particularly after Oslo that the Palestinian groups began to develop sustained relationships, sometimes formalized in networks. Besides the opening up of communications and the fact that al-Haq had met and worked with some of its Arab counterparts in the lead-up to the Vienna World Conference, these groups were beginning to meet together more frequently, and the establishment of the PA meant that al-Haq had many more political and governance issues in common with human rights groups in Arab states.[67] After initial disagreements about how al-Haq might approach the PA and something of a honeymoon period with the newly established authority, patterns of executive overreach and interference, security abuses, and judicial shortcomings and lack of capacity began to manifest and to be challenged by Palestinian civil society. The struggle with the PA over the NGO law has already been noted; more recent years have seen an encroachment of executive interference and threats of further closure of space for dissent, inter alia with the Cybercrimes Law. Across the region (and indeed elsewhere), with the "war on terror" and particularly after the Arab Spring, draconian legislation and arbitrary implementation put human rights organizations and individual defenders at substantial risk—for example, laws criminalizing libel or slander of public institutions or heads of government or "disseminating false information," severe restrictions on the freedom to legally constitute associations, and constraints on the receipt of funding for human rights work, in particular foreign funding.

The "foreign funding debate" has been particularly vehement in Egypt, with some early human rights actors there arguing against taking funds from outside agencies, both for pragmatic political reasons (how it looks to the constituency) and for reasons of principle—that it should be possible to raise sufficient funds from internal sources, to rely on the voluntarism of participants in the movement, and to avoid the risk of locally determined human rights priorities being overtaken by donor-driven agendas.[68] As the Arab movement professionalized (often at the pressing of funders) and European and US governmental and private (foundation) donors made funds increasingly available for human rights work in the Middle East, and indeed for human-rights-and-democracy work (this the elision noted by Zalaquett in his report to al-Haq), governments hostile to scrutiny from their domestic groups used the fact of foreign funding to allege a range of dubious intentions and suspect backers and to impugn the patriotism of those in receipt of funds aimed (according to that narrative) at changing the nature of the national identity and priorities at the behest of foreign powers. There appears to be widespread acceptance of official discourses to the effect that human rights is a fundamentally Western concept, that the discourse is deployed in a power struggle against authentic national values, and that foreign funds (at least potentially) work against the sovereign interests of the state.[69] In Palestine, Eyad El Sarraj, head of Gaza's Community Mental Health Programme and one of the first commissioners general of the national human rights institution (ICHR), noted in a reflection on his arrest and detention by the PA that "the usual line is that human rights are Western and used in particular by the United States to control Palestinians and Arabs. A human rights activist is, therefore, suspect."[70] According to Hajjar, for many Palestinians there is "an enduring perception that human rights remain an instrument of Western governments, often invoked in ways that discriminate against Arabs and Muslims."[71]

And indeed there is plenty of evidence that the human rights discourse has been very inconsistently deployed by European powers and the United States.[72] Indeed, one of the major obstacles to promoting human rights in Palestine and the wider Arab state region is the selectivity in approach to enforcement of international law displayed by powerful third-party state actors. Often these precedents are related to inaction on Palestine/Israel compared with action on (against) Arab states; one example often cited (and noted by al-Haq at the time) is the West's response to Iraq's 1991 invasion and occupation of Kuwait, while Chase refers to "the counterproductivity of a US invasion of Iraq [in 2003] that invoked human rights as one of its justifications—albeit in passing and artificially."[73] As Megally observes, "double standards of this kind were and are recited all over the Middle East and North Africa," with considerable negative impact on the idea of "human rights."[74]

These debates have infused and conditioned the human rights debate in Palestine since Oslo. Raji Sourani told the 1998 meeting on the Arab human rights movement, for example, that "nobody raised the question of foreign funding before the Oslo accords" but that now the Palestinian groups were being "accused by the Palestinian National Authority of being organisations with secret agendas, implementing the will of foreign governments, even though their activities are fully transparent and accountable."[75] The point about transparency was made in contrast to widespread corruption in the PA. There was Palestinian executive interest in controlling the inflow and use of funds from abroad, as well as, probably, in distracting attention from stories about internal PA corruption, and the general objection of a government (in this case, recently installed, and itself heavily dependent on foreign support, financial and other) to criticism from domestic human rights groups about violative practices. A 1999 report from the office of the UN's Special Coordinator for the Occupied Territories (UNSCO) on support to the rule-of-law sector in Palestine showed some twenty million dollars (of a total of something over one hundred million) having gone to NGOs focused broadly on human rights, legal development, and civil education.[76] Hammami and Hajjar have both analyzed the attacks against the NGO sector that followed in the public arena, with NGOs "vilified as 'fat cats' exploiting donor funds for their own enrichment and at the cost of an increasingly destitute population."[77] Hammami further noted:

> In quiet, some sectors of the NGO community noted the alarming disparity between the amount of donor money channelled through NGOs to human rights and legal issues (even if the most conservative estimates are used), and the paltry impact these NGOs have had on the rule of law and the protection of human rights.[78]

This remains key. Al-Haq, alongside its peers in the Palestinian human rights movement, was and is implicated not only by public distrust of and resentment at funds coming in from abroad, but also by a lack of belief in the capacity of the human rights and international law effort to have any impact in improving salient features of life in the oPt.[79] In 2012, Shawan Jabarin acknowledged that "in the Occupied Palestinian Territories, there is little faith in the principles of human rights. Notions of justice, accountability and international law mean too little to too many."[80] If the chief factor for this was Israel's repeated performance, the second was "the international community's apathy and what often amounts to complicity in the deteriorating situation" across the oPt. Jabarin's piece insisted nevertheless on holding the PA to account, in that "human rights should not simply be a by-product of good governance" (part of Allen's "performance" of human rights), but rather should be fundamental to the governance project itself: "Ultimately, for as long as the PA continues to dismiss its obligations and refuses to respect the rule of law, neither liberation nor justice will ever come to Palestine."

The challenges are enormous, and for many the situation appears bleaker than ever. Al-Haq is not alone in arguing that it may no longer be adequate or appropriate to frame what is happening in the oPt as "merely" occupation. Note has already been made of the developments in the law of armed conflict particularly since the 2003 US-led invasion and subsequent military occupation of Iraq. But the recent recognition of "the transformative goals of certain occupations" (such as the project in Iraq with its "stated purpose of reforming their political systems in a democratic direction") does not apply to Israel's purpose in the oPt; and nor yet has Israel conformed to the "conservationist principle" which requires minimal intervention in the existing legal and economic order of occupied territory.[81] John Dugard, an eminent South African jurist and at the time UN Special Rapporteur on the situation of human rights in the Palestinian territories occupied since 1967, summarized his argument in his 2007 report (when the occupation reached forty) as follows:

> The international community has identified three regimes as inimical to human rights—colonialism, apartheid and foreign occupation. Israel is clearly in military occupation of the OPT. At the same time elements of the occupation constitute forms of colonialism and of apartheid, which are contrary to international law. What are the legal consequences of a regime of prolonged occupation with features of colonialism and apartheid for the occupied people, the occupying Power and third States?[82]

For Dugard, the question was whether an occupation that may have begun as a lawful (if temporary) regime becomes unlawful when it clearly "acquires some of the characteristics of colonialism and apartheid" and continues for, then, nearly forty, now over fifty years – and if so "what are the legal consequences?"[83] Dugard said that "clearly none of the obligations imposed on the occupying Power are reduced as a result of such a prolonged occupation." He referenced a 1990 paper by Adam Roberts, a reprise of the latter's paper to Palestine's first international law conference convened by al-Haq in January 1988.[84] Dugard argued for these questions to be put to the International Court of Justice for an advisory opinion. Meanwhile, popular references to "Israeli apartheid" increased after the second intifada.[85] In the event, Dugard's home state, South Africa, provided follow-up to the questions in his report through a major international law research project led by a South African–funded team and involving researchers from al-Haq, under the title *Occupation, Colonialism, Apartheid?*[86]

Dugard concluded his 2007 report with a vehement indictment of the failure of the West to "demonstrate a real commitment to the human rights of the Palestinian people. [. . .] There is no other case of a Western-affiliated regime that denies self-determination and human rights to a developing people and that has done so for so long."[87] References to colonialism as a frame through which to view Israel's treatment of the oPt have increased in the face of Israel's relentless expropriation and exploitation of land and water resources for use by Israeli settlers, and its denial of the Palestinian right to self-determination. Al-Haq's 2017 call on the international community to act to end the occupation fifty years on invoked Israel's "broad colonial aims" and stated that "Israel's occupation and associated policies and practices fragment the Occupied Palestinian Territory, violate the collective and individual rights of Palestinians and amount to colonialism."[88]

The year 2017 also saw the publication and then withdrawal of a report commissioned by ESCWA from a team comprising Richard Falk, who followed Dugard as Special Rapporteur, and Virginia Tilley, editor of the report and the book from the South African–led project on occupation, colonialism, and apartheid. The ESCWA-commissioned report was specifically to consider the question of apartheid in relation to Israel's treatment of the Palestinian people.[89] The authors declared that they were "aware of the seriousness of this allegation" but that "available evidence establishes beyond a reasonable doubt that Israel is guilty of policies and practices that constitute the crime of apartheid as legally defined in instruments of international law."[90] The reaction from Israel and the United States was, according to Falk, "what can only be described as hysteria."[91] UN secretary-general Antonio Guterres instructed the ESCWA head, Rima Khalaf, to have the report taken off the website; she refused and resigned; the report was withdrawn. Falk said it reminded him of the US reaction to the Goldstone report. The PHROC expressed its dismay at this "political pressure," declared that the member organizations (including al-Haq) would adopt the report's conclusions and analysis, and called on the prosecutor's office at the ICC "to take [the report] into account during its preliminary examination into the situation in Palestine."[92] Besides intense hostility and sensitivity to any invocation of apartheid as a descriptor for Israeli policies and practices, because of the image of apartheid South Africa, the fact that apartheid (as a crime against humanity) falls within the ICC jurisdiction raises again for Israel and its allies the red flag of criminal proceedings in a tribunal governed (at least in theory) by a conception of the rule of law not compatible with that developed and projected by Israel as part of its narrative of state lawfare.

Facing the upcoming fiftieth anniversary of the occupation, in his 2016 panel interview alongside Sourani, Jabarin insisted that "Palestine, in its legal and jurisprudential aspects, is a test for the whole system of international law."[93] The anniversary-laden year of 2017 started with the Israeli Knesset purporting to "regularize" the status of Israeli settlements built on expropriated private Palestinian land in the West Bank, and ended with the United States declaring recognition of Jerusalem as the capital of Israel and the imminent relocation of its embassy from Tel Aviv; both are surely indications of annexation rather than occupation.[94] Protests in Jerusalem and a sustained hunger strike by Palestinian prisoners marked the months in between. Al-Haq's public response to the so-called "Trump Declaration" denounced the violations of principles of international law that Trump's move endorsed, including the prohibition of the acquisition of territory by force, and asserted that "the recognition of Israel's unlawful annexation of East Jerusalem amounts to complicity in an unlawful settlement enterprise which was condemned by Security Council Resolution 2334 in 2016."[95] It called on the UN General Assembly to refer a request for an advisory opinion to the ICJ on "the question of Israel's annexation, colonization and apartheid," notably substituting "annexation" for "occupation"; it called on High Contracting Parties to the Geneva Conventions to convene a meeting to address Israel's breaches; and EU states to take the lead in facilitating peace negotiations in the place of the United States. Its call on the Palestinian political authorities can be compared with its intervention in 1991 with the Palestinian delegation setting off for Madrid when it emphasized the limits set by IHL on representatives of a protected population, but took "no position with regard to the merits of the political process in question."[96] Faced with the so-called Trump Declaration on Jerusalem, al-Haq insisted:

> It is imperative that the Palestine Liberation Organization immediately and permanently end peace negotiations with US President Trump, who is positioning the US as a transgressor of international law. In light of the deliberate sabotage of the status of East Jerusalem, Al-Haq calls [for] the disbandment of the Palestinian Authority's security coordination and all political coordination with Israel, which is effectively entrenching the occupation and facilitating Israel's colonial agenda.[97]

This is a weighty call made in light of a reckoning that, on balance, the gains of Oslo are more than outweighed by losses both already inflicted and on the horizon. It is not one that al-Haq would have made in its formative years; it illustrates the urgency felt at the risk that the Trump declaration and subsequent action pose, as al-Haq put it, to "the entire international legal system [. . .] and the reciprocal maintenance of peace and security."

In April 2020 there followed a more detailed "Open Letter to the UN Security Council on Israel's Plans to Annex the West Bank" in the wake of the release by the US administration of its Peace to Prosperity Plan and reports of an agreement on the future of the occupied Palestinian territory between the two men poised to lead Israel's government (Netanyahu and Benny Gantz) after successive inconclusive elections. US secretary of state Mike Pompeo was reported as stating that "the annexation of parts of the West Bank is ultimately Israel's decision to make." Al-Haq's intervention presented many of the mechanisms available to third states set out in its 1990 "Representation to States Signatory to the Fourth Geneva Convention" discussed in chapter 5. Reminding the Security Council of the "obligation to ensure respect as an essential component of third state responsibility" under IHL, al-Haq insisted that "to fail in this obligation is to legitimise colonialism, consolidate apartheid, and to fatally undermine efforts at securing enjoyment of human rights through the rule of law." Thus, al-Haq invokes key elements of its resistance agenda dating back to its establishment in 1979, and forward to a future which, post COVID-19, many hope will involve a reconfiguration or reconstruction of the lawful means through which peoples and communities seek more generous, more inclusive conceptions of peace and justice.

INTRODUCTION

1. Over fifty interviews were conducted in 2009, with some additions and updates in 2018. Most were in person in the West Bank; some were by Skype, and a few by email exchange. A number of interviewees chose not to speak on the record. The following gave their permission for my use, under their name, of approved extracts of their interviews: Raqiya Abu Ghosh, Nina Atallah, Sami 'Ayad, Fateh Azzam, Khaled Batrawi, Grazia Careccia, Claudio Cordone, Judith Dueck, George Giacaman, Iyad Haddad, Roger Heacock, Tim Hillier, Joost Hiltermann, Shawan Jabarin, Zahi Jaradat, 'Abdel Karim Kan'an, Jonathan Kuttab, Mustafa Mar'i, Anne Massagee, Emma Playfair, Joanna Oyediran, Hanan Rabbani, Mouin Rabbani, Naser Rayyes, Mervat Rishmawi, Mona Rishmawi, Marty Rosenbluth, Donatella Rovera, Jacqueline Shahinian, Charles Shammas, Ghazi Shashtari, Raja Shehadeh, Randa Siniora, Marc Stephens, Nidal Taha, Candy Whittome, Issam Younis, and Said Zeedani.

2. Raja Shehadeh's later legal works include *Occupier's Law: Israel and the West Bank* (Washington, DC: Institute for Palestine Studies, 1985); and *From Occupation to Interim Accords: Israel and the Palestinian Territories* (The Hague: Kluwer Law International, 1997).

3. Shehadeh, *The Sealed Room* (London: Quartet, 1992); *When the Bulbul Stopped Singing* (London: Profile Books, 2003); *Occupation Diaries* (London: Profile Books, 2012). A different exploration is in *A Rift in Time: Travels with My Ottoman Uncle* (London: Profile Books Ltd, 2010).

4. Of particular note for this study are "Human Rights and the Israeli Occupation," *CR: The New Centennial Review* 8/1 (2008): 33–55; and Vincent Bernard, Michael Siegrist, and Anton Camen, "Interview with Raja Shehadeh," *International Review of the Red Cross* 94/885 (2012): 13–28.

5. Fateh Azzam, "Al-Haq in 2004: A Twenty-Five Year Retrospective," in *Waiting for Justice: Annual Report 2004* (Ramallah: al-Haq, 2005), 12–13.

6. Newsletter no. 9 (1985), no. 16 (1986), and no. 19 (1987). The Newsletters are available in hard copy at al-Haq's library in Ramallah. The very first one was reproduced as an appendix to the ICJ Newsletter (Quarterly Report, no. 21, April 1–June 30, 1984). After mostly regular publication from the first issue in May 1984 to no. 21 of September–December 1987, only five (22–26) were issued up to October–December 1992, none of which I was able to locate in al-Haq's files. Publication was rather sporadic thereafter; al-Haq's archives appeared to hold only the Arabic texts and to have gaps for later years' issues. I found no Newsletters after no. 38 (September 1998), which opened with the announcement of the "restructuring and rebuilding" of al-Haq after the 1997 organizational crisis.

7. For example, Joost Hiltermann, "Human Rights and the Politics of Computer Software," *Middle East Report* 150 (January–February 1988): 8–9; and "Deaths in Israeli Prisons," *Journal of Palestine Studies* 19/3 (Spring 1990): 101–10. Emma Playfair also published articles based on her al-Haq work; at the time, this was one way of ensuring a wider audience for al-Haq's occasional papers than was reached through the unreliable postal service from the West Bank. See, for example, Playfair, "Administrative Detention in the Israeli-Occupied West Bank," *SIM Newsletter* 13 (February 1986): 5–26.

8. "Palestinian Human Rights Activism under Israeli Occupation: The Case of Al-Haq," *Arab Studies Quarterly* 16/2 (1994): 27–53.

9. Lisa Hajjar, "Human Rights in Israel/Palestine: The History and Politics of a Movement," *Journal of Palestine Studies* 30/4 (2001): 21.

10. Hajjar, 25.

11. Lisa Hajjar, *Courting Conflict: The Israeli Military Court System in the West Bank and Gaza* (London: University of California Press, 2005), 158.

12. Hajjar, *Courting Conflict*, 46.

13. Lori Allen, *The Rise and Fall of Human Rights: Cynicism and Politics in Occupied Palestine* (Stanford: Stanford University Press, 2013), 25.

14. Tom Buchanan, "'The Truth Will Set You Free': The Making of Amnesty International," *Journal of Contemporary History* 37/4 (2002): 576.

15. Buchanan, 577. The "flash of inspiration" moment draws on the memoir of Peter Benenson, Amnesty's founder, sitting on an underground train in 1960s London and reading in a newspaper about two Portuguese students being sentenced to prison for toasting liberty in a Lisbon restaurant.

16. Allen, *Rise and Fall of Human Rights*, 58. Jan Eckel notes the "sardonic" use of the term *human rights industry* term in the 1970s by "contemporary commentators [. . .] amazed by the sudden upsurge." Eckel, "The Rebirth of Politics from the Spirit of Morality: Explaining the Human Rights Revolution of the 1970s," in *The Breakthrough: Human Rights in the 1970s*, ed. Jan Eckel and Samuel Moyn (Philadelphia: University of Pennsylvania Press, 2013), 228. In that same volume, see also Samuel Moyn, "The Return of the Prodigal: The 1970s as a Turning Point in Human Rights History," 1–14. On the "displacement" of other languages of struggle or resistance, see Paul O'Connell, "Human Rights: Contesting the Displacement Thesis," *Northern Ireland Legal Quarterly* 69/1 (2018): 19–36.

17. Paul O'Connell reviews the first sustained academic critique of rights by critical legal studies scholars in the 1980s United States. He dates the emergence of the current, broader wave of critique to the period after the US-led invasion of Iraq in 2003 (when, as discussed later, academic commentary on international humanitarian law also took off exponentially). O'Connell, "On the Human Rights Question," *Human Rights Quarterly* 40/4 (2018): 962–88.

18. Christine Bell, "Human Rights and the Struggle for Change: A Study in Self-Critical Legal Thought," in *Examining Critical Perspectives on Human Rights*, ed. Rob Dickinson, Elena Katselli, Colin Murray, and Ole W. Pederson (Cambridge: Cambridge University Press, 2012), 245. Bell worked for years with the Committee for the Administration of Justice in Belfast, and her chapter is a reflection on two pieces by David Kennedy: "The International Human Rights Movement: Part of the Problem?," *Harvard Human Rights Journal* 15 (2002): 101–25; and "The International Human Rights Regime: Still Part of the Problem?," in Dickinson et al., eds., *Examining Critical Perspectives on Human Rights*, 19–34.

19. Philip Alston, "The Populist Challenge to Human Rights," *Journal of Human Rights Practice* 9 (2017): 13.

20. Makau Mutua, *Human Rights Standards: Hegemony, Law and Politics* (Albany: SUNY Press, 2016), ix.

21. Fateh Azzam, "NGOs vs. Grassroots Movements: A False Dichotomy," Al-Shabaka Palestinian Policy Network, February 6, 2014, https://al-shabaka.org/commentaries /ngos-vs-grassroots-movements-a-false-dichotomy/; "Why Should We Have to Represent Anyone?," *Sur—International Journal on Human Rights* 20 (2014): 273–82; and "In Defense of 'Professional' Human Rights Organizations," openDemocracy, January 13, 2014.

22. Anthony Tirado Chase, "Human Rights and the Middle East and North Africa: Indivisibility, Social Rights, and Structural Change," in *Routledge Handbook on Human Rights and the Middle East and North Africa*, ed. Anthony Tirado Chase (Abington: Routledge, 2017), 22. For those on the ideology side of the argument, see for example Stephen Hopgood, *The Endtimes of Human Rights* (Ithaca, NY: Cornell University Press, 2013); and Samuel Moyn, *The Last Utopia: Human Rights in History* (Cambridge, MA: Harvard University Press, 2010).

23. B.S. Chimni, "Legitimating the International Rule of Law," in *Cambridge Companion to International Law*, ed. James Crawford (Cambridge: Cambridge University Press, 2012), 290.

24. Hajjar, *Courting Conflict*, 49. See also George Bisharat, "Courting Justice? Legitimation in Lawyering under Israeli Occupation," *Law and Social Enquiry* 20/2 (1995): 391–92.

25. INSIGHT, "Israel Tortures Arab Prisoners: Special Investigation by INSIGHT," *Sunday Times*, June 19, 1977, archived as UN doc. A/32/132 S/12356, July 5, 1977, available online, including the cover story about the report (1–2) and the *Sunday Times* editorial at 36–38. The permanent representative of the Sudan (then chairing the Arab Group) submitted the (retyped) text of the report for circulation at the UN. The report is reproduced in the *Journal of Palestine Studies* 6/4 (1977): 191–210, with the response of the Israeli embassy in London (July 3, 1977) at 210–15 and the response to that from the INSIGHT team at 215–19.

26. Editorial, *Sunday Times*, June 19, 1977, UN doc. A/32/132 S/12356, July 5, 1977, 36.

27. INSIGHT, *Sunday Times*, June 19, 1977, UN doc. A/32/132 S/12356, July 5, 1977, 11.

28. Editorial, *Sunday Times*, June 19, 1977, UN doc. A/32/132 S/12356, July 5, 1977, 37.

29. Editorial, *Sunday Times*, June 19, 1977, UN doc. A/32/132 S/12356, July 5, 1977, 37; INSIGHT, *Sunday Times*, June 19, 1977, UN doc. A/32/132 S/12356, July 5, 1977, 11.

30. I switch to the current designation, occupied Palestinian territory (oPt), in the later chapters on the time when this usage took over after Oslo.

31. David Kretzmer, *The Occupation of Justice: The Supreme Court of Israel and the Occupied Territories* (New York: SUNY Press, 2002), 76. See also Kathleen Cavanaugh, "Narrating Law: Israel and the Occupied Territories," in Chase, ed., *Routledge Handbook*

on Human Rights, 136; and Virginia Tilley, ed., *Occupation, Colonialism, Apartheid? A Re-Assessment of Israel's Practices in the Occupied Palestinian Territories under International Law*, Middle East Project (Cape Town: HSRC, 2009).

32. Patrick Wolfe, "Settler Colonialism and the Elimination of the Native," *Journal of Genocide Research* 8/4 (2006): 387–409. See also Nicola Perugini and Neve Gordon, "Israel/Palestine, Human Rights and Domination," in Chase, ed., *Routledge Handbook on Human Rights*, 419–30; Omar Jabary Salamanca, Mezna Qato, Kareem Rabie, and Sobhi Samour, "Past Is Present: Settler Colonialism in Palestine," *Settler Colonial Studies* 2/1 (2012): 1–8; Mazen Masri, "Colonial Imprints: Settler-Colonialism as a Fundamental Feature of Israeli Constitutional Law," *International Journal of Law in Context* 13/3 (2017): 388–407. On "colonial erasures," see Noura Erakat, *Justice for Some: Law and the Question of Palestine* (Stanford: Stanford University Press, 2019), 23–60.

33. See Tilley, ed., *Occupation, Colonialism, Apartheid?*; John Dugard and John Reynolds, "Apartheid, International Law, and the Occupied Palestinian Territory," *European Journal of International Law* 24/3 (2013): 867–913. See also John Dugard, *Confronting Apartheid: A Personal History of South Africa, Namibia and Palestine* (Johannesburg: Jacana Media, 2018).

34. Shehadeh, *Occupier's Law*, 46.

35. Newsletter no. 19 (May–June 1987), 3.

36. Shehadeh makes that comparison in "The Legal System of the Israeli Settlements in the West Bank," *Review of the ICJ* 27 (December 1981): 59–74; and Kuttab in his "Statement [. . .] for the Palestine Human Rights Campaign, Foreign Affairs Committee, US House of Representatives, 7 March 1985," al-Haq archives.

37. Erakat, *Justice for Some*, xi, 7. See Duncan Kennedy, "A Left Phenomenological Alternative to the Hart/Kelson Theory of Legal Interpretation," In Kennedy, *Legal Reasoning: Collected Essays* (Aurora: The Davies Group, 2008), 153–73.

38. Erakat, *Justice for Some*, 95–134.

39. George Bisharat, *Palestinian Lawyers and Israeli Rule: Law and Disorder in the West Bank* (Austin: University of Texas Press, 1989), 168. Compare how Tunisian lawyers conducted themselves before and after the 2011 revolution, achieving "considerable symbolic influence over the post-uprising government": Eric Gobe and Lena Salaymeh, "Tunisia's 'Revolutionary' Lawyers: From Professional Autonomy to Political Mobilization," *Law and Social Inquiry* 41/2 (2016): 311. Lawyers and legal professionals were prominent in the Sudanese Professionals Association, which took a high profile in and after the protests that led to the ousting of President Omar al-Bashir in 2019.

40. Charles Tripp, *The Power and the People: Paths of Resistance in the Middle East* (New York: Cambridge University Press, 2013). *Sumud* is usually translated as steadfastness.

41. Bisharat, *Palestinian Lawyers and Israeli Rule*, 164. See further in the next chapter.

42. Eckel, "Rebirth of Politics," 239. Ilias Bantekas and Lutz Oette credit efforts by "Third World" states with the UN Declaration on the Right to Development (1986). Bantekas and Oette, *International Human Rights Law and Practice*, 2nd ed. (Cambridge: Cambridge University Press, 2016), 21.

43. "Twenty Years of Occupation: A Time to Reflect," Newsletter no. 19 (May–June 1987). Talhami's 1987 consideration of "The Palestinian Perception of the Human Rights Issue" starts with an exposition of the right to self-determination. *Syracuse Journal of International Law and Commerce* 13 (1987): 475–88.

44. Emma Playfair, ed., *International Law and the Administration of Occupied Territories: Two Decades of Israeli Occupation of the West Bank and Gaza Strip* (Oxford: The Clarendon Press, 1992).

45. Aziz Shehadeh, Fuad Shehadeh, and Raja Shehadeh, *Israeli Proposed Road Plan for the West Bank: A Question for the International Court of Justice* (Ramallah: LSM, 1984).

46. Erakat, *Justice for Some*, xii.

CHAPTER 1. CONTEXT

1. Noura Erakat, however, rightly observes that the Trump administration's decision "did not mark an abrupt and ruinous rupture in US policy; it made it unambiguously coherent." Erakat, *Justice for Some*, 223.

2. Raja Shehadeh (assisted by Jonathan Kuttab), *The West Bank and the Rule of Law* (New York: International Commission of Jurists, 1980), 84.

3. Gabi Baramki, *Peaceful Resistance: Building a Palestinian University under Occupation* (London: Pluto Press, 2010), 85–86.

4. Article 5 of Military Proclamation no. 101, "Concerning the prohibition of incitement and adverse propaganda," as reproduced in Shehadeh, *West Bank and the Rule of Law*, 126–28, esp. 127.

5. Tripp, *Power and the People*, 117.

6. Armed struggle was renounced by the Palestine National Council at its Algiers summit in November 1988, in response to US demands as conditions for opening negotiations with the PLO. Erakat, *Justice for Some*, 142.

7. Lisa Taraki, "The Development of Political Consciousness among Palestinians in the Occupied Territories, 1967–1987," in *Intifada: Palestine at the Crossroads*, ed. Jamal Raji Nassar and Roger Heacock (New York: Praeger Publishers, 1990), 53–72. Taraki was closely involved with al-Haq at different stages of the organization's development.

8. Hiltermann, *Behind the Intifada: Labor and Women's Movements in the Occupied Territories* (Princeton: Princeton University Press, 1991), 5.

9. Hiltermann, 12. The 7th Arab League Summit at Rabat in October 1974 affirmed "the right of the Palestinian people to establish an independent national authority under the command of the Palestine Liberation Organisation, the sole legitimate representative of the Palestinian people, in any territory that is liberated." Hiltermann observes that this position "later evolved into the two-state solution." Hiltermann, *Behind the Intifada*, 45.

10. UN doc. A/PV.2282 & Corr.1, November 13, 1974, UNGA 29th Session, New York, para 82.

11. Erakat, *Justice for Some*, 112–22, quotations from 117, 114.

12. Hiltermann, *Behind the Intifada*, 47.

13. Taraki, "Development of Political Consciousness," 60. The National Guidance Committee was banned in 1982. Members of the first National Guidance Committee ("the de facto Palestinian leadership in the Occupied Territories of that time") had been targets of Israel's deportation policy in the mid-1970s. Joost Hiltermann, *Israel's Deportation Policy in the Occupied West Bank and Gaza* (Ramallah: al-Haq, 1986), 6.

14. Hamas began in 1988 as the "intifada wing" of the Muslim Brotherhood in Palestine. Graham Usher, *Palestine in Crisis* (London: Pluto Press, 1995), 5. See also Tripp, *Power and the People*, 32–33.

15. Shehadeh, "Human Rights and the Israeli Occupation," 33–55.

16. Bisharat, *Palestinian Lawyers and Israeli Rule*, 164. The author credits his internship with LSM in the summer of 1982 as helping to spark his research interest.

17. Shehadeh, *West Bank and the Rule of Law*, 46. The chapter on "The Legal Profession" focuses entirely on the strike. Lawyers elsewhere in the region have taken different forms of strike action against abuses by their governments, for example in Tunisia and Yemen. See Welchman, "Human Rights, Law and Politics."

18. George Bisharat reports that Gazan lawyers told him that "it simply never occurred to them to strike like their West Bank counterparts." Bisharat, "Courting Justice?," 362n55.

19. Bisharat, *Palestinian Lawyers and Israeli Rule*, 138.

20. Shehadeh, *West Bank and the Rule of Law*, 48.

21. Raja Shehadeh, *The Third Way: A Journal of Life in the West Bank* (London: Quartet Books, 1982), 118.

22. Shehadeh, *West Bank and the Rule of Law*, 75–76.

23. Shehadeh, *Third Way*.

24. Raja Shehadeh, *Strangers in the House* (London: Profile Books, 2002), 168. On the Village Leagues, see Shehadeh, *Occupier's Law*, 174–84.

25. Erakat, *Justice for Some*, 130.

26. Avi Shlaim, *The Iron Wall: Israel and the Arab World* (London: Penguin, 2001), 364.

27. The second provided for the withdrawal of Israeli settlements and military forces from Egypt's Sinai Peninsula (occupied since 1967), with certain constraints remaining on the deployment of Egyptian military in the Sinai.

28. On the 1977 Begin Plan for autonomy, see David Ott, *Palestine in Perspective: Politics, Human Rights and the West Bank* (London: Quartet Books, 1980), 3. On the implementation of Camp David "autonomy," see Jonathan Kuttab and Raja Shehadeh, *Civilian Administration in the Occupied West Bank: Analysis of Israeli Military Government Order No. 947* (Ramallah: LSM, 1982).

29. Hiltermann, *Behind the Intifada*, 43.

30. Kuttab and Shehadeh, *Civil Administration in the Occupied West Bank*.

31. Bernard et al., "Interview with Raja Shehadeh," 17.

32. Erakat, *Justice for Some*, 132–34.

33. Taraki, *Development of Political Consciousness*. Gabi Baramki describes Camp David as "a great disappointment to us, as the accords failed to even mention Palestinian national aspirations." Baramki, *Peaceful Resistance*, 78. See also Zachary Lockman, "Israel at a Turning Point," *Middle East Report* 92 (1980), describing the Palestinian population as "united in rejecting Begin's 'autonomy' plan and Sadat's claim to negotiate on its behalf."

34. Amnesty International *Annual Report 1977*, "Israel and the Occupied Territories," 94–95.

35. Hiltermann, *Behind the Intifada*, 43, 13.

36. Hiltermann, 13, drawing on Eqbal Ahmad, "Revolutionary Warfare and Counterinsurgency," in *National Liberation: Revolution in the Third World*, ed. Norman Miller and Roderick Aya (New York: Free Press, 1971), 137–213.

37. Hiltermann, 51–52.

38. Hiltermann, 50–51.

39. Shehadeh, *Third Way*, vii.

40. Hiltermann, *Behind the Intifada*, 48. See also Baramki, *Peaceful Resistance*, 65–67.

41. Hiltermann, *Behind the Intifada*, 49.

42. Bisharat, *Palestinian Lawyers and Israeli Rule*, 155.

43. Hiltermann, "Al-Haq: The First Twenty Years," in *Twenty Years Defending Human Rights* (Ramallah: al-Haq, 1999), 9–11. See also Tripp, *Power and the People*, 279–84, on the 1979 establishment in Ramallah of Gallery 79 to host art exhibitions.

44. The Jerusalem Legal Aid Centre (JLAC, now the Jerusalem Legal Aid and Human Rights Centre) formally separated from QPS in 1997; its website situates its services now in the core of the human rights movement. See www.jlac.ps/.

45. Hajjar, "Human Rights in Israel/Palestine," 26.

46. For some of the documents produced by the Israeli League, see Adnan Amad, ed., *The Israeli League for Human and Civil Rights (The Shahak Papers)* (Beirut: Near East Bureau for Information and Interpretation, 1973). A review of these documents by Hugh Harcourt and Charles Glass appears in the *Journal of Palestine Studies* 5/1–2 (1975): 150–58. On the circumstances of the ILHR decision in 1973, see Nabeel Abraham, Janice Terry, Cheryl Rosenberg, Lisa Hajjar, and Hilary Shadroui, "International Human Rights Organizations and the Palestine Conflict," *MERIP Middle East Report* 150 (1988): 18. For one early evaluation of the ILHR, see Laurie S. Wiseberg and Harry M. Scobie, "The International League for Human Rights: The Strategy of a Human Rights NGO," *Georgia Journal of International and Comparative Law* 7 (1977): 289–313. The authors are uncritical of the League's move to disaffiliate the Israeli League for Human and Civil Rights in 1973; see 297–98n17. Samuel Moyn describes the ILHR as "ineffectual." Moyn, *The Last Utopia: Human Rights in History* (Cambridge, MA: Belknap Press of Harvard University Press, 2010), 60. Writing in the first intifada, Abraham et al. identify the ILHR as "the most notable offender" among a particular set of international human rights organizations "that claim to cover Israeli violations of Palestinian rights but in reality disregard, ignore or downplay many cases." "International Human Rights Organizations," 13.

47. Hajjar, "Human Rights in Israel/Palestine," 23. In particular, Hajjar identifies Israeli lawyer Felicia Langer as a "catalysing agent" in this regard through the 1970s.

48. Hajjar, 21.

49. Eckel, "Rebirth of Politics," 230.

50. See Moyn, *Last Utopia*, 8, and Moyn, "Return of the Prodigal." Howard B. Tolley Jr. invokes but a few of the "extraordinary atrocities in the 1970s" after which "the human rights movement came of age." Tolley, *The International Commission of Jurists: Global Advocates for Human Rights* (Philadelphia: University of Pennsylvania Press, 1994), 137. See also Aryeh Neier, *The International Human Rights Movement* (Princeton: Princeton University Press, 2012), 143–45, 161–69, and 1–25 for an account of the movement's development by this cofounder of Helsinki Watch.

51. Upendra Baxi, *The Future of Human Rights*, 2nd ed. (New Delhi: Oxford University Press, 2006), 42–43, cited in Joseph R. Slaughter, "Hijacking Human Rights: Neoliberalism, the New Historiography, and the End of the Third World," *Human Rights Quarterly* 40 (2018): 735–75. See also Steven L.B. Jensen, *The Making of International Human Rights: The 1960s, Decolonization, and the Reconstruction of Global Values* (Cambridge: Cambridge University Press, 2016).

52. Vasuki Nesiah, "The Rise and Fall of the Human Rights Empire," *Foreign Policy in Focus*, June 28, 2012, 3.

53. And LSM/al-Haq did have at least one volunteer from the Centre for Applied Legal Studies (Wits University) in the mid- to late 1980s.

54. Joe Stork, "Three Decades of Human Rights Activism in the Middle East and North Africa: An Ambiguous Balance Sheet," in *Social Movements, Mobilization, and Contestation in the Middle East and North Africa*, ed. Joel Beinin and Frédéric Vairel (Stanford: Stanford University Press 2011), 83; Susan E. Waltz, *Human Rights and Reform: Changing the Face of North African Politics* (Berkeley: University of California Press, 1995), 151.

55. David Weissbrodt. "The Role of International Nongovernmental Organizations in the Implementation of Human Rights," *Texas International Law Journal* 12 (1977): 293–94. FIDH stands for La Fédération internationale des ligues des droits de l'homme. I use the term "international human rights movement" here to encompass the relations and alliances sought and made primarily by LSM/al-Haq in its early years, and my examination here is of their engagement with Palestine in the late 1970s.

56. Weissbrodt, 297.

57. Amnesty International Annual Reports, 1970–71 (67) and 1979; Amnesty International, "Report and Recommendations of an AI Mission to the Government of the State of Israel" (London, 1979); Jonathan Power, *Amnesty International: The Human Rights Story* (New York: McGraw-Hill, 1981).

58. Amnesty's membership is still concentrated in Western Europe and North America. Power's 1981 book lists sections in Israel and Turkey but not elsewhere in the region. In 2011, Joe Stork reported "active" Amnesty sections in Algeria, Tunisia (where the section was the first in an Arab state), Morocco, and Israel, with "more or less active groups" in Bahrain, Jordan, Lebanon, and Yemen. A Palestinian section established after Oslo faded. Stork, "Three Decades of Human Rights Activism," 259n3.

59. See Slaughter, "Hijacking Human Rights," 743, on other non–North Atlantic events of 1977.

60. INSIGHT in the *Sunday Times* in 1977, recalled inter alia by Baramki in *Peaceful Resistance*, 56. Amnesty reported the piece in its annual report of 1978. The INSIGHT team carefully invoked Amnesty research methodologies in explaining their approach to their material; this was the decade when Amnesty was very much focused on torture. Buchanan, "'The Truth Will Set You Free,'" 590.

61. The LCHR came from an initiative from the older International League for Human Rights.

62. See Neier's insider's account: *International Human Rights Movement*, 204–32. According to HRW's website, www.hrw.org/history (accessed February 22, 2017), Helsinki Watch (established in 1978) was "designed to support the citizens' groups formed throughout the Soviet bloc to monitor government compliance with the 1975 Helsinki Accords." Here again, Jensen locates the "pre-history" of the accords away from Europe and the United States; he does agree with the importance of the Helsinki Final Act as "a new beginning for human rights politics." Jensen, *Making of International Human Rights*, 210.

63. Americas Watch was founded in 1981, Asia Watch in 1985, Africa Watch in 1988, and finally Middle East Watch in 1989, a year after the organization adopted the wider HRW name and well into the first intifada.

64. At the end of 2018, the ICJ's website listed one national section in the Middle East/North Africa, Sisterhood Is Global in Jordan; no Israel section was listed. The following were listed as "ICJ affiliated organisations": in the occupied territories, al-Haq and the

Palestinian Centre for Human Rights (PCHR, in Gaza); the Tunisian League of Human Rights (LTDH); the Moroccan Organisation for Human Rights (OMDH); and in Egypt the Egyptian Organisation for Human Rights (EOHR) and the Arab Centre for the Independence of the Judiciary and the Legal Profession. www.icj.org.

65. Weissbrodt, "Role of International Nongovernmental Organizations," 301.

66. *Treatment of Palestinians in the Israeli-Occupied West Bank and Gaza* (New York: National Lawyers Guild, 1978). See review by Anis F. Kassim in the *Journal of Palestine Studies* 9/4 (1980): 142–46.

67. Neier, *International Human Rights Movement*, 23; see also his chapter on IHL, 117–37.

68. Cavanaugh, "Narrating Law," 132, referring also to Eyal Benvenisti, *The International Law of Occupation*, 2nd ed. (Oxford: Oxford University Press, 2012). By way of example, the *Yearbook of International Humanitarian Law* issued its first volume in 1998, the *Journal of Armed Conflict Law* in 1996; and before the 1990s, according to Laurie R. Blank and David Kaye, IHL "rarely appeared in American law school curricula." Blank and Kaye, "Direct Participation: Law School Clinics and International Humanitarian Law," *International Review of the Red Cross* 96/895–96 (2014): 945.

69. Yehuda Blum, "The Missing Reversioner: Reflections on the Status of Judea and Samaria," *Israel Law Review* 3/2 (1968): 279–301. See Erakat, *Justice for Some*, 79–83.

70. Adam Roberts, "Transformative Military Occupation: Applying the Laws of War and Human Rights," *American Journal of International Law* 100 (2006): 580–82.

71. Erakat, *Justice for Some*, 109–112, esp. 110.

72. Margaret E. Keck and Kathryn Sikkink, *Activists beyond Borders: Advocacy Networks in International Politics* (Ithaca, NY: Cornell University Press, 1998), 96. The Office of the High Commissioner for Human Rights (OHCHR) was established in 1993.

73. Roberts, "Transformative Military Occupation," 582. Scholars cite International Court of Justice support for the continued application of the ICCPR in times of war, alongside IHL as the *lex specialis*, in the international court's 1996 advisory opinion on the *Legality of the Threat or Use of Nuclear Weapons*, an opinion substantially expanded upon in the 2004 advisory opinion on the *Legal Consequences of the Construction of a Wall in the Occupied Palestinian Territory*. For an introduction to the topic, see Bantekas and Oette, *International Human Rights Law and Practice*, 649–81: "The jurisprudence of the ICJ, human rights treaty bodies and UN institutions is unequivocal that human rights are an integral part of the international law of occupation—provided of course that they do not clash with a *lex specialis* rule of IH" (quotation on 664).

74. Tolley, *International Commission of Jurists*, 98; Anthony Tirado Chase, *Human Rights, Revolution, and Reform in the Muslim World* (Boulder: Lynne Rienner, 2012), 32–33. The four states Chase names here are Afghanistan, Syria, Egypt, and Saudi Arabia; in fierce opposition were Britain and France. See also Moyn, *Last Utopia*, 96–98.

75. Chase, *Human Rights, Revolution, and Reform*, 27.

76. Moyn, *Last Utopia*, 107–8, 134.

77. Mouin Rabbani, "Palestinian Human Rights Activism under Israeli Occupation: The Case of Al-Haq," *Arab Studies Quarterly* 16/2 (1994): 29.

78. Hajjar, "Human Rights in Israel/Palestine," 23.

79. José Zalaquett, "Evaluation of al-Haq's Programs, Strategy and Work," February 1994, 18, al-Haq archives.

80. Hanny Megally, "Human Rights in the Arab World: Reflections on the Challenges Facing Human Rights Activism," in *Human Rights in the Arab World: Independent Voices*, ed. Anthony Chase and Amr Hamzawy (Philadelphia: University of Pennsylvania Press, 2006), 107. See also Stork, "Three Decades of Human Rights Activism," 83. Fateh Azzam attributes the start of the human rights movement in the Arab region to politically disenchanted Marxists and nationalists and to "lawyers and intellectuals who believed that a focus on the law would liberate the struggle for freedoms from its political manipulations and machinations." Azzam, "Reflections on Three Decades of Human Rights Work in the Arab Region," in Chase, ed., *Routledge Handbook on Human Rights*, 463.

81. See Waltz, *Human Rights and Reform*, 133–50. Waltz and others writing on this subject do not include for consideration in their study of other Arab human rights groups the earlier Moroccan League of Human Rights, founded in 1972 by the ruling Istiqlal party, its lack of political independence placing it outside the idea of the "human rights organisation." See Stork, "Three Decades of Human Rights Activism," 97, and Kevin Dwyer, *Arab Voices: The Human Rights Debate in the Middle East* (London: Routledge, 1991), 161.

82. See Dwyer, *Arab Voices*, 159.

83. Anthony Tirado Chase, "Human Rights and Agency in the Arab World," in Chase and Hamzawy, eds., *Human Rights in the Arab World*, 12; Dwyer, *Arab Voices*, 159–60 (interview with Saad ed-Din Ibrahim).

84. Stork, "Three Decades of Human Rights Activism," 90.

85. Waltz, *Human Rights and Reform*, 135.

86. Hani Shukrallah, quoted in Stork, "Three Decades of Human Rights Activism," 91. See similarly Megally, "Human Rights in the Arab World," 108.

87. Jill Crystal. "The Human Rights Movement in the Arab World," *Human Rights Quarterly* 16/3 (1994): 449.

88. *The Reply of Law in the Service of Man / al-Haq to the US Report on Human Rights Practices in the Territories Occupied by Israel for 1982* (Ramallah: LSM, 1983), prepared by Timothy Hiller. See also chapter 5 of the present work. For discussion of the establishment and development of the country reports under Carter and Reagan by an author who worked with the State Department on them in 1980, see Judith de Neufville, "Human Rights Reporting as a Policy Tool: An Examination of the State Department Country Reports," *Human Rights Quarterly* 8 (1986): 681–99.

89. See Moyn, *Last Utopia*, 155. He later observed that Carter "almost wandered into using the language." Moyn, "Return of the Prodigal," 9. See Neier, *International Human Rights Movement*, 94, 165–68, for his assessment, and Power, *Amnesty International*, for a contemporary view of the significance (to Amnesty's work) of Carter's human rights policy more broadly. Waltz argues that Carter "gave the concept new rhetorical life." Waltz, *Human Rights and Reform*, 25. Daniel Sargent describes Carter as "moved by a humanitarian spirit and strong (some said rigid) moral commitments." Sargent, "Oasis in the Desert? America's Human Rights Rediscovery," in Eckel and Moyn, eds., *Breakthrough*, 143.

90. John Dumbrell, *American Foreign Policy: Carter to Clinton* (London: MacMillan, 1997), 17. Jan Eckel notes a similar reaction among some European conservatives to the Helsinki process, viewing it "as a new venue for discrediting the socialist system." Eckel, "Rebirth of Politics," 249.

91. Dumbrell, *American Foreign Policy*, 17.

92. Sari Hanafi and Linda Tabar comment similarly in "Palestinian Human Rights Organisations: Agenda and Praxis," *Palestine-Israel Journal* 10/2 (2003): 24.

93. B'Tselem (the Israeli Information Centre for Human Rights in the Occupied Territories) was established in February 1989. See further chapter 5.

94. Jimmy Carter, "Israel, Palestine, Peace or Apartheid," *The Guardian*, December 12, 2006.

CHAPTER 2. BEGINNINGS

1. The correspondence between the Palestinian group and the ICJ quoted here was provided from the personal archive of Nidal Taha.

2. Letter of April 7, 1977, from Nidal Taha, Raja Shehadeh, and two others.

3. Shehadeh, "Human Rights and the Israeli Occupation," 37.

4. On ICJ commissioners, see http://www.icj.org.

5. Untitled document of January 7, 1970, headed International Commission of Jurists, Israel National Section, under the names of Haim Cohn and Adv. Daniel Jacobson, ICJ archives.

6. "The Middle East: War or Peace," *ICJ Review* 3 (September 1969): 10–14. See also Tolley, *International Commission of Jurists*, 127.

7. MacBride also went on to head a panel of international jurists (the MacBride Commission) to investigate alleged war crimes in the Israeli invasion of Lebanon in 1982, including the massacre at Sabra and Shatila. See *Israel in Lebanon: The Report of the International Commission to Inquire into Reported Violations of International Law by Israel during Its Invasion of Lebanon* (London: Ithaca Press, 1984); and Edward Said's reflection on this report in *London Review of Books*, February 16, 1984, 13–17. See also Neier, *International Human Rights Movement*, 188; and Power, *Amnesty International*, 12–13.

8. International Commission of Jurists, Israeli National Section, January 7, 1970, reporting a decision taken at its general meeting the previous day "to register its protest" against *The Review*'s publication of the report, ICJ archives.

9. Lisa Hajjar, *Courting Conflict: The Israeli Military Court System in the West Bank and Gaza* (London: University of California Press, 2005), 63.

10. Tam Dalyell, "Obituary: Niall MacDermot." *The Independent*, February 27, 1996.

11. Richard Norton-Taylor considers MacDermot a "notorious example" of people who were "blacklisted by MI5 on grounds of putative or past communist affiliation"—in this case because MacDermot's second wife had worked with the Italian resistance during the Second World War "and must, therefore, have been a communist." Norton-Taylor, "Official MI5 History Sheds Little Light," *The Guardian*, October 6, 2009, reviewing Christopher Andrew, *The Defence of the Realm: The Authorized History of MI5* (London: Penguin, 2009).

12. Howard B. Tolley Jr., "Popular Sovereignty and International Law: ICJ Strategies for Human Rights Standard-Setting," *Human Rights Quarterly* 11/4 (1989): 571. The quotation is sourced to a study by Iain Guest, *Behind the Disappearances: Argentina's Dirty War against Human Rights and the United Nations* (Philadelphia: University of Pennsylvania Press, 1990). See also Tolley, 577.

13. *ICJ Revew* 19 (December 1977): 27–36.

14. "Speech by Mr. Niall MacDermot, Secretary-General of the International Commission of Jurists, at a Meeting in the Palais des Nations, Geneva, on the Occasion of the International Day of Solidarity with the Palestinian People," November 29, 1979, in ICJ Newsletter no. 4 (October 1—December 31, 1979), Appendix A, 27–30, quotation from 29.

15. ICJ Newsletter no. 4, 28.

16. "Speech at the UN Headquarters, Geneva, on 29 November 1980, the International Day of Solidarity with the Palestinian People, by Niall MacDermot, Secretary-General of the ICJ," ICJ Newsletter no. 7 (October 1–December 31, 1980), 22–25, quotation on 24–25. The study he was referring to is Ann Mosely Lesch, *Political Perceptions of the Palestinians of the West Bank and Gaza Strip* (Washington, DC: Middle East Institute, 1980).

17. Hiltermann, "Al-Haq: The First Twenty Years," 11. In the 1972 *Chambers Twentieth Century Dictionary* (ed. A.M. Macdonald, Edinburgh, repr. 1974), the second definition for the noun *Palestinian* was "a member of a guerrilla movement one of whose aims is to reclaim former Arab lands from Israelis."

18. Speech by Niall MacDermot, November 29, 1979, 27.

19. Tolley, *International Commission of Jurists*, 196.

20. Richard Pierre Claude, review of Tolley, *International Commission of Jurists*, in *Human Rights Quarterly* 16/3 (1994): 576.

21. Tolley, *International Commission of Jurists*, 144. See *ICJ Review* 26 (1981) reporting an ICJ conference and commission meeting on development and the rule of law.

22. Claude, Review of *International Commission of Jurists*, 576. The ICJ was not the only recipient of these funds.

23. Tolley, *International Commission of Jurists*, 125. Tolley covers these events at 125–30.

24. Neier, *International Human Rights Movement*, 248. The *ICJ Review* of 1970 states that a funding crisis had caused past issues not to appear.

25. Jean Ziegler, "Justice et oppression," *Afrique-Asie*, January 18, 1981.

26. Letter of May 9, 1977, from Niall MacDermot.

27. Letter of August 7, 1977, from Raja Shehadeh, Nidal Taha, and two others to Niall MacDermot. The reference to "occupied territories of Jordan" should be read in its time, as seeking cautiously to avoid raising the issue of Palestinian self-determination and Israel's anticipated reaction.

28. Letter of November 16, 1977, from Niall MacDermot.

29. According to Noura Erakat, "Israel contemplated dealing with Palestinians but not a Palestinian people. The latter would imply the establishment of an independent state, whereas the former implied dealings with a scattered polity with whom a host of arrangements could be conceived, including a self-governing authority." Erakat, *Justice for Some*, 131.

30. Tolley, *International Commission of Jurists*, 149; he records on 150 that the Israeli ICJ section "discontinued its limited chapter" in 1988.

31. Shehadeh, "Human Rights and the Israeli Occupation," 36.

32. Letter of March 13, 1978, from Niall MacDermot.

33. Letter of November 9, 1978, from Hans Thoolen (office of Niall MacDermot) to Charles Shammas.

34. Letter of October 8, 1979, from Niall Macdermot to Jonathan Kuttab.

35. Shehadeh, "Human Rights and the Israeli Occupation," 37.

36. Letter of February 18, 1978, from Raja Shehadeh, Charles Shammas, Nidal Taha, and three others to Niall MacDermot.

37. After the arrival of the PA, al-Haq joined an eventually successful civil society campaign seeking revision of a draft by the Palestinian executive of a similarly intrusive text aimed at constraining the responsible functioning of the NGO sector. See Rema Hammami, "Palestinian NGOs since Oslo: From NGO Politics to Social Movements?," *Middle East Report* 214 (2000): 16–19.

38. Letter of March 13, 1978, from Niall MacDermot.

39. Letter of September 20, 1978, from Charles Shammas, Raja Shehadeh, Nidal Taha, and three others to Niall MacDermot.

40. Letter of November 9, 1978, from Hans Thoolen (office of Niall MacDermot) to Charles Shammas.

41. Letter of September 26, 1979, from Jonathan Kuttab "on behalf of Mssrs" Taha, Shehadeh, Shamas, and six others to Niall MacDermot.

42. In the early 1980s, LSM invested considerable energy in working with Gazan colleagues towards the establishment of an ICJ affiliate—including assigning a staff member with this specific brief—an objective first realized in the relatively short-lived Gaza Centre for Rights and Law (established in 1985). Newsletter no. 9 (July–October 1985). The Palestinian Centre for Human Rights (established in 1995) has been the ICJ affiliate ever since. PCHR's director, Raji Sourani, was elected as an ICJ commissioner in 2003 and reelected in 2008 and 2013; in 2006, he was elected to the Executive Committee.

43. Waltz, *Human Rights and Reform*, 138, 165.

44. Dwyer, *Arab Voices*, 167–70, interviews with Khémais Chammari and Muhammad Charfi; and 162–64 with Abderrahim Jamai. See Stork, "Three Decades of Human Rights Activism," 93, on similar challenges in the EOHR peaking in 1994, and 97 on the "competition of the leftist parties for hegemony over the organisations" in Morocco. See also Crystal, "Human Rights Movement in the Arab World," 449, on the AOHR and its Egyptian section. Hanny Megally pays tribute to the LTDH and the EOHR as "two unusual examples of organisations that have attempted to develop along membership lines." Megally, "Human Rights in the Arab World," 295n2.

45. ICJ archives.

46. Gabi Baramki describes in his memoir of Birzeit the different way that he and the exiled head of the University, Hanna Nasir, approached relations with the PLO over the same period. Baramki, *Peaceful Resistance*.

47. See ICJ Newsletter No. 7 (October 1–December 31, 1980), 22.

48. Letter of October 8, 1979, from Niall MacDermot to Jonathan Kuttab; "Agreement Made between the ICJ (The Commission) and Law in the Service of Man (The Company)," January 22, 1980.

49. Letters of February 11, 1980, and February 15, 1980, from Niall MacDermot to Nidal Taha, notifying availability of grants of $1,000 and an expected $10,000, respectively.

50. Letter of March 10, 1980, from Nidal Taha to Niall MacDermot.

51. Shehadeh, *West Bank and the Rule of Law*, 81.

52. Shehadeh, *Third Way*, 128–29.

53. Tolley, *International Commission of Jurists*, 205.

54. *ICJ Review* 24 (June 1980): 9–11. During that time MacDermot was deeply involved in deliberations at the UN Commission on Human Rights that led eventually to the adoption of the UN Convention against Torture in 1984. See Howard B. Tolley Jr., "Popular Sovereignty and International Law: ICJ Strategies for Human Rights Standard-Setting,"

Human Rights Quarterly 11/4 (1989): 570–72. MacDermot had also been involved in drafting the UN Declaration on Protection from Torture, G.A. Res. 3462 (XXX), 1978.

55. *ICJ Review* 24 (June 1980): 9. MacDermot may have met Gazan lawyers but they were not yet affiliated with the ICJ.

56. *ICJ Review* 24: 10.

57. The reference is to Menachem Begin, *White Nights: The Story of a Prisoner in Russia* (New York: Harper and Row, 1979).

58. See Melissa Phillips, *Torture for Security: The Systematic Torture and Ill-Treatment of Palestinians by Israel* (Ramallah: al-Haq, 1995), 54–58.

59. Interviews with Mona Rishmawi and Shawan Jabarin.

60. See Neier, *International Human Rights Movement*, 346n6. A former CIA agent publicly accused the ICJ of having been "CIA-controlled" in past years, after the organization published a report highly critical of the CIA-supported Pinochet regime in Chile.

61. Established by G.A. Res. 2443 (XXIII), 1748th Plenary Meeting, December 19, 1968.

62. See also Shehadeh, *Strangers in the House*, 144.

63. UN doc. A/AC.145/RT.296/Add.1, May 20, 1980, 1.

64. See also Shehaheh, *Strangers in the House*, 132.

65. Shehadeh, *Third Way*, 44–48.

66. Shehadeh, 50 (journal extract from May 13, 1980).

67. Shehadeh, "Human Rights and the Israeli Occupation," 37–38.

68. Shehadeh, *Third Way*, 52.

69. Shehadeh, "Human Rights and the Israeli Occupation," 38.

70. I have used here quotations from *The Third Way* that refer to "the book" and are footnoted as referring to *The West Bank and the Rule of Law*. Given the timing of the committee hearings and subsequently the proposal made by MacDermot for publication, related by Shehadeh in his 2008 article as well as in interview, I assume that the diary extracts were at the time referring to the manuscript of notes compiled for the committee hearings, which became the basis for the book. Shehadeh did not refer to the committee hearings in his public writings until much later.

71. UN docs. A/AC.145.RT.296/Add.1, May 20 1980 (296th meeting); A/AC.145/RT.298, May 21, 1980 (298th meeting); A/AC.145/RT.299, May 21, 1980 (299th meeting); A/AC.145/RT.300, May 22, 1980); A/AC.145/RT.301, May 22, 1980 (301st meeting); A/AC.145/RT.302, May 23, 1980 (302nd meeting). From Shehadeh's personal archives.

72. UN doc. A/AC.145/RT.296/Add.1, May 20, 1980, 10.

73. Un doc. A/AC.145/RT.299, May 21, 1980, 17.

74. UN doc. A/AC.145/RT.302, May 23, 1980, 4–5.

75. Roberts, "Transformative Military Occupation," 620. Shehadeh and Kuttab also note this development (in Military Order 268 of July 24, 1968) with approval. Shehadeh, *West Bank and the Rule of Law*, 122. Commendation of Israel's abolition of the judicial death penalty in local law in the West Bank and Gaza does not remove condemnation of its policies and practices of extrajudicial executions and unlawful targeted killings, as documented by al-Haq and others down the decades and as publicly sanctioned in more recent times by Israel's highest court. The judicial death penalty remained theoretically available to Israeli military courts in certain cases, although it has not been implemented; for the role this plays and the debate around it in Israeli public discourse, see Ron Dudai, "Restraint, Reaction, and Penal Fantasies: Notes on the Death Penalty in Israel, 1967–2017," *Law and Social Inquiry* 43/3 (2017): 862–88.

76. Shehadeh, *Human Rights and the Israeli Occupation*, 38.

77. UN doc. A/AC.145/RT.300, May 22, 1980, 3. This was in April 1980. Shehadeh, *West Bank and the Rule of Law*, 49.

78. Bisharat, *Palestinian Lawyers and Israeli Rule*, 152.

CHAPTER 3. FOUNDERS

1. The first section is considerably longer than the other two, partly because the two first publications were authored by both Shehadeh and Kuttab, and partly because of Shehadeh's published output.

2. Interview with Marc Stephens.

3. Shehadeh, *Strangers in the House*, 133–34.

4. See chapter 1 and the further discussion in the epilogue of this refusal as a fundamental plank of Israel's lawfare narrative to avoid important constraints of IHL on an occupying power's conduct. On the lawfare narrative, see Lisa Hajjar, *Lawfare and Armed Conflict: Comparing Israeli and US Targeted Killing Policies and Challenges against Them* (Beirut: Issam Fares Institute for Public Policy and International Affairs, American University of Beirut, 2013).

5. Shehadeh, *West Bank and the Rule of Law*, 11.

6. On "rightful resistance," see Tripp, *Power and the People*, 9, 216; and Kevin O'Brien, "Rightful Resistance," *World Politics* 49/1 (1996): 31–55.

7. Tolley, *International Commission of Jurists*, 150, 206.

8. "Israel Accused of Extending Rule in West Bank," *International Herald Tribune*, October 3, 1980; "Israel Denounced on West Bank," *The Guardian*, October 3, 1980; John Quigley, review of Shehadeh, *West Bank and the Rule of Law*, *International Lawyer* 15/2 (1981); Musa Mazzawi, review of Shehadeh, *West Bank and the Rule of Law*, *Middle East International*, November 21, 1980.

9. Shehadeh, *Third Way*, 106.

10. Shehadeh, "Human Rights and the Israeli Occupation," 38.

11. Shehadeh, *Third Way*, 102.

12. Jean Ziegler, "Justice et Oppression," *Afrique-Asie*, January 18, 1981.

13. Edward Grossman, "Thyme and Occupation," *Jerusalem Post Magazine*, January 2, 1981.

14. Israeleft Bi-Weekly News Service, no. 181, January 22, 1981.

15. Shehadeh, *Third Way*, 126–27. The "either" at the end of the quote refers to an earlier entry describing the reaction of an officer of the military government; 107–8 (emphasis in the original).

16. MacDermot, preface to Shehadeh, *West Bank and the Rule of Law*, 7; Tolley, *International Commission of Jurists*, 149. There is some anecdotal evidence that MacDermot had to deal with adverse reactions from some of his commissioners following the launch of the book and its attendant publicity.

17. Rabbani, "Palestinian Human Rights Activism," 30.

18. Rabbani, 31; he has a list of compilations at note 13.

19. Letter from Lieutenant Colonel Joel Singer, head, International Law Branch, Israel Defence Forces, to Raja Shehadeh and Jonathan Kuttab, LSM Ramallah, March 30, 1983, al-Haq archives.

20. *The Rule of Law in the Areas Administered by Israel* (Tel Aviv: Israeli National Section of the International Commission of Jurists, 1981), vii–viii.

21. Shehadeh, "Human Rights and the Israeli Occupation," 40.

22. *Rule of Law in the Areas Administered by Israel*, viii.

23. *Rule of Law in the Areas Administered by Israel*, ix.

24. *Rule of Law in the Areas Administered by Israel*, xi.

25. *Rule of Law in the Areas Administered by Israel*, xii.

26. In a 1981 article, Raja Shehadeh responded to the Israeli ICJ publication on the specific issue on amendments made to local law to the benefit of Israeli settlements in the West Bank in the context of Camp David and noting "strong similarities" with certain of the practices of the apartheid government in South Africa. Shehadeh, "The Legal System of the Israeli Settlements in the West Bank," *ICJ Review* 2 (December 1981): 59–74.

27. Michael Reisman, "International Law and the Israeli Occupation," *The Nation*, December 5, 1981.

28. *Human Rights Internet Reporter* 7/1 (1981): 159–63. For an appraisal of this organization's interventions during the 1980s, see Abraham et al, "International Human Rights Organizations," 16–17.

29. "This took place on January 9th, 1982." Letter from Raja Shehadeh to Laurie Wiseberg, March 13, 1982, al-Haq archives. In his 1981 response in the *ICJ Review*, Shehadeh had also taken up the dismissal by the Israeli study's "anonymous authors" of his own statement as to the nonavailability to the public of military orders, with further details on this subject. Shehadeh, "Legal System of the Israeli Settlements," 60–61.

30. *Al-Quds*, October 3, 1980; *Al-Fajr*, October 26–November 1, 1980.

31. *Al-diffa al-gharbiyya wa hukm al-qanun*, translated by Wadi' Khouri and published by Dar al-Kilma li'l-Nashr, 1982. A note at the front states, "in cooperation with the ICJ and the LSM group."

32. Shehadeh, *Strangers in the House*, 148.

33. Shehadeh, *West Bank and the Rule of Law*, 50.

34. Shehedeh, *Rift in Time*, 6.

35. Shehadeh, *Strangers in the House*, 131, 133.

36. Shehadeh, *Strangers in the House*, 129.

37. Shehadeh, *Strangers in the House*, 128.

38. Bisharat, *Palestinian Lawyers and Israeli Rule*, 3. He notes that when he first went, he assumed that the LSM founders were "typical" and was unaware of the conflict around the issue of practicing/striking lawyers.

39. Bisharat, "Courting Justice?," 349.

40. Shehadeh, *Third Way*, 118–19.

41. Bisharat, "Courting Justice?," 359. See also Bisharat, *Palestinian Lawyers and Israeli Rule*, 145–61, on "Disintegration of the Profession."

42. Bisharat, "Courting Justice?," 397.

43. Bisharat, 350.

44. Bisharat, 359. See also Hajjar, *Courting Conflict*, 177. Israeli human rights lawyers and scholars continue to publish about the dilemmas involved in their work.

45. Bisharat, "Courting Justice?," 395. On the diverging views of some Israeli human rights advocates and the Palestinians they were representing, see also Talhami, "The Palestinian Perception of the Human Rights Issue."

46. Al-Haq was to publish a study of this later: Martha Roadstrum Moffett, *Perpetual Emergency: A Legal Analysis of Israel's Use of the British Defence (Emergency) Regulations, 1945, in the Occupied Territories* (Ramallah: al-Haq, 1989).

47. Shehadeh, *Third Way*, 101. The Israeli government had moved to allow appeals in accordance with the Defence (Emergency) Regulations in 1977; the first appeal against a deportation order had been turned down in 1979 in *Abu 'Awad v. IDF Commander of Judea and Samaria* (1979); see Hiltermann, *Israel's Deportation Policy*, 10, and see 13 for extracts from the affidavit of Aziz Shehadeh in the 1980 case. Justice Haim Cohn dissented from his colleagues to hold in a minority opinion that the "prohibition of deportation is absolute," and Hiltermann reproduces interviews with him in the Israeli press on 35, 86, 88. Cohn also publicly deplored the use of the Defence (Emergency) Regulations.

48. Hiltermann, *Israel's Deportation Policy*, 58–59. The two deportees were Mahmud Da'is and Yunis al-Rujub. Gabi Baramki reproduces the deportation statement (from Beirut) of Hanna Nasir, the president of Birzeit University who was deported before appeal to the Israeli Supreme Court was granted, in *Peaceful Resistance*, 169–72.

49. Al-Haq/LSM Newsletter no. 17 (January–February 1987), 5. The deportee was Muhammad Yusuf Dahlan.

50. Michael Sfard, "The Human Rights Lawyer's Existential Dilemma," *Israel Law Review* 38/3 (2005) 154–69. The article is a review of Kretzmer, *Occupation of Justice*. See also Michael Sfard, *The Wall and The Gate: Israel, Palestine and the Legal Battle for Human Rights* (New York: Metropolitan Books, 2017).

51. Sfard, 156 (emphasis in the original).

52. Sfard, 156n2. A different approach is set out by Hassan Jabareen, who describes the efforts of Adalah—The Legal Centre for Arab Minority Rights in Israel. Jabareen argues for a reformulated understanding of legal victory in light of new dimensions of transnational rights lawyering in "Transnational Lawyering and Legal Resistance in National Courts: Palestinian Cases before the Israeli Supreme Court," *Yale Human Rights and Development Law Journal* 13 (2010): 239–80.

53. Shehadeh, *Rift in Time*, 60. See also Raja Shehadeh, *Palestinian Walks: Notes on a Vanishing Landscape* (London: Profile Books, 2007), 53.

54. Shehadeh. "Human Rights and the Israeli Occupation," 38–42.

55. Shehadeh, 50. Article XIX of the 1995 Israeli-Palestinian Interim Agreement on the West Bank and Gaza Strip (having otherwise avoided mention of international law) states that Israel and the PA "shall exercise their powers and responsibilities pursuant to this Agreement with due regard to internationally accepted norms and principles of human rights and the rule of law."

56. Shehadeh, "Human Rights and the Israeli Occupation," 39. See Hajjar, "Human Rights in Israel/Palestine"; and on the "meta-conflict" involving the law, see Cavanaugh, "Narrating Law." For battles over control of other narratives, see Edward Said, "Permission to Narrate: Edward Said Writes about the Story of the Palestinians," *London Review of Books*, February 16, 1984, 13–17. See Tripp, *Power and the People*, 223–37 on Israeli "critical sociologists" and "new historians."

57. Stanley Cohen, *States of Denial: Knowing about Atrocities and Suffering* (Cambridge: Polity Press, 2001), 7–8. An examination of "the Israeli culture of denial" is examined in Cohen's work on 157–59 with a focus on reactions of the Israeli Jewish public to publicized human rights violations during the first intifada.

58. Kuttab and Shehadeh, *Civilian Administration in the Occupied West Bank*, quoted material on 22. This 1982 study was translated into Arabic by Mona Rishmawi and published by LSM in 1983.

59. Kuttab and Shehadeh, 12.

60. Letter from Lieutenant Colonel Joel Singer, head, International Law Branch, Israel Defence Forces General Staff, to Raja Shehadeh, LSM, Ramallah, March 30, 1983, enclosing copies of Joel Singer, "The Establishment of a Civil Administration in the Areas Administered by Israel," *Israel Yearbook on Human Rights* 12 (1982): 259–337. Shehadeh also examines the role played by Singer in the preparations for the Declaration of Principles in "Human Rights and the Israeli Occupation," 46.

61. Shehadeh, "Human Rights and the Israeli Occupation," 42. He explains his use of the term *apartheid*: "different laws applicable to different groups with different and unequal distribution of resources and opportunities for development."

62. UN Division for Palestinian Rights, "The First International NGO Meeting on the Question of Palestine," United Nations Offices, Geneva, August 20–22, 1984, 53–56.

63. Shehadeh, Shehadeh, and Shehadeh, *Israeli Proposed Road Plan.*

64. Al-Haq/LSM Newsletter no. 6 (January–February 1985), 5. A decade later al-Haq reexamined this issue in Samira Shah, *The By-Pass Road Network in the West Bank* (Ramallah: al-Haq, 1997). See also Shah, "On the Road to Apartheid: The Bypass Road Network in the West Bank," *Columbia Human Rights Law Review* 29 (1997–98): 221–377. A later secretary-general of the International Commission of Jurists, Adama Dieng, also lobbied the commission to seek a ruling from the International Court of Justice, this time on the issue of Israeli settlements. Tolley notes that the commission "deferred action" in 1992. Tolley, *International Commission of Jurists,* 226.

65. Shehadeh, "Advice to the Palestinian Leadership." *London Review of Books*, July 3, 2014, 10–13. This comment is part of Shehadeh's critique of the PLO leadership for paying insufficient attention to the legal mechanisms of control and expropriation that Israel was implementing in the oPt.

66. "Legal Consequences of the Construction of a Wall in the Occupied Palestinian Territory," advisory opinion, *ICJ Reports* 2004, 136.

67. According to the Orwell Prize website: http://theorwellprize.co.uk/the-orwell-prize/.

68. Shehadeh, *Palestinian Walks,* 58–62.

69. This order was taken up in LSM's work; see Newsletter no. 11 (January–February 1986). West Bank lawyers from outside Jerusalem had been excluded from practice in Jerusalem; Jerusalem lawyers could continue to practice in Jerusalem but had to be admitted to the Israeli bar to do so. See Bisharat, *Palestinian Lawyers and Israeli Rule,* 146.

70. "Statement of Jonathan Kuttab, Esquire, for the Palestine Human Rights Campaign, Foreign Affairs Committee, US House of Representatives, 7 March 1985," al-Haq archives, reported in al-Haq Newsletter no. 7 (March–April 1985), 4–5.

71. See Mubarak Awad, "Non-Violent Resistance: A Strategy for the Occupied Territories," *Journal of Palestine Studies* 13/4 (Summer 1984): 22–36. See also Victoria Mason and Richard Falk, "Assessing Nonviolence in the Palestinian Rights Struggle," *State Crime Journal* 5/1 (2016): 163–86.

72. Based in Jerusalem, the center was directed by Mubarak Awad until his deportation by the Israeli authorities in 1988. Kuttab has also been chair of the board of directors of the Holy Land Trust, which incorporated the Palestinian Center for the Study of Non-Violence in 1998. Background at www.holylandtrust.org/index.php (accessed August 11, 2012). He is also a co-founder, wth Awad, of Nonviolence International (see www.nonviolenceinternational.net/).

73. Jim Wallis, "Interview with Palestinian Christian, Jonathan Kuttab: Inside Israeli Apartheid," *Sojourners Magazine*, September–October 2001.

74. See the HURIDOCS website, www.huridocs.org/ (accessed December 19, 2020).

75. On HURIDOCS, see Hans Thoolen, "We Were Breaking New Ground," interview conducted by Friedhelm Weinberg, HURIDOCS, November 30, 2012, www.huridocs .org/2012/11/we-were-breaking-new-ground/. Thoolen was a founder of HURIDOCS after working at the International Commission of Jurists. In an earlier article, "A Biased History of Huridocs" (May 3, 2002; this piece was no longer available on the HURIDOCS site when accessed November 23, 2020), Thoolen mentioned Judith Dueck, who joined HURIDOCS after a stint managing the expansion of LSM/al-Haq in the mid-1980s. Al-Haq's database coordinator, Nina Atallah, also served on the International Advisory Board of HURIDOCS.

76. Accreditation of this report is to "the staff of Law in the Service of Man."

77. *Al-Fara'a Report*, 1985, 1. This report and its predecessor, issued in paper copy only by LSM in 1984, are regarded as milestones in LSM's early work by many staffers from the time. An earlier collection of affidavits on selected subjects had been published by the World Council of Churches as *Human Rights Violations in the West Bank: In Their Own Words; Affidavits Collected by Law in the Service of Man* (Geneva: Commission of the Churches on International Affairs, World Council of Churches, 1983).

78. Niall MacDermot, editorial, *The Review* 34 (June 1985): 1.

79. MacDermot, editorial.

80. "Statement by Ambassador Ephraim Dowek on the Report of Law in the Service of Men," Commission on Human Rights, 41st session, February 1985, al-Haq archives.

81. Letter of March 23, 1985, from Jonathan Kuttab, director, LSM, to the Israeli Ministry of Foreign Affairs, copy to Israeli ambassador Ephraim Dowek in Geneva. Text reproduced by MacDermot in *ICJ Review* 34 (June 1985) by way of a right of reply to the attack on the ICJ and LSM by the Israeli ambassador. Following the launch of the 1985 report and the allegations made against LSM by the Israeli ambassador at the Human Rights Commission, Israeli MK Matti Peled sent a parliamentary question to then foreign minister Yitzhak Shamir, asking him "to indicate exactly which evidence provided by LSM was not based on facts." In a response, Shamir's deputy claimed that "evidence provided by LSM had been used by others to attack the Israeli government's policy in the Occupied Territories," referring specifically to "presentations made by LSM directors Raja Shehadeh and Jonathan Kuttab during their tours abroad, and to materials given by LSM to such organisations as the World Council of Churches and the United Nations Human Rights Commission." Newsletter no. 10 (November–December 1985), 5–6. LSM noted that the response "failed [. . .] to answer directly the issue of the alleged falsity of LSM's report on al-Fara'a."

82. The papers from the conference were published in *International Law and the Administration of Occupied Territories: Two Decades of Israeli Occupation of the West Bank and Gaza Strip*, ed. Emma Playfair (Oxford: Clarendon Press, 1992).

83. Jonathan Kuttab, "Avenues Open for Defence of Human Rights in the Israeli-Occupied Territories," in Playfair, ed., *International Law and the Administration of Occupied Territories*, 498.

84. Kuttab, "Avenues Open for Defence of Human Rights," 499.

85. Shehadeh makes a similar point: "We weren't going to be another organisation that condemns things, it doesn't bring anything; we were distinguishing ourselves from that." See also Allen, *Rise and Fall of Human Rights*, 49.

86. Kuttab, "Avenues Open for Defence of Human Rights," 499–500.

87. See Megally, "Human Rights in the Arab World," 109; Waltz, *Human Rights and Reform*, 21; and Dwyer, *Arab Voices*, 167–69, on recognition by other human rights groups and actors in the Arab world of the significance of universality.

88. One notable exception to this came in the form of a letter to then president Bourghiba of Tunisia asking him to intervene against the detention of Khémais Chammari, then vice-president of the FIDH and secretary-general of the LTDH, on charges of slandering the Tunisian prime minister. Al-Haq was acting on the basis of information received from Amnesty International. Al-Haq Newsletter no. 19 (May–June 1987), 5. See Waltz, *Human Rights and Reform*, 13.

89. Kuttab, "Avenues Open for Defence of Human Rights," 500–501.

90. Different scholars examine the way in which human rights is so perceived and presented, for example Moyn, *Last Utopia* (internationally and historically); Stephen Hopgood, *Keepers of the Flame: Understanding Amnesty International* (Ithaca, NY: Cornell University Press, 2006) (at Amnesty International); and Waltz, *Human Rights and Reform* (among North African activists).

91. Kuttab, "Avenues Open for Defence of Human Rights," 502.

92. Kuttab, 502.

93. Hiltermann, "Al-Haq: The First Twenty Years," 10.

94. Ron Dudai discusses this in the particular context of the death penalty debate in Israel. Dudai, "Restraint, Reaction, and Penal Fantasies." See also Cohen, *States of Denial*; and James Ron's consideration of the conduct of the Israeli military in the first intifada, which "views security forces as decoupled organizations embedded in environments saturated by concerns for legitimacy and norms." Ron, "Savage Restraint: Israel, Palestine and the Dialectics of Legal Repression," *Social Problems* 47/4 (2000): 446.

95. Letter of November 6, 1982, from Jonathan Kuttab to Niall MacDermot of the ICJ, copied to Justice Haim Cohn and a number of other Israeli and international human rights contacts.

96. Letter of August 24, 1983, from Jonathan Kuttab to Justice Haim Cohn, responding to letter of July 7 from Cohn to Kuttab.

97. *Markaz tatbiqat al-tanmiya al-intajiyya.*

98. Newsletter no. 20 (July–August 1987).

99. The continued work of Shammas and colleagues focused on EU commitments and domestic regulations, eventually (in the summer of 2013) winning a breakthrough with the commission and EU states in regard to EU states' regulation of entry to their markets of Israeli settlement goods (see chapter 5). See Emily Harris, "An Israeli-Palestinian Battle with Roots in Lingerie," NPR, August 6, 2016.

100. Charles Shammas, "The Role of the Enforcement of International Law in the Processes of Dispute Settlement," in *Towards a Strategy for the Enforcement of Human Rights in the Israeli Occupied West Bank and Gaza: A Working Symposium*, London, July 25, 1989 (London: Labour Middle East Council and Conservative Middle East Council, 1989), 35–38.

101. "Manual of the Al-Haq Database—Draft," undated internal al-Haq document, circa 1984–85, emphasis in the original.

102. Hiltermann, "Human Rights and the Politics of Computer Software," 8–9.

103. The HURIDOCS conference was reported in al-Haq Newsletter no. 12 (March–April 1986). Kuttab had by then been institutionally involved with HURIDOCS for some years, as noted above.

104. Manuel Guzman, "The Investigation and Documentation of Events as a Methodology in Monitoring Human Rights Violations," *Statistical Journal of the United Nations ECE* 18 (2001): 249–57. The task force's work resulted in a 1993 HURIDOCS publication on standard formats coedited by Judith Dueck, formerly an al-Haq staffer.

105. Allen, *Rise and Fall of Human Rights*, 34.

106. Rabbani, "Palestinian Human Rights Activism," 49n46.

CHAPTER 4. ORGANISATION

1. The Jerusalem-based Palestine Human Rights Information Centre was established in 1986 through the Arab Studies Society. For other human rights initiatives during this period (such as Birzeit University's Human Rights Action Project), see Penny Johnson, "The Routine of Repression: Notes on the Struggle for Rights in the West Bank and Gaza," *Middle East Report* 150 (January–February 1988): 3–11.

2. See John Quigley, *The Case for Palestine: An International Law Perspective* (Durham, NC: Duke University Press, 2005), 200.

3. Hiltermann, *Israel's Deportation Policy*, 70.

4. Hiltermann, 81. The deportation of Qawasme, Milhem, and Tamimi had been the last until 1985, after what Hiltermann calls the "fracas" of the arguments at the Supreme Court, particularly opposition from Haim Cohn. Hiltermann, 74.

5. Hilterman, 72; Johnson, "Routine of Repression," 6.

6. Shehadeh, in *Twenty Years Defending Human Rights*, 6.

7. This founding year was also given in a few of the earliest publications; later, all referred to 1979.

8. Newsletter no. 6 (January–February 1985), 5–6.

9. Rabbani, "Palestinian Human Rights Activism," 27–28.

10. Respectively, in 1982 and 1983 (Arabic texts).

11. Compare the role of the newsletter issued by the Belfast-based Committee on the Administration of Justice (established in 1980) as described by Maggie Beirne, *A Beacon of Light: The Story of CAJ* (Belfast: Committee on the Administration of Justice, 2016), 13–14.

12. Or more usually "al-Haq institution" (*mu'assasat al-haqq*). In Palestine, the usual Arabic term for organization (*munazhzhama*) was generally reserved for "*the* Organization," the PLO.

13. Newsletter no. 11 (January–February 1986).

14. Hiltermann, "Al-Haq: The First Twenty Years," 9. LSM's first office staffer, Paulein Hanna née Natour, worked with al-Haq throughout her professional life until her untimely death in 2002.

15. The arrival of the phone line was announced in Newsletter no. 4 (September–October 1984). Bisharat notes that in 1984–85, the waiting time for a new telephone line could be three to four years. Bisharat, *Palestinian Lawyers and Israeli Rule*, 207n13.

16. Newsletter no. 9 (July–October 1985), 1: "Many of our associates have reported that they do not receive our publications, even when sent out for the second time."

17. See also Virgil Falloon, *Excessive Secrecy, Lack of Guidelines: A Report on Military Censorship in the West Bank* (Ramallah: LSM, 1986), reprinted from *Index on Censorship* 13/4 (1984): 32–36.

18. By 1986 the organization was funded by "ten European and North American organisations concerned with human rights and the rule of law," had project-specific funding from the European Human Rights Foundation, and had secured a three-year grant from the then EEC through OXFAM. Al-Haq, Programme Report, 1986, 30.

19. According to Margaret E. Keck and Kathryn Sikkink, Ford's turn to human rights funding in the late 1970s was directly prompted by Ford field offices in South America. Keck and Sikkink, *Activists beyond Borders*, 98.

20. "Draft Study of al-Haq's Structure: Past, Present and Future," internal memo, 1988, al-Haq archives.

21. The same point was made by other field researchers. See also Allen, *Rise and Fall of Human Rights*, 41.

22. Fateh Azzam, "Non-Governmental Organisations between the Field of Politics and the Field of Human Rights," *al-Quds*, June 25 1993, reproduced in *Zawiyat huquq al-insan* [Human rights corner] (Ramallah: al-Haq, 1993), 131–32.

23. Emma Playfair, *Administrative Detention in the Occupied West Bank* (Ramallah: al-Haq, 1986).

24. LSM Newsletter no. 9 (July–October 1985), 4. In the first year of the uprising, both were given further administrative detention orders and were adopted as "prisoners of conscience" by Amnesty International. Three other al-Haq field workers (Abdel Karim Kan'an, Shawan Jabarin, Iyad Haddad) and researcher Riziq Shuqair were also detained during that first year. *Punishing a Nation: Human Rights during the Palestinian Uprising, December 1987–December 1988* (Ramallah: al-Haq, 1989), 290–92.

25. Newsletter no. 19 (May–June 1987), 6.

26. Letter of December 17, 1987, from Shehadeh to MacDermot, in response to letter from MacDermot of September 9, 1987.

27. Iain Guest, "Defending Human Rights in the Occupied Palestinian Territory—Challenges and Opportunities: A Discussion Paper on Human Rights Work in the West Bank and Gaza Strip," report and conclusions of a mission conducted for Friedrich Ebert Foundation (Jerusalem, February 2007), 35.

28. Compare also Allen, *Rise and Fall of Human Rights*, 50–51.

29. Shehadeh, *Strangers in the House*, 174.

30. Shehaheh, "Human Rights and the Israeli Occupation," 37.

31. Shehadeh, *Strangers in the House*, 178.

32. According to Newsletter no. 16 (November–December 1986), human rights courses were introduced in Birzeit University and in Hebron University in March 1986.

33. Jabarin recalled putting the allegations about al-Haq's CIA connections to Jonathan Kuttab during his interview with the organization in 1987. Joe Stork quotes Moroccan human rights defender Driss al-Yazami as recalling that the key constituency around whom the human rights movement grew in Morocco in the 1970s was the prisoners, and "the prisoners themselves were mainly Marxists then, and for them human rights was a bourgeois issue." Stork, "Three Decades of Human Rights Activism," 96.

34. International Commission of Jurists, *The Rule of Law and Human Rights: Principles and Definitions* (Geneva: International Commission of Jurists, 1966; translated as *Siyadat*

al-qanun wa huquq al-insan by Wadi' Salim Khouri, Ramallah: LSM, 1985). Newsletter no. 9 (July–September 1985) reported the publication of the translation of this "book of primary importance" and a launch of the publication, with discussion, at the Hakawati Theatre in East Jerusalem.

35. Bisharat, "Courting Justice?," 397.

36. See also Allen, *Rise and Fall of Human Rights*, 51–53.

37. Rabbani, "Palestinian Human Rights Activism," 29. See also Allen, *Rise and Fall of Human Rights*, 47.

38. By comparison, Ghada Talhami's 1987 consideration of Palestinian perceptions of human rights starts with an exposition of the right to self-determination. Talhami, "Palestinian Perception of the Human Rights Issue."

39. Shawan Jabarin, "Peace and Human Rights: Palestine as a Case Study," University Centre Saint-Ignatius, Antwerp, Belgium, October 17, 2008, available online from al-Haq's website (accessed March 6, 2017). See also Hajjar, "Human Rights in Israel/Palestine," 22.

40. Newsletter no. 10 (November–December 1985) annexes the article the organization published in *al-Fajr*, December 13, 1985, titled "Commitment to UN Declaration."

41. *Punishing a Nation*, 476.

42. *A Nation under Siege: Al-Haq Annual Report on Human Rights in the Occupied Palestinian Territories 1989* (Ramallah: al-Haq, 1990), 669. See also *A Human Rights Assessment of the Declaration of Principles on Interim Self-Government Arrangements for Palestinians* (Ramallah: al-Haq, 1993).

43. UN doc. E/CN.4/2006/95/Add.3, March 10, 2006, report submitted by the Special Rapporteur on the situation of human rights defenders, Hina Jilani, 3. On Palestinians' right to resist, see Quigley, *Case for Palestine*, 189–205.

44. Zalaquett, "Evaluation of al-Haq's Programs," 2. See also chapter 7 of the present volume.

45. Some scholars hold the "human rights industry" at least partially responsible for the demise of "politics proper" in Palestine; see Allen, *Rise and Fall of Human Rights*.

46. Undated response to the February 1987 orientation process, al-Haq archives.

47. Newsletter no. 9 (July–October 1985), 14.

48. A farmer from Beit Ijza village in the Ramallah district who for decades fought Israel's expropriation of his land; see also chapter 6.

49. Stork, "Three Decades of Human Rights Activism," 93.

50. Waltz, *Human Rights and Reform*, 184. Asked in an interview whether with the changing times al-Haq should now become a membership organization, Shehadeh replied that "a membership organisation is more susceptible to political pressure." *Twenty Years Defending Human Rights*, 6.

51. Megally, "Human Rights in the Arab World," 110. In specific reference to Egypt, see Nicola Pratt, "Human Rights and the 'Foreign Funding Debate' in Egypt," in Chase and Hamzawy, eds., *Human Rights in the Arab World*, 114–26. See also *International Aspects of the Arab Human Rights Movement: An Interdisciplinary Discussion Held in Cairo in March 1998* (Cambridge, MA: Human Rights Program, Harvard Law School; Cairo: Centre for the Study of Developing Countries, Cairo University, 2000), 45–65, for a discussion in 1998 on "foreign funding." The situation became considerably more fraught for Egyptian human rights NGOs under President Sisi.

52. Interview in *Twenty Years Defending Human Rights*, 5.

53. See also Allen, *Rise and Fall of Human Rights*, 70–71.

54. Compare the original similar role of the general meeting at CAJ in its early years, with the difference that CAJ was a membership organization and the general meeting comprised members. Beirne, *Beacon of Light*, 10.

55. Shawan Jabarin recalls the first field researcher telling him that the atmosphere at the organization was positive, that "the way they deal with internal relations is new."

56. The critiques of "professionalization" of human rights and more generally the NGO spheres came later.

57. Howard B. Tolley Jr. reports this also from an interview with Mona Rishmawi. Tolley, *International Commission of Jurists*, 150.

58. LSM, Programme Report, 1985, 10–11.

59. Al-Haq, Programme Report, 1986, 29.

60. "Draft Study of al-Haq's Structure."

61. Newsletter no. 16 (November–December 1986), 1–3.

62. The first on workers in the West Bank and the second on Palestinians working for Israeli employers, both published in 1986.

63. Newsletter no. 16 (November–December 1986), 10.

64. Al-Haq Orientation, February–March 1987, internal document. It is unclear who authored the document, and it reads very much like a group effort.

65. "Orientation February/March 1987—The Critical Evaluation of al-Haq's Work 1979–1987: Critical Comments Following First Session." Al-Haq archives.

66. The description "volunteer" in relation to foreign staffers does not mean that they were unpaid. The term *volunteer* (as in the British Volunteer Programme) included the idea that the individuals could command substantially better terms and conditions in the commercial market elsewhere. Some non-Palestinian staffers at al-Haq were paid by al-Haq but formally affiliated with certain of al-Haq's partners. A number of both Palestinian and non-Palestinian staff did begin their work at al-Haq as volunteers in the original sense of not receiving remuneration; several subsequently became paid staff, remunerated at the organization's standard rates. See Azzam, "Al-Haq in 2004," 13.

67. Al-Haq, Programme Report, 1986, 31.

68. Tolley, *International Commission of Jurists*, 150.

69. The 1985 training day covered issues such as the rule of law, the origin of rights, universality, the right to development and international organizations, as well as research methods, LSM's library and field research. Newsletter no. 10 (November–December 1985). An internal schedule for the day included a lunch discussion of "the role of foreign volunteers." Al-Haq archives. The term foreign/foreigner was the term in use then both in English and in Arabic to refer to non-Palestinians working at LSM/al-Haq; it was considerably later that a move was generally made to "internationals," probably drifting over from UN usage. An argument could be made that the foreigner-Palestinian binary privileges the power of the former less than the international-Palestinian binary.

70. Rabbani, "Palestinian Human Rights Activism," 39. See also Hanafi and Tabar, "Palestinian Human Rights Organisations," 29, critiquing reliance among Palestinian human rights groups on foreign interns and volunteers.

71. The exception was Mona Rishmawi, *Muqaddimat hawl al-mar'a al-filastiniyya bayn al-tajriba wa'l-nass al-qanuni* [Palestinian women between experience and legal text], Occasional Paper no. 3 (Ramallah: al-Haq, 1986).

72. Hanny Megally records the first conference of the Arab human rights movement in Casablanca in 1999. Megally, "Human Rights in the Arab World," 113.

73. Interviews with Playfair and Dueck.

74. In addition, Issam Younis noted the relative isolation from the organization of short-term foreign researchers and wondered whether the studies produced were the best use of al-Haq's resources.

75. Newsletter no. 7 (March–April 1985), 7.

76. Al-Haq, Programme Report, 1986, 32.

77. As suggested by Roger Heacock and others.

78. "Acknowledgements," in Playfair, *International Law and the Administration of Occupied Territories*, vii.

79. Playfair, introduction to *International Law and the Administration of Occupied Territories*, 1–22, quotation from 12.

80. Newsletter no. 19 (May–June 1987), 1–3.

CHAPTER 5. INTERVENTIONS AND ALLIES

1. Al-Haq, Programme Report, 1986, 9.

2. Al-Haq, Programme Report, 1986, 9.

3. Al-Haq, Programme Report, 1986, 9–10.

4. Newsletter no. 17 (January–February 1987), 4–5.

5. Al-Haq, Programme Report, 1986, 9.

6. Kuttab, "Avenues Open for Defence of Human Rights," 502–3. Rabbani, in "Palestinian Human Rights Activism," describes al-Haq's correspondence with the Israeli occupation authorities as "both vital and ineffectual."

7. Timothy Hiller, *The Reply of Law in the Service of Man / Al-Haq to the US Report on Human Rights Practices in the Territories Occupied by Israel for 1982* (Ramallah: LSM, 1983); Joost Hiltermann, *Al-Haq's Response to the Chapter on Israel and the Occupied Territories in the US State Department's "Country Reports on Human Rights Practices for 1984"* (Ramallah: al-Haq, 1986).

8. The Washington-based Palestine Human Rights Campaign had the previous year produced a *Report on Israeli Human Rights Practices in the Occupied Territories in 1981* (Washington, DC: Americans for Mid-East Understanding, 1982). Keck and Sikkink identify the State Department country reports as "a focal point for human rights groups" in *Activists beyond Borders*, 103. More recent scholarship continues to note criticisms by NGOs "especially in relation to highly controversial issues or to states with which the US has especially close or especially strained relations" while holding them overall to be a useful source. Philip Alston and Colin Gillespie, "Global Human Rights Monitoring, New Technologies, and the Politics of Information," *European Journal of International Law* 23/4 (2012): 1098.

9. Newsletter no. 1 (May 1984), 3.

10. Hiller, *Reply of Law in the Service of Man*, 1.

11. Hiller, 3.

12. Hiller, 5.

13. Newsletter no. 14 (July–August 1986), 9; Hiltermann, *Al-Haq's Response*, ii. A critique of LSM's response to the 1982 report noted that "LSM hoists the State Department on its own petard in its reply" but lamented the "reluctance of the organisation to pass through the 'political' door [. . .] With the growth in the human rights business, the area cries out

for a consciously political analysis of the situation here." John Richardson, "When the US Gets to Monitoring Human Rights," *Al-Fajr* (Palestinian English weekly), December 23, 1983. LCHR had published a critique of some sections of the 1984 Department of State Reports jointly with Helsinki Watch and Americas Watch. This joint critique is referenced in de Neufville, "Human Rights Reporting as a Policy Tool," 692.

14. Hiltermann, *Al-Haq's Response*, ii–Iii.

15. Hiltermann, 2–3.

16. Hiltermann, 7; the quote is referenced to the *Jerusalem Post*, February 15, 1985.

17. Hiltermann, 11–12.

18. Hiltermann, iv.

19. Letter of December 1, 2009, available on al-Haq's website.

20. UN doc. A/HRC/12/48, September 15, 2009. Israel termed this attack Operation Cast Lead.

21. *An Examination of the Detention of Human Rights Workers and Lawyers from the West Bank and Gaza and Conditions of Detention at Ketziot* (New York: Lawyers' Committee for Human Rights, 1988).

22. The bombs were defused by the police, but al-Haq noted that "it did not appear as if the police were carrying out a very full investigation." Newsletter no. 1 (May 1984), 5.

23. Newsletter no. 1, 5.

24. Newsletter no. 13 (May–June 1986).

25. Al-Haq submitted an announcement to the local Arabic press asking all *tawjihi* students whose arrests had prevented them from taking their exams to contact the organization; the notice was censored by the Israeli authorities. Newsletter no. 17 (January–February 1987), 8.

26. Newsletter no. 17, 2–3.

27. See *Israel's War on Education in the Occupied West Bank: A Penalty for the Future* (Ramallah: al-Haq, 1988).

28. Henry Steiner, *Diverse Partners: Non-Governmental Organizations in the Human Rights Movement; The Report of a Retreat of Human Rights Activists* (Harvard: Harvard Law School Human Rights Program and Human Rights Internet, 1991), 15.

29. Shehadeh, *Occupier's Law*, 11. Extracts from the Israeli press on publication of extracts of the Karp Report are in "The Karp Report," *Journal of Palestine Studies* 13/4 (1984): 156–61.

30. Shehadeh, *Occupier's Law*, 11.

31. Newsletter no. 20 (July–August 1987), 5.

32. Newsletter no. 20, 5–6.

33. Newsletter no. 11 (January–February 1986).

34. Newsletter no. 21 (September–December 1987), 2–4. See also Jonathan Kuttab, "Comment on Military Order no. 1164," *Palestine Yearbook of International Law* 2 (1985) 158–61; and "Military Order Threatens the Independence of the Bar Association," CIJL Bulletin no. 17 (April 1986), 17–22. John Quigley notes this as the only time the Court had upheld a challenge to a military order. Quigley, *Case for Palestine*, 202.

35. See chapter 3.

36. Niall MacDermot, "Torture in al-Fara`a Prison: A Reply to the Israeli Ambassador," editorial, *ICJ Review* 34 (June 1985): 3.

37. MacDermot, 4.

38. Mustafa Mar'i, *The Right to Freedom of Assembly: An Analysis of the Position of the Palestinian Authority* (Ramallah: al-Haq, May 1995 in Arabic, March 1997 in English).

39. Newsletter no. 1 (May 1984), 6.

40. Newsletter no. 2 (July 1984), 1.

41. Newsletter no. 8 (May–June 1985), 7.

42. Newsletter no. 32 (April–June 1994) 2. Israel ratified the Convention against Torture in 1991. Amnesty International, "'Under Constant Medical Supervision': Torture, Ill-Treatment and the Health Professions in Israel and the Occupied Territories," April 1996, AI Index: MDE 15/37/96.

43. *Nation under Siege*, 572.

44. Margaret E. Keck and Kathryn Sikkink note the creation in Argentina of "a new profession—what one might call 'human rights forensic science'" with the response of transnational networks to calls from Argentinian activists in the mid-1980s. Keck and Sikkink, *Activists beyond Borders*, 93–94, 110.

45. Derrick Pounder, "Death in Detention of Ibrahim al-Mtour: Text of Autopsy Report by Dr. Derrick Pounder," in *Nation under Siege*, 229.

46. Pounder, 231.

47. Hiltermann, "Deaths in Israeli Prisons," 102.

48. *Punishing a Nation*, 351.

49. See *Nation under Siege*, 572–79.

50. *Nation under Siege*, 572.

51. *Nation under Siege*, 547–90 (chap. 16, "Investigations").

52. *Nation under Siege*, 575

53. *Nation under Siege*, 579, citing Felicia Langer, "The Death of Ibrahim al-Umtour, or: The Closed File That Remains Open" (Tel Aviv: presentation to Israeli League for Human and Civil Rights, 1989, in Hebrew).

54. Pounder, "Death in Detention of Ibrahim al-Mtour," 230.

55. *Nation under Siege*, 672. Hiltermann opens his 1990 report "Deaths in Israeli Prisons" with the same quotation, and it is also recalled by engineer Khaled Batrawi in "Al-tashrih ka juz' min al-tahqiq fi hawadith istishhad dakhil al-sujun al-isra'iliyya" [Autopsy as part of investigations into incidents of martyrdom in Israeli prisons] (text of paper, 2009).

56. Batrawi, "Al-tashrih ka juz' min al-tahqiq."

57. The Karp report had pointed to "a vicious circle in which occurrences aren't investigated for lack of complaint, while complaints aren't submitted because of a lack of proper investigation. The rule of law and public order surely do not come out the winners in this matter." Cited in *Nation under Siege*, 559.

58. Paul Hunt, *Justice? The Military Court System in the Israeli-Occupied Territories* (Ramallah: al-Haq and GCRL, 1987).

59. Johnson, "Routine of Repression," 10.

60. Rabbani, "Palestinian Human Rights Activism," 44.

61. Rabbani, 44. In 2018, on International Human Rights Day, against the backdrop of increasingly hostile campaigns by Israeli official and nonofficial actors against individual and organizational defenders of Palestinian rights under occupation, al-Haq and B'Tselem were joint recipients of the Human Rights Award of the French Republic.

62. Steiner, *Diverse Partners*, 57.

63. Rabbani, "Palestinian Human Rights Activism," 44.

64. Steiner, *Diverse Partners*, 56.

65. Johnson, "Routine of Repression," 10.

66. "Amnesty International's Response to the Comments of the Israeli Ministry of Justice on the Amnesty International Reports 1990 and 1991," October 1991, 5.

67. In *Occupier's Law*, Shehadeh invoked Amnesty's disagreement with Israel over membership of the PLO when explaining that "Israeli propaganda outside and inside Israel has made unfounded use of its security needs. What has come to be accepted is that the PLO is a terrorist organisation whose sole aim is the destruction of Israel and that all Palestinians are supporters of the PLO and are bent deep down on destroying Israel. As it is morally and legally justifiable to destroy in self-defence an enemy bent on your destruction, it is legitimate to destroy all Palestinians" (9).

68. "Amnesty International's Response," 5. The piece goes on to remind the Israeli government of Amnesty's application of these standards inter alia to members of the ANC; famously, Amnesty had not adopted Nelson Mandela as a prisoner of conscience "because of his acknowledged advocacy of violence," but other individual ANC members had been so adopted.

69. *Examination of the Detention of Human Rights Workers and Lawyers*; Amnesty International, *Israel and the Occupied Territories: Administrative Detention during the Palestinian Intifada* (London: AI Index MDE 15/06.89, June 1989).

70. Letter from Ian Martin, secretary-general of Amnesty International, to Minister of Defence Moshe Arens, September 6, 1990, AI ref. TG MDE 15/90.11. I am grateful to Claudio Cordone and Ian Martin for permission to quote it.

71. Further details of this and later detention hearings were also reproduced in *Nation under Siege*, which made clear that al-Haq and Jabarin himself were convinced that Jabarin's human rights work was the reason behind his detention.

72. Interview with Claudio Cordone. The 1989 and 1991 Amnesty reports set out ICRC positions on IHL, for example considering the holding of administrative detainees from the occupied territories in detention facilities inside Israel (such as Ansar 3) to be a breach of the Fourth Geneva Convention, but the concluding findings are all based on international human rights standards.

73. "Amnesty International's Response," 6; interview with Cordone.

74. "Amnesty International's Response," 2, 6.

75. Steiner, *Diverse Partners*, 24.

76. Mustapha Al-Sayyid, Peter Rosenblum, and Henry Steiner, eds., *International Aspects of the Arab Human Rights Movement* (Cambridge, MA: Harvard Law School Human Rights Program, 2000), 75 (reporting on a meeting in Cairo, 1998).

77. Rabbani, "Palestinian Human Rights Activism," 51n74.

78. Neier, *International Human Rights Movement*, 219, 222–24; "Human Rights Watch Should Not Be Criticized for Doing Its Job," *Huffington Post*, November 2, 2009; Robert L. Bernstein, "Rights Watchdog, Lost in the Mideast," *New York Times*, October 20, 2009.

79. Steiner, *Diverse Partners*, 66.

80. Interviews with Abdel Karim Kan'an and Zahi Jaradat. See Beirne, *Beacon of Light*, 29–30, on similar demands on time in CAJ's relationship with international allies.

81. Palestinian public transport did not run on strike days in the first intifada.

82. Keck and Sikkink note the "considerable tensions" that can arise in relationship between "third world actors and northern groups" in transnational human rights advocacy networks. *Activists beyond Borders*, 12–13.

83. Keck and Sikkink, 12–13. See Posner and Whittome, "The Status of Human Rights Non-Governmental Organisations," *Columbia Human Rights Law Review* 25 (1994): 269–90, on the significance of the role of local human rights NGOs.

84. Caroline Moorehead, *Dunant's Dream: War, Switzerland and the History of the Red Cross* (New York: Carroll & Graf, 1998), 636.

85. Daniel Palmieri, "An Institution Standing the Test of Time? A Review of 150 Years of the History of the International Committee of the Red Cross," *International Review of the Red Cross* 94/888 (2012): 1288 (emphasis in the original). A second conflict identified as a turning point is the 1967 Biafran War.

86. Moorehead, *Dunant's Dream*, 637.

87. Moorehead, 638.

88. Vincent Bernard, "The Quest for Humanity: 150 Years of International Humanitarian Law and Action" (editorial), *International Review of the Red Cross* 94/888 (2012): 1203.

89. Moorehead, *Dunant's Dream*, 705.

90. Moorehead, 638.

91. Article 11, Fourth Geneva Convention. Al-Haq's examination of protecting powers and the ICRC is in *Nation under Siege*, 645–48.

92. "The ICRC Action in the Middle East," *International Review of the Red Cross* 8/92 (1968): 588–590, esp. 589. For a discussion of the protecting powers system as seen in the mid-1970s, see David Forsythe, "Who Guards the Guardians: Third Parties and the Law of Armed Conflict," *American Journal of International Law* 70/1 (1976): 41–61.

93. *ICRC Annual Report* 1972, 69–70. The ICRC had also made the same offer to Egypt, Jordan, Lebanon, and Syria, none of which accepted. *Nation under Siege*, 647.

94. *Nation under Siege*, 647.

95. Shehadeh, *Occupier's Law*, 151, citing *ICRC Annual Report* 1978, 31. Moorehead, *Dunant's Dream*, 637, states that "Israel is the country where the Committee fought hardest to get their delegates to see detainees as soon as possible after arrest."

96. Shehadeh, *Occupier's Law*, 152.

97. Shehadeh, 52.

98. Shehadeh, 52.

99. Newsletter no. 8 (May–June 1985), 8. It notes that "both Amnesty International and the ICJ have at different times challenged the government of Israel itself to disclose these reports, after reliance had been placed on them in this way to demonstrate that other allegations were unfounded."

100. *Nation under Siege*, 647–48. See 665n21 for details of three public interventions by the ICRC in the context of the Iran-Iraq war. In its usual practical manner, however, al-Haq in the same publication (at 301) proposed that a permanent presence of the ICRC should be established at the Israeli prison camp called Ansar 3 (or officially Ketziot) until such time as the camp was closed, in light of the severe risk to the detainees held there.

101. Cited in Amnesty International, "'Under Constant Medical Supervision,'" 10; ICRC Press Release, May 22, 1992.

102. Moorehead, *Dunant's Dream*, 637–38.

103. See ICRC Resource Centre, "Israel and the Occupied Territories: Protection, Prevention and Assistance—2013," www.icrc.org/eng/resources/documents/fact-figures/05 -15-israel-palestine-2013.htm (accessed August 18, 2014).

104. Bernard et al., "Interview with Raja Shehadeh," 13–28. Shehadeh's answer to the specific question on the ICRC is at 25–26.

105. Bernard, "Quest for Humanity," 1206. Maurer's piece comes at the end of the third section, titled "The ICRC Today."

106. Peter Maurer, "Challenges to International Humanitarian Law: Israel's Occupation Policy," *International Review of the Red Cross* 94/888 (Winter 2012): 1504.

107. Maurer, 1508.

108. See, for example, "Statement by the International Committee of the Red Cross to the Conference of High Contracting Parties to the Fourth Geneva Convention," Geneva, December 5, 2001, para. 5, annexed to Pierre-Yves Fux and Mirko Zambelli, "Mise en oeuvre de la quatrième Convention de Genéve dans les territoires palestiniens occupés: Historique d'un processus multilatéral (1997–2001)," *International Review of the Red Cross*, 84/847 (2002): 661–97. See also Marcin Monko, "The ICRC in the Palestinian Territories: Double Role, Single Aim," *Humanitarian Exchange Magazine* 37 (March 2007): 22–24. For a statement from a former ICRC president at the start of the occupation, see Léopold Boissier, "The Silence of the ICRC," *International Review of the Red Cross* 8/85 (April 1968): 178–80.

109. Bernard, "Quest for Humanity," 1200. See also "The International Committee of the Red Cross's (ICRC's) Confidential Approach," Policy Document, December 2012, *International Review of the Red Cross* 94/887 (2012): 1135–44.

110. Alan Baker, "International Humanitarian Law and Israel's Status in the Territories," *International Review of the Red Cross* 94/888 (2012): 1511–21. At the start of the first intifada, Baker had addressed the ICJ's Niall MacDermot on the subject of al-Haq's continuing ability to operate; see *Nation under Siege*, 622, and Rabbani, "Palestinian Human Rights Activism," 42 and 51n69.

111. After contesting the ICRC view on the illegality of settlements, Baker states that "Israel has never expressed any intention to colonise the territories, to confiscate land, or to displace the local population for political or racial reasons, nor to alter the demographic nature of the area" (1518).

112. Baker, "International Humanitarian Law," 1513.

113. Baker, 1520–21.

114. Draft Programme Objectives 1987, 2, al-Haq archives.

115. Press Release no. 10, December 13, 1987: "An Appeal to State Signatories to the Fourth Geneva Convention to Intervene after Recent Killings."

116. Over the course of summer 1987, an al-Haq legal researcher had researched and written a study on the implications of common Article 1 which was subsequently published as an occasional paper. Marc Stephens, *Enforcement of International Law in the Israeli-Occupied Territories*, Occasional Paper no. 7 (Ramallah: al-Haq, 1989).

117. Cover letter, Memorandum to Member States of the European Community as State Parties to the Fourth Geneva Convention, January 14, 1988.

118. Memorandum, January 14, 1988.

119. *Punishing a Nation*, 474–75. It goes on to note that "enforcement of the law regulating occupation" is not an end in itself but an "interim measure" pending the realization of the right to self-determination.

120. "Memorandum of Protest and Appeal re: Grave Breaches of the Fourth Geneva Convention," April 15, 1989; "Representation to State Signatories of the Fourth Geneva Convention—Israeli Tax Policies in the West Bank: The Case of Beit Sahour," September 27, 1989, al-Haq archives.

121. *Nation under Siege*, 661.

122. *Nation under Siege*, 667.

123. *Hansard*, House of Commons debates, February 7, 1990, columns 884–85.

124. Letter from Yves Sandoz, director, Principles, Law and Relations with the Movement, ICRC, of October 18, 1989, to Sir Dennis Walters, MP, and Ernie Ross, MP. The letter also referred to "problems of grave humanitarian concern" in the territories occupied by Israel, "which have been the subject of numerous representations by the ICRC."

125. *Towards a Strategy for the Enforcement of Human Rights in the Israeli Occupied West Bank and Gaza: A Working Symposium*, London, July 25, 1989 (London: Labour Middle East Council and Conservative Middle East Council, 1989).

126. My paper to the London Symposium dealt with this issue in regard to the UK: "Repression of Grave Breaches of the Geneva Conventions through the Domestic Judicial System: The Case of the UK," in *Towards a Strategy for the Enforcement of Human Rights*, 68–79.

127. See the epilogue for developments in al-Haq's work on universal jurisdiction and international criminal law.

128. As Rabbani observes, the Enforcement Project thus already represented a progression in the way al-Haq was thinking about the law. PAN had not used grave breaches as a category in its analytical framework. Rabbani, "Palestinian Human Rights Activism," 36–37.

129. This is taken from my part of a paper on enforcement work—at al-Haq, CIHRE, and MATTIN—that goes into greater detail than is possible here. The paper was drafted for al-Haq's twenty-fifth-year conference, but not published. Salwa Du'aybis, Charles Shammas, and Lynn Welchman, "The Invocation of International Humanitarian Law in NGO Advocacy in the Occupied Palestinian Territory: A Diagnostic Analysis," draft paper (2007), on file.

130. "Fifteenth Round Table of the International Institute of Humanitarian Law (San Remo, September 4–8, 1990)," *International Review of the Red Cross* 31/280 (1991): 59–60, esp. 59.

131. Frits Kalshoven, "The Undertaking to Respect and to Ensure Respect," *Yearbook of International Humanitarian Law* 2 (1999): 57. The argument over the nature of the obligation "to ensure respect" continues; see, for example, Knut Dormann and Jose Serralvo, "Common Article 1 to the Geneva Conventions and the Obligation to Prevent International Humanitarian Law Violations," *International Review of the Red Cross* 96/895–96 (2014): 707–36; Carlo Focarelli, "Common Article 1 of the 1949 Geneva Conventions: A Soap Bubble?," *European Journal of International Law* 21/1 (2010): 125–71. Dormann and Serralvo's narrative makes it clear how central the Israel-Palestine conflict has been to developments in the Article 1 obligation "to ensure respect."

132. Dormann and Serralvo, "Common Article 1 to the Geneva Convention," 730.

133. See *Protection Denied*, chap. 18 (authored by myself), "Ensuing Israel's Respect for International Law in the Occupied Palestinian Territories: Third Party Practice During 1990," 173–213.

134. *Protection Denied*, 206–7. See also Rabbani, "Palestinian Human Rights Activism," on this. Lisa Hajjar describes the 1991 Gulf War as "the most glaring example" of the double

standards of Western states' application of "human rights rhetoric." Hajjar, "Human Rights in Israel/Palestine," 30.

135. "Representation to States Signatory to the Fourth Geneva Convention," June 7, 1990, accompanied by a supplement, "The Need for International Protection." On the "protection resolution" (UN doc. S/21326, of May 31, 1990), see Lynn Welchman, "International Protection and International Diplomacy: Policy Choices for Third-Party States in the Occupied Palestinian Territories," in *International Human Rights Enforcement: The Case of the Occupied Palestinian Territories in the Transitional Period* (Ramallah: Centre for International Human Rights Enforcement, 1996) 225–77.

136. For the Tenth Emergency Session, see www.un.org/en/ga/sessions/emergency10th .shtml.

137. There are more positive evaluations of these conferences, notably by Swiss staffers involved: see Fux and Zambelli, "Mise en oeuvre de la quatrième Convention de Genéve," and Matthias Lanz, Emilie Max, and Oliver Hoehne, "The Conference of High Contracting Parties to the Fourth Geneva Convention of 17 December 2014 and the Duty to Ensure Respect for international Humanitarian Law," *International Review of the Red Cross* 98/895–96 (2014): 1115–33.

138. For a critique of TIPH's initial setup and mandate, see Lynn Welchman, "Consensual Intervention: A Case Study on the TIPH," in *International Human Rights Enforcement: The Case of the Occupied Palestinian Territories in the Transitional Period* (Ramallah: Centre for International Human Rights Enforcement, 1996), 279–314. The paper was also republished by al-Haq. TIPH had its own website: www.tiph.org/ (accessed March 23, 2017).

139. Al-Haq's enforcement team worked with Irish jurists, politicians, and others to convene a symposium in Dublin in 1990 and began a productive engagement with foreign affairs officials. An earlier draft of the statement had urged states parties to the Fourth Geneva Convention "to respect and ensure respect for its provisions," a stronger wording that was toned down in the final statement, probably at the urging of the United Kingdom. *Protection Denied*, 187.

140. See Daniel Machover and Kate Maynard, "Prosecuting Alleged Israeli War Criminals in England and Wales," *Denning Law Journal* 18 (2006): 95–114. Machover was an early ally of the Enforcement Project and attended the 1989 London Symposium.

141. For a review of these developments from the first intifada to 1994, see Welchman, "International Protection and International Diplomacy."

142. Hajjar, "Human Rights in Israel/Palestine," 28.

143. Charles Shammas made this point frequently.

144. Shammas and his MATTIN colleague Susan Rockwell produced three annual reviews on human rights in EU-Israel relations over the period 2003–6 for the Euro-Mediterranean Human Rights Network, which includes al-Haq as well as other Palestinian human rights organizations.

145. Du'aybis, Shammas, and Welchman, "Invocation of International Humanitarian Law," 15.

146. Alessandro Tonatti, *Feasting on the Occupation* (Ramallah: al-Haq, January 2013).

147. As welcomed by the PHROC, see below. Valentina Azarov (then an associate at MATTIN) explicitly attributes the EU's July 2013 Guidelines to MATTIN's strategic lobbying and advocacy work at the EU: "Legal House-Keeping in the EU," *openDemocracy*, July

31, 2013; "Making Human Rights Work for the Palestines of the World," *openDemocracy*, November 4, 2013.

148. "PHROC Welcome the EU's Adherence to International Law through the Adoption of EU Guidelines on EU Support to Israeli Entities or Activities in Illegal Settlements," Palestinian Human Rights Organizations Council, al-Haq, July 17, 2013, www.alhaq.org/palestinian-human-rights-organizations-council/6734.html.

149. Variations on these paragraphs appeared in various papers and presentations related to the Enforcement Project and CIHRE, and the original articulation no doubt came from Charles Shammas.

150. Rabbani, "Palestinian Human Rights Activism," 38; see also Hajjar, "Human Rights in Israel/Palestine," 25.

151. The critiques and challenges to the project enumerated here are drawn from interviews and from my own experience of events.

152. Email from Khaled Batrawi. In his unpublished "Dhikriyat Al-Haq" [Memories of al-Haq] (November 27, 2009), Batrawi pays tribute to "Charlie Shammas, who drove us all mad on the subject of the enforcement of international law." Batrawi presented a paper on "The Responsibilities of European States as Co-Signatories of the Fourth Geneva Convention" at the 5th European Regional NGO Symposium on the Question of Palestine in Vienna, August 26–27, 1991.

153. According to Shammas, "All the funders thought this was the most effective thing al-Haq was doing, they saw the effect on their own governments." Letters from donors in the archives confirm their interest in the project, including concern when the project was terminated. Commenting on this, Nina Atallah observed that "Charles brought the money in for it, but the project was vague, ambiguous for us, we couldn't see clearly where it was taking us."

154. Memo of June 10, 1992, from Said Zeedani and Naila Hazboun to Lynn Welchman. On file with author.

155. Azzam, "Al-Haq in 2004," 15.

156. Another non-Palestinian al-Haq staffer, Melissa Phillips, also later joined the redesigned enforcement project at CIHRE.

157. In 2018 Younis was elected commissioner at the Palestinian national human rights institution, the Independent Commission for Human Rights.

158. Newsletter no. 38 (July 1999). And al-Haq's website lists the 1988 launch of the Enforcement Project as one of the organization's "milestones" (accessed April 30, 2020).

CHAPTER 6. FIELD AND LEGAL RESEARCH

1. Batrawi, "Dhikriyat Al-Haq."

2. Batrawi, "Dhikriyat Al-Haq." Iyad Haddad recalls Batrawi's predecessor, Riziq Shuqair, implementing this system and "going over my material word by word." Interviews with Zahi Jaradat, Issam Younis.

3. The fieldwork material would be reviewed again at the further stages of entry into the database and use by the research unit.

4. See *Protection Denied*, 34–38. To Israel the site is Temple Mount.

5. *Protection Denied*, 34.

6. Ahmad Jaradat, "Thirty Years of Persistent Production," in *Thirty Years Defending Human Rights* (Ramallah: al-Haq, 2009), 79.

7. S/21919/Add.2; al-Haq, "Reconstruction of Events (Revised): al-Haram al-Sharif, Jerusalem, Monday 8 October 1990," October 28, 1990, reproduced as "Addendum 2" to the UN secretary-general's report submitted to the Security Council in accordance with Security Council Resolution 672 (1990), November 1, 1990. See *Protection Denied*, 197. The report of the Israeli official inquiry was also appended. The statement was reproduced in the secretary-general's report of October 31, 1990; *Protection Denied*, 201. Al-Haq dedicated *Protection Denied* to the "memory of those martyred during the al-Haram al-Sharif massacre 8 October 1990."

8. See also Allen, *Rise and Fall of Human Rights*, 42–44.

9. Batrawi, "Dhikriyat Al-Haq"; interviews with Shawan Jabarin, Jonathan Kuttab, and Abdel Karim Kan'an.

10. Sabri Gharib's sworn statement is reproduced in *Thirty Years Defending Human Rights*, 18–24. Sabri Gharib's son accepted an award on behalf of his father at the al-Haq thirty years event. This introduction and the affidavit were the first entry in *In Their Own Words: Affidavits Collected by LSM* (Geneva: Commission of the Churches on International Affairs, World Council of Churches, 1983), 13–16.

11. Raja Shehadeh, "The House That Sabri Built," *International Herald Tribune*, May 3, 2012, http://latitude.blogs.nytimes.com/2012/05/03/israels-progress-with-settlements -in-the-west-bank-is-really-its-loss/.

12. Newsletter no. 1 (May 1984), 4.

13. See Diane Orentlicher, "Bearing Witness: The Art and Science of Human Rights Fact-Finding." *Harvard Human Rights Journal* 3 (1990): 83–135; and see Allen, *Rise and Fall of Human Rights*, 43–44. Nancy Hawker traces "testimonies" ("witness accounts of violence, suffering and/or historic events presented in the first person"—thus not necessarily sworn statements) through the MENA section of Amnesty International. Hawker, "The Journey of Arabic Human Rights Testimonies, from Witnesses to Audiences via Amnesty International," *Translation Spaces* 7/1 (2018): 65–91.

14. "We *samidin*" means "we who are steadfast"—see chapter 3 for Shehadeh's focus on this concept. Shehadeh, *Third Way*, 67–68.

15. LSM staff, *Torture and Intimidation in the West Bank: The Case of Al-Fara'a Prison* (Ramallah: ICJ and LSM, 1985), 5.

16. Preface by LSM to *In Their Own Words*, 9.

17. The colloquial Palestinian Arabic saying is *idha gharimak al-qadi, li-min biddak tishki?*

18. Interviews with 'Ayad, Jaradat, and Kan'an.

19. See Ron Dudai, "Advocacy with Footnotes: The Human Rights Report as a Literary Genre," *Human Rights Quarterly* 28/3 (2006): 790. Dudai points out that the insertion of "first person unedited testimonies" into reports of human rights organizations is now "one of the trademarks of the genre." See also Allen, *Rise and Fall of Human Rights*.

20. See Richard Wilson, "Representing Human Rights Violations: Social Contexts and Subjectivities," in *Human Rights, Culture and Context: Anthropological Perspectives*, ed. Richard Wilson (London: Pluto Press, 1997), 134–60.

21. Newsletter no. 1 (May 1984), 4.

22. Interviews with 'Ayad, Kan'an, and Batrawi, along with Batrawi's "Dhikriyat Al-Haq."

23. Paul Gready, "Introduction—Responsibility to the Story," *Journal of Human Rights Practice* 2/2 (2010): 178.

24. Batrawi, "Dhikriyat Al-Haq."

25. Batrawi, "Dhikriyat Al-Haq." Compare Allen, *Rise and Fall of Human Rights*, 49–50.

26. Newsletter no. 9 (July–October 1985), 2.

27. Newsletter no. 9. See also Playfair, "Administrative Detention in the Occupied West Bank."

28. Newsletter no. 9, 4.

29. Shuqair was to spend four-and-a-half months in administrative detention after his original six-month order was reduced on appeal. The field-workers were Ghazi Shashtari, Shawan Jabarin, Zahi Jaradat, Iyad Haddad, and Abdel Karim Kan'an. In 1989, another al-Haq field-worker, Ahmad Jaradat, was detained for two months. Updates on these cases were provided in *Nation under Siege*, 615, and include also the administrative detention of a PHRIC worker.

30. Jaradat, Shashtari, and Jabarin. See *Nation under Siege*, 615, and Amnesty's letter to the Israeli government regarding Jabarin.

31. For example, LCHR director Michael Posner's visit to four al-Haq field-workers detained in Ansar III in August 1988.

32. See Shravati Reddy, "Palestinian Human Rights Activist Continues His Work Despite Obstacles," interview with Shawan Jabarin, Digital Freedom Network (n.d.).

33. *Nation under Siege*, 615; the cases are discussed on 616–18.

34. Hiltermann, "Deaths in Israeli Prisons," 103.

35. Statement on "Sha'wan Jabrin" from the Israeli embassy in Washington, DC, October 25, 1989, reported in *Nation under Siege*, 617 and 623.

36. *Nation under Siege*, 618.

37. For details, see *Nation under Siege*, 618.

38. The occasion was Carter's presentation of the Carter-Menil award to al-Haq: Jabarin, interviewed in Reddy, *Palestinian Human Rights Activist*. Jabarin received the Reebok Human Rights Award for young activists in 1990: see www.youtube.com/watch?v=TB7I9SxPG4o. He recalls that it took another intervention from Carter to get him a laissez-passer to travel, with his wife and son, to receive the award.

39. *Protection Denied*, 157–69. In 2002, al-Haq published the detention memoirs of another of its workers, Yaser al-Disi, who was taken from the office by Israeli soldiers at the start of Israel's invasion and reoccupation of Ramallah (and other West Bank cities) in the second intifada. See *Screaming in the Dark* (Ramallah: al-Haq, 2002, combined English and Arabic text).

40. *Punishing a Nation*, 1. PCHR and al-Mizan both document violations in the Gaza Strip; neither was in existence in the late 1980s.

41. In explaining the methodology of the fieldwork carried out for al-Haq's first systematic report on torture, the author attributed the low number of documented torture cases involving women to, inter alia, "the reluctance of former female detainees to discuss their treatment with al-Haq's predominantly male team of fieldworkers." Phillips, *Torture for Security*, 18.

42. *Nation under Siege*, 503–41. The chapter dealt with the use of force against women, including misuse of tear gas and miscarriages, sexual harassment, detention, expulsion, and the suppression of women's organizational activities.

43. Newsletter no. 16 (November–December 1986), 15, and no. 21 (September – December 1987), 17; *Punishing a Nation*, 216.

44. Ninan Koshy, introduction to *In Their Own Words*, 5–7.

45. LSM, preface to *In Their Own Words*, 10.

46. Newsletter no. 1 (May 1984), 6–7.

47. Rabbani, "Palestinian Human Rights Activism," 33.

48. Riziq Shuqair and Randa Siniora, eds., *Application Denied: Separated Palestinian Families Tell Their Stories* (Ramallah: al-Haq, 1991).

49. From the brochure for the 1992 campaign "Stop Destroying Palestinian Homes"; the aims are given as "cessation of demolition and sealing [of homes]; recognition that these measures are in violation of international law; compensation for the affected families; and permission for the re-opening of sealed houses and re-building on the site of demolished houses."

50. Adama Dieng, preface to Candy Whittome, *The Right to Unite: The Family Reunification Question in the Palestinian Occupied Territories* (Ramallah: al-Haq, 1990), i–ii.

51. Whittome, *Right to Unite*, 1.

52. Shuqair and Siniora, *Application Denied*, 5.

53. It was listed as one of "other projects" in the LSM preface to *In Their Own Words*, 8.

54. Newsletter no. 16 (November–December 1986); the following edition (no. 17, January–February 1987) leads with an editorial on restrictions on family life.

55. See Azzam, "Al-Haq in 2004," 8; and Newsletter no. 27 (October–December 1992) and no. 33 (July–September 1994) on the campaign and concluding conference on "Women, Justice and the Law" (published as *Al-Mar'a wa'l-'Adala wa'l-Qanun*, Ramallah: al-Haq, 1995).

56. *Palestinian Victims of Torture Speak Out: Thirteen Accounts of Torture during Interrogation in Israeli Prisons* (1993). The Arabic version (1992) was edited by Riziq Shuqair, the English by Tom Taylor.

57. Its press release (no. 67, of February 26, 1994) invokes Security Council Resolution 681 (1990) and in particular its call on state parties to the Fourth Geneva Convention.

58. Khamis Shalabi and Zahi Jaradat, eds., *'Amm 'ala ahdath majzarat al-haram al-Ibrahimi bi'l-khalil* [One year after the massacre at the Ibrahimi sanctuary in Hebron] (Ramallah: Al-Haq, 1995). The sanctuary includes the Tomb of the Patriarchs. Shalabi died tragically young during his employment with al-Haq.

59. This is not to suggest that this was new; Batrawi notes that the field-workers would take al-Haq's publications to those whose cases were related in them.

60. Interview with Joanna Oyediran.

61. Newsletter no. 30 (December 1993).

62. Interviews with Jaradat and Kan'an.

63. Rabbani, "Palestinian Human Rights Activism," 32.

64. Tolley, *International Commission of Jurists*, 167–68.

65. Letter of May 27, 1987, to the editor of *al-Fajr*, al-Haq archives.

66. *A Report on the Treatment of Security Prisoners at the West Bank Prison of al-Fara'a* (Ramallah: al-Haq, April 1984), 2.

67. LSM staff, *Torture and Intimidation in the West Bank*, 3, citing a policy document issued by the Israeli chief of staff's office after a visit to the West Bank.

68. LSM staff, 3. This policy had come to light during the trial in 1982 of seven Israeli army members. *Newsweek*, February 14, 1983, included the following account: "Beyond

constant police controls, the most common manifestations of tertur are the wholesale roundups that take place whenever West Bank Arabs stage nationalist demonstrations. Israeli border police have been witnessed forcing Arabs to sing the Israeli national anthem, slap each other's faces and crawl and bark like dogs."

69. *Report on the Treatment of Security Prisoners*, 9.

70. LSM staff, *Torture and Intimidation in the West Bank*, 1–2.

71. LSM Newsletter no. 2 (May–June 1984).

72. LSM Newsletter no. 2, 5–6; *Jerusalem Post*, March 26, 1984. Niall MacDermot's 1985 reply to the Israeli ambassador notes Israeli newspapers *Haaretz* and *Ma'ariv* publishing interviews with detainees from al-Fara'a in March 1985. MacDermot, "Torture in al-Fara`a Prison," 3.

73. LSM staff, *Torture and Intimidation in the West Bank*, 2.

74. LSM staff, 5.

75. In the 1984 al-Fara'a report, LSM had explained that "by political prisoners we are referring to those convicted or detained on suspicion of committing offences against the 'security' laws of the Israeli military government in the occupied West Bank." *Report on the Treatment of Security Prisoners*, 2.

76. That is apart from an introductory reference to West Bank Palestinians held in prisons inside Israel in violation of Article 76 of the Fourth Geneva Convention. This was a major point of argument in the 1988 report on Ansar 3.

77. LSM, *Jnaid: The New Israeli Prison in Nablus* (Ramallah: al-Haq, October 1984), 2. The Standard Minimum Rules were approved by the Economic and Social Council in resolutions 663 C (XX!V) 1957 and 2076 (LXII) 1; they were revised and adopted by the UN General Assembly in 2015 as the Nelson Mandela Rules (A/RES/70/175).

78. There are short references to the Standard Minimum Rules and Israeli Military Order 29 in the introduction to the section on medical care at al-Fara'a, and a reference to the agreement between the ICRC and the Israeli authorities in the section regarding complaints to the ICRC.

79. Phillips, *Torture for Security*, 12. The figure was further explained as representing approximately 24 percent of the male population of the occupied territories aged 15–54.

80. Al-Haq, *Dhahiriyyeh: Centre for Punishment* (Ramallah: al-Haq), 13.

81. Al-Haq Briefing Papers, 1987.

82. See Playfair, *International Law and the Administration of Occupied Territories*.

83. Playfair in *Twenty Years Defending Human Rights*, 16.

84. Eitan Felner, "Human Rights Leaders in Conflict Situations: A Case Study of the Politics of 'Moral Entrepreneurs,'" *Journal of Human Rights Practice* 4/1 (2012): 75.

85. Felner appears to be locating B'Tselem in a certain category of "traditional human rights groups" largely based in the Global North.

86. Tolley, *International Commission of Jurists*, 144.

87. Tolley, 144.

88. Shehadeh, introduction to the first edition of *Occupier's Law* (1985), 3. See also Rabbani, "Palestinian Human Rights Activism," 31.

89. Shehadeh, *Occupier's Law*, 8.

90. Shehadeh, introduction to revised edition of *Occupier's Law* (1988), x.

91. Raja Shehadeh, "Analyzing Palestine: Post-Mortem or Prognosis?," in *Waiting for the Barbarians: A Tribute to Edward Said*, ed. Basak Ertur and Muge Gursoy Sokmen (London: Verson, 2008).

92. Mona Rishmawi, *Planning in Whose Interest?*, Occasional Paper no. 4 (Ramallah: al-Haq/LSM, 1986).

93. Anthony Coon, *Town Planning under Military Occupation: An Examination of the Law and Practice of Town Planning in the Occupied West Bank* (Aldershot: Dartmouth, 1992), ix.

94. Coon, 3.

95. Coon, 212.

96. Coon, 213.

97. See "LSM Publications," in Playfair, *Administrative Detention in the Occupied West Bank*, 52–53.

98. Newsletter no. 1 (May 1984), 3; Falloon, *Excessive Secrecy*, 19–39.

99. The substance of Rishmawi's paper was published in English in an academic journal. See Rishmawi, "Palestinian Women—Experience and Legal Text," *International Review of Comparative Public Policy* 4 (1992).

100. Newsletter no. 20 (July–August 1987), 11.

101. Newsletter no. 14 (July–August 1986), 1–2.

102. Emma Playfair, *Demolition and Sealing of Houses as a Punitive Measure in the Israeli-Occupied West Bank*, Occasional Paper no. 5 (Ramallah: al-Haq, 1987), 30.

103. High Court of Justice 698/85, *Mazen Abdullah Said Daghlas and Others v. The Military Commanders of the Judea and Samaria Region* (para. 3), reproduced in Playfair, *Demolition and Sealing of Houses*, 37–41, 38.

104. Cohen, *States of Denial*, and see Dudai, *Advocacy with Footnotes*.

105. Playfair, *Demolition and Sealing of Houses*, 30.

106. Tom Taylor, *Missiles and Dynamite: The Israeli Military Forces' Destruction of Palestinian Homes with Anti-Tank Missiles and High-Powered Explosives*, Occasional Paper no. 10 (Ramallah: al-Haq, 1993); and Lynn Welchman, *A Thousand and One Homes: Israel's Demolition and Sealing of Houses in the Occupied Palestinian Territories*, Occasional Paper no. 11 (Ramallah: al-Haq, 1993). The latter was based on campaign field research.

107. Martha Roadstrum Moffett, *Perpetual Emergency: A Legal Analysis of Israel's Use of the British Defence (Emergency) Regulations, 1945, in the Occupied Territories*, Occasional Paper no. 6 (Ramallah: al-Haq, 1989); Stephens, *Enforcement of International Law*.

108. LSM, Programme Report, 1985.

109. Al-Haq, Programme Report, 1986, 15.

110. Interview with Joanna Oyediran: "There are very few NGOs in the world where you can go in and see a library like the one al-Haq had."

111. Newsletter no. 16 (November–December 1986), 8. In cases where court procedures were needed, the organization would advise the client to get a lawyer from outside al-Haq. It cited financial restrictions for this position.

112. Newsletter no. 16, 9.

113. Newsletter no. 1 (May 1984) and no. 12 (March–April 1986).

114. *Zawiyat huquq al-insan.*

115. In English translation, these 1992 leaflets were titled "They confiscated my ID Card: What do I do?" "They imposed Kafala on me: What do I do?" and "They confiscated my car: What do I do?"

116. Hiltermann, "Al-Haq: The First Twenty Years."

117. *Al-Muwatin* literally means fellow countrymen/women; in a state, it could be citizens.

118. Mona Rishmawi, introduction to *Al-Muwatin* [The citizen], Know Your Rights (KYR) no. 3 (Ramallah: al-Haq, 1983), i–ii.

119. Draft Programme Objectives for 1987, 3.

120. Gazan labor law was different.

121. Newsletter no. 15 (September–October 1986), 1.

122. Newsletter no. 15, 3.

123. Newsletter no. 19 (May–June 1987), 5.

124. Newsletter no. 19, 8.

125. Draft Programme Objectives for 1987, 3.

126. The most prominent women's rights organization currently, the Women's Centre for Legal Aid and Counselling, was established in 1991. On the women's and the labor movements before the intifada, see Hiltermann, *Behind the Intifada*.

127. Randa Siniora, "Al-Haq and Its Societal Programs: The Women's Rights Program," in *Twenty Years Defending Human Rights*, 21.

128. Al-Haq's second annual report in the uprising, *A Nation under Siege*, includes a separate chapter (by Siniora) on the violation of women's rights by the occupying authorities.

129. Siniora, "Al-Haq and Its Societal Programs," 22.

130. The publication (in Arabic) of this effort was produced under the lead editorship of Mervat Rishmawi, who had taken over the project when Siniora left for her LLM studies. Mervat Rishmawi and Intisar Qawwas represented al-Haq in a delegation of Palestinian women who attended the Beijing World Conference on Women in 1995.

131. Newsletter no. 28 (January–April 1993).

132. Anthony Tirado Chase agrees on the significance of Vienna, noting also a series of regional meetings that followed among the Arab NGOs in the late 1990s and early 2000s. Chase, *Human Rights, Revolution, and Reform*, 41.

133. Riziq Shuqair, *Al-Qatl al-ʿAmd* [Willful killing], KYR no. 7 (Ramallah: al-Haq, 1989).

134. Riziq Shuqair, *Lamm Shaml* [Israeli policy on family reunification], KYR no. 8 (Ramallah: al-Haq: 1990); Riziq Shuqair, *Nahu munahadat al-taʿdhib* [Towards the elimination of torture], KYR no. 9 (Ramallah: al-Haq, 1991).

135. Code of Conduct for Law Enforcement Officials, adopted by UN General Assembly resolution 34/169 of December 17, 1979.

136. The Declaration of Principles on Interim Self-Government Arrangements, September 13, 1993; Article VIII on "public order and security."

137. *Mudawwana li-qawaʾid suluk al-muwazhzhafin al-mukallafin bi-infadh al-qanun* [Code of Conduct for Law Enforcement Officials], KYR no. 10 (Ramallah: al-Haq, 1993), 1–4.

138. Newsletter no. 30 (September–December 1993), 8, 10; Mustafa Marʾi and Riziq Shuqair, *Al-muwatin. Al-taftish waʾl-ʿitiqal waʾl-muhakama al-ʿaskariyya* [The citizen: Search, arrest, military trial], KYR no. 11 (Ramallah: al-Haq, 1993).

139. *Majmuʿat al-mabadiʾ al-mutaʿalliqa bi-himaya jamiʿ al-ashkhas alladhina yataʿarridun li-ayy shakl min ashkal al-ihtijaz au al-sijn* [Body of Principles on the Protection of All Persons Subjected to Any Form of Detention or Imprisonment], KYR no. 13 (Ramallah: al-Haq, August 1994), 7.

140. Randa Siniora and Rim 'Abd al-Hadi, 'Abd al-Hadi. *Al-'unf didd al-mar'a – zhahira 'amma au khassa?* [Violence against women: A general or particular phenomenon?], KYR no. 12 (Ramallah: al-Haq, 1994). WCLAC and the Palestinian Counselling Centre were given as resources.

141. Riziq Shuqair, *Al-khususiyya al-thaqafiyya: 'uqba haqiqiyya amama 'alamiyyat huquq al-insan am ghita' li-tabrir intihakatiha?!* [Cultural relativism: A real obstacle to the universality of human rights or a cover to justify violations?!], KYR no. 14 (Ramallah: al-Haq, November 1995).

142. Megally, "Human Rights in the Arab World," 111–12.

143. Rabbani, "Palestinian Human Rights Activism," 27–28. In 1984 LSM began preparing a substantial collection of sources published on microfiche in Switzerland by the Inter Documentation Centre (IDC) and titled *Palestine: The Legal Background*; the collection included "rare reference works and texts long since out of print" from Ottoman, British Mandate, and Jordanian rule as well as Israeli military orders on the West Bank and Gaza Strip. Newsletter no. 1 (May 1984), 2.

144. Newsletter no. 12 (March–April 1986), 5.

145. In support of this last statement, al-Haq gave the example of the position of the United States in its 1980 State Department report. Newsletter no. 21 (September–December 1987), 7.

146. *Punishing a Nation*, 1, 6.

147. *Punishing a Nation*, 7.

148. *Punishing a Nation*, 5.

149. *Nation under Siege*, 1.

150. Phillips *Torture for Security*.

151. See Methodology section of Phillips, 15–16.

152. Phillips, 12. The footnotes reference questionnaires and affidavits collected by al-Haq field-workers and stored in the database.

153. Phillips, 19.

154. Phillips, 12.

155. Phillips, 14.

156. Shehadeh, Occupier's Law, 227.

157. Johnson, "Routine of Repression," 10n12.

158. *Punishing a Nation*, 243. See Phillips. *Torture for Security*, 54–58. B'Tselem published a report in March 1991 by Stanley Cohen and Daphna Golan titled *The Interrogation of Palestinians during the Intifada: Ill-Treatment, "Moderate Physical Pressure" or Torture?* In the 1990s, repeated (and failed) petitions to the Israeli HCJ challenging this position (and seeking publication of the secret guidelines) finally provoked a Supreme Court ruling that the GSS "lacks the required authority under Israeli law to employ certain methods of 'moderate physical and psychological pressure' when interrogating Palestinian 'security' suspects." But see Ardi Imseis, "Moderate Torture on Trial: Critical Reflections on the Israeli Supreme Court Judgement Concerning the Legality of General Security Services Interrogation Methods," *Berkeley Journal of International Law* 19 (2001): 330.

159. Also the ICCPR, the ICESCR, CEDAW, and the Convention on the Rights of the Child.

160. Phillips, *Torture for Security*, 10. The committee asked Israel to submit a further report on the Landau guidelines, and in 1997, having reviewed this special report, concluded

that the methods of interrogation as described by the NGO evidence presented to the committee were in violation of Article 16 of the convention (regarding cruel, inhuman, and degrading treatment) and constituted torture according to the definition in Article 1. "Concluding Observations of the Committee against Torture: Israel," A/52/44, May 9, 1997, paras. 253–60.

161. Linda Bevis, *The Applicability of Human Rights Law to Occupied Territories: The Case of the Occupied Territories* (Ramallah: al-Haq, 1994). A 2003 reprint is available on al-Haq's website.

162. Newsletter no. 32 (April–June 1994), 1–2. Amnesty International also submitted evidence to the committee.

163. Newsletter no. 32 (1994); Amnesty International Annual Report 1994, 173; Bevis, *Applicability of Human Rights Law*, 95. The PLO had earlier (in 1989) deposited instruments of accession to the Geneva Conventions and their protocols. The Swiss government "refused to decide whether the communication could be considered an instrument of accession" given the lack of agreement internationally as to whether the State of Palestine existed, but noted that the unilateral declaration "remains valid" (Bevis, 94–95). The State of Palestine was to ratify in 2014.

164. Azzam, preface to Bevis, *Applicability of Human Rights Law*, 6.

165. Azzam, preface to Phillips, *Torture for Security*, 10–11.

CHAPTER 7. FALLOUTS

1. See Aeyal Gross, *The Writing on the Wall: Rethinking the International Law of Occupation* (Cambridge: Cambridge University Press, 2017), 256–59, on "the story of freedom of movement as the story of the occupation."

2. See Shehadeh, *From Occupation to Interim Accords*, 103–31, on the Washington and then the Oslo negotiations, including reflection on the challenges as he saw them as legal adviser to the Palestinian delegation.

3. The legacy of the first intifada arguably lived on "in the power of memory" and served to "provide the repertoires of meaningful resistance in ongoing confrontations with power over many decades." Tripp, *Power and the People*, 15–16.

4. Speaking as an experienced donor, in contexts other than the Middle East, Michael Shifter notes as inevitable the strains placed on NGOs arising from "the sensitivity of law-related work in changing political contexts." Shifter, "Weathering the Storm: NGOs Adapting to Major Political Transitions," in *Many Roads to Justice* (New York: Ford Foundation, 2000), 327.

5. Christine Bell and Johanna Keenan. "Human Rights Nongovernmental Organisations and the Problems of Transition," *Human Rights Quarterly* 26 (2004): 330.

6. Zalaquett, "Evaluation of al-Haq's Programs," 8–9. This paper was available on al-Haq's website for many years but then removed. See also Newsletter no. 30 (September–December 1993), 15. Al-Haq had also commissioned a review from the Bisan Centre for Research and Development on the structural functioning of the organization. On Zalaquett's stature in the international human rights movement, see Neier, *International Human Rights Movement*, 164, and Keck and Sikkink, *Activists beyond Borders*, 90–91.

7. Compare Bell and Keenan, "Human Rights Nongovernmental Organisations," 375.

8. Compare Bell and Keenan, 366.

9. Mona Rishmawi, "Judicial Independence under Palestinian Rule," in *The Arab-Israeli Accords: Legal Perspectives*, ed. Eugene Cotran and Chibli Mallat (London: Kluwer Law International, 1996), 259.

10. Article V/3, Declaration of Principles. The five year "transitional period" was to start when Israeli troops redeployed from Gaza and Jericho. Edward Said, "The Morning After— October 1993," *Al-Hayat*, October 13 and 14, 1993, in *Peace and Its Discontents: Gaza-Jericho 1993–1995* (London: Vintage, 1995). 5–18.

11. See chapter 5. LSM included among its questionnaires one that addressed violence by members of the Village Leagues, and one set of affidavits in *In Their Own Words* (1983) addressed the same theme.

12. *Nation under Siege*, 151–52.

13. "To the extent that collaborators are armed and trained by the Israeli authorities, and receive the latter's instructions" (152).

14. Azzam, "Al-Haq in 2004," 12.

15. *Nation under Siege* 154. See *Collaborators in the Occupied Territories: Human Rights Abuses and Violations* (Jerusalem: B'Tselem [The Israeli Information Centre for Human Rights in the Occupied Territories], 1994).

16. For a contemporary examination, see Adrien Katherine Wing, "Legal Decision-Making during the Palestinian Intifada: Embryonic Self-Rule," *Yale Journal of International Law* 18 (1993): 95–153.

17. See *A License to Kill: Israeli Operations against "Wanted" and "Masked" Palestinians* (New York: Human Rights Watch, 1993).

18. Hammami, "Palestinian NGOs since Oslo," 4.

19. "The Killing of Alleged 'Collaborators,'" Amnesty International Newsletter 20/1 (January 1990): 5, quoted in *Nation under Siege*, 153. B'Tselem gave a figure from the Israeli army of 942 from December 1987 to November 1993 (*Collaborators in the Occupied Territories*, 14), while the Associated Press reported 771.

20. It was at its Yokohama meeting in 1991 that Amnesty's International Council formally agreed to "expand the work of the organization" on nonstate actors, specifically "abuses by opposition groups such as [. . .] deliberate and arbitrary killings." Its response to the Israeli Ministry of Justice acknowledges the fact that the ministry had noted Amnesty's reference to the issue of the killing of alleged collaborators as part of setting the context in its reports of 1990 and 1991. Amnesty International, "Amnesty International's Response to the Comments of the Israeli Ministry of Justice on the Amnesty International Reports 1990 and 1991," October 1991. International NGO attention to abuses by armed groups grew in the 1990s; earlier endeavors were made by Americas Watch in the 1980s, reporting on abuses by armed opposition groups (some sponsored by Reagan's administration) in Central America. See *Ends and Means: Human Rights Approaches to Armed Groups* (Geneva: International Council on Human Rights Policy, 2000), 11–12; and David Petrasek, "A Road Less Travelled: International Human Rights Advocacy and Armed Groups," *Journal of Human Rights Practice* 4/1 (2012): 129. Aryeh Neier notes a 1982 Americas Watch report on Guatemala as the first to focus on IHL including "guerrilla abuses." Neier, *International Human Rights Movement*, 210–11.

21. Rabbani, "Palestinian Human Rights Activism," 44. B'Tselem refers to the "complex political reality" surrounding the subject of its report on collaborators. *Collaborators in the Occupied Territories*, 20.

22. Azzam, "Al-Haq in 2004," 12.

23. Sari Hanafi and Linda Tabari credit al-Haq with denouncing the killing of collaborators as against the right to life, while others remained silent. Hanafi and Taber, "Palestinian Human Rights Organisations," 25.

24. A footnote to this text notes that "Additional Protocol I is the accepted international standard regulating attacks on 'collaborators' in the Occupied Territories. [. . .] Additional Protocol I was neither signed nor ratified by Israel. The PLO, as a resistance movement, has signed it."

25. *Nation under Siege*, 153.

26. *Nation under Siege*, 13–14.

27. Rabbani, "Palestinian Human Rights Activism," 45.

28. Azzam, "Al-Haq in 2004," 12.

29. Azzam, 12. B'Tselem doubted the effectiveness of the public criticism at the time. In 2014, during Israel's fifty-day onslaught on Gaza, the issue of the killing of suspected collaborators again drew intense attention from the international press when, after the assassination of three senior military leaders by Israeli attacks, a number of Palestinians suspected of having collaborated with the Israeli authorities were executed by firing squads in the Hamas-controlled Gaza Strip. Palestinian human rights groups (notably the Gaza-based PCHR and the Independent Commission) were swift to call for an end to the executions and a commitment to the rule of law, including fair trial and due process. *Collaborators in the Occupied Territories*, 165–70.

30. Azzam, "Al-Haq in 2004," 12–13.

31. Azzam, 13.

32. Occasional letters from the very earliest days of LSM stated that the organization opposed all forms of violence, but this did not develop into a general principle articulated as part of organizational identity.

33. See Richard R. Baxter, "The Duty of Obedience to the Belligerent Occupant," *British Yearbook of International Law* 27 (1950): 255–57: "Underground movements carrying on clandestine activities and persons who individually make armed attacks on occupying military forces are presumably left to the common law of war, subject to the protection afforded by the Geneva Civilians Convention" (257). Baxter's statement of the law obviously predates the Additional Protocols to the Geneva Convention.

34. Erakat, *Justice for Some*, 133.

35. Steiner, *Diverse Partners*, 57–58. See also Petrasek, "Road Less Travelled," 129.

36. Stork, "Three Decades of Human Rights Activism," 103.

37. Felner, "Human Rights Leaders in Conflict Situations."

38. Bell, "Human Rights and the Struggle for Change," 227.

39. Felner, "Human Rights Leaders in Conflict Situations," 61.

40. Bell, "Human Rights and the Struggle for Change," 228.

41. Beirne, *Beacon of Light*, 47.

42. Hanafi and Tabar, "Palestinian Human Rights Organisations," 25. See Waltz, *Human Rights and Reform*, 169–70, on the debate in North African human rights organizations on the same issue, and with the same tenor.

43. Hiltermann, *Behind the Intifada*, 51.

44. Hajjar, "Human Rights in Israel/Palestine," 9.

45. Shehadeh, "The Weight of Legal History: Constraints and Hopes in the Search for a Sovereign Legal Language," in *The Arab-Israeli Accords: Legal Perspectives*, ed. Eugene Cotran and Chibli Mallat (London: Kluwer Law International, 1996), 4–7. See also "Expanded

Outline: Palestinian ISGA: Concepts, Preliminary Measures and Elections Modalities," *Journal of Palestine Studies* 21/3 (1992): 135–41.

46. Shehadeh, "Weight of Legal History," 7–9. Shehadeh has reflected extensively on his experience with the negotiations process, including in *Palestinian Walks*, 120–31 (with Oslo, "we had been defeated, we had lost"); in "Human Rights and the Israeli Occupation"; and in Bernard et al., "Interview with Raja Shehadeh," 15 (referring to the Oslo agreements as "surrender documents").

47. See the website of Nonviolence International, www.nonviolenceinternational.net /beyond2states (accessed December 16, 2020).

48. Al-Haq, "Memorandum to the Palestinian Delegation Attending the Regional Conference in Madrid," October 24, 1991. Maggie Beirne reports CAJ similarly evaluating the Anglo-Irish Agreement (of 1985) on the basis of "civil liberties issues" and declining to make political statements on the process. Beirne, *Beacon of Light*, 11.

49. Shehadeh, "Weight of Legal History"; Shehadeh, *Palestinian Walks*; Shehadeh, "Human Rights and the Israeli Occupation."

50. Al-Haq, January 1, 1993, reported in Newsletter no. 28 (January–April 1993), 4 (Arabic text).

51. Erakat, *Justice for Some*, 139.

52. Erakat, 139.

53. See also Azzam, "Al-Haq in 2004," 15.

54. Bell and Keenan. "Human Rights Nongovernmental Organisations," 372.

55. Newsletter no. 27 (October–December 1992), 14. The Newsletter set the challenges of the intifada years as the context for the need for a reconsideration of structure.

56. Azzam, "Al-Haq in 2004," 10.

57. Newsletter no. 30 (September–December 1993) indicates the range of activities over this period, and includes a report of a study meeting with the ICJ on the future of the civilian judicial system in the occupied territory.

58. *A Human Rights Assessment of the Declaration of Principles on Interim Self-Government Arrangements for Palestinians* (Ramallah: al-Haq, 1993). Al-Haq noted that the Arabic and English versions available to them at the time "differ on key matters" (2).

59. "While debates continue on the exact scope of the right to self-determination, its interpretation in the case of the Palestinian People clearly includes sovereignty without ex-ternal interference, and the free pursuit of economic, social and cultural development, with free disposition of natural wealth and resources without prejudice to any obligations arising out of international economic cooperation." *Human Rights Assessment*, 3–4.

60. *Human Rights Assessment*, 1–2.

61. *Human Rights Assessment*, 9. See also Bell and Keenan, "Human Rights Nongovern-mental Organisations," 345.

62. *Human Rights Assessment*, 11, 4.

63. *Human Rights Assessment*, 10.

64. Al-Haq Press Release no. 63, October 7, 1993. Claudio Cordone (then of Amnesty) recalls consulting with al-Haq and with Raji Sourani in Gaza and going to Tunis where, to-gether with Hanny Megally, then Amnesty's MENA director, he met with Arafat and elicited this statement of commitment to international instruments.

65. On NHRIs, see *Performance and Legitimacy: National Human Rights Institutions*, 2nd ed. (Geneva: International Council on Human Rights Policy, 2004).

66. See www.ichr.ps. Azzam reports that President Arafat handed a copy of the decree establishing the PICCR to his visitors from Amnesty International in September 1993. "Update: The Palestinian Independent Commission for Citizens' Rights," *Human Rights Quarterly* 20/2 (1998): 340. For a more recent consideration, see Allen, *Rise and Fall of Human Rights*, 133–47.

67. Azzam, "Al-Haq in 2004," 11.

68. Azzam, 11.

69. Bell and Keenan, "Human Rights Nongovernmental Organisations," 334.

70. Compare Raja Shehadeh's more general recollection of the PLO's response: "Okay, you people who were working on human rights, you were part of the resistance against the Israeli occupation; now the resistance should be stopped because we have reached an agreement with Israel. Go home." Bernard et al., "Interview with Raja Shehadeh," 21–22.

71. Azzam, "Al-Haq in 2004," 10.

72. Bell and Keenan, "Human Rights Nongovernmental Organisations," 335.

73. Azzam, "Al-Haq in 2004," 10; Allen, *Rise and Fall of Human Rights*, 64. For a 2009 observation of a human rights training with security officers, see Allen, 99–130.

74. Newsletter no. 33 (July–September 1994), 6.

75. The consequences were also potentially significant, as the incoming PA and established civil society organizations met on contested ground: in Gaza, after the PCHR similarly issued a press release criticizing the establishment of the State Security Court, director Raji Sourani was arrested by the PA.

76. Zalaquett, "Evaluation of al-Haq's Programs," 5.

77. Zalaquett, 6. For the "boomerang effect" at which much transnational human rights advocacy is aimed, see Keck and Sikkink, *Activists beyond Borders*, 12–13.

78. Zalaquett, "Evaluation of al-Haq's Programs," 6.

79. Zalaquett, 7–8.

80. Al-Haq Press Release no. 71 (June 2, 1994). See also *License to Kill*.

81. Zalaquett "Evaluation of al-Haq's Programs," 11–12.

82. Newsletter no. 33 (July–September 1994).

83. Newsletter no. 33.

84. Zalaquett, "Evaluation of al-Haq's Programs," 2.

85. Zalaquett, 18. See also Samuel Moyn, "Reflections on 'The Last Utopia': A Conversation with Samuel Moyn," interview with Brian Phillips, *Journal of Human Rights Practice* 3/2 (2011): 129–38. Moyn is critical of the conflation of human rights with democracy promotion.

86. Newsletter no. 33 (July–September 1994). See Newsletter no. 38 (July 1999) (lead article: "All NGOs, and Human Rights NGOs in Particular, Targeted by Direct Campaign"). The amended draft text was finally signed into law in the year 2000 and was described in a comparative study as "by a wide margin the most liberal and least restrictive NGO law in the Middle East." Kareem Elbayar, "NGO Laws in Selected Arab States," *International Journal of Not-for-Profit Law* 7/4 (2005): 21. Encroachments on this law by decrees issued by President Abbas and by practices of closure and seizure against certain NGOs followed in the Fatah-Hamas division after the 2006 elections.

87. Hajjar, "Human Rights in Israel/Palestine," 30.

88. Zalaquett, "Evaluation of al-Haq's Programs," 15.

89. Zalaquett, 13.

90. Zalaquett, 13.

91. *Al-Mar'a wa'l-'Adala wa'l-Qanun.* Other major conferences also took place that summer, convened by PCHR (on Human Rights and Political Transition) and by CIHRE, the spin-off of al-Haq's Enforcement Project (on International Human Rights Enforcement: The oPts under Political Transition).

92. Angela Gaff, *The Human Rights of Persons with Disabilities* (Ramallah: al-Haq 1994). Interviewees also referred to work on the Palestinian Charter of Patients' Rights.

93. Zalaquett, "Evaluation of al-Haq's Programs," 21.

94. Zalaquett, 22.

95. Zalaquett, 24.

96. Oyediran similarly noted, "There was too much democracy, I realize now."

97. See also Allen, *Rise and Fall of Human Rights.*

98. "Memorandum: Appeal to Save al-Haq," addressed to Members of the Board of Trustees by the Union of Workers in al-Haq, September 17, 1996.

99. This is reminiscent of the complaints around the board that resigned in 1992 before the period of staff management and ownership.

100. "Tajawazat majlis al-umana," unsigned and undated.

101. "Letter to Human Rights Organisations in the oPt," April 23, 1997 (unsigned), referring to the attempted "coup" of March 13, 1997. While the various documents allege politicization evidenced in the action of individual board members, risking al-Haq's reputation and standing, they do not seem to allege an impact on the substantive program of the organization.

102. Agreement of May 8, 1997, between a "representative and delegate" of the board, another of the governing council of LSM, and two employees' representatives (presumably coming from the two sides to the dispute).

103. Shukri Nashashibi and James Fine, "Preliminary Report: Consultancy on the Future of al-Haq," August 10, 1997.

104. Nashashibi and Fine, "Preliminary Report," 9.

105. Nashashibi and Fine, 9–10.

106. Nashashibi and Fine, 10.

107. Nashashibi and Fine, 11.

108. Nashashibi and Fine, 12.

109. Nashashibi and Fine, 14.

110. Shahinian observed that it helped that she was generally considered to be non-aligned politically. Randa Siniora also continued into December with a specific training project that she was organizing with external funding already received.

111. The point here was that the six employee-owners had been mandated by the whole of al-Haq's staff when they accepted to hold the LSM company shares, and that the group of four should probably have given that fact greater weight in their considerations.

112. Shawan Jabarin stressed the same point.

113. Newsletter no. 36 (English: Arabic is unnumbered) (September 1998).

114. Newsletter no. 36, 11–12 (Arabic text, slightly different, at 3–4).

EPILOGUE

1. Law on Charitable Associations and Civil Society Organizations (Law no. 1 of 2000). Follow-up work on this law included response to amendments and additions by decree

laws issued by President Abbas in 2011 and 2012 and challenges to closure decisions by the minister of the interior made under the law against various NGOs.

2. Al-Haq By-Laws, Article 7.

3. Al-Haq Vision, Mission, and Goals, www.alhaq.org/about-al-haq/vision-mission-and-goals (accessed January 5, 2018).

4. Al-Haq, Addameer, Al Dameer Association for Human Rights, Badil, the Community Action Center (at al-Quds University), the Civic Coalition for Palestinian Rights in Jerusalem, and the Jerusalem Legal Aid and Human Rights Center, "International Community Must Act to End the Occupation." June 8, 2017.

5. Hajjar, *Courting Conflict*, 15.

6. Tripp, *Power and the People*, 32–33. See chapter 7 on al-Haq's response to attacks against civilian Israeli targets in the later '90s.

7. Erakat, *Justice for Some*, 196.

8. Iain Guest, "Defending Human Rights in the Occupied Palestinian Territory—Challenges and Opportunities: A Discussion Paper on Human Rights Work in the West Bank and Gaza Strip," report and conclusions of a mission conducted for the Friedrich Ebert Foundation, Jerusalem, February 2007, 7, www.advocacynet.org/wp-content/uploads/2015/06/2007-report-on-human-rights-in-the-OPT.pdf.

9. Ziyad Humaidan, *Al-inqisam al-falastini: Safha suda' fi masar al-huquq wa'l-hurriyat* (Ramallah: al-Haq, 2011).

10. The military attacks that Israel named Operations Cast Lead (December 2008–January 2009), Pillar of Defence (November 2012), and Protective Edge (June–August 2014).

11. Al-Haq Center for Applied International Law, www.alhaq.org/alhaq-center/7019.html.

12. Al-Haq Centre for Applied International Law: First Regional Human Rights Seminar in Tunis, September 2011, www.alhaq.org/alhaq-center/6994.html.

13. *Dalil hawl tawthiq intihakat huquq al-insan* (Ramallah: al-Haq, 2011), 12.

14. Shawan Jabarin, introduction to Chris Cobb-Smith, *A Guide to Field Investigation* (Ramallah: al-Haq, 2012), 5.

15. So-called after the head of the four-person inquiry team, Richard Goldstone. The other members were Hina Jilani, Christine Chinkin, and Desmond Travers. UN doc. A/HRC/12/48, September 25, 2009.

16. UN doc. A/HRC/12/48, 421–22 para 1957.

17. See Stephen Zunes, "The United States and Israeli Violations of International Humanitarian Law," in Chase, ed., *Routledge Handbook on Human Rights*, 142–54. See also articles by Falk, Quigley, Reynolds, and Kearney in *Palestine Yearbook of International Law* 16 (2010).

18. It also provided impetus for the boycott, divestment, and sanctions movement: Ardi Imseis, "Introduction: The Goldstone Report and Beyond," *Palestine Yearbook of International Law* 16: 2.

19. See al-Haq 2006 Narrative Report, 2–3.

20. Naser Rayyes, who was appointed legal researcher at al-Haq in 1998, provided me with an extensive collection of these communications. On human rights training for law enforcement officials, see for example Al-Haq 2007 Narrative Report, 4–5.

21. On the "statehood bid," see Valentina Azarov, "An International Legal Demarche for Human Rights? Perils and Prospects of the Palestinian UN Bid," *International Journal of Human Rights* 18/4–5 (2014): 527–44; and Erakat, *Justice for Some*, 221–22

22. Those treaties were ICCPR, ICESCR, CAT and Optional Protocol, CEDAW, CERD, CRC and two Optional Protocols, and CRPD. This was against Israel's objections after Israel reneged on an agreed prisoner release. In early 2015 Palestine ratified Additional Protocol Two to the Geneva Conventions, along with the statute of the International Criminal Court, and in 2019 the CEDAW Optional Protocol. For IHL ratifications, see International Committee of the Red Cross, "States, Parties and Commentaries," https://ihl-databases.icrc.org/applic/ihl/ihl.nsf/vwTreatiesByCountrySelected.xsp?xpcountrySelected=PS.

23. "Al-Haq's Comments on the Draft Law by Decree Amending the Law by Decree on Cybercrimes," January 25, 2018.

24. Allen, *Rise and Fall of Human Rights*, 142, 20–21.

25. This was in addition to many criticisms of the substance of the decree law. See "Civil Society Organisations Demand That the Law by Decree on the High Criminal Court Be Repealed" (al-Haq, January 28, 2018). The Palestinian Basic Law (2003, Article 43) allows the president to "issue decrees that have the power of law" when the Legislative Council is not sitting, "in cases of necessity that cannot be delayed." For a contemporary consideration of how to respond to executive (presidential) control of legislative initiatives, see al-Haq 2008 Narrative Report, 7–8. See also Isam Abdeen, "Al-Haq's Comment on the Draft Law by Decree on the Creation of the National Preventative Mechanism for the Prevention of Torture in Palestine," April 25, 2020, www.alhaq.org/advocacy/16393.html, similarly insisting that a freshly elected PLC must be closely involved in the establishment of the mechanism.

26. Guest, "Defending Human Rights," 6.

27. Originally the Land and Water Establishment, it became the Palestinian Society for the Protection of Human Rights and the Environment.

28. Guest, "Defending Human Rights," 45; Allen, *Rise and Fall of Human Rights*, 83.

29. See Abigail B. Bakan and Yasmeen Abu-Laban, "Palestinian Resistance and International Solidarity: The BDS Campaign," *Race and Class* 51/1 (2009): 29–54, on the BDS campaign, and Erakat, *Justice for Some*, 228–34, on the Palestinian leadership position. Israeli authorities have elided those advocating BDS with security threats to Israel and called on donors not to fund organizations endorsing BDS—see further below.

30. Noura Erakat, "Palestinian Human Rights Defenders on the Limits and Horizons for the International Criminal Court: Interview with Raji Sourani and Shawan Jabarin," *Status Hour* 3/2 (Arab Studies Institute: December 2016), www.statushour.com/en/Interview/187.

31. In January 2009, the Palestinian leadership had submitted a declaration recognizing ICC jurisdiction over its territory, ahead of acquiring the status of a state allowing it to sign up to the Rome treaty as such; see Kearney and Denayer, "Al-Haq Position Paper on Issues Arising from the Palestinian Authority's Submission of a Declaration to the Prosecutor of the International Criminal Court under Article 12(3) of the Rome Statute," October 13, 2010.

32. UN News at https://news.un.org/en/story/2014/12/487342-un-security-council-action-palestinian-statehood-blocked#.VKWNgNLF-68. Negotiations on the resolution showed the draft resolution one vote short of the nine needed, and in addition, the United States threatened to use its veto. See Noah Gordon, "Why the Palestinians Joined the International Criminal Court," *The Atlantic*, December 31, 2014. Palestine became a state party to the treaty (following its accession) on April 1, 2015.

33. Erakat, *Justice for Some*, 208.

34. The State of Palestine formally referred the situation in Palestine to the ICC Prosecutor General in May 2018 against the background of the weekly Great Return March events on the borders of Gaza, and one week after the seventieth anniversary of the *Nakba*. See "State of Palestine Submits State Referral to the ICC," al-Haq, May 22, 2018, www.alhaq .org/advocacy/targets/international-criminal-court-icc/1257-state-of-palestine-submits -state-referral-to-the-icc. In April 2018, it had submitted a complaint against Israel under the UN CERD.

35. "Four Palestinian Human Rights Organisations Submit File to ICC Prosecutor: Israel is Unable and Unwilling to Conduct Genuine Investigations and Prosecutions," press release from PCHR, Al Mezan, Al-Haq, and Al-Dameer, December 23, 2017. Previous quotations from the organizations' press releases from 2015, 2016, 2016, and 2017.

36. "After Five Years the Prosecutor of the ICC Finally Advances the Situation of Palestine from Preliminary Examination to the Pre-Trial Chamber for Questions on Jurisdiction," al-Haq, December 29, 2019, www.alhaq.org/advocacy/16323.html.

37. "Palestinian Human Rights Organizations Submit Amicus on Territorial Jurisdiction," March 19, 2020, text at www.alhaq.org/advocacy/16609.html. For the ICJ submission, see www.icc-cpi.int/CourtRecords/CR2020_01108.pdf. Developments continued apace into the summer of 2020 against the background of Israel's announced annexation plans and sanctions laid against the ICC prosecutor through a US executive order (see condemnation by al-Haq at www.alhaq.org/advocacy/16609.html).

38. See "No Accountability," B'Tselem, November 11, 2017, www.btselem.org/account ability. B'Tselem's position is set out in full in *The Occupation's Fig Leaf: Israel's Military Law Enforcement System as a Whitewash Mechanism* (Jerusalem: B'Tselem, 2016).

39. According to Grazia Careccia, who established the war crimes project when she joined the organization as a legal researcher in 2006 and later headed al-Haq's Legal Research and Advocacy Department.

40. Hajjar, *Lawfare and Armed Conflict*, 11, 21–22. See also Michael Kearney, "Lawfare, Legitimacy and Resistance: The Weak and the Law." *Palestine Yearbook of International Law* 16 (2010): 97–100.

41. *Al-Haq v. Secretary of State for Foreign and Commonwealth Affairs* (2009) EWHC 1910. This was in cooperation with Phil Shiner of Public Interest Lawyers; refusal of permission for al-Haq to seek judicial review was ruled on July 29, 2009, by the Divisional High Court of Justice in England and Wales. See "Judgment Handed Down in the Case of Al-Haq v. Secretary of State for Foreign and Commonwealth Affairs," al-Haq, July 29, 2009, www .alhaq.org/advocacy/targets/accountability/69-al-haq-vs-uk/249-judgment-handed -down-in-the-case-of-al-haq-v-secretary-of-state-for-foreign-and-commonwealth-affairs.

42. Kearney, "Lawfare, Legitimacy and Resistance," 99.

43. Al-Haq, "Business and Human Rights Resource Centre, Response to Heidelberg Cement," October 10, 2017.

44. See Ali Abunimah, "UN Holds Back Names of Israeli Settlement Profiteers," *Electronic Intifada*, February 4, 2018; and "Israel/Palestine: UN Settlement Business Data Can Stem Abuse," Human Rights Watch, November 28, 2017, www.hrw.org/news/2017/11/28 /israel/palestine-un-settlement-business-data-can-stem-abuse. See also UN doc. A/ HRC/43/71 of February 12, 2020; and "Al-Haq and CIHRS Welcome Publication of the UN Database on Settlement Business Activities," February 13, 2020.

45. Interview with Naser Rayyes, who was in the forefront of this work. See also al-Haq Newsletter no. 38 (September 1998). In 2008 al-Haq hosted "the first ever Palestinian Conference against the Death Penalty" along with the Palestinian Coalition against the Death Penalty (Al-Haq 2008 Narrative Report, 7). In 2018, the Palestinian president signed Palestine's accession to the Second Optional Protocol to the ICCPR: see PCHR, "Accession to Protocol Aiming at Abolition of Death Penalty Is Step in Right Direction," June 10, 2018.

46. The Copenhagen-based Euro-Mediterranean Human Rights Network.

47. Shawan Jabarin was elected secretary-general of FIDH for the second time in October 2019.

48. In 2018 Shawan Jabarin was elected to the ICJ's Executive Committee during his second term as an ICJ Commissioner.

49. Keck and Sikkink, *Activists beyond Borders*, 12–14, 107.

50. Observatory for the Protection of Human Rights Defenders (FIDH & OMCT), "Open Letter to UNSG Regarding Slandering Statements against Palestinian NGOs al-Haq and Al Mezan," July 4, 2017. See also PHROC and PNGO, March 26, 2018, www.pngo.net /position-paper-on-the-ongoing-campaign-to-silence-delegitimize-and-de-fund-palestinian -civil-society-organizations-and-human-rights-defenders/ (accessed March 29, 2018).

51. "Al-Haq under Attack—Staff Member's Life Threatened," March 5, 2016, That statement notes that in the early stages the harassers claimed to be acting from within the Palestinian Authority—"a fact categorically refuted by an official statement from the State of Palestine." Al-Haq declared itself "convinced that the source of these attacks, as the case was in previous years, is the Israeli side."

52. Ron Dudai makes this point in regard to the United Kingdom and the United States. Dudai, *Advocacy with Footnotes*, 795.

53. On this, see Erakat, *Justice for Some*, 175–210, describing Israel's "legal work" in moving (with US support) from a sui generis characterization of its engagement as "short of war" to an "explicitly warfare" model.

54. Kearney, "Lawfare, Legitimacy and Resistance," 88. Most ascribe the original use of the term to US major general Charles Dunlap; for his updated views, see Dunlap, "Lawfare Today: A Perspective," *Yale Journal of International Affairs* (Winter 2008): 146–54.

55. Neve Gordon, "Human Rights as a Security Threat: Lawfare and the Campaign against Human Rights NGOs," *Law and Society Review* 48/2 (2014): 313, 312.

56. Kearney, "Lawfare, Legitimacy and Resistance," 81. Key nongovernmental proponents of this "lawfare narrative" include the NGO Monitor and The Lawfare Project. See also Gordon, "Human Rights as a Security Threat," 312–13, 322–23.

57. Kearney, "Lawfare, Legitimacy and Resistance," 113. Law and colonialism scholar John Comaroff uses lawfare to indicate "the effort to conquer and control indigenous peoples by the coercive use of legal means." Comaroff, "Colonialism, Culture, and the Law: A Foreword," *Law and Social Inquiry* 26 (2001): 306.

58. Gordon, "Human Rights as a Security Threat," 328. Livni was summoned by the police during a 2016 visit to Great Britain, with the summons withdrawn after diplomatic contacts; see "Israeli Politician Tzipi Livni 'Summonsed by UK Police,'" BBC, July 3, 2016, www.bbc.co.uk/news/world-middle-east-36697324.

59. Eyal Weizman, "Short Cuts," *London Review of Books*, December 6, 2012, 28.

60. The New Israel Fund, according to Gordon, denied that this change in policy was a direct result of the anti-NGO campaign that was unleashed after Goldstone. Gordon, "Human Rights as a Security Threat," 335.

61. Gordon, 332–33.

62. "Palestinian Human Rights Organisations Condemn Israel's Unremitting Attempts to Silence Them," May 25, 2018, www.alhaq.org/advocacy/6197.html. See also, "Al-Haq Condemns Attempt to Smear al-Haq, Its Staff and Partners in Recent Report," May 11, 2020, www.alhaq.org/advocacy/16854.html.

63. Hajjar, "Lawfare and Armed Conflict."

64. Erakat, *Justice for Some*, 178.

65. Hajjar, "Lawfare and Armed Conflict," 25. See also Eyal Weizman, "Lawfare in Gaza: Legislative Attack," *openDemocracy*, March 1, 2009; Richard Falk, "The Goldstone Report: Neither Implemented nor Ignored," *Palestine Yearbook of International Law* 16 (2010): 11; and Zunes, "United States and Israeli Violations," 151 on US support for Israel's positions.

66. Hajjar, "Lawfare and Armed Conflict," 11; see also Cavanaugh, "Narrating Law," and Erakat, *Justice for Some*, 175–210.

67. See contributions by Bahey el-Din Hassan at the 1998 meeting about the Arab human rights movement in *International Aspects of the Arab Human Rights Movement*, 22; and see Lisa Hajjar, "Law against Order: Human Rights Organizations and (Versus?) the Palestinian Authority," *University of Miami Law Review* 56 (2002): 60; and Chase, *Human Rights, Revolution and Reform*, 41, on the increasing frequency and profile of Arab regional human rights meetings in the late 1990s and early 2000s.

68. See Pratt, "Human Rights NGOs." See also the disagreement among Egyptian activists in the chapter on "Foreign Funding and Partnership in the Arab Human Rights Movement" in *International Aspects of the Arab Human Rights Movement*, 45–65.

69. Megally, "Human Rights in the Arab World," 107.

70. Eyad El Sarraj, "Justice in Heaven," in Chase and Hamzawy, eds., *Human Rights and the Arab World*, 133.

71. Hajjar, "Law against Order," 67.

72. See generally Hopgood, *Endtimes of Human Rights*.

73. Megally, "Human Rights in the Arab World," 110; Hajjar, "Human Rights in Israel/Palestine," 30; Chase, *Human Rights, Revolution and Reform*, 43. See also chapter 5 of the present work.

74. Megally, "Human Rights in the Arab World," 110.

75. *International Aspects of the Arab Human Rights Movement*, 49.

76. UN Office of the Special Coordinator in the Occupied Territories, "Rule of Law Development Support in the West Bank and Gaza Strip: Survey and State of the Development Effort," May 31, 1999, https://unispal.un.org/DPA/DPR/unispal.nsf/2ee9468747556b2d85256 cf60060d2a6/7968e954038f503785256b1f0058556f?OpenDocument.

77. Hammami, "Palestinian NGOs since Oslo," 16; Hajjar, "Law against Order," 70–71; Hajjar, "Human Rights in Israel/Palestine," 33. See also Bell and Keenan, "Human Rights Nongovernmental Organisations," 347.

78. Hammami, "Palestinian NGOs since Oslo," 19.

79. See Azzam, "Al-Haq in 2004," 2; Allen, *Rise and Fall of Human Rights*; Hanafi and Tabar, "Palestinian Human Rights Organisations," 27; Perugini and Gordon, "Israel/Palestine, Human Rights and Domination," 426.

80. Jabarin, "The PA's West Bank Abuses Weaken Resistance to Israel," *The National*, July 31, 2012. More broadly, Usha Natarajan notes the "heavily negative perception of international law in the Arab world." Natarajan, "TWAIL and the Environment: The State of

Nature, the Nature of the State, and the Arab Spring," *Oregon Review of International Law* 14/1 (2012): 177.

81. Roberts, "Transformative Military Occupation," 580.

82. "Report of the Special Rapporteur on the Situation of Human Rights in the Palestinian Territories Occupied by Israel since 1967," UN doc. A/HRC/4/14, January 29, 2007, 3.

83. "Report of the Special Rapporteur," 23, para 62.

84. Adam Roberts, "Prolonged Military Occupation: The Israeli-Occupied Territories since 1967," *American Journal of International Law* 84 (1990): 44.

85. Dugard and Reynolds, "Apartheid, International Law, and the Occupied Palestinian Territory," 868.

86. Tilley, ed., *Occupation, Colonialism, Apartheid?*, and see also Virginia Tilley, ed., *Beyond Occupation: Apartheid, Colonialism and International Law in the Occupied Palestinian Territories* (London: Pluto Press, 2012). Al-Haq, together with Adalah, hosted a seminar to launch the findings of the research project. See Dugard's personal account of his engagement with this issue in *Confronting Apartheid*.

87. UN doc. A/HRC/4/14, 24, para. 63.

88. Al-Haq, "International Community Must Act to End the Occupation," June 8, 2017.

89. The authors considered the question in relation to the different regimes exercised over Palestinian citizens of Israel, Palestinians in East Jerusalem, in the rest of the West Bank and the Gaza Strip, and Palestinians living as refugees and in exile. See also Erakat, *Justice for Some*, 213–19.

90. Economic and Social Commission for Western Asia (ESCWA), *Israeli Practices towards the Palestinian People and the Question of Apartheid* (Beirut: United Nations, 2017), quotation from the Executive Summary.

91. Richard Falk. "The Inside Story on Our UN Report Calling Israel an Apartheid State," *The Nation*, March 22, 2017.

92. PHROC letter to UN Secretary-General Antonio Guterres, March 21, 2017. Accordingly, al-Haq and its allies regularly invoke the apartheid framework in public interventions such as that released on World Health Day in the spring of 2020 and the midst of the COVID-19 pandemic: "Israeli Apartheid Undermines Palestinian Right to Health." On the particular vulnerability to COVID-19 of Palestinian refugees in the West Bank (due to disproportionately high and structurally produced rates of diabetes), see Wispelwey and Al-Orzza, "Underlying Conditions," LRB blog, April 18, 2020, www.lrb.co.uk/blog/2020 /april/underlying-conditions.

93. Erakat, "Palestinian Human Rights Defenders."

94. The US Department of State Country Reports for 2017 (released in March 2018) addressed human rights in "Israel, Golan Heights, West Bank and Gaza" in a studied departure from the previous heading of "Israel and the Occupied Territories." www.state.gov/j /drl/rls/hrrpt/2017humanrightsreport/index.htm#wrapper.

95. "Al-Haq Condemns United States Recognition of Jerusalem, in the Occupied State of Palestine, as Israel's Capital," December 6, 2017. The passage of SCR 2334 in December 2016, condemning Israel's settlement activities, had been welcomed as hugely significant, mostly for the fact that the United States (at the end of Barack Obama's presidency) had abstained and had thus, for once, not used its veto to prevent the Council from reasserting its established position on the unlawful nature of Israeli settlement activity including

in East Jerusalem. Erakat opens her book *Justice for Some* with the passage of SCR 2334. On the Trump declaration, she observes, "For the vast majority of Palestinians the affront is not the loss of a would-be capital, but the imperial rejection of Palestinian belonging and the formalization of their erasure" (235). In 2019, Trump formally recognized Israeli sovereignty over the occupied Syrian Golan Heights; see "Golan Heights: Trump Signs Order Recognising Occupied Area as Israeli," BBC, March 25, 2019, www.bbc.co.uk/news/world-middle-east-47697717.

96. "Al-Haq Memorandum to the Palestinian Delegation Attending the Regional Conference in Madrid," October 24, 1991. See above, chapter 7.

97. Al-Haq, December 6, 2017.

LSM/AL-HAQ PUBLICATIONS AND SOURCES

Al-Haq Publications Referred To in Text

"Al-Haq Condemns United States Recognition of Jerusalem, in the Occupied State of Palestine, as Israel's Capital." December 6, 2017.

"Al-Haq's Comments on the Draft Law by Decree Amending the Law by Decree on Cybercrimes." January 25, 2018.

Al-Haq's Response to the US State Department Country Reports on Human Rights Practices for 1990: The Occupied Territories. May 1991.

Al-Mar'a wa'l-'Adala wa'l-Qanun [Women, justice, and the law]. 1995.

Ansar 3: A Case for Closure. 1988.

"An Appeal to State Signatories to the Fourth Geneva Convention to Intervene after Recent Killings." Press Release no. 10. December 13, 1987.

Briefing Papers on Twenty Years of Israeli Occupation of the West Bank and Gaza. 1987.

Critique of the US Department of State Country Reports on Human Rights Practices for 1991: Israel and the Occupied Territories. March 1992.

Dalil hawl intihakat huquq al-insan. 2011.

Dhahiriyyeh: Centre for Punishment. 1988.

A Human Rights Assessment of the Declaration of Principles on Interim Self-Government Arrangements for Palestinians. 1993.

"International Community Must Act to End the Occupation." June 8, 2017.

Israel's War on Education in the Occupied West Bank: A Penalty for the Future. 1988.

"Memorandum of Protest and Appeal re: Grave Breaches of the Fourth Geneva Convention, 15 April 1989."

"Memorandum to Member States of the European Community as State Parties to the Fourth Geneva Convention, January 14, 1988."

"Memorandum to the Palestinian Delegation Attending the Regional Conference in Madrid." October 24, 1991.

"Open Letter to Palestinian Public Opinion." January 1, 1993.

Palestinian Victims of Torture Speak Out: Thirteen Accounts of Torture during Interrogation in Israeli Prisons. 1993 (Arabic text, 1992, edited by Riziq Shuqair, English by Tom Taylor).

"Reconstruction of Events (Revised): Al-Haram al-Sharif, Jerusalem, Monday 8 October 1990," October 28, 1990. S/21919/Add.2. Reproduced as "Addendum 2" to the UN Secretary-General's Report submitted to the Security Council in accordance with Security Council Resolution 672 (1990), November 1, 1990.

"Representation to State Signatories of the Fourth Geneva Convention—Israeli Tax Policies in the West Bank: The Case of Beit Sahour." September 27, 1989.

"Representation to States Signatory to the Fourth Geneva Convention, 7 June 1990," accompanied by a Supplement, "The Need for International Protection."

Screaming in the Dark. 2002 (combined English and Arabic text).

Zawiyat huquq al-insan [Human rights corner]. 1993.

Al-Haq Annual Reports and Anniversary Publications

In Need of Protection: An Investigation into Israeli Practices in the Occupied Palestinian Territories during the Intifada: 29 September 2000 to 1 October 2001. 2002.

A Nation under Siege: Al-Haq Annual Report on Human Rights in the Occupied Palestinian Territories 1989. 1990.

Protection Denied: Continuing Israeli Human Rights Violations in the Occupied Palestinian Territories, 1990. 1991.

Punishing a Nation: Human Rights during the Palestinian Uprising, December 1987–December 1988. 1989.

Thirty Years Defending Human Rights. 2009.

Twenty Years Defending Human Rights. 1999.

Waiting for Justice: Al-Haq: Twenty-Five Years Defending Human Rights (1979–2004). 2005.

Al-Haq Know Your Rights (KYR) series (in Arabic)

Please note that these entries are listed in order of their publication in al-Haq's Know Your Rights series. I did not locate a publication for KYR no. 15.

Mona Rishmawi. *Al-Ard: al-subul al-qanuniyya li'l-hifazh 'alayha* [The land: Legal means to protect it]. 1982 (KYR no. 1).

———. *Al-Muwatin. Al-taftish wa'l-i'tiqal wa'l-muhakama al-'askariyya* [The citizen: Search, arrest and military trial]. 1983 (KYR no. 2).

———. *Al-Iqama al-jabriyya—ma'naha—wasa'il al-ta'n bi-ha* [Forced residence—what does it mean—ways of challenging it]. 1984 (KYR no. 3).

Al-i'lan al-'alami li-huquq al-insan [The Universal Declaration of Human Rights]. 1986 (KYR no. 4).

Huquq al-'ummal al-'amilin fi al-daffa al-gharbiyya [Rights of workers working in the West Bank]. 1986 (slightly updated and republished 1989) (KYR no. 5).

Huquq al-'ummal al-'amilin laday arbab al-'amal al-israiliyin [Rights of Palestinian workers working for Israeli employers]. 1986 (KYR no. 6).

Riziq Shuqair. *Al-qatl al-'amd* [Willful killing]. 1989 (KYR no. 7).

———. *Lamm Shaml* [Israeli policy on family reunification]. 1990 (KYR no. 8).

————. *Nahu munahadat al-taʿdhib* [Towards the elimination of torture]. 1991 (KYR no. 9).

Mudawwana li-qawaʾid suluk al-muwazhzhafin al-mukallafin bi-infadh al-qanun [Code of Conduct for Law Enforcement Officials, adopted by UN General Assembly Resolution 34/169 of 17 December 1979]. 1993 (KYR no. 10).

Mustafa Marʾi and Riziq Shuqair. *Al-muwatin. Al-taftish waʾl-iʿtiqal waʾl-muhakama al-ʿaskariyya* [The citizen: Search, arrest, military trial]. 1993 (second printing, KYR no. 11).

Randa Siniora and Rim. ʿAbd al-Hadi. *Al-ʿunf didd al-marʾa—zhahira amma au khassa?* [Violence against women: A general or particular phenomenon?]. 1994 (KYR no. 12).

Majmuʿat al-mabadiʾ al-mutaʿalliqa bi-himaya jamiʿ al-ashkhas alladhina yataʿarridun li-ayy shakl min ashkal al-ihtijaz au al-sijn [Body of Principles on the Protection of All Persons Subjected to Any Form of Detention or Imprisonment]. 1994 (KYR no. 13).

Riziq Shuqair. *Al-khususiyya al-thaqafiyya: ʿuqba haqiqiyya amama ʿalamiyyat huquq al-insan am ghitaʾ li-tabrir intihakatiha?!* [Cultural relativism: A real obstacle to the universality of human rights or a cover to justify violations?!]. 1995 (KYR no. 14).

Hana Husam Amir. *Ittifaqiyya huquq al-tifl* [The Convention on the Rights of the Child]. N.d. (KYR no. 16).

————. *Huquq al-sujanaʾ bi-muqtada qanun marakiz al-islah waʾl-taʾhil al-falastini bi-muqarana maʿa al-qawaʾid al-namudhajiyya al-dunya li-muʿamalat al-sujanaʾ* [Prisoners' rights under the Palestinian Law of Correction and Rehabilitation Centers compared with the Standard Minimum Rules for the Treatment of Prisoners]. 2007 (KYR no. 17).

Al-Haq Published / Al-Haq Originated

Published by LSM or al-Haq unless otherwise indicated.

Abdeen, Isam. "Al-Haq's Comment on the Draft Law by Decree on the Creation of the National Preventative Mechanism for the Prevention of Torture in Palestine." April 25, 2020.

Azzam, Fateh. "Al-Haq in 2004: A Twenty Five Year Retrospective." In *Waiting for Justice: Annual Report 2004*, 2–17. 2005.

————. "Non-Governmental Organisations between the Field of Politics and the Field of Human Rights." *Al-Quds*, June 25, 1993. Reproduced in al Haq, *Zawiyat huquq al-insan*, 1993, 129–33.

Batrawi, Khaled. "Al-tashrih ka juzʾ min al-tahqiq fi hawadith istishhad dakhil al-sujun al-israʾiliyya" [Autopsy as part of investigations into incidents of martyrdom in Israeli prisons]. Personal experience recalled by engineer Khaled Batrawi. Text of paper, 2009.

————. "Dhikriyat al-Haq" [Memories of al-Haq]. November 27, 2009 (unpublished).

Bevis, Linda. *The Applicability of Human Rights Law to Occupied Territories: The Case of the Occupied Territories*. 1994 (reprinted 2003).

Cobb-Smith, Chris. *A Guide to Field Investigation*. 2012.

Coon, Anthony. *Town Planning under Military Occupation: An Examination of the Law and Practice of Town Planning in the Occupied West Bank*. Aldershot: Dartmouth, 1992.

Falloon, Virgil. *Excessive Secrecy, Lack of Guidelines: A Report on Military Censorship in the West Bank*. Ramallah: LSM, 1986. Reprinted from *Index on Censorship* 13/4 (1984): 32–36.

Gaff, Angela. *The Human Rights of Persons with Disabilities*. 1994.

Hillier, Tim. *The Reply of Law in the Service of Man / Al-Haq to the US Report on Human Rights Practices in the Territories Occupied by Israel for 1982*. 1993.

Hiltermann, Joost. "Al-Haq's Response to the Chapter on Israel and the Occupied Territories in the State Department's 'Country Reports on Human Rights Practices for 1984.'" 1986.

———. "Al-Haq: The First Twenty Years." In *Twenty Years Defending Human Rights*, 9–11. 1999.

———. *Israel's Deportation Policy in the Occupied West Bank and Gaza*. 1986.

Humaidan, Ziyad. *Al-inqisam al-falastini: Safha suda' fi masar al-huquq wa'l-hurriyat*. 2011.

Hunt, Paul. *Justice? The Military Court System in the Israeli-Occupied Territories*. Ramallah: al-Haq and GCRL, 1987.

In Their Own Words: Affidavits Collected by LSM. Geneva: Commission of the Churches on International Affairs, World Council of Churches, 1983.

Jabarin, Shawan. "The PA's West Bank Abuses Weaken Resistance to Israel." *The National*, July 31, 2012.

———. "Peace and Human Rights: Palestine as a Case Study." University Centre Saint-Ignatius, Antwerp, Belgium. October 17, 2008 (conference, "The Local Relevance of Human Rights"). Available online from Al-Haq's website (accessed March 6, 2017).

Jaradat, Ahmad. "Thirty Years of Persistent Production." In *Thirty Years Defending Human Rights*. 2009.

Kearney, Michael, and Stijn Denayer. "Al-Haq Position Paper on Issues Arising from the Palestinian Authority's Submission of a Declaration to the Prosecutor of the International Criminal Court under Article 12(3) of the Rome Statute." October 13, 2010.

Kuttab, Jonathan. *Analysis of Military Order no. 854 and Related Military Orders Concerning Educational Institutions in the West Bank*. 1981.

———. "Avenues Open for Defence of Human Rights in the Israeli-Occupied Territories." In Playfair, ed., *International Law and the Administration of Occupied Territories*, 489–504.

———. "A Comment on Military Order no. 1164." *Palestine Yearbook of International Law* 2 (1985): 158–61.

———. "Military Order 1164 Threatens the Independence of the Bar Association." CIJL Bulletin no. 17 (April 1986), 17–22.

———. "Statement of Jonathan Kuttab, Esquire, for the Palestine Human Rights Campaign, Foreign Affairs Committee, US House of Representatives, 7 March 1985."

Kuttab, Jonathan, and Raja Shehadeh. *Civilian Administration in the Occupied West Bank: Analysis of Israeli Military Government Order no. 947*. 1982.

LSM, *The Reply of Law in the Service of Man / Al-Haq to the US Report on Human Rights Practices in the Territories Occupied by Israel for 1982*. Prepared by Timothy Hiller. 1983.

———. *Jnaid: The New Israeli Prison in Nablus*. 1984.

LSM Staff. *Torture and Intimidation in the West Bank: The Case of Al-Fara'a Prison*. Ramallah: ICJ and LSM, 1985.

Mar'i, Mustafa. *The Right to Freedom of Assembly: An Analysis of the Position of the Palestinian Authority*. Ramallah: al-Haq, 1995 (Arabic), 1997 (English) (Occasional Paper no. 12).

Moffett, Martha Roadstrum. *Perpetual Emergency: A Legal Analysis of Israel's Use of the British Defence (Emergency) Regulations, 1945, in the Occupied Territories*. 1989 (Occasional Paper no. 6).

Nashashibi, Shukri, and James Fine. "Preliminary Report on the Future of Al-Haq." August 10, 1997.

Phillips, Melissa. *Torture for Security: The Systematic Torture and Ill-Treatment of Palestinians by Israel.* 1995.

Playfair, Emma. "Administrative Detention in the Israeli-Occupied West Bank." *ICJ Review* 35 (December 1985): 31–44, and SIM Newsletter no. 13 (February 1986), 5–26.

———. *Administrative Detention in the Occupied West Bank.* 1986 (Occasional Paper no. 1).

———. *Demolition and Sealing of Houses as a Punitive Measure in the Israeli-Occupied West Bank.* 1987 (Occasional Paper no. 5).

———. "Israel's Security Needs in the West Bank, Real and Contrived." *Arab Studies Quarterly* 10 (1988): 406–23.

Playfair, Emma, ed. *International Law and the Administration of Occupied Territories: Two Decades of Israeli Occupation of the West Bank and Gaza Strip.* Oxford: The Clarendon Press, 1992.

Pounder, Derrick. "Death in Detention of Ibrahim al-Mtour: Text of Autopsy Report by Dr. Derrick Pounder." In *A Nation under Siege: Al-Haq Annual Report on Human Rights in the Occupied Palestinian Territories 1989,* 218–31. 1990.

A Report on the Treatment of Security Prisoners at the West Bank Prison of al-Fara'a. 1984.

Rishmawi, Mona. *Muqaddimat hawl al-mar'a al-filastiniyya bayn al-tajriba wa'l-nass al-qanuni* [Palestinian women between experience and legal text]. 1986 (Occasional Paper no. 3).

———. *Planning in Whose Interest?* 1984 (Occasional Paper no. 4).

Shah, Samira. *The By-Pass Road Network in the West Bank.* 1997.

Shalabi, Khamis, and Zahi Jaradat, eds., *'Amm 'ala ahdath majzarat al-haram al-Ibrahimi bi'l-khalil* [One year after the massacre at the Ibrahimi sanctuary in Hebron]. 1995.

Shammas, Charles. "The Role of the Enforcement of International Law in the Processes of Dispute Settlement." In *Towards a Strategy for the Enforcement of Human Rights in the Israeli Occupied West Bank and Gaza: A Working Symposium,* London, July 25, 1989, 35–40. London: Labour Middle East Council and Conservative Middle East Council, 1989.

Shehadeh, Aziz, Fuad Shehadeh, and Raja Shehadeh, *Israeli Proposed Road Plan for the West Bank: A Question for the International Court of Justice.* 1984.

Shehadeh, Raja (assisted by Jonathan Kuttab). *The West Bank and the Rule of Law.* New York: International Commission of Jurists, 1980.

Shuqair, Riziq, and Randa Siniora, eds. *Application Denied: Separated Palestinian Families Tell Their Stories.* 1991.

Siniora, Randa. "Al-Haq and Its Societal Programs: The Women's Rights Program." In *Twenty Years Defending Human Rights,* 21–22. 1999.

Stephens, Marc. *Enforcement of International Law in the Israeli-Occupied Territories.* 1989 (Occasional Paper no. 7).

Taylor, Tom. *Missiles and Dynamite: The Israeli Military Forces' Destruction of Palestinian Homes with Anti-Tank Missiles and High-Powered Explosives.* 1993 (Occasional Paper no. 10).

Tonatti, Alessandro. *Feasting on the Occupation.* 2013.

Towards a Strategy for the Enforcement of Human Rights in the Israeli Occupied West Bank and Gaza: A Working Symposium. London, July 25, 1989. London: Labour Middle East Council and Conservative Middle East Council, 1989.

Welchman Lynn. "Repression of Grave Breaches of the Geneva Conventions through the Domestic Judicial System: The Case of the UK." In *Towards a Strategy for the Enforcement of Human Rights in the Israeli Occupied West Bank and Gaza: A Working Symposium, London, July 25, 1989, 68–79.* London: Labour Middle East Council and Conservative Middle East Council, 1989.

———. *A Thousand and One Homes: Israel's Demolition and Sealing of Houses in the Occupied Palestinian Territories.* 1993 (Occasional Paper no. 11).

Whittome, Candy. *The Right to Unite: The Family Reunification Question in the Palestinian Occupied Territories.* 1990.

Zalaquett, José. "Evaluation of Al-Haq's Programs, Strategy and Work." February 1994.

OTHER SOURCES

Abraham, Nabeel, Janice Terry, Cheryl Rosenberg, Lisa Hajjar, and Hilary Shadroui. "International Human Rights Organizations and the Palestine Conflict." *MERIP Middle East Report* 150 (January–February 1988): 12–20.

Ahmad, Eqbal. "Revolutionary Warfare and Counterinsurgency." In *National Liberation: Revolution in the Third World*, edited by Norman Miller and Roderick Aya, 137–213.New York: Free Press, 1971.

Allen, Lori. *The Rise and Fall of Human Rights: Cynicism and Politics in Occupied Palestine.* Stanford: Stanford University Press, 2013.

Al-Sayyid, Mustapha K., Peter Rosenblum, and Henry Steiner, eds. *International Aspects of the Arab Human Rights Movement.* Cambridge, MA: Harvard Law School Human Rights Program, 2000.

Alston, Philip. "The Populist Challenge to Human Rights." *Journal of Human Rights Practice* 9 (2017): 1–15.

Alston, Philip, and Colin Gillespie. "Global Human Rights Monitoring, New Technologies, and the Politics of Information." *European Journal of International Law* 23/4 (2012): 1089–1123.

Amad, Adnan, ed. *The Israeli League for Human and Civil Rights (The Shahak Papers).* Beirut: Near East Bureau for Information and Interpretation, 1973.

Amnesty International. "Amnesty International's Response to the Comments of the Israeli Ministry of Justice on the Amnesty International Reports 1990 and 1991." October 1991.

———. *Israel and the Occupied Territories: Administrative Detention during the Palestinian Intifada.* AI Index MDE 15/06/89, June 1989.

———. *Report and Recommendations of an AI Mission to the Government of the State of Israel.* London, 1979.

———. "'Under Constant Medical Supervision': Torture, Ill-Treatment and the Health Professions in Israel and the Occupied Territories." AI Index: MDE 15/37/96, April 1996.

Andrew, Christopher. *The Defence of the Realm: The Authorized History of MI5.* London: Penguin, 2009.

Awad, Mubarak. "Non-Violent Resistance: A Strategy for the Occupied Territories." *Journal of Palestine Studies* 13/4 (1984): 22–36.

Azarov, Valentina. "An International Legal Demarche for Human Rights? Perils and Prospects of the Palestinian UN Bid." *International Journal of Human Rights* 18/4–5 (2014): 527–44.

———. "Legal House-keeping in the EU." *openDemocracy*, July 31, 2013.

———. "Making Human Rights Work for the Palestines of the World." *openDemocracy*, November 3, 2013.

Azzam, Fateh. "The Duty of Third States to Implement and Enforce International Humanitarian Law." *Nordic Journal of International Law* 66 (1997): 55–75.

———. "In Defense of 'Professional' Human Rights Organizations." *openDemocracy*, January 13, 2014.

———. "NGOs vs. Grassroots Movements: A False Dichotomy." Al-Shabaka Palestinian Policy Network, February 6, 2014. https://al-shabaka.org/commentaries/ngos-vs-grassroots-movements-a-false-dichotomy/.

———. "Reflections on Three Decades of Human Rights Work in the Arab Region." In Chase, ed., *Routledge Handbook on Human Rights*, 463–73.

———. "Update: The Palestinian Independent Commission for Citizens' Rights." *Human Rights Quarterly* 20/2 (1998): 338–47.

———. "Why Should We Have to Represent Anyone?" *Sur—International Journal on Human Rights* 20 (2014): 273–82.

Bakan, Abigail B., and Yasmeen Abu-Laban. "Palestinian Resistance and International Solidarity: The BDS Campaign." *Race and Class* 51/1 (2009): 29–54.

Baker, Alan. "International Humanitarian Law and Israel's Status in the Territories." *International Review of the Red Cross* 94/888 (2012): 1511–21.

Balyis, Elena. "Tribunal-Hopping with the Post-Conflict Justice Junkies." *Oregon Review of International Law* 10 (2008): 361–90.

Bantekas, Ilias, and Lutz Oette. *International Human Rights Law and Practice*. 2nd ed. Cambridge: Cambridge University Press, 2016.

Baramki, Gabi. *Peaceful Resistance: Building a Palestinian University under Occupation*. London: Pluto Press, 2010.

Baxi, Upendra. *The Future of Human Rights*. 2nd ed. New Delhi: Oxford University Press, 2006.

Baxter, Richard R. "The Duty of Obedience to the Belligerent Occupant." *British Yearbook of International Law* 27 (1950): 235–66.

Begin, Menachem. *White Nights: The Story of a Prisoner in Russia*. New York: Harper and Row, 1979.

Beinin, Joel, and Frédéric Vairel, eds. *Social Movements, Mobilization, and Contestation in the Middle East and North Africa*. Stanford: Stanford University Press, 2011.

Beirne, Maggie. *A Beacon of Light: The Story of CAJ*. Belfast: Committee on the Administration of Justice, 2016.

Bell, Christine. "Human Rights and the Struggle for Change: A Study in Self-Critical Legal Thought." In *Examining Critical Perspectives on Human Rights*, edited by Rob Dickinson, Elena Katselli, Colin Murray, and Ole W. Pederson, 217–46. Cambridge: Cambridge University Press, 2012.

Bell, Christine, and Johanna Keenan. "Human Rights Nongovernmental Organisations and the Problems of Transition." *Human Rights Quarterly* 26 (2004): 330–74.

Benvenisti, Eyal. *The International Law of Occupation*. 2nd ed. Oxford: Oxford University Press, 2012.

Bernard, Vincent. "The Quest for Humanity: 150 Years of International Humanitarian Law and Action." *International Review of the Red Cross* 94/888 (2012): 1195–1207.

Bernard, Vincent, Michael Siegrist, and Anton Camen. "Interview with Raja Shehadeh." *International Review of the Red Cross* 94/885 (2012): 13–28.

Bernstein, Robert L. "Rights Watchdog, Lost in the Mideast." *New York Times*, October 20, 2009.

Bisharat, George. "Courting Justice? Legitimation in Lawyering under Israeli Occupation." *Law and Social Enquiry* 20/2 (1995): 349–405.

———. *Palestinian Lawyers and Israeli Rule: Law and Disorder in the West Bank*. Austin: University of Texas Press, 1989.

Blair, William G. "Seán MacBride Is Dead at 83." *New York Times*, June 16, 1988.

Blank, Laurie R., and David Kaye. "Direct Participation: Law School Clinics and International Humanitarian Law." *International Review of the Red Cross* 96/895–96 (2014): 943–68.

Blum, Yehuda. "The Missing Reversioner: Reflections on the Status of Judea and Samaria." *Israel Law Review* 3/2 (1968): 279–301.

Boissier, Léopold. "The Silence of the ICRC." *International Review of the Red Cross* 8/85 (1968): 178–80.

Braumen, Rony. "Médicins Sans Frontières and the ICRC: Matters of Principle." *International Review of the Red Cross* 94/888 (2012): 1523–35.

Brysk, Alison. "The Question for Constructive Criticism: Critical Approaches to Human Rights." In Chase, ed., *Routledge Handbook on Human Rights*, 431–43.

Buchanan, Tom. "'The Truth Will Set You Free': The Making of Amnesty International." *Journal of Contemporary History* 37/4 (2002): 575–97.

Cavanaugh, Kathleen. "Narrating Law: Israel and the Occupied Territories." In Chase, ed., *Routledge Handbook on Human Rights*, 129–41.

Chase, Anthony Tirado, "Human Rights and Agency in the Arab World." In Chase and Hamzawy, eds., *Human Rights in the Arab World*, 1–17.

———. "Human Rights and the Middle East and North Africa: Indivisibility, Social Rights, and Structural Change." In Chase, ed., *Routledge Handbook on Human Rights*, 3–25.

———. *Human Rights, Revolution, and Reform in the Muslim World*. Boulder: Lynne Rienner, 2012.

———, ed. *Routledge Handbook on Human Rights and the Middle East and North Africa*. Abingdon: Routledge, 2017.

Chase, Anthony, and Amr Hamzawy, eds. *Human Rights in the Arab World: Independent Voices*. Philadelphia: University of Pennsylvania Press, 2006.

Chimni, B.S. "Legitimating the International Rule of Law." In *Cambridge Companion to International Law*, edited by James Crawford, 290–308. Cambridge: Cambridge University Press, 2012.

Claude, Richard Pierre. Review of Howard B. Tolley, *The International Commission of Jurists*. *Human Rights Quarterly* 16/3 (1994): 576–77.

Cohen, Stanley. *States of Denial: Knowing about Atrocities and Suffering*. Cambridge: Polity Press, 2001.

Cohen, Stanley, and Daphna Golan. *The Interrogation of Palestinians during the Intifada: Ill-Treatment, "Moderate Physical Pressure" or Torture?* Jerusalem: B'Tselem, 1991.

Collaborators in the Occupied Territories: Human Rights Abuses and Violations. Jerusalem: B'Tselem, 1994.

Comaroff, John L. "Colonialism, Culture, and the Law: A Foreword." *Law and Social Inquiry* 26 (2001): 305–14.

Crystal, Jill. "The Human Rights Movement in the Arab World." *Human Rights Quarterly* 16/3 (1994): 435–54.

Dalyell, Tam. "Obituary: Niall MacDermot." *The Independent*, February 27, 1996.

David, Barak. "EU: Future Agreements with Israel Won't Apply to Territories." *Ha'aretz*, July 16, 2013.

de Neufville, Judith Innes. "Human Rights Reporting as a Policy Tool: An Examination of the State Department Country Reports." *Human Rights Quarterly* 8 (1986): 681–99.

Dormann, Knut, and Jose Serralvo. "Common Article 1 to the Geneva Conventions and the Obligation to Prevent International Humanitarian Law Violations." *International Review of the Red Cross* 96/895–96 (2014): 707–36.

Du'aybis, Salwa, Charles Shammas, and Lynn Welchman. "The Invocation of International Humanitarian Law in NGO Advocacy in the Occupied Palestinian Territory: A Diagnostic Analysis." Unpublished draft paper, 2007, on file.

Dudai, Ron. "Advocacy with Footnotes: The Human Rights Report as a Literary Genre." *Human Rights Quarterly* 28/3 (2006): 783–95.

———. "Restraint, Reaction, and Penal Fantasies: Notes on the Death Penalty in Israel, 1967–2017." *Law and Social Inquiry* 43/3 (2017): 862–88.

Dugard, John. *Confronting Apartheid: A Personal History of South Africa, Namibia and Palestine*. Johannesburg: Jacana Media, 2018.

Dugard, John, and John Reynolds. "Apartheid, International Law, and the Occupied Palestinian Territory." *European Journal of International Law* 24/3 (2013): 867–913.

Dumbrell, John. *American Foreign Policy: Carter to Clinton*. London: MacMillan, 1997.

Dunlap, Charles. "Lawfare Today: A Perspective." *Yale Journal of International Affairs* 3 (2008): 146–54.

Dwyer, Kevin. *Arab Voices: The Human Rights Debate in the Middle East*. London: Routledge, 1991.

Eckel, Jan. "The Rebirth of Politics from the Spirit of Morality: Explaining the Human Rights Revolution of the 1970s." In Eckel and Moyn, eds., *Breakthrough*, 226–59.

Eckel, Jan, and Samuel Moyn, eds. *The Breakthrough: Human Rights in the 1970s*. Philadelphia: University of Pennsylvania Press, 2013.

Economic and Social Commission for Western Asia. *Israeli Practices towards the Palestinian People and the Question of Apartheid*. Beirut: United Nations, 2017.

Eichensher, Kirsten. "On Target? The Israeli Supreme Court and the Expansion of Targeted Killings." *Yale Law Journal* 116 (2007): 1873–81.

Elbayar, Kareem. "NGO Laws in Selected Arab States." *International Journal of Not-for-Profit Law* 7/4 (2005): 3–27.

El Sarraj, Eyad. "Justice in Heaven." In Chase and Hamzawy, eds., *Human Rights in the Arab World*, 127–34.

Ends and Means: Human Rights Approaches to Armed Groups. Geneva: International Council on Human Rights Policy, 2000.

Erakat, Noura. *Justice for Some: Law and the Question of Palestine*. Stanford: Stanford University Press, 2019.

———. "Palestinian Human Rights Defenders on the Limits and Horizons for the International Criminal Court: Interview with Raji Sourani and Shawan Jabarin." *Status Hour* (Arab Studies Institute) 3/2 (December 2016). www.statushour.com/en/Interview/187.

An Examination of the Detention of Human Rights Workers and Lawyers from the West Bank and Gaza and Conditions of Detention at Ketziot. New York: Lawyers' Committee for Human Rights, 1988.

Falk, Richard. "The Goldstone Report: Neither Implemented nor Ignored." *Palestine Yearbook of International Law* 16 (2010): 5–23.

———. "The Inside Story on Our UN Report Calling Israel an Apartheid State." *The Nation*, March 22, 2017.

Felner, Eitan. "Human Rights Leaders in Conflict Situations: A Case Study of the Politics of 'Moral Entrepreneurs.'" *Journal of Human Rights Practice* 4/1 (2012): 57–81.

Focarelli, Carlo. "Common Article 1 of the 1949 Geneva Conventions: A Soap Bubble?" *European Journal of International Law* 21/1 (2010): 125–71.

Forsythe, David. "Who Guards the Guardians: Third Parties and the Law of Armed Conflict." *American Journal of International Law* 70/1 (1976): 41–61.

Fux, Pierre-Yves, and Mirko Zambelli, "Mise en oeuvre de la quatrième Convention de Genéve dans les territoires palestiniens occupés: Historique d'un processus multilateral (1997–2001)." *International Review of the Red Cross* 84/847 (2002): 661–97.

Gobe, Eric, and Lena Salaymeh. "Tunisia's 'Revolutionary' Lawyers: From Professional Autonomy to Political Mobilization." *Law and Social Inquiry* 41/2 (2016): 311–45.

Gordon, Neve. "Human Rights as a Security Threat: Lawfare and the Campaign against Human Rights NGOs." *Law and Society Review* 48/2 (2014): 311–44.

Gordon, Noah. "Why the Palestinians Joined the International Criminal Court." *The Atlantic*, December 3, 2014.

Gready, Paul. "Introduction—Responsibility to the Story." *Journal of Human Rights Practice* 2/2 (2010): 177–90.

Gross, Aeyal. *The Writing on the Wall: Rethinking the International Law of Occupation.* Cambridge: Cambridge University Press, 2017.

Grossman, Edward. "Thyme and Occupation." *The Jerusalem Post* magazine, January 2, 1981.

Guest, Iain. *Behind the Disappearances: Argentina's Dirty War against Human Rights and the United Nations.* Philadelphia: University of Pennsylvania Press, 1990.

———. "Defending Human Rights in the Occupied Palestinian Territory—Challenges and Opportunities: A Discussion Paper on Human Rights Work in the West Bank and Gaza Strip." Report and conclusions of a mission conducted for Friedrich Ebert Foundation, Jerusalem, February 2007. www.advocacynet.org/wp-content/uploads/2015/06/2007 -report-on-human-rights-in-the-OPT.pdf.

Guzman, Manuel Mario. "The Investigation and Documentation of Events as a Methodology in Monitoring Human Rights Violations." *Statistical Journal of the United Nations ECE* 18 (2001): 249–57.

Hajjar, Lisa. *Courting Conflict: The Israeli Military Court System in the West Bank and Gaza.* London: University of California Press, 2005.

———. "Human Rights in Israel/Palestine: The History and Politics of a Movement." *Journal of Palestine Studies* 30/4 (2001): 21–38.

———. "Law against Order: Human Rights Organizations and (Versus?) the Palestinian Authority." *University of Miami Law Review* 56 (2002): 59–76.

———. *Lawfare and Armed Conflict: Comparing Israeli and US Targeted Killing Policies and Challenges against Them.* Beirut: Issam Fares Institute for Public Policy and International Affairs, American University of Beirut, 2013.

Hammami, Rema. "Palestinian NGOs since Oslo: From NGO Politics to Social Movements?" *Middle East Report* 214 (2000): 16–19, 27.

Hanafi, Sari, and Linda Tabar. "Palestinian Human Rights Organisations: Agenda and Praxis." *Palestine-Israel Journal* 10/2 (2003): 23–31.

Harcourt, Hugh, and Charles Glass. "Israeli League for Human and Civil Rights (The Shahak Papers) by Adnan Amad. Review." *Journal of Palestine Studies* 5/1–2 (1975): 150–58.

Harris, Emily. "An Israeli-Palestinian Battle with Roots in Lingerie." National Public Radio, August 2, 2016. www.npr.org/sections/parallels/2016/08/06/488249269/an-israeli-palestinian-battle-with-roots-in-lingerie.

Hawker, Nancy. "The Journey of Arabic Human Rights Testimonies, from Witnesses to Audiences via Amnesty International." *Translation Spaces* 7/1 (2018): 65–91.

Hiltermann, Joost. *Behind the Intifada: Labor and Women's Movements in the Occupied Territories.* Princeton: Princeton University Press, 1991.

———. "Deaths in Israeli Prisons." *Journal of Palestine Studies* 19/3 (1990): 101–10.

———. "Human Rights and the Politics of Computer Software." *Middle East Report* 150 (1988): 8–9.

Hopgood, Stephen. *The Endtimes of Human Rights.* Ithaca, NY: Cornell University Press, 2013.

———. *Keepers of the Flame: Understanding Amnesty International.* Ithaca, NY: Cornell University Press, 2006.

Imseis, Ardi. "Introduction: The Goldstone Report and Beyond." *Palestine Yearbook of International Law* 16 (2010): 1–4.

———. "Moderate Torture on Trial: Critical Reflections on the Israeli Supreme Court Judgement Concerning the Legality of General Security Services Interrogation Methods." *Berkeley Journal of International Law* 19 (2001): 328–49.

———. "On the Fourth Geneva Convention and the Occupied Palestinian Territory." *Harvard Journal of International Law* 44 (2003): 65–138.

International Aspects of the Arab Human Rights Movement: An Interdisciplinary Discussion Held in Cairo in March 1998. Cambridge, MA: Human Rights Program, Harvard Law School; Cairo: Centre for the Study of Developing Countries, Cairo University, 2000.

International Commission of Jurists. "The Middle East: War or Peace." *ICJ Review* 3 (September 1969): 10–14.

———. *The Rule of Law and Human Rights: Principles and Definitions.* Geneva: International Commission of Jurists, 1966 (translated as *Siyadat al-qanun wa huquq al-insan* by Wadi' Salim Khouri; Ramallah: LSM, 1985).

International Committee of the Red Cross. "The International Committee of Red Cross' (ICRC's) Confidential Approach: Specific Means Employed by the ICRC to Ensure Respect for the Law by State and Non-State Authorities; Policy Document." *International Review of the Red Cross* 94/887 (2012): 1135–44.

International Court of Justice. *Legal Consequences of the Construction of a Wall in the Occupied Palestinian Territory.* Advisory Opinion, ICJ Reports 136 (2004).

———. *Legality of the Threat or Use of Nuclear Weapons,* Advisory Opinion, ICJ Reports 226 (1996).

International Human Rights Enforcement: The Case of the Occupied Palestinian Territories in the Transitional Period. Ramallah: Centre for International Human Rights Enforcement, 1996.

INSIGHT. "Israel Tortures Arab Prisoners: Special Investigation by INSIGHT." *Sunday Times*, June 19, 1977. Archived as UN doc. A/32/132 S/12356, July 5, 1977 (available online, including *Sunday Times* editorial); also in *Journal of Palestine Studies* 6/4 (Summer 1977): 191–210, with response of Israeli embassy in London (July 3, 1977) at 210–15, and response from the INSIGHT team at 215–19.

Israel in Lebanon: Report of the International Commission to Inquire into Reported Violations of International Law by Israel during Its Invasion of Lebanon. London: Ithaca Press, 1984.

Jabareen, Hassan. "Transnational Lawyering and Legal Resistance in National Courts: Palestinian Cases before the Israeli Supreme Court." *Yale Human Rights and Development Law Journal* 13 (2010): 239–80.

Jabary Salamanca, Omar, Mezna Qato, Kareem Rabie, and Sobhi Samour. "Past Is Present: Settler Colonialism in Palestine." *Settler Colonial Studies* 2/1 (2012): 1–8.

Jensen, Steven L.B. *The Making of International Human Rights: The 1960s, Decolonization, and the Reconstruction of Global Values*. Cambridge: Cambridge University Press, 2016.

Johnson, Penny. "The Routine of Repression: Notes on the Struggle for Rights in the West Bank and Gaza." *Middle East Report* 150 (January–February 1988): 3–11.

Kalshoven, Frits. "The Undertaking to Respect and to Ensure Respect." *Yearbook of International Humanitarian Law* 2 (1999): 3–61.

"The Karp Report." *Journal of Palestine Studies* 13/4 (Summer 1984): 156–61.

Kassim, Anis F. "Review of National Lawyers Guild Report." *Journal of Palestine Studies* 9/4 (Summer 1980): 142–46.

Kearney, Michael. "Lawfare, Legitimacy and Resistance: The Weak and the Law." *Palestine Yearbook of International Law* 16 (2010): 79–130.

Keck, Margaret E., and Kathryn Sikkink. *Activists beyond Borders: Advocacy Networks in International Politics*. Ithaca, NY: Cornell University Press, 1998.

Kennedy, David. "The International Human Rights Movement: Part of the Problem?" *Harvard Human Rights Journal* 15 (2002): 101–25.

———. "The International Human Rights Regime: Still Part of the Problem?" In *Examining Critical Perspectives on Human Rights*, edited by Rob Dickinson, Elena Katselli, Colin Murray, and Ole W. Pederson, 19–34. Cambridge: Cambridge University Press, 2012.

Kennedy, Duncan. "A Left Phenomenological Alternative to the Hart/Kelson Theory of Legal Interpretation." In Kennedy, *Legal Reasoning: Collected Essays*. Aurora: The Davies Group, 2008: 153–73.

Kretzmer, David. "The Law of Belligerent Occupation in the Supreme Court of Israel." *International Review of the Red Cross* 94/885 (2012): 207–36.

———. *The Occupation of Justice: The Supreme Court of Israel and the Occupied Territories*. New York: SUNY Press, 2002.

Langer, Felicia. "The Death of Ibrahim al-Umtour, or: The Closed File That Remains Open." Tel Aviv: presentation to Israeli League for Human and Civil Rights, 1989 (in Hebrew).

Lanz, Matthias, Emilie Max, and Oliver Hoehne. "The Conference of High Contracting Parties to the Fourth Geneva Convention of 17 December 2014 and the Duty to Ensure Respect for International Humanitarian Law." *International Review of the Red Cross* 98/895–96 (2014): 1115–33.

Lerner, Antony. "Why Turning to Jewish Exceptionalism to Fight Antisemitism Is a Failing Project." *openDemocracy*, July 16, 2018.

Lesch, Ann Mosely. *Political Perceptions of the Palestinians of the West Bank and Gaza Strip.* Washington, DC: Middle East Institute, 1980.

A License to Kill: Israeli Operations against 'Wanted' and 'Masked' Palestinians. New York: Human Rights Watch, 1993.

Lockman, Zachary. "Israel at a Turning Point." *Middle East Report* 92 (1980): 3–6.

MacDermot, Niall. "Speech at the UN Headquarters, Geneva, on 29 November 1980, the International Day of Solidarity with the Palestinian People, by Niall MacDermot, Secretary-General of the ICJ." ICJ Newsletter no. 7 (October 1–December 31, 1980), 22–25.

———. "Speech by Mr. Niall MacDermot, Secretary-General of the International Commission of Jurists, at a Meeting in the Palais des Nations, Geneva, on the Occasion of the International Day of Solidarity with the Palestinian People, 29 November 1979." ICJ Newsletter no. 4 (October 1–December 31, 1979), Appendix A, 27–30.

———. "Torture in al-Fara`a Prison: A Reply to the Israeli Ambassador." Editorial, *ICJ Review* 34 (June 1985): 1–4.

Machover, Daniel, and Kate Maynard. "Prosecuting Alleged Israeli War Criminals in England and Wales." *Denning Law Journal* 18 (2006): 95–114.

Mason, Victoria, and Richard Falk, "Assessing Nonviolence in the Palestinian Rights Struggle." *State Crime Journal* 5/1 (Spring 2016): 163–86.

Masri, Mazen. "Colonial Imprints: Settler-Colonialism as a Fundamental Feature of Israeli Constitutional Law." *International Journal of Law in Context* 13/3 (2017): 388–407.

Maurer, Peter. "Challenges to International Humanitarian Law: Israel's Occupation Policy." *International Review of the Red Cross* 94/888 (Winter 2012): 1503–10.

Megally, Hanny. "Human Rights in the Arab World: Reflections on the Challenges Facing Human Rights Activism." In Chase and Hamzawy, eds., *Human Rights in the Arab World*, 107–13.

Monko, Marcin. "The ICRC in the Palestinian Territories: Double Role, Single Aim." *Humanitarian Exchange Magazine* 37 (March 2007): 22–24.

Moorehead, Caroline. *Dunant's Dream: War, Switzerland and the History of the Red Cross.* New York: Carroll & Graf, 1998.

Moyn, Samuel. *The Last Utopia: Human Rights in History.* Cambridge, MA: Belknap Press of Harvard University Press, 2010.

———. "Reflections on 'The Last Utopia': A Conversation with Samuel Moyn." Interview with Brian Phillips, *Journal of Human Rights Practice* 3/2 (2011): 129–38.

———. "The Return of the Prodigal: The 1970s as a Turning Point in Human Rights History." In Eckel and Moyn, eds., *Breakthrough*, 1–14.

Mutua, Makau. *Human Rights Standards: Hegemony, Law and Politics.* Albany: SUNY Press, 2016.

Natarajan, Usha. "TWAIL and the Environment: The State of Nature, the Nature of the State, and the Arab Spring." *Oregon Review of International Law* 14/1 (2012): 177–202.

Neier, Aryeh. "Human Rights Watch Should Not Be Criticized for Doing Its Job." *Huffington Post*, November 2, 2009.

———. *The International Human Rights Movement.* Princeton: Princeton University Press, 2012.

Nesiah, Vasuki. "The Rise and Fall of the Human Rights Empire." *Foreign Policy in Focus*, June 28, 2012.

Norton-Taylor, Richard. "Official MI5 History Sheds Little Light." *The Guardian*, October 6, 2009.

O'Brien, Kevin J. "Rightful Resistance." *World Politics* 49/1 (1996): 31–55.

The Occupation's Fig Leaf: Israel's Military Law Enforcement System as a Whitewash Mechanism. Jerusalem: B'Tselem, 2016.

O'Connell, Paul. "Human Rights: Contesting the Displacement Thesis." *Northern Ireland Legal Quarterly* 69/1 (2018): 19–36.

———. "On the Human Rights Question." *Human Rights Quarterly* 40/4 (2018): 962–88.

Orentlicher, Diane. "Bearing Witness: The Art and Science of Human Rights Fact-Finding." *Harvard Human Rights Journal* 3 (1990): 83–135.

Ott, David. *Palestine in Perspective: Politics, Human Rights and the West Bank*. London: Quartet Books, 1980.

Palmieri, Daniel. "An Institution Standing the Test of Time? A Review of 150 Years of the History of the International Committee of the Red Cross." *International Review of the Red Cross* 94/888 (2012): 1273–98.

Patel, Ian. "The Role of Testimony and Testimonial Analysis in Human Rights Advocacy and Research." *State Crime Journal* 1/2 (2012): 235–65.

Pendas, Devin O. "Towards a New Politics? On the Recent Historiography of Human Rights." *Contemporary European History* 21/1 (2012): 95–111.

Performance and Legitimacy: National Human Rights Institutions. 2nd ed. Geneva: International Council on Human Rights Policy, 2004.

Perugini, Nicola, and Neve Gordon. *The Human Right to Dominate*. New York: Oxford University Press, 2015.

———. "Israel/Palestine, Human Rights and Domination." In Chase, ed., *Routledge Handbook on Human Rights*, 419–30.

Petrasek, David. "A Road Less Travelled: International Human Rights Advocacy and Armed Groups." *Journal of Human Rights Practice* 4/1 (2012): 128–40.

Posner, Michael, and Candy Whittome. "The Status of Human Rights Non-Governmental Organisations." *Columbia Human Rights Law Review* 25 (1994): 269–90.

Power, Jonathan. *Amnesty International: The Human Rights Story*. New York: McGraw-Hill, 1981.

Pratt, Nicola. "Human Rights NGOs and the 'Foreign Funding' Debate in Egypt." In Chase and Hamzawy, eds., *Human Rights in the Arab World*, 114–26.

Quigley, John. *The Case for Palestine: An International Law Perspective*. Durham, NC: Duke University Press, 2005.

Rabbani, Mouin. "Palestinian Human Rights Activism under Israeli Occupation: The Case of Al-Haq." *Arab Studies Quarterly* 16/2 (1994): 27–53.

Rayyes, Naser. "The Rule of Law and Human Rights within Palestinian National Authority Territories." *Palestine-Israel Journal* 10/2 (2003): 50–57.

Reisman, Michael. "International Law and the Israeli Occupation." *The Nation*, December 5, 1981.

Richardson, John. "When the US Gets to Monitoring Human Rights." *Al-Fajr*, December 23, 1983.

Rishmawi, Mona. "Judicial Independence under Palestinian Rule." In *The Arab-Israeli Accords: Legal Perspectives*, edited by Eugene Cotran and Chibli Mallat, 259–67. London: Kluwer Law International, 1996.

Roberts, Adam. "Prolonged Military Occupation: The Israeli-Occupied Territories 1967–1988." In Playfair, ed., *International Law and the Administration of Occupied Territories*, 25–85.

———. "Prolonged Military Occupation: The Israeli-Occupied Territories since 1967." *American Journal of International Law* 84 (1990): 44–103.

———. "Transformative Military Occupation: Applying the Laws of War and Human Rights." *American Journal of International Law* 100 (2006): 508–622.

Roberts, Adam, with Boel Jorgensen and Frank Newman. *Academic Freedom under Israeli Military Occupation: Report of a WUS/ICJ Mission of Enquiry into Higher Education in the West Bank and Gaza*. London: World University Service, 1984.

Ron, James. "Savage Restraint: Israel, Palestine and the Dialectics of Legal Repression." *Social Problems* 47/4 (2000): 445–72.

The Rule of Law in the Areas Administered by Israel. Tel Aviv: Israeli National Section of the International Commission of Jurists, 1981.

Said, Edward. *The End of the Peace Process: Oslo and After*. 2nd ed. London: Granta, 2002.

———. "The Morning After—October 1993." *Al-Hayat*, October 13 and 14, 1993. In Said, *Peace and Its Discontents: Gaza-Jericho, 1993–1995*. London: Vintage, 1995: 5–18.

———. "Permission to Narrate: Edward Said Writes about the Story of the Palestinians." *London Review of Books*, February 16, 1984, 13–17.

Sargent, Daniel. "Oasis in the Desert? America's Human Rights Rediscovery." In Eckel and Moyn, eds., *Breakthrough*, 125–45.

Sfard, Michael. "The Human Rights Lawyer's Existential Dilemma." *Israel Law Review* 38/3 (2005): 154–69.

———. *The Wall and the Gate: Israel, Palestine and the Legal Battle for Human Rights*. New York: Metropolitan Books, 2017.

Shah, Samira. "On the Road to Apartheid: The Bypass Road Network in the West Bank." *Columbia Human Rights Law Review* 29 (1997–98): 221–90.

Sharif, Regina. "The United Nations and Palestinian Rights, 1974–1979." *Journal of Palestine Studies* 9/1 (1979): 21–45.

Shehadeh, Raja. "Advice to the Palestinian Leadership." *London Review of Books*, July 3, 2014, 10–13.

———. "Analyzing Palestine: Post-Mortem or Prognosis?" In *Waiting for the Barbarians: A Tribute to Edward Said*, edited by Basak Ertur and Muge Gursoy Sokmen. London: Verson, 2008.

———. "Can the Declaration of Principles Bring About a 'Just and Lasting Peace'?" *European Journal of International Law* 4/5 (1993): 555–63.

———. *From Occupation to Interim Accords: Israel and the Palestinian Territories*. The Hague: Kluwer Law International, 1997.

———. "Human Rights and the Israeli Occupation." *CR: The New Centennial Review* 8/1 (2008): 33–55.

———. "The Legal System of the Israeli Settlements in the West Bank." *ICJ Review* 2 (December 1981): 59–74.

———. *Occupation Diaries*. London: Profile Books, 2012.

———. *Occupier's Law*. Rev. ed. Washington: Institute for Palestine Studies, 1988.

———. *Palestinian Walks: Notes on a Vanishing Landscape*. London: Profile Books, 2007.

———. *A Rift in Time: Travels with My Ottoman Uncle*. London: Profile Books, 2010.

———. *The Sealed Room*. London: Quartet, 1992.

———. *Strangers in the House*. London: Profile Books, 2002.

———. *The Third Way: A Journal of Life in the West Bank*. London: Quartet Books, 1982.

———. "The Weight of Legal History: Constraints and Hopes in the Search for a Sovereign Legal Language." In *The Arab-Israeli Accords: Legal Perspectives*, edited by Eugene Cotran and Chibli Mallat, 3–20. London: Kluwer Law International, 1996.

———. *When the Bulbul Stopped Singing: A Diary of Ramallah under Siege*. London: Profile Books, 2003.

Shestack, Jerome J. "Sisyphus Endures: The International Human Rights NGO." *New York Law School Review* 24 (1978): 89–123.

Shifter, Michael. "Weathering the Storm: NGOs Adapting to Major Political Transitions." In *Many Roads to Justice*, 327–37. New York: Ford Foundation, 2000.

Shlaim, Avi. *The Iron Wall: Israel and the Arab World*. London: Penguin, 2001.

Siegman, Henry. "Gaza and the Palestinian Struggle for Statehood." NOREF (Norwegian Peacebuilding Resource Centre), August 2014, www.peacebuilding.no/Regions/Middle-East-and-North-Africa/Israel-Palestine/Publications/Gaza-and-the-Palestinian-struggle-for-statehood.

Singer, Joel. "The Establishment of a Civil Administration in the Areas Administered by Israel." *Israel Yearbook on Human Rights* 12 (1982): 259–337.

Slaughter, Joseph R. "Hijacking Human Rights: Neoliberalism, the New Historiography, and the End of the Third World." *Human Rights Quarterly* 40 (2018): 735–75.

Steiner, Henry. *Diverse Partners: Non-Governmental Organizations in the Human Rights Movement; The Report of a Retreat of Human Rights Activists*. Cambridge, MA: Harvard Law School Human Rights Program and Human Rights Internet, 1991.

Stork, Joe. "Three Decades of Human Rights Activism in the Middle East and North Africa: An Ambiguous Balance Sheet." In *Social Movements, Mobilization, and Contestation in the Middle East and North Africa*, edited by Joel Beinin and Frédéric Vairel, 83–106. Stanford: Stanford University Press, 2011.

Talhami, Ghada. "The Palestinian Perception of the Human Rights Issue." *Syracuse Journal of International Law and Commerce* 13 (1987): 475–88.

Taraki, Lisa. "The Development of Political Consciousness among Palestinians in the Occupied Territories, 1967–1987." In *Intifada: Palestine at the Crossroads*, edited by Jamal Raji Nassar and Roger Heacock, 53–72. New York: Praeger Publishers, 1990.

Thompson, Andrew S. "Beyond Expression: Amnesty International's Decision to Oppose Capital Punishment, 1973." *Journal of Human Rights* 7 (2008): 327–40.

Thoolen, Hans. "We Were Breaking New Ground." Interview conducted by Friedhelm Weinberg. HURIDOCS, November 30, 2012. www.huridocs.org/2012/11/we-were-breaking-new-ground/.

Tilley, Virginia, ed. *Beyond Occupation: Apartheid, Colonialism and International Law in the Occupied Palestinian Territories*. London: Pluto Press, 2012.

———, ed. *Occupation, Colonialism, Apartheid? A Re-Assessment of Israel's Practices in the Occupied Palestinian Territories under International Law*. Cape Town: Human Sciences Research Council (Middle East Project), 2009.

Tolley, Howard B., Jr. *The International Commission of Jurists: Global Advocates for Human Rights*. Philadelphia: University of Pennsylvania Press, 1994.

———. "Popular Sovereignty and International Law: ICJ Strategies for Human Rights Standard-Setting." *Human Rights Quarterly* 11/4 (1989): 561–85.

Treatment of Palestinians in the Israeli-Occupied West Bank and Gaza. New York: National Lawyers Guild, 1978.

Tripp, Charles. *The Power and the People: Paths of Resistance in the Middle East.* New York: Cambridge University Press, 2013.

UN Office of the Special Coordinator in the Occupied Territories. "Rule of Law Development Support in the West Bank and Gaza Strip: Survey and State of the Development Effort." UNSCO, May 31, 1999.

Usher, Graham. *Palestine in Crisis.* London: Pluto Press, 1995.

Wallis, Jim. "Interview with Palestinian Christian, Jonathan Kuttab: Inside Israeli Apartheid." *Sojourner Magazine*, September–October 2001.

Waltz, Susan E. *Human Rights and Reform: Changing the Face of North African Politics.* Berkeley: University of California Press, 1995.

Weissbrodt, David. "The Role of International Nongovernmental Organizations in the Implementation of Human Rights." *Texas International Law Journal* 12 (1977): 293–320.

Weizman, Eyal. "Lawfare in Gaza: Legislative Attack." *openDemocracy*, March 1, 2009.

———. "Short Cuts." *London Review of Books*, December 6, 2012, 28.

Welchman, Lynn. "Consensual Intervention: A Case Study on the TIPH." In *International Human Rights Enforcement*, 279–314.

———. "Human Rights, Law and Politics: A Reflection on Human Rights Work in the Middle East and North Africa." In Chase, ed., *Routledge Handbook on Human Rights*, 502–11.

———. "International Protection and International Diplomacy: Policy Choices for Third-Party States in the Occupied Palestinian Territories." In *International Human Rights Enforcement*, 225–77.

Wilson, Richard. "Representing Human Rights Violations: Social Contexts and Subjectivities." In *Human Rights, Culture and Context: Anthropological Perspectives*, edited by Richard Wilson, 134–60. London: Pluto Press, 1997.

Wing, Adrien Katherine. "Legal Decision-Making during the Palestinian Intifada: Embryonic Self-Rule." *Yale Journal of International Law* 18 (1993): 95–153.

Wiseberg, Laurie S., and Harry M. Scobie. "The International League for Human Rights: The Strategy of a Human Rights NGO." *Georgia Journal of International and Comparative Law* 7 (1977): 289–313.

Wispelwey, Bram, and Amaya Al-Orzza. "Underlying Conditions." LRB blog, April 18, 2020. www.lrb.co.uk/blog/2020/april/underlying-conditions.

Wolfe, Patrick. "Settler Colonialism and the Elimination of the Native." *Journal of Genocide Research* 8/4 (2006): 387–409.

Ziegler, Jean. "Justice et Oppression." *Afrique-Asie*, January 18, 1981.

Zunes, Stephen. "The United States and Israeli Violations of International Humanitarian Law." In Chase, ed., *Routledge Handbook on Human Rights*, 142–54.

Abbas, Mahmoud, 217
Abu Ghosh, Raqiya, 87
accountability, 5, 16, 84, 117, 123, 135, 180, 187, 194,
    196, 203, 207, 210, 212, 214, 218, 219, 224
accuracy, 5, 63, 64, 84, 111, 112, 148, 150, 151,
    161, 200
acquisition, 7, 57, 168, 226
Adalah, 216, 245n52, 280n86
administered territories, 15, 51, 52, 58
administrative detention, 55, 73, 156, 164, 165;
    al-Haq fieldworkers and, 81–82, 97, 127,
    153–55, 156, 206, 250n24, 263n29; Amnesty
    International on, 127–28, 256n72
administrative penalties, 73, 97, 106, 128, 166,
    173, 199
affidavits, 55, 63, 64, 129, 153, 162, 164, 179; LSM's
    first, 3, 149, 262n10; as documentation tool,
    76, 148–50, 155, 161; collection of, 86, 147,
    150–52; published collections of, 120, 156–60,
    162–63, 247n77
Al-Dameer, 217
Al-Haq: and Oslo, 8, 25, 90, 120, 146, 182, 184,
    185, 195–96, 199, 200, 203, 208, 226; and the
    Palestinian Authority, 159, 177, 182, 187, 194,
    195, 196–97, 199, 208, 209, 213, 214, 218, 226;
    contribution, 8–11; name, 76; organizational
    culture, 90–97; origins, 28–46; structure and
    governance, 8, 74, 77, 78–79, 89, 101–3, 183,
    185, 191–95, 202–5, 207–8, 211

"Al-Haq's Action to Defend the Right to
    Education," 115
al-haram al-sharif massacre-, 139, 140, 148,
    262n7; "Reconstruction of Events," 148
Ali, Khaled al-Sheikh, 123
Allen, Lori, 4–5, 72, 215, 224, 251n45, 273n66,
    272n73
allies, 2, 3, 15, 31, 36, 77, 82, 98, 108, 110, 111,
    121–135, 137, 138, 142, 158, 169, 206, 212, 218, 219
Al-Marsad, 216
Al Mezan, 103, 145, 216–17, 219
Alston, Philip, 5, 253n8
American Academy for the Advancement of
    Science (AAAS), 122
Amnesty International, 2, 4, 22, 30, 66, 110, 115,
    121, 122, 129, 130, 175, 181, 186, 213, 256n67,
    262n13, 270n20, 272n64, 273n66; and al-Haq
    fieldworkers, 126–27, 153; on administrative
    detention, 127–28, 256n72
annexation, 57, 59, 60, 113, 134, 143, 192, 226, 227;
    of East Jerusalem, 16, 51, 143, 222, 226
annexationist agenda, 9, 23, 61, 75, 76, 108, 143
Ansar 3, 123, 164, 165, 257n100
apartheid, 7, 19, 21, 26, 58, 60, 217, 224, 225,
    226, 227
"Appeal to State Signatories to the Fourth
    Geneva Convention 1987," 135
Application Denied, 157. *See also* family
    reunification

Founded in 1893,
UNIVERSITY OF CALIFORNIA PRESS
publishes bold, progressive books and journals
on topics in the arts, humanities, social sciences,
and natural sciences—with a focus on social
justice issues—that inspire thought and action
among readers worldwide.

The UC PRESS FOUNDATION
raises funds to uphold the press's vital role
as an independent, nonprofit publisher, and
receives philanthropic support from a wide
range of individuals and institutions—and from
committed readers like you. To learn more, visit
ucpress.edu/supportus.

9 780520 379756